Golf Courses of the
PGA  TOUR

Golf Courses of the

PHOTOGRAPHS BY
BRIAN D. MORGAN,
JAMES MORIARTY AND
ANTHONY ROBERTS

MAPS BY ELIZABETH PEPER

PGA TOUR

BY GEORGE PEPER
EDITOR OF GOLF MAGAZINE

FOREWORD BY DEANE R. BEMAN
COMMISSIONER, PGA TOUR

HARRY N. ABRAMS, INC. NEW YORK
A GOLF MAGAZINE BOOK

CONTENTS

Project Director: Margaret L. Kaplan
Copy Editor: Pauline Crammer
Designer: Bob McKee

Library of Congress Cataloging-in-Publication Data
Peper, George.
    Golf courses of the PGA Tour.
    Bibliography: p.
    Includes index.
    1. Golf courses—United States. 2. Professional
Golfers' Association of America. I. Title.
GV975.P465 1986   796.352′06   86–3588
ISBN 0–8109–0994–4
Text copyright © 1986, 1988 George Peper.
Illustrations copyright © 1986, 1988
Harry N. Abrams, Inc.
Published in 1986 by Harry N. Abrams, Incorporated,
New York. All rights reserved. No part of the contents
of this book may be reproduced without the written
permission of the publishers.
Times Mirror Books
Printed and bound in Japan

FOREWORD
DEANE R. BEMAN, COMMISSIONER, PGA TOUR

Few players have ever tamed the beasts described in these pages, but through the efforts of George Peper you are about to stroll the fairways of some of the most storied and prestigious golf courses in the world.

This ambitious undertaking will take you out on the PGA Tour. Its courses are as diverse as their locales, but all share one thing—for one week a year they test the best golfers in the world, the players of the PGA Tour.

Golf Courses of the PGA Tour is the only book of its kind, and I am sure it will be a much valued addition to

Frontmatter illustrations:

Endpapers: Doral Country Club, 18th hole
Half title: Oakwood Country Club, 3rd hole
Title: Cypress Point Golf Club, 16th hole
Contents: Harbour Town Golf Links, 18th hole
Foreword: Glen Abbey Golf Club, 18th hole

your golf library. Within these pages you will see and read about some of the most venerated courses in the world and relive some of the most exciting moments in the Tour's history.

The beautiful color photographs and course maps give you a sense of knowing each course and can only enhance your appreciation of the sport, as well as your appreciation for the masterful way that the course architects have molded the land into something timeless in its beauty.

It was my distinct pleasure to play many of these fine courses during my days on the Tour, and I am pleased that through this effort many Tour fans will now have the opportunity to "walk along" in the footsteps of the legends of the game of golf. I think you will enjoy seeing in full color the weekly challenge that the best courses in North America have provided our players.

You will be there at "Amen Corner" at Augusta National; you will face the treacherous par-four 18th at Doral, and will wonder at the splendor of Pebble Beach's 18th. The 16th at Cypress Point awaits you, as does the startling island 17th at the Tournament Players Club at Sawgrass.

The lush green fairways, sparkling waters, and brilliant white bunkers that have faced the attacks of Ben Hogan, Sam Snead, Arnold Palmer, and Jack Nicklaus now await your inspection on the pages within.

The true measure of a champion's skill is how well he stands the test of time. This book will show you the golf courses that have not only withstood the challenge of the world's finest shotmakers, but the test of time as well.

It is to these great courses that the PGA Tour returns year after year, and I invite you to join with us now as we walk the fairways of the PGA Tour.

Hours of pleasure await you.

Deane R. Beman
Commissioner, PGA Tour

LA COSTA *Country Club*

MONY TOURNAMENT OF CHAMPIONS CALIFORNIA

For some pros, merely qualifying for the Tournament of Champions is the thrill of a lifetime. Invitation to this exclusive tournament is secured in only one way—by winning a Tour event.

In 1953, Tournament Director Allard Roen came up with the idea of assembling all the winners of events during the previous twelve months on the professional circuit to determine the champion of champions. To show he was serious, Roen put up a purse of $35,000 with a first prize

17th hole

of $10,000 to be paid in silver dollars. In those days, $10,000 was a huge amount—about the same as the combined total Ben Hogan collected that year for winning The Masters, the U.S. Open, and the British Open.

The T of C today is a fixture in men's professional golf, with the elite groups of winners from the PGA Tour and the PGA Senior Tour each holding a four-day shoot-out and the total prize in excess of half a million dollars.

Not the least of the attractions for the pros.is that everyone who arrives a winner also goes home a winner. With an average field of about twenty-five players, there is no cut in the T of C; every entrant is guaranteed a four-figure check regardless of how he plays. One year, Phil Hancock finished 40 strokes behind the winner and still took home $3,400.

For the players' wives, this is unquestionably the most popular stop on the Tour. During the T of C, each pro and family are treated to an all-expenses-paid week at the

READING ROUGH
BY LANNY WADKINS

La Costa would be a relatively easy course were it not for one factor—deep, dense rough. The thick grass is on everyone's mind during every hole of the Tournament of Champions.

Ninety-nine percent of the lies in the fairway can be played the same way, but in the rough no two lies are alike. Indeed, the most important aspect of playing from rough is being able to read the lie and choose the shot that offers the best promise of success.

Remember a couple of rules. If the ball is sitting in deep rough, you won't be able to hit it as far as you would from the fairway; but if the ball is sitting cleanly in light or moderate rough, you'll likely get a "flyer," a spinless shot that can travel as much as 30 yards farther than a shot hit with the same club from a fairway lie. In either case you'd almost never use the same club for, say, a 170-yard shot from rough that you'd use for a 170-yard shot from the fairway.

Bermudagrass usually is more tangly than bent or rye rough. Lies in which the rough grows against the direction of the shot are more difficult than those in which the grass grows with the shot. And remember that, unless you have a very clean lie, you'll have almost no chance of maneuvering the ball from left-to-right or right-to-left or of applying any backspin to the shot.

Lanny Wadkins is a back-to-back winner (1982 and 1983) of the MONY Tournament of Champions.

5th hole

6th hole

15th hole

18th hole

famous La Costa Country Club and Spa, a sort of YMCA for millionaires.

Some guests stay at La Costa for a week and never realize that it adjoins a golf course. The fact is, it adjoins one of America's finest. The La Costa Country Club course has hosted the T of C since 1969.

That inaugural tournament was something of a surprise to many of the players. For thirteen years, they had played the T of C at the demanding Desert Inn Country Club course in Las Vegas. Coming to La Costa, which is nearly 300 yards shorter, many thought they were in for an easier time. But no one figured on the five-inch rough. Jack Nicklaus was among the notable victims, taking an 80 in the opening round as Gary Player won with a four-under-par 284. He and Lee Trevino, two strokes back, were the only players to finish better than par.

The first four holes on the course are relatively tame, but on the fifth tee the golfer confronts a 424-yard par four that is the hardest hole on the course. A stream runs down the left side of the landing area, then cuts diagonally across the fairway at about the 300-yard mark. The green is the smallest on the golf course and is bunkered to the left and back. Even the strongest players need long irons—and straight ones—to get home.

The sibling to that hole is number 10—a 437-yard par four—where water crosses the fairway. In this case the water does not come into play off the tee, but, with a long bunker on the left and several large trees on the right, the drive is nonetheless one of the tightest in town.

The finishing holes at La Costa—15 through 18—are called the Last Mile, and when the prevailing north wind is up it is easy to see why.

The 15th is the easiest of the four. A classic, short-dogleg par four, it is played from an elevated tee. The drive must be shaded to the right to avoid a large sycamore protecting the left corner of the dogleg. The approach is generally played with a short iron, but it is not an easy shot, particularly when played into the teeth of the wind. Five bunkers surround this elevated green.

There is no sand to worry about on the tee shot at 16, but pine trees on the inside corner of this left-to-right dogleg have proved nettlesome to many a competitor. It was here in 1982 that Ron Streck suffered a costly penalty after violating one of the Rules of Golf. In the final round Streck was in a tight battle with Lanny Wadkins when he came to this hole. He hit his tee shot into the trees, and then, as he addressed the ball, he unconsciously brushed aside a branch of one of the trees, a violation of the Rule that prohibits improving one's lie. None of the officials on the scene noticed, but a television viewer did and called NBC to report what he saw.

Streck parred 16 and 17, then bogeyed 18. When Wadkins parred 18, Streck became the runner-up until word of the violation reached the scorer's tent. Streck was immediately assessed a two-stroke penalty, which dropped him into a four-way tie for second. The difference in earnings was $14,000.

The 17th hole at La Costa is consistently one of the most difficult par fives on the Tour and one of the few that does not play under par for the pros. The reasons are its tremendous length into the wind and the nearly 200-yard-long water hazard that flanks the right side and comes into play on both the second and third shots. Pros seldom write the number seven on their cards, but this hole produces a couple of dozen each year.

A good tee shot is important on 18, where the long approach must be played to an elevated, well-bunkered, severely sloping green.

Since 1979 the Tournament of Champions has been dominated by Tom Watson with three victories (1979, 1980, and 1984) and Lanny Wadkins with two (1982 and 1983). Like Ron Streck, Watson committed a Rules infraction in 1980. On the final hole he was assessed a two-stroke penalty when he gave a "lesson" to his fellow competitor, Lee Trevino, thereby violating the Rule that prohibits a player from giving advice to other players. At the time, Watson was clearly in command of the tournament and Trevino had had a miserable day. Even after the penalty, Watson's victory margin was three strokes better than Jim Colbert's score.

The lesson must have helped because a year later Trevino came back to La Costa and won.

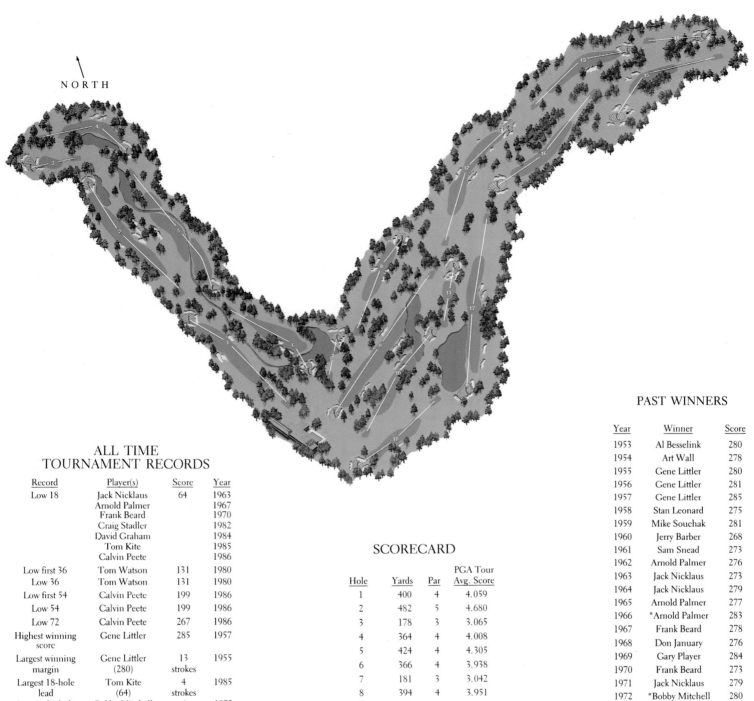

NORTH

ALL TIME
TOURNAMENT RECORDS

Record	Player(s)	Score	Year
Low 18	Jack Nicklaus	64	1963
	Arnold Palmer		1967
	Frank Beard		1970
	Craig Stadler		1982
	David Graham		1984
	Tom Kite		1985
	Calvin Peete		1986
Low first 36	Tom Watson	131	1980
Low 36	Tom Watson	131	1980
Low first 54	Calvin Peete	199	1986
Low 54	Calvin Peete	199	1986
Low 72	Calvin Peete	267	1986
Highest winning score	Gene Littler	285	1957
Largest winning margin	Gene Littler (280)	13 strokes	1955
Largest 18-hole lead	Tom Kite (64)	4 strokes	1985
Largest 36-hole lead	Bobby Mitchell (136)	4 strokes	1972
	Bud Allin (135)		1974
Largest 54-hole lead	Jack Nicklaus (209)	5 strokes	1971
	Don January (208)		1976
	Tom Watson (203)		1980
Lowest start by winner	Tom Kite	64	1985
Highest start by winner	Johnny Miller	75	1974
Lowest finish by winner	Gary Player	67	1978
	Tom Watson		1984
Highest finish by winner	Al Geiberger	73	1975
	Tom Watson		1980
	Lanny Wadkins		1982
Best final-round comeback	Gary Player	7 back	1978
Lowest 36-hole cut score	No cut		

SCORECARD

Hole	Yards	Par	PGA Tour Avg. Score
1	400	4	4.059
2	482	5	4.680
3	178	3	3.065
4	364	4	4.008
5	424	4	4.305
6	366	4	3.938
7	181	3	3.042
8	394	4	3.951
9	531	5	4.840
OUT	3320	36	35.888
10	437	4	4.181
11	164	3	2.921
12	510	5	4.649
13	400	4	4.000
14	183	3	3.108
15	375	4	4.071
16	400	4	4.208
17	535	5	5.086
18	398	4	4.208
IN	3402	36	36.432
TOTAL	6722	72	72.320

PAST WINNERS

Year	Winner	Score
1953	Al Besselink	280
1954	Art Wall	278
1955	Gene Littler	280
1956	Gene Littler	281
1957	Gene Littler	285
1958	Stan Leonard	275
1959	Mike Souchak	281
1960	Jerry Barber	268
1961	Sam Snead	273
1962	Arnold Palmer	276
1963	Jack Nicklaus	273
1964	Jack Nicklaus	279
1965	Arnold Palmer	277
1966	*Arnold Palmer	283
1967	Frank Beard	278
1968	Don January	276
1969	Gary Player	284
1970	Frank Beard	273
1971	Jack Nicklaus	279
1972	*Bobby Mitchell	280
1973	Jack Nicklaus	276
1974	Johnny Miller	280
1975	*Al Geiberger	277
1976	Don January	277
1977	*Jack Nicklaus	281
1978	Gary Player	281
1979	Tom Watson	275
1980	Tom Watson	276
1981	Lee Trevino	273
1982	Lanny Wadkins	280
1983	Lanny Wadkins	280
1984	Tom Watson	274
1985	Tom Kite	275
1986	Calvin Peete	267
1987	Mac O'Grady	278
1988	Steve Pate	‡202

*Playoff

‡Rain-curtailed

BERMUDA DUNES
Country Club

INDIAN WELLS
Country Club

LA QUINTA
Country Club

ELDORADO
Country Club

TAMARISK
Country Club

Tamarisk, 5th hole

BOB HOPE
CHRYSLER CLASSIC, CALIFORNIA

California is the wealthiest, glitziest state in the Union. Palm Springs is the wealthiest, glitziest part of California. And the fairways of Palm Springs are the wealthiest, glitziest acreage in the world. The businessmen who gather here each January could, if they so desired, pool their resources to buy Albania or start their own space program or finance the paving of Lake Superior or simply pay off the national debt.

Instead, they play golf. For four straight days they play golf in the desert, trading shots and stories and stock tips with an assortment of actors, athletes, politicians, and pros in the Bob Hope Chrysler Classic, the wealthiest, glitziest show on the PGA Tour.

The entry fee for this pro-am is several thousand dollars, but it buys a lot—four days of golf, from Wednesday through Saturday, each day on a different course, each day with a different Tour pro. On Sunday the low-70 pros go it alone in the final 18 of this 90-hole event.

Five country clubs stage the Hope—Bermuda Dunes, Indian Wells, La Quinta, Eldorado, and Tamarisk. The last two are used alternately, Eldorado one year, Tamarisk the next; the three permanent sites take turns as the host club.

Tamarisk, one of the first Palm Springs courses, was designed in 1953 by William P. "Billy" Bell, the caddie-master who apprenticed as a construction superintendent

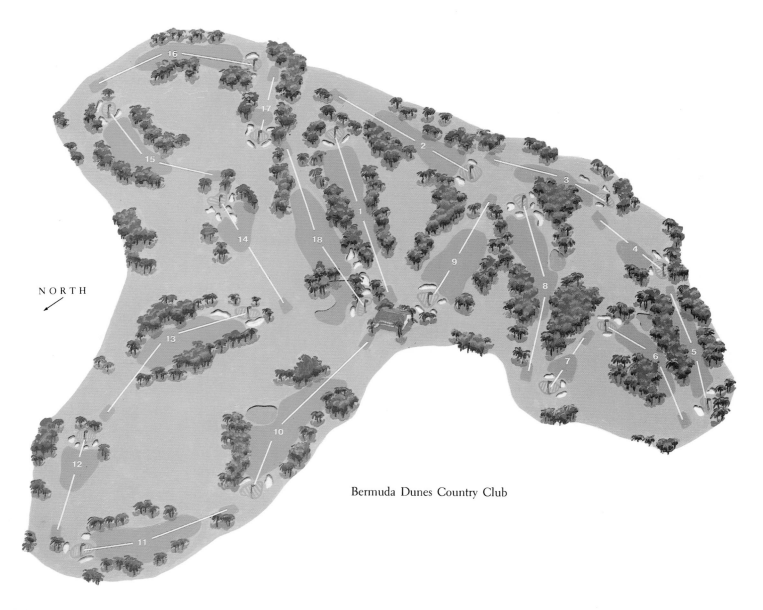

NORTH

Bermuda Dunes Country Club

Bermuda Dunes, 9th hole

BERMUDA DUNES CC
SCORECARD

Hole	Yards	Par	PGA Tour Avg. Score
1	534	5	4.720
2	418	4	4.035
3	372	4	3.874
4	208	3	3.112
5	432	4	4.083
6	361	4	3.939
7	170	3	2.911
8	536	5	4.613
9	386	4	3.900
OUT	3417	36	35.187
10	411	4	4.148
11	376	4	4.017
12	154	3	2.946
13	554	5	4.793
14	375	4	3.968
15	391	4	3.947
16	446	4	4.133
17	208	3	3.172
18	505	5	4.647
IN	3420	36	35.771
TOTAL	6837	72	70.958

Bermuda Dunes, 18th hole

INDIAN WELLS CC SCORECARD

Hole	Yards	Par	PGA Tour Avg. Score
1	388	4	3.978
2	355	4	3.928
3	382	4	4.021
4	162	3	3.061
5	517	5	4.552
6	140	3	2.820
7	338	4	3.900
8	515	5	4.734
9	398	4	3.983
OUT	3195	36	34.977
10	446	4	4.244
11	398	4	4.129
12	343	4	3.814
13	197	3	3.114
14	483	5	4.559
15	163	3	2.956
16	354	4	3.911
17	398	4	4.002
18	501	5	4.589
IN	3283	36	35.318
TOTAL	6478	72	70.295

LA QUINTA CC SCORECARD

Hole	Yards	Par	PGA Tour Avg. Score
1	382	4	3.914
2	433	4	4.224
3	186	3	2.994
4	397	4	4.073
5	492	5	4.700
6	521	5	4.565
7	174	3	3.046
8	395	4	4.013
9	391	4	3.970
OUT	3371	36	35.499
10	389	4	4.101
11	556	5	4.808
12	201	3	3.300
13	521	5	4.620
14	445	4	4.153
15	202	3	3.092
16	411	4	3.979
17	419	4	4.105
18	396	4	4.041
IN	3540	36	36.199
TOTAL	6911	72	71.698

ELDORADO CC SCORECARD

Hole	Yards	Par	PGA Tour Avg. Score
1	507	5	4.632
2	175	3	3.066
3	439	4	4.103
4	393	4	4.118
5	379	4	4.029
6	368	4	3.912
7	189	3	3.147
8	394	4	4.059
9	502	5	4.596
OUT	3346	36	35.662
10	377	4	3.985
11	437	4	4.338
12	217	3	3.132
13	518	5	4.816
14	412	4	4.265
15	403	4	4.066
16	194	3	3.169
17	425	4	4.213
18	511	5	4.985
IN	3494	36	36.969
TOTAL	6840	72	72.631

TAMARISK CC SCORECARD

Hole	Yards	Par	PGA Tour Avg. Score
1	483	5	4.198
2	166	3	2.897
3	433	4	4.144
4	503	5	4.768
5	199	3	3.053
6	375	4	4.034
7	330	4	3.867
8	389	4	3.886
9	435	4	4.038
OUT	3312	36	34.885
10	404	4	4.131
11	188	3	3.106
12	542	5	4.779
13	417	4	4.147
14	234	3	3.125
15	420	4	4.141
16	401	4	4.023
17	389	4	3.954
18	522	5	4.692
IN	3517	36	36.098
TOTAL	6829	72	70.983

for architect George C. Thomas and then rose to become the most prolific course designer in the West.

Tamarisk's alternate, Eldorado Country Club, hosted the 1959 Ryder Cup Matches and for many years was the western home of President and Mrs. Eisenhower. Set at the foot of the majestic Santa Rosa Mountains, Eldorado is far more lush than one would expect of a desert course, its long, slender fairways lined with orange, grapefruit, olive, and peach trees and dotted with cool lakes. It also boasts the only bentgrass greens of any Hope venue.

At 6,911 yards, La Quinta is the longest of the five Hope courses, and with lakes bordering seven of its fairways this tropical layout can be as difficult as it is beautiful.

Interestingly, the hole that annually surfaces as the toughest on the course, according to Tour statistics, is a par three, the 201-yard 12th. The boomerang-shaped pond, several yards short of the green, does not bother the pros much, but the rolling green and large flanking bunkers do. When the pin is up front, in the narrow neck between those bunkers, this hole tags the pros for more fours than threes.

The shortest of the Hope courses—indeed, the shortest golf course on the PGA Tour—is Indian Wells at just 6,478 yards, but in 1985 it was toughened up a bit.

The major change came at number 18, a par five that architect Ted Robinson lengthened from 478 to 501 yards and made much more hazardous at the same time. The elevated tee was extended backward, in the fairway a bunker on the left was elongated, and eucalyptus trees were added on the right. Today, any player who hopes to reach the home hole in two will have to begin with a drive that is both longer and straighter than it had to be in years past.

The same demands have been stiffened on the second shot. Formerly a small pond (Robinson called it a bird bath) to the left of the green did little to deter gambling golfers. Today that pond is a five-level, cascading waterfall. Another elongated bunker lines the right side of the green, with a small oval bunker at the rear.

Robinson also added rigor to the other back-nine par five at Indian Wells, number 14. Until 1985, it had been one of the ten easiest holes on the Tour, averaging less than 4.5 strokes for the pros. But Robinson recontoured and narrowed the fairway by adding two drive-threatening bunkers in the landing area. Today birdies and eagles come less easily.

It is surprising that no one has renamed Bermuda Dunes "Palmer's Playground." In 1962, the first year Bermuda Dunes hosted the Palm Springs Golf Classic (as it was called then), Arnold won. In 1965, the second time through the rotation, Palmer finished second when Billy

ALL-TIME TOURNAMENT RECORDS

Record	Player(s)	Score	Year
Low 18	Bert Yancey	61	1974
Low first 36	Craig Stadler	129	1983
Low 36	Jodie Mudd	65–63 (rounds 3–4)	1986
Low first 54	Bruce Lietzke	196 (65–66–65)	1981
Low 54	Keith Fergus	195 (65–65–65)	1983
Low first 72	Bruce Lietzke	266 (65–66–65–70)	1981 (rounds 2–3–4–5)
Low 72	Keith Fergus	264 (69–65–65–65)	1983
Low 90	Lanny Wadkins	333 (67–67–68–66–65)	1985
	Craig Stadler		1985
Highest winning score	Doug Sanders Tom Nieporte	349	1966 1967
Largest winning margin	Rik Massengale (337)	6 strokes	1977
Largest 18-hole lead	Rik Massengale (64)	3 strokes	1977
	Craig Stadler (63)		1983
Largest 36-hole lead	Craig Stadler (129)	6 strokes	1983
Largest 54-hole lead	Jack Nicklaus (207)	5 strokes	1963
	Bruce Lietzke (196)		1981
Largest 72-hole lead	Rik Massengale (270)	6 strokes	1977
Lowest start by winner	Johnny Miller Rik Massengale	64	1975 1977
Highest start by winner	Tom Nieporte	76	1967
Lowest finish by winner	Johnny Miller	63	1976
Highest finish by winner	Jack Nicklaus Billy Casper	72	1963 1965
Best final-round comeback	Tommy Jacobs (283)	4 back	1964
	Doug Sanders (283)		1966
	John Mahaffey (274)		1984
Lowest 72-hole cut score		281	1986
Highest 72-hole cut score		295	1976

PAST WINNERS

Year	Winner	Score	Year	Winner	Score
1960	Arnold Palmer	338	1975	Johnny Miller	339
1961	Billy Maxwell	345	1976	Johnny Miller	344
1962	Arnold Palmer	342	1977	Rik Massengale	337
1963	*Jack Nicklaus	345	1978	Bill Rogers	339
1964	*Tommy Jacobs	348	1979	John Mahaffey	343
1965	Billy Casper	348	1980	Craig Stadler	343
1966	*Doug Sanders	349	1981	Bruce Lietzke	335
1967	Tom Nieporte	349	1982	*Ed Fiori	335
1968	*Arnold Palmer	348	1983	*Keith Fergus	335
1969	Billy Casper	345	1984	*John Mahaffey	340
1970	Bruce Devlin	339	1985	*Lanny Wadkins	333
1971	*Arnold Palmer	342	1986	*Donnie Hammond	335
1972	Bob Rosburg	344	1987	Corey Pavin	341
1973	Arnold Palmer	343	1988	Jay Haas	338
1974	Hubert Green	341	*Playoff		

Indian Wells, 5th hole

ON BREAKING PUTTS
BY JOHN MAHAFFEY

With four different courses at the Bob Hope Chrysler Classic, it's often hard to get a feel for the greens. Just when you have one course figured out, it's time to play another one. To make matters more difficult, the grass on most of the greens in the desert area is a hybrid bermuda that doesn't have as strong a grain as normal bermuda or even bentgrass.

However, the local knowledge says that all greens break toward Indio, a town down in the valley just southeast of the tournament area. Armed with this knowledge and a sense of direction, a pro can save himself a few shots along the way.

No matter where you play golf, you should make a point of knowing how the general terrain flows and in what way that flow influences putts. In Colorado, greens break away from the mountains; on the coasts, greens break toward the shore. And in most areas, the grain grows toward the setting sun and pushes all putts, to a greater or lesser degree, in a westerly direction.

So on your home course, get all the local knowledge you can. Then once you've made up your mind about the way a putt will break, don't change it. Don't second-guess yourself as you stand over the ball. Go ahead and give it a firm, confident stroke. More than likely your first reading was right.

———————

John Mahaffey is a two-time winner (1979, 1984) of the Bob Hope Chrysler Classic.

Indian Wells, 18th hole

Casper's closing birdie edged him by a stroke. In 1968, Palmer won again, beating Deane Beman on the first hole of sudden death. In 1971 he again won, and again in sudden death, this time over Raymond Floyd. Finally, and certainly most satisfying for Arnold, he won the 1974 tournament hosted at Bermuda Dunes, this time with a closing birdie to edge his nemesis, Jack Nicklaus. It was the last of Palmer's 61 career victories.

Set in the middle of the sandy, barren desert, Bermuda Dunes is an oasis of rolling fairways and lofty palms and pines. At 6,837 yards it is not a long par 72, but it is an honest course with no tricks or unnecessary punishments.

The number one handicap hole is the fifth, a par four of 432 yards. Bunkers on the left side of the fairway put pressure on the drive, and the second shot will have to negotiate more sand on both sides of the green.

Water comes into play at four holes, notably the par-four 10th, a dogleg left where a big draw will be rewarded but a big fade will be punished by the lake on the right of the fairway.

The final hole at Bermuda Dunes is the type of finisher every Tour event likes to have: a reachable but menacing par five. Out-of-bounds looms on the left, and a lake greets any approach shot that strays to the right of the long, narrow green. Almost as many balls find that water as find the green on the second shot.

Bob Hope became associated with the tournament in 1965, and his magnetism has been the key to its success. Superstars such as Arnold Palmer and Jack Nicklaus annually suffer the gauntlet of four days of pro-am competition purely because of their loyalty and gratitude to Hope, an avid 15-handicapper even in his eighties, and one of the game's greatest ambassadors. Of course, the substantial prize money at this tournament is no deterrent. As the host himself puts it, "This is the only event in the world where guys can get money out of the desert without drilling for oil."

La Quinta, 7th hole

Eldorado, 8th hole

TPC of SCOTTSDALE

Two million cubic yards of dirt. Try to imagine that. If you cannot, then go play the Tournament Players Club of Scottsdale, because that is how this course was made—by digging, dumping, piling, sculpting, seeding, and cultivating 200 million cubic yards of dirt.

When the PGA Tour selected Jay Morrish and Tom Weiskopf as the designers for this project, the two men knew it was good news and bad news. The good news: They had carte blanche in routing the holes. The bad news: The terrain was absolutely barren.

Funded by the City of Scottsdale, this TPC was the first municipal facility to join the family of Stadium Courses. As such its design posed unique challenges to designers Morrish and Weiskopf and their player consultants Jim Colbert and Howard Twitty.

The course had to be sufficiently difficult from the back tees to test the world's best players in the Phoenix Open and yet provide enjoyment to the golf-playing residents of Scottsdale. It had to include enough challenges to give the pros pause, yet encourage a swift pace of play from the thousands of average golfers who would annually assault it.

ALL TIME TOURNAMENT RECORDS

Record	Player(s)	Score	Year
Low 18	Johnny Miller	61	1970, 1975
	Homero Blancas		1972
	Ben Crenshaw		1979
	Don Pooley		1986
Low first 36	Johnny Miller	128 (67–61)	1975
	Ben Crenshaw	128 (67–61)	1979
	Hal Sutton	128 (64–64)	1986
Low 36	Johnny Miller	128 (67–61)	1975
	Ben Crenshaw	128 (67–61)	1979
	Lanny Wadkins	128 (63, 65)	1982 (rounds 3–4)
	Hal Sutton	128 (64–64)	1986
Low first 54	Johnny Miller	196 (67, 61, 68)	1975
Low 54	Johnny Miller	193 (61–68–64)	1975 (rounds 2–3–4)
Low 72	Johnny Miller	260 (67–61–68–64)	1975
Highest winning score	Jimmy Demaret	278	1949
	Dudley Wysong	278	1966
Largest winning margin	Johnny Miller (260)	14 strokes	1975
Largest 18-hole lead	Arnold Palmer (64)	3 strokes	1962
Largest 36-hole lead	Byron Nelson (133)	6 strokes	1939
	Johnny Miller (128)	6 strokes	1975
Largest 54-hole lead	Byron Nelson (198)	12 strokes	1939
Lowest start by winner	Jimmy Demaret	64	1950
	Arnold Palmer	64	1962
	Hal Sutton	64	1986
Highest start by winner	Dudley Wysong	73	1966
Lowest finish by winner	Ed Oliver	64	1940
	Johnny Miller	64	1975
Highest finish by winner	Jimmy Demaret	64	1949
	Jerry Pate	73	1977
Best final-round comeback	Dudley Wysong	6 back	1966
Lowest 36-hole cut score		141	1979, 1981, 1983
Highest 36-hole cut score		153	1953

DUELING WITH THE DESERT
BY TOM WEISKOPF

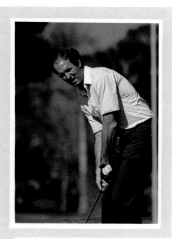

When you hit the ball off the playing areas of the TPC course, you're basically in the desert. It's maintained terrain, but it's also very rugged in spots, grown over with cactus, creosote bushes, brittle brush, red threon, and other species of desert flora.

Don't try to be a hero from that stuff. It's similar to the ice plant in Monterey—it's a lot tougher to hit out of than it looks. So focus on getting the ball back into play, not on ripping it 200 yards or knocking it stiff to the pin.

Indeed, your best alternative may be to resort to the Rules of Golf and seek relief under the provisions for an unplayable lie. Let's say the ball's in the middle of a patch of brittle brush. You have three options: 1. Go back to the point from which you hit the previous shot and play again; 2. Drop a ball within two club lengths of the spot in the bush where the ball lays (but not closer to the hole) and play from there; 3. Drop a ball behind the spot where the ball lays, keeping that spot directly between you and the hole, with no limit to how far behind that spot the ball may be dropped.

In any of these situations there is a penalty of one stroke. Still, that may be less painful than dueling with the desert.

Tom Weiskopf is a co-designer of the TPC of Scottsdale.

SCORECARD

Hole	Yards	Par
1	400	4
2	416	4
3	576	5
4	166	3
5	466	4
6	390	4
7	228	3
8	470	4
9	416	4
OUT	3528	35
10	406	4
11	450	4
12	200	3
13	570	5
14	436	4
15	515	5
16	180	3
17	303	4
18	450	4
IN	3510	36
TOTAL	7038	71

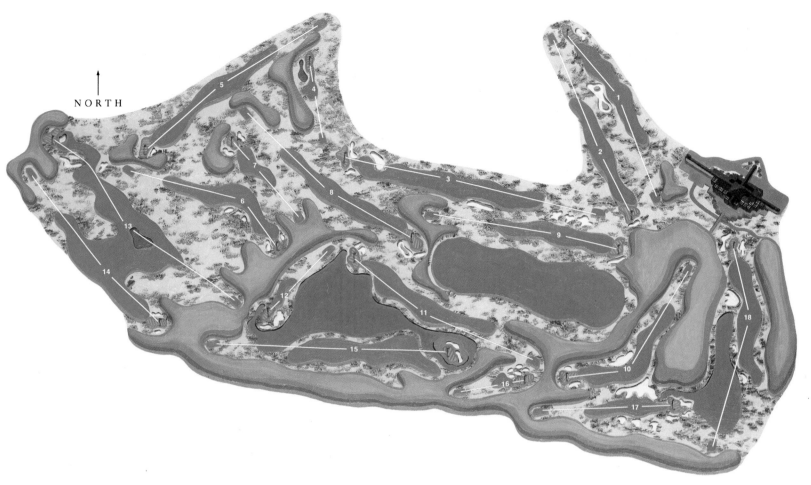

NORTH

PAST WINNERS

Year	Winner	Score	Year	Winner	Score
1935	Ky Laffoon	281	1964	Jack Nicklaus	271
1936–			1965	Rod Funseth	274
1938	No Tournaments		1966	Dudley Wysong	278
1939	Byron Nelson	198	1967	Julius Boros	272
1940	Ed Oliver	205	1968	George Knudson	272
1941–			1969	Gene Littler	263
1943	No Tournaments		1970	Dale Douglass	271
1944	*H. McSpaden	273	1971	Miller Barber	261
1945	Byron Nelson	274	1972	Homero Blancas	273
1946	*Ben Hogan	273	1973	Bruce Crampton	268
1947	Ben Hogan	270	1974	Johnny Miller	271
1948	Bobby Locke	268	1975	Johnny Miller	260
1949	*Jimmy Demaret	278	1976	Bob Gilder	268
1950	Jimmy Demaret	269	1977	*Jerry Pate	277
1951	Lew Worsham	272	1978	Miller Barber	272
1952	Lloyd Mangrum	274	1979	‡Ben Crenshaw	199
1953	Lloyd Mangrum	272	1980	Jeff Mitchell	272
1954	*Ed Furgol	272	1981	David Graham	268
1955	Gene Littler	275	1982	Lanny Wadkins	263
1956	C. Middlecoff	276	1983	*Bob Gilder	271
1957	Billy Casper	271	1984	Tom Purtzer	268
1958	Ken Venturi	274	1985	Calvin Peete	270
1959	Gene Littler	268	1986	Hal Sutton	267
1960	*Jack Fleck	273	1987	Paul Azinger	268
1961	*Arnold Palmer	270	1988	Sandy Lyle	269
1962	Arnold Palmer	269	*Playoff		
1963	Arnold Palmer	273	‡Rain-curtailed		

With a late 1986 opening and debut on the Tour for the 1987 Phoenix, the amateur and professional juries are still out. Certainly, with holes such as the 466-yard (upwind) fifth and the 228-yard seventh, this TPC would seem to be a pro-sized challenge. However, at least two holes suggest that the architects have successfully met the dual demands of the Tour and the public.

The 15th hole is a par five of 515 yards—reachable in two by every pro on the Tour (and a good many amateurs as well). But most handicap players (and many Tour players) will think twice before they blast their tee shots. A lake on the left side cautions against an overactive right hand in the hitting area. Even after a good drive, the second shot will have to be as high and straight as it is long, because this green sits on an island. Fifteen is an excellent three-shot par five for the locals and a fine opportunity for the aggressive pros to make 4—or 6.

Another subtly challenging hole is the tiny 17th, at 303 yards a *drivable par four* for the Tour's longest hitters. But the chances are, few will try. With bunkers in the center of the fairway and water to the left of the green, that 300-yard tee shot will have to be hit with the accuracy of a 9-iron.

PEBBLE BEACH
Golf Links

CYPRESS POINT
Golf Club

SPYGLASS HILL
Golf Club

AT&T
PEBBLE BEACH
NATIONAL
PRO—AM
CALIFORNIA

Robert Louis Stevenson called it "the most felicitous meeting of land and sea in Creation." Stevenson, the nineteenth-century author of *Treasure Island*, was describing the Monterey Peninsula. Had he lived 100 years later, he might have called it "the most felicitous meeting of land, sea, and *golf.*"

Stevenson died in 1894, several years after the birth of a man named Samuel F. B. Morse, the grandnephew and namesake of the telegraph inventor. It was Morse, a visionary and conservationist, who introduced golf—grand, compelling, spectacular golf—to this savagely beautiful stretch of northern California.

It was Morse who in 1919 unveiled Pebble Beach, the layout that is, by universal consent, the finest seaside course in North America and, very likely, the world. A few years later that big, brawling layout was joined by a compact, devilish jewel called Cypress Point. Together with the Monterey Peninsula Country Club, they became the tripartite playing ground for the Pebble Beach National Pro-Am.

Bing Crosby originated this event, which carried his name until 1985, when his widow, Kathryn, withdrew the family name because of what she deemed "overcommercialization" of the event. Officially or not, the tournament is still known as "The Crosby." A member and several-time club champion of Lakeside Country Club near Los Angeles, Crosby got the idea of staging a pro-am event for Lakeside members as a chance to get the average hacks together with a few of the pros. This was in 1937, when Bing owned a home on the golf course at Rancho Santa Fe, and it was there that the first tournament was held—in a deluge of rain, an appropriate beginning for the event that is notorious for its unpredictable weather. In a foreword to Dwayne Netland's book *The Crosby: Greatest Show in Golf*, Bing reminisced about the festivities that capped his first tournament:

Pebble Beach, 7th hole

Spyglass, 1st hole

Spyglass, 4th hole

The rain stopped in time that evening for the big barbecue down under the pepper trees of the ranch, with suitable potables, edibles, and impromptu entertainment. . . . I just say it was a pretty good little soiree, lasting far into the night and necessitating the aid of the highway patrol to guide some of the more bibulous guests to their pads in Del Mar, LaJolla, Oceanside and San Clemente. Thus was born what was to become known as "The Clambake."

That first Crosby was won by Sam Snead. As Bing handed him the winner's check of $500, the legendarily tightfisted Snead is reputed to have said, "Thank you very much, Mr. Crosby, but if you don't mind, I'd rather have cash."

The tournament stayed at Rancho Santa Fe for five years before it was discontinued during World War II. By the time it reappeared in 1947, Crosby was a member of Cypress Point. A group of locals from Monterey urged him to move The Clambake to the peninsula, and so he did, spreading the play over Cypress, Pebble, and the Monterey Peninsula Country Club. It remained on those three until 1967, when Spyglass Hill Golf Club took the place of Monterey.

The Crosby was the first Tour event to employ more than one course, and it was also the first of the big celebrity pro-ams. Under its unique format an amateur partners with the same professional for three straight days, playing one round on each of the three courses. After the third round a cut is made of both the professionals and the pro-am teams, and the survivors play at Pebble Beach on Sunday for both the pro-am team and individual pro championships.

An invitation to the Crosby is a major status symbol. Only 168 amateurs may play each year, but the tournament annually receives nearly 10,000 requests. For decades

Spyglass, 5th hole

Bing selected the lucky group, rotating in a group of fifty newcomers each year. After Bing's death his son Nathaniel took over the bittersweet chore of saying "yes" to a few hopefuls and "no" to the majority.

Maury Luxford, for years the tournament chairman and official starter, claimed he was once approached in the men's room of the Los Angeles Airport by a stranger who had recognized him. "I've got $25,000 in my pocket," the man said, "and if you can get me into the Crosby, it's yours."

The offer was declined. But certain amateurs are granted entry every year. These are the core celebrities, stars like Jack Lemmon, Clint Eastwood, James Garner, George C. Scott, Telly Savalas, Glen Campbell, and Andy Williams, along with a smattering of athletes, politicians, and corporate kingpins. All that is required of them is a comparatively modest entrance fee and a handicap of 18 or lower.

The fact is that many of the big names also have big handicaps. Raymond Floyd, a good friend and a longtime Crosby partner to Clint (18-handicap) Eastwood, claims he can count on one hand the number of holes where Clint has helped the team. And Jack Lemmon, although he claims to have a 16, has been known to use up most of that on a single hole.

One year Lemmon slashed at the ball nine times before reaching the 18th green at Pebble Beach. As he lined up his lengthy putt for a 10, he asked his caddie, "Which way does this break?"

"Who cares?" replied the caddie.

Then there's the classic story of Lemmon and the dog, an episode that illustrates the type of terror that consumes most amateurs involved in the Crosby. On one tee Lemmon was preparing to hit his drive when out of the gallery tore a big, scruffy dog. It ran straight through Lemmon's legs and disappeared into the crowd on the other side of the tee. Without batting an eye, Lemmon played a fine tee shot.

Jimmy Demaret was doing color commentary on television at the time, and after Lemmon's round he went up to Jack.

"Jack, that was really remarkable, the composure you displayed back there on the 15th tee," said Demaret. "That dog ran right between your legs and you didn't let it disturb you at all."

Lemmon looked at Demaret in absolute surprise and said, "You mean, that was a *real* dog?"

A subtle caste system exists with regard to the three groups of pro-am teams rotating among the courses. The "A" group plays Cypress Point on Thursday, moves to Spyglass Hill on Friday, and finishes at Pebble Beach on Saturday—the day that play on Pebble is televised. It is

ego-bruising for a celebrity to discover that his Saturday round is at Cypress or Spyglass.

There are some pros and amateurs, in fact, who would just as soon avoid Spyglass altogether. In the view of many players, it is simply too hard.

"Pebble and Cypress make you want to play golf," says Jack Nicklaus, a three-time champion. "They're such interesting and enjoyable layouts. Spyglass Hill, that's different. That makes you want to go fishing."

Jim Murray, the demon columnist for the *Los Angeles Times*, once wrote:

> If it were human, Spyglass would have a knife in its teeth, a patch on its eye, a ring in its ear, tobacco in its beard and a blunderbuss in its hands. It's a privateer plundering the golfing main, an amphibious creature, half ocean, half forest. You play through seals to squirrels, sand dunes to pine cones, pounding surf to mast-high firs. It's a 300-acre unplayable lie.

And Lee Trevino put it as only he can: "They ought to hang the man who designed this course," he said. "Ray Charles could have done better."

The man who designed Spyglass is Robert Trent Jones, dean of American golf course architects and the most prolific practitioner in the history of his profession. Jones was commissioned by the Pebble Beach Company in 1966 to construct this public course, which now is headquarters for the Northern California Golf Association.

Jones envisioned Spyglass as his crowning achievement, an opportunity to blend the sea, the dunes, and the forest into an exhilarating 18-hole package. To his credit, he used restraint. In the past Jones had been accused of bulldozing courses to death, but at Spyglass he left the best land—the dunes areas of holes two through five—virtually untouched as a sort of Pine Valley of the Pacific.

The golfer reaches that seaside area via the first hole, a mammoth par five that winds 600 yards downhill in a gentle leftward turn. Generally played into the ocean breeze, this is one of the toughest starting holes on the Tour. It is a formidable place to have to make five, whether your name is Jack Lemmon or Jack Nicklaus

The next four holes weave through the sand dunes: the 350-yard second winding uphill, followed by the picturesque par-three third played straight at the windy sea. Number four, one of the finest mid-length fours anywhere, demands accurate placement of both the tee shot and the approach. Miss either one even slightly and you will find yourself in the unraked sand or, worse yet, in the ice plant.

Ice plant is the meanest flora in golf. The feeling at impact with this asparagus is about the same as when hitting a 1-iron out of a pile of old sneakers. Simply moving the ball is an achievement, getting it to the fairway a miracle, and approximating your target an accident.

After another windy par three, the course meanders back uphill, where it stays for the rest of the round, threading through thick stands of Monterey pines. The best-known hole on the back nine is the 12th, a downhill par three that Jones modeled after the famous Redan Hole of North Berwick in Scotland. With the canted green wedged between water left and a steep, bunkered rise on the right, careful club selection is vital.

The 14th is a rare double-dogleg par five with water in front of the green, a relatively easy par for the pros but a tough birdie. And the longest, toughest four on the course is number 16, a 465-yard dogleg left with trees lining the entire fairway on both sides. Tall trees encroach on the last two holes as well, both par fours. No one is out of the woods on this course until he leaves the parking lot.

A short drive down the road is the place that former USGA President Sandy Tatum called "The Sistine Chapel of Golf": Cypress Point. Most of those fortunate enough to have had a round there would agree that it is akin to a religious experience.

Designed in 1928 by Alister Mackenzie and Robert Hunter, Cypress is a layout that breaks many of the canons of golf course design and does it with panache. The opening drive plays across a road, two back-to-back holes on the front nine are par fives, two back-to-back holes on the back nine are par threes, and from the tips of the pro tees the course measures only 6,506 yards. Yet this is undisputedly one of the finest courses since St. Andrews. In the decade since *Golf Magazine* began its biennial list of "The 100 Greatest Courses in the World," Cypress Point has never ranked lower than fifth.

Certainly no course has a more beautiful natural setting. Its emerald green fairways wind up and down the rugged dunes and hills lined with cathedral pines and cypress. Wild deer and elk roam the holes, sea gulls hover overhead, and the Pacific waves crash and spray as sea lions bark from their misty perches in the bay.

But when the wind blows, as normally it does, the 6,500 yards can seem like 7,500, and the fairways can look like catwalks. The first hole, a straightforward par four of 418 yards, exacts three times as many bogeys as birdies from the pros.

Three of the next five holes are par fives, and this is where the players make their scores. The sixth hole, at 522 yards, is the longest but probably the least troublesome. All are reachable in two, and most pros get through holes five and six in nine shots.

The eighth and ninth holes at Cypress are on every discerning golfer's list of classic, short par fours. At 355

and 291 yards, respectively, they provide a compact one-two punch that is as staggering as any pair of 450-yard brutes. Set in the rolling dunes, both holes call for long-iron tee shots followed by surgically sure wedges to the well-bunkered, plateau greens. One of them always plays downwind, complicating the second shot. Once, during a Crosby practice round, Tom Watson took out his driver on the ninth and nailed a bullet through the narrow opening to the green. It finished a few feet from the hole.

"Is that the club you'll hit when the bell rings?" a member of the gallery asked.

"Sure," answered Watson, adding "if I want to be certain of making a 7."

Par for the front nine at Cypress is 37, the back nine 35, but it is likely that most amateurs' scores on the second nine are higher. The reasons: holes 16 and 17.

Having handled the cute little 15th with a short iron and two putts, the golfer strolls around the corner and runs into its big brother. This is in fact the big brother of par threes everywhere, the most photographed and arguably the most difficult hole in the world, a howling, frothing behemoth that ravages all except those who can slug a driver down its throat. In every year since scoring statistics have been compiled, the 16th at Cypress has ranked as the hardest of the almost 1,000 holes on the PGA Tour.

"It took me ten years of playing the Crosby before I made a birdie on that hole," says Ben Crenshaw, "and when I did, it was by sinking a 45-foot putt."

For most players, par three feels like a birdie. The distance from the back tee is 233 yards, and there is no front tee. Anyone hoping to hit the green will have to play his shot at least 220 of those yards across the crashing surf. There is a bail-out area to the left, but for those who hit into the Pacific, there is no drop area. They just keep on slugging.

That is what Porky Oliver did in 1953. Oliver was in contention during the third round of the Crosby when he came to 16. That day it was playing into the teeth of a fifty-mile-per-hour gale. Porky slapped five straight shots out to sea, then knocked one into a patch of ice plant and spent some time there. When he finally holed out he had a 16.

Occasionally, someone will attempt to play a recovery shot from the rocky beach below. One year Henry Ransom climbed down there. He hit three consecutive shots into the rocks; the third one bounced back and struck him in the stomach. Disgusted, Ransom ordered his caddie to pick up the ball and stalked off. "When they start hitting back at you," he said, "it's time to quit."

A handful of golfers have actually mastered 16. One is Jerry Pate, who knocked his orange ball into the hole

Spyglass, 12th hole

Spyglass, 14th hole

during the 1982 Crosby. Another, appropriately, is Bing Crosby, who aced it during a casual round in 1947.

The 17th is thought by many players to be the best hole on the peninsula. From a tee directly behind and above the 16th green, it plays back across the inlet to a sharply doglegging fairway that skirts the craggy cliffs all the way to the green 376 yards away. Thus one may cut off as much or as little as he dares. To complicate matters, a stand of large, gnarly cypress trees sits in the right-center of the landing area about 250 yards out.

It was here in 1951 that Byron Nelson hit the most daring shot of his professional life. Nelson was leading the Crosby that year when he knocked his drive dead-behind those cypress trees. From there he played a hook out over the surf. It finished twelve feet from the pin, and Nelson went on to win the tournament by a shot. It was the last of his 54 career victories.

Jerry Pittman was not as lucky—or maybe he was. In 1967 Pittman was tied for the lead when he pushed his second shot into the ice plant on the edge of the cliff. As he stepped in to determine whether to play the ball or take a penalty drop, the ground suddenly gave way, and he began to fall sixty feet onto the jagged rocks below. Fortunately, Tour official George Walsh was nearby. He reached out and grabbed the sinking golfer just in time. Shaken, Pittman bogeyed the next two holes and was never seen on the leaderboard again.

Cypress Point is traditionally in the best condition of the three Crosby venues, and why not? Whereas Pebble Beach and Spyglass Hill get tens of thousands of rounds by the public each year, ultra-private Cypress, with 240 widely scattered members, sees almost no play. Except for the Crosby, it has hosted only one event of consequence: the 1981 Walker Cup Matches. The tone of the club is low-key and protective. Bob Hope, who has been a member for forty years, sums it up: "One year we had a big membership drive—and drove out fifty members."

Pebble Beach is a public golf course. Anyone can play it. Anyone, that is, who has the requisite time and money. At last count, the cost of a cart and green fee was a nice, round $125, and the duration of an average round was about five-and-a-half hours. But people from all over the world happily pay the price and endure the traffic. And well they should. At twice the cost and twice the wait, Pebble Beach is a bargain.

When Samuel Morse sought an architect for his project, he did not look far. The job went to Jack Neville, a real estate salesman in Morse's Del Monte Properties company. Neville was a scratch player, and Morse reasoned that anyone who could play that well had to be able to design a course. In this case, he was right.

Some have argued that the first five holes of the course lack the splendor of the last 13. From a scenic standpoint, this is inarguable. But all five are nonetheless solid tests of shotmaking, beginning with the slender first—such a good opening four and such a tough three. The long second, its second shot over a gulch complicated by a large tree blocking the left side, is a good gambler's par five that varies greatly with every change in the wind.

The third may seem a mundane dogleg four until the drive draws a bit too much. Then the trees and sand can quickly turn par into a major assignment. Likewise at the deceptive fourth, where bunkers to the left and the sea cliffs hard by the right demand a string-straight drive. As for the fifth hole, its tunnel of trees makes this uphill 166-yard shot one of the most claustrophobically daunting vistas in golf.

Lee Trevino calls the fifth hole a pivotal one because, "If you're five over when you get to the sixth hole at Pebble, it's a good time to commit suicide." When the golfer emerges from the leafy cocoon of number five, he is on the threshold of a stretch of the most dramatically beautiful and testing holes in the world.

The easiest of them may be the first, number six. From the tee the hole looks like a playground for dinosaurs. Halfway to the green of this 516-yard par five, the fairway swoops dramatically upward, leaving a sheer drop to the ocean on the right. A good drive leaves a blind second shot up that steep hill. It also leaves most golfers wondering whether they can possibly hit a ball high enough and hard enough to reach the top and, if so, whether that ball can possibly stay on the shelf. The pros play the shot as a drive, a long iron or wood, and a pitch. Into the wind, add another long iron or wood.

The tiny seventh is the shortest hole on any championship golf course, and yard for yard it also may be the hardest. On a mild day it is merely a crisp wedge to the tiny green embraced by rock, sand, and Pacific. But catch it during a hard blow, and you will have to summon one of the firmest, straightest, bravest iron shots of your life. Eddie Merrins, "The Little Pro" from Bel Air, aced this hole during one blustery Crosby—with a 3-iron. And one year Sam Snead was so intimidated by what he faced that he *putted* the ball down the dirt path to the green.

Number eight begins the most awesome sequence of three par-four holes anywhere. Tony Lema stood on this tee the year he was the defending Crosby champion and said to his pro-am cohort, "Partner, you'll have to make bogeys on the next three holes, and with your strokes we'll get out alive. There is no way I can par all three of them."

At the eighth hole, most of the fours are one-putt pars. It begins with a blind tee shot uphill to the edge of a cliff.

Cypress Point, 3rd hole

From there the challenge is to play an approach of more than 200 yards across a chasm that drops a rugged 100 feet, and hold the ball on one of the narrowest, fastest greens on a course that is known for its narrow, fast greens. Nicklaus calls it the greatest second shot in golf.

The hardest hole on this nine is the last one, a brawling 464-yard par four that plays downhill while falling left to right toward the menacing cliffs. Those who seek to avoid the perils of the right side may find equally severe trouble in the thick rough and bunkers on the left. The green sits on the brink of the precipice. Occasionally, even a putt has been known to fall off the edge and onto the beach below. In the 1963 Crosby, Dale Douglass took a 19 here. Yes, 19.

Cypress Point, 6th hole

Cypress Point, 9th hole

Cypress Point, 17th hole

Cypress Point, 15th hole

Pebble Beach, 6th, 7th, and 8th holes

Only slightly less difficult is the 10th, another long (426-yard) tightrope walk along the ocean bluffs. Again, the green hugs the edge of disaster; this time, though, it is partly cradled in sand. Jack Nicklaus won the 1972 U.S. Open despite hitting the beach twice and making 6 on this hole in the final round.

On a day when a Monterey bluster is in full cry, anyone who can go par-par-par at eight, nine, and ten will pick up several shots on the field.

Bobby Jones once complained that on most par fives "you don't start playing golf until the third shot." On the 14th at Pebble Beach, you start playing from the moment you stick the tee in the ground. This is a classically strategic hole, demanding a well-placed tee shot to maneuver the second into the ideal position from which to skirt the yawning bunker at the front of this acutely two-tiered green.

Sixteen is a left-to-right dogleg par four to a green that is fronted by a deep barranca and closely encircled by cypress trees. The trees encroach to such a degree that only a very well-placed tee shot will allow an unobstructed shot to the green.

Pebble Beach, 8th hole

Pebble Beach, 7th hole

Nicklaus has had more success than anyone on Pebble, the course he has always called his favorite. Jack won his second U.S. Amateur here in 1961 and later added three Crosbys and the 1972 U.S. Open. He was the first player—and probably will be the last—to win both the U.S. Amateur and U.S. Open on the same golf course. In Britain the feat was accomplished only by Bobby Jones at St. Andrews.

At least some of Nicklaus's good fortune has occurred at the par-three 17th. It was at this 209-yard hole during the 1972 U.S. Open that Jack stung a 1-iron into a stiff wind and incredibly hit the flagstick, leaving a tap-in putt for the birdie that clinched the title.

But it was this hole also that spelled Nicklaus's demise in the same championship a decade later. Anyone who follows golf knows that the 17th hole at Pebble Beach was the site of Tom Watson's miracle chip from heavy rough. At the time Watson and Nicklaus were tied for the championship, with Jack safely in the clubhouse. When Watson's tee shot strayed into heavy rough to the left of the green, Jack's chances for a record fifth U.S. Open title looked excellent.

"Get it close," said Watson's caddie to his boss.

"I'm not going to get it close," said Tom. "I'm going to sink it."

And he did, flipping the ball over the fringe and down the bank of the hard green into the back of the hole, one of the most electrifying strokes in the history of championship golf. It gave Watson a one-stroke edge and the adrenaline to birdie 18 for a two-stroke victory.

Pebble Beach, 16th hole

Pebble Beach, 18th hole

The best of this great course is the last. By almost unanimous agreement, the 18th at Pebble has no parallel as a long finishing hole. Curved gracefully along 548 yards of the rockbound coast, it is as demanding as it is beautiful, as exciting as it is treacherous. The best tee shot bites off a bit of the water, as bunkers and a stand of trees impede progress down the dry right side. Then the second shot must be banged down the right center, ideally leaving a full wedge to the small, firm green. On every one of the three shots, water is in mind even more than it is in view.

This tournament annually attracts one of the largest television audiences of the golf year. Two ingredients make that happen. First, the time of year. Many golfers cannot play, so they watch. Second, the show itself, and this in turn breaks down into three elements: the beautiful scenery, the entertaining amateurs and professionals, and invariably the weather.

As Crosby himself said, "I think the galleryites enjoy draping themselves in every manner of rain gear, parkas, mukluks, hip boots, balbriggans, pea jackets, space suits, ski pants, Antarctic survival gear, and woolen long johns, and watching with fiendish relish while great players, actors, athletes, and executives lurch through the rain, lashing out desperately against the elements with only occasional success."

That is the Crosby, 336 of golf's most dogged victims acting out their inexorable fate in some of the most splendid settings—and most execrable conditions—God and golf can produce.

ALL-TIME TOURNAMENT RECORDS

Record	Player(s)	Score	Year
Low 18	Tom Kite	62	1983
Low first 36	Bob Rosburg	132 (65–67)	1958
Low 36	Bob Rosburg	132 (65–67)	1958
	Mike Morley	(65–67)	1982 (rounds 3–4)
Low first 54	Cary Middlecoff	202 (66–68–68)	1956*
	Tom Watson	(66–69–67)	1977
Low 54	Cary Middlecoff	202 (66–68–68)	1956*
	Tom Watson	(66–69–67)	1977
Low 72	Tom Watson	273 (66–69–67–71)	1977
Highest winning score	Ken Venturi	286 (70–71–68–77)	1960
	Doug Ford	(70–73–69–74)	1962
Largest winning margin	Lloyd Mangrum	5 strokes	1948*
	Cary Middlecoff		1956*
	Jack Nicklaus		1967
Largest 18-hole lead	Jack Nicklaus (66)	3 strokes	1972
	Billy Casper (66)		1973
	Tom Watson (66)		1978
Largest 36-hole lead	Bob Rosburg (132)	5 strokes	1958
Largest 54-hole lead	Ted Kroll (203)	5 strokes	1961
	Lon Hinkle (207)		1979
	Fuzzy Zoeller		1986
Lowest start by winner	John Dawson**	66	1942†
	Cary Middlecoff		1956*
	Jack Nicklaus		1972
	Tom Watson		1977–1978
	John Cook		1981*
Highest start by winner	Jack Burke	75	1950*
	Bruce Crampton		1965
	Ben Crenshaw		1976
Lowest finish by winner	Jim Simons	66	1982
	Johnny Miller		1987
Highest finish by winner	Ken Venturi	77	1960
	Lon Hinkle		1979
Best final-round comeback	Bob Rosburg	7 back	1961
Lowest 54-hole cut score		216	1983
Highest 54-hole cut score		227	1967

*54-hole tournament
**amateur
†36-hole tournament

PAST WINNERS

Year	Winner	Score	Year	Winner	Score
1937	Sam Snead	68	1963	Billy Casper	285
1938	Sam Snead	139	1964	Tony Lema	284
1939	Dutch Harrison	138	1965	Bruce Crampton	284
1940	Ed Oliver	135	1966	D. Massengale	283
1941	Sam Snead	136	1967	Jack Nicklaus	284
1942	Tie-Lloyd Mangrum		1968	*Johnny Pott	285
	Leland Gibson	133	1969	George Archer	283
1943-			1970	Bert Yancey	278
1946	No Tournaments		1971	Tom Shaw	278
1947	Tie-Ed Furgol		1972	*Jack Nicklaus	284
	George Fazio	213	1973	*Jack Nicklaus	282
1948	Lloyd Mangrum	205	1974	Johnny Miller	208
1949	Ben Hogan	208	1975	Gene Littler	280
1950	Tie-Sam Snead		1976	Ben Crenshaw	281
	Jack Burke, Jr.		1977	Tom Watson	273
	Smiley Quick		1978	*Tom Watson	280
	Dave Douglas	214	1979	Lon Hinkle	284
1951	Byron Nelson	209	1980	George Burns	280
1952	Jimmy Demaret	145	1981	*John Cook	209
1953	Lloyd Mangrum	204	1982	Jim Simons	274
1954	Dutch Harrison	210	1983	Tom Kite	276
1955	C. Middlecoff	209	1984	*Hale Irwin	278
1956	C. Middlecoff	202	1985	Mark O'Meara	283
1957	Jay Hebert	213	1986	‡Fuzzy Zoeller	205
1958	Billy Casper	277	1987	Johnny Miller	278
1959	Art Wall	279	1988	Steve Jones	280
1960	Ken Venturi	286			
1961	Bob Rosburg	282	*Playoff		
1962	*Doug Ford	286	‡Rain-curtailed		

Pebble Beach Golf Links

PEBBLE BEACH GL SCORECARD

Hole	Yards	Par	PGA Tour Avg. Score
1	373	4	4.163
2	502	5	4.475
3	388	4	4.016
4	327	4	3.957
5	166	3	3.091
6	516	5	4.803
7	107	3	3.070
8	431	4	4.281
9	464	4	4.368
OUT	3274	36	36.224
10	426	4	4.289
11	384	4	4.065
12	202	3	3.179
13	392	4	4.065
14	565	5	5.172
15	397	4	4.055
16	402	4	4.164
17	209	3	3.004
18	548	5	5.140
IN	3525	36	37.133
TOTAL	6799	72	73.357

CYPRESS POINT GC SCORECARD

Hole	Yards	Par	PGA Tour Avg. Score
1	418	4	4.235
2	551	5	4.897
3	161	3	2.963
4	385	4	4.239
5	491	5	4.829
6	522	5	4.736
7	163	3	3.175
8	355	4	4.401
9	291	4	4.197
OUT	3337	37	37.672
10	491	5	4.622
11	434	4	4.253
12	409	4	4.191
13	362	4	4.091
14	383	4	4.431
15	139	3	2.966
16	233	3	3.636
17	376	4	4.287
18	342	4	4.219
IN	3169	35	36.696
TOTAL	6506	72	74.368

SPYGLASS HILL GC SCORECARD

Hole	Yards	Par	PGA Tour Avg. Score
1	600	5	5.158
2	350	4	4.140
3	150	3	3.108
4	365	4	4.054
5	180	3	3.287
6	415	4	4.333
7	515	5	4.849
8	395	4	4.441
9	425	4	4.221
OUT	3395	36	37.591
10	400	4	4.183
11	520	5	4.879
12	180	3	2.980
13	440	4	4.205
14	555	5	5.006
15	130	3	3.014
16	465	4	4.391
17	320	4	4.010
18	405	4	4.327
IN	3415	36	36.995
TOTAL	6810	72	74.586

PITCHING FROM ROUGH
BY TOM WATSON

Probably the one shot of my golfing career that will be most remembered was the short but difficult pitch that I holed from heavy rough to the left of the 71st green in the 1982 U.S. Open at Pebble Beach. When playing such a shot, I use a sand wedge and hit the ball much the same way I would a sand shot. I open both my setup and clubface. I take the club up more abruptly and away from my body on the backswing by hinging my wrists sooner, to avoid as much grass as possible on the takeaway. On the forward swing I slide the club under the ball with the clubface held firmly open by the last three fingers of my left hand. I can even hit slightly behind the ball, as if it were in the sand, with good results. Remember that the ball will tend to run farther out of rough than from a regular lie.

Tom Watson won back-to-back victories in the AT&T Pebble Beach National Pro-Am (1977, 1978) as well as the 1982 U.S. Open at Pebble Beach.

TORREY PINES *Golf Course*

Torrey Pines North, 6th hole

Let us say you are a golf nut, you have a week's vacation, and you want to cram your days with as much play as possible. Where should you go?

Go to San Diego. The weather is perfect for golf nearly 365 days a year, and the city boasts more than seventy courses.

Now let us say you are a golf gourmet. Quality is more important than quantity. You still have a week, but you want to spend your time on courses that are scenic, challenging, and first class.

Go to San Diego anyway. And go to Torrey Pines.

Set along a row of cliffs at the edge of the Pacific Ocean, the North and South courses of Torrey Pines constitute one of the finest municipal golf facilities in the world. Fifty-one weeks out of the year, they are operated by the city of San Diego for the enjoyment of the public. One week each winter, they host the PGA Tour.

Few courses in America, and perhaps no municipal course, can boast a more spectacular natural setting. The ocean is in view from many of the holes and in play on a couple of them, where the fairways cling to the ledges of steep canyons dropping 300 feet to the sea. Most of the trees on the course are the starkly beautiful Torrey pines for which the club is named, an ancient variety of long-needled fir that is native only to San Diego and the Channel Islands off Santa Barbara.

Both courses were designed during the early fifties by William P. "Billy" Bell, a protégé of George C. Thomas, the famed designer of the Riviera and Los Angeles Country Club courses. Bell died before he could see completion of his work, but his son, William F. Bell, oversaw the construction.

Par for both courses is 72, but the South is nearly 350 yards longer and plays roughly two strokes harder than the North. The pros play both courses on Thursday and Friday of the tournament; after the cut, the competition is restricted to the South course.

Wind is a major factor here, particularly in the afternoon, when it gusts through the canyons and lengthens the holes that play toward the sea. The greens are not fast, but their breaks are subtle and often confounding. Raymond Floyd was once asked about the most unforgettable putt of his career, and he recalled not one but two putts at Torrey Pines.

"The first was in 1975, in the first hole of a sudden-death playoff with J.C. Snead and Bobby Nichols," said Floyd.

"On the first hole [15 on the South course], I had a chance to win. I hit a putt that was going down. No way I was going to miss. I went to get it, convinced it was in the hole. Then it just lipped out. I was amazed. It was the weirdest thing I'd ever seen. In fact, for a long time after that, I actually had nightmares about it. I kept seeing it in my mind, over and over.

"Then, unbelievably, the same thing happened on the same hole and under the same circumstances in 1981 when I was in a playoff with Bruce Lietzke and Tom Jenkins. As had been the case six years earlier, they both missed their birdie putts. I hit mine, and it was breaking right into the center of the hole again. Then, just at the lip, it swerved away and missed."

Not many birdies are made on the fourth hole, a 445-yard uphill buster that runs along the cliff on the left. Generally regarded as the second hardest hole on the course, it can produce high numbers, particularly when a shot tumbles off the cliff to the clay beach below. It is still playable down there, but the prognosis for complete recovery is grave. Imagine trying to hit a 9-iron off a sidewalk to the roof of a skyscraper across the street, and you get a feel for the assignment.

Still, Johnny Miller calls number four "my lucky hole," and for good reason. In 1982, when he won the tournament, Miller somehow birdied it four days in a row.

The longest par four and the hardest hole on the South course—or either course for that matter—is the 12th. Its 467 yards play uphill and into a prevailing wind off the ocean. Tall trees and four-inch rough line both sides of the fairway, a bunker on the right catches fades that fade too much, and another one a bit farther down the fairway snares draws that draw too much. A ball in either of them almost inevitably means a shot lost on the way to the sand-flanked green. Number 15, where Floyd had his double trouble, is an excellent, short par four of 389 yards. Formerly a straight hole, it is now a slight dogleg left for the pros, thanks to a tee, added in 1973, that tacked 50 yards onto the hole. The smart drive is shaded to the right to avoid a large eucalyptus tree on the left side of the fairway.

Number 17 is the type of hole that gives even the straightest hitters pause. The canyons gape on the left, and a thick fence of trees runs down the right.

The 18th, a reachable par five fronted by water, has beckoned both the best and worst from those who have toyed with it. The key to the hole is the elongated pond, which was added to the left-front of the green in 1968. The pond became known as (Bruce) Devlin's Billabong in 1975 after the Australian played six shots from its near shore in an attempt to blast his ball onto the green. Only three strokes off the lead when he hit water in the final round, Devlin lost $3,000—$600 per swing—and finished tied for 30th. A plaque marks the spot.

Unless wind is dead in the face on this 501-yard par five, most of the pros go for the green in two. Many of them make birdies, and a few do even better. In 1968 Tom Weiskopf inaugurated the pond hole by sinking a 25-foot eagle putt from off the green to edge Al Geiberger by a stroke. Since then the hole has produced a string of dramatic finishes that rival any on the Tour.

In 1970 Pete Brown made up six shots in the final round on defending champion Jack Nicklaus, then by his own admission "choked" on a four-foot putt at 18 to move into a playoff with Tony Jacklin (Nicklaus also missed a short one at 18 that would have put him into the playoff). Brown won on the first extra hole, thus becoming the second black golfer to win a PGA Tour event (the first was Charlie Sifford).

Nicklaus almost returned to the winner's circle in 1982 after playing one of the greatest shots of his life. He had trailed Johnny Miller by seven strokes at the start of the final round, but reeled off five birdies and an eagle, then, from a bad lie on the 18th fairway, slugged a 3-wood across the pond to within eight feet of the cup. Down went the putt for his second eagle of the day and a course-record-tieing 64.

It forced Miller to play cautiously on 18. After a huge, straight drive, he laid up short of the water with a 7-iron, then pitched on and two-putted for the par that gave him a one-stroke victory over Jack. It was the 21st PGA Tour win for Miller and it gave him the distinction of having at least one victory in every Tour event west of the Rockies.

The San Diego event has been on the Tour since 1952 and has always had its dramatic moments. In 1954 local boy Gene Littler outplayed a full field of pros and won the tournament as an amateur. In 1961 Arnold Palmer shot 65 in the final round to tie Al Balding and then won in a playoff. And in 1963 it was Gary Player's turn, sinking an 18-footer on the final hole to edge Tony Lema.

In those days the event was played at a variety of courses in the San Diego area. Andy Williams joined up in 1968, the same year the tournament was first played at Torrey Pines. With the move to those two cliffhanging courses, the tradition of golf theatrics has continued.

ALL TIME TOURNAMENT RECORDS

Record	Player(s)	Score	Year
Low 18	Gene Littler	62	1965
	Craig Stadler	62	1987
Low first 36	Gary Player	130	1963
Low 36	Billy Casper	127 (63–64)	1965 (rounds 3–4)
Low first 54	Woody Blackburn	198 (66–66–66)	1985
Low 54	Woody Blackburn	198 (66–66–66)	1985
Low 72	George Burns	266	1987
Highest winning score	Jack Nicklaus	284 (68–72–71–73)	1969
Largest winning margin	Tom Watson (269)	5 strokes	1977
	Fuzzy Zoeller (282)		1979
Largest 18-hole lead	Jimmy Powell (64)	2 strokes	1968
	Gene Littler (66)		1972
	Tommy Aaron (69)		1979
Largest 36-hole lead	Jay Haas (136)	3 strokes	1978
	Johnny Miller (132)		1982
	Tom Kite (133)		1983
Largest 54-hole lead	J.C. Snead (200)	5 strokes	1976
Lowest start by winner	George Burns	63	1987
Highest start by winner	Pete Brown	76	1970
	Fuzzy Zoeller		1979
Lowest finish by winner	Billy Casper	64	1966
Highest finish by winner	Jack Nicklaus	73	1969
Best final-round comeback	Pete Brown (210)	7 back	1970
Lowest 36-hole cut score		139	1985
Highest 36-hole cut score		150	1969

PAST WINNERS

Year	Winner	Score	Year	Winner	Score
1952	Ted Kroll	276	1972	Paul Harney	275
1953	Tommy Bolt	274	1973	Bob Dickson	278
1954	**Gene Littler	274	1974	Bobby Nichols	275
1955	Tommy Bolt	274	1975	*J. C. Snead	279
1956	Bob Rosburg	270	1976	J. C. Snead	272
1957	Arnold Palmer	271	1977	Tom Watson	269
1958	No Tournament		1978	Jay Haas	278
1959	Marty Furgol	274	1979	Fuzzy Zoeller	282
1960	Mike Souchak	269	1980	*Tom Watson	275
1961	*Arnold Palmer	271	1981	*Bruce Lietzke	278
1962	*Tommy Jacobs	277	1982	Johnny Miller	270
1963	Gary Player	270	1983	Gary Hallberg	271
1964	Art Wall	274	1984	*Gary Koch	272
1965	*Wes Ellis	267	1985	*Woody Blackburn	269
1966	Billy Casper	268	1986	*‡Bob Tway	204
1967	Bob Goalby	269	1987	George Burns	266
1968	Tom Weiskopf	273	1988	Steve Pate	269
1969	Jack Nicklaus	284	*Playoff		
1970	Pete Brown	275	**Amateur		
1971	George Archer	272	‡Rain-curtailed		

Torrey Pines South, 3rd hole

Torrey Pines North, 5th hole

Torrey Pines South, 13th hole

Torrey Pines South, 18th hole

Torrey Pines South Golf Club

TORREY PINES GC— NORTH SCORECARD

Hole	Yards	Par	PGA Tour Avg. Score
1	522	5	4.610
2	335	4	3.935
3	158	3	2.910
4	396	4	4.049
5	377	4	3.957
6	170	3	3.073
7	401	4	4.208
8	436	4	4.038
9	497	5	4.323
OUT	3292	36	35.103
10	419	4	4.025
11	434	4	4.231
12	179	3	3.061
13	435	4	4.118
14	503	5	4.493
15	399	4	3.971
16	338	4	3.796
17	178	3	2.939
18	490	5	4.357
IN	3375	36	34.991
TOTAL	6667	72	70.094

TORREY PINES GC— SOUTH SCORECARD

Hole	Yards	Par	PGA Tour Avg. Score
1	430	4	4.190
2	334	4	3.897
3	173	3	3.003
4	445	4	4.242
5	412	4	3.941
6	527	5	4.656
7	461	4	4.226
8	174	3	2.966
9	541	5	4.550
OUT	3497	36	35.671
10	371	4	3.968
11	216	3	3.039
12	467	4	4.241
13	535	5	4.717
14	399	4	4.057
15	389	4	4.021
16	202	3	3.036
17	425	4	4.073
18	501	5	4.688
IN	3505	36	35.840
TOTAL	7002	72	71.511

CUT SHOTS
BY GARY HALLBERG

To my knowledge, Torrey Pines is the only course on the PGA Tour where the list of natural hazards includes canyons. Beautiful to look at, they can do some ugly things to a golfer's score. Occasionally, even a pro will hit a ball down into one of these deep, steep-sided monsters. He'll have a shot back, but only one—the fast-climbing cut.

When you have to make a ball climb quickly, begin by picturing the ideal shot. Address the ball with an open stance—knees, hips, and shoulders pointing about 25 degrees left of the target. Play the ball up off your left heel to ensure catching it on the upswing. If the ball is sitting on relatively soft turf, you can add a little height to the shot by opening the face, pointing it a couple of degrees right of the target.

During the swing, keep most of your weight on your right side. Flexing your right knee a little extra will help you do this and will also give you the feeling that you're "under" the ball at address and during the swing. Reach for the sky as you swing back. High hands lead to high shots, so swing down, through, and back up to a high-handed finish.

Gary Hallberg won the 1983 Shearson Lehman Brothers Andy Williams Open.

45

WAIALAE *Country Club*

17th hole

Waialae Country Club is 3,000 miles from its nearest neighbor on the PGA Tour. But who cares? The way the pros see it, eleven hours of air travel is a small price to pay for the annual boondoggle to Paradise.

While the wives and families bask on Waikiki Beach the players enjoy the fairways and greens of Waialae, where birdies and eagles are as plentiful as coconuts and pineapples.

Waialae is the work of Seth Raynor, sole protégé of C.B. Macdonald, the St. Andrews-trained gentleman-golfer whose autocratic personality and daunting designs spearheaded the growth of golf in turn-of-the-century America. Raynor visited Oahu and drew up the Waialae plans in November of 1926. But he never saw his vision take shape, for in February of the following year he died.

His design, however, prevailed. It incorporated several ideas from Macdonald's American courses and from the original Scottish links. On the first hole, for example, Raynor plotted a short par five whose doglegging fairway and severely front-bunkered green recalled the "Road Hole" at St. Andrews, often called the toughest par four in the world.

Waialae was immediately hailed as the finest course in the islands, and for more than fifty years it has remained virtually unchanged.

At 6,881 yards, Waialae is one of the shortest par 72s on the Tour. Its four par fives—the first, ninth, thirteenth and fifteenth holes—are particularly vulnerable, averaging just 515 yards. But these holes are the key to the excitement at the Hawaiian Open. Witness the performance of Bruce Lietzke, who scored three eagles in a single round. Or Andy Bean, who won the 1980 event with a record score of 22-under-par 266 by playing the par fives in 13-under par. Or Hale Irwin, who bettered Bean's total by one a year later when he eagled the final hole. Or the ultimate example, Isao Aoki, who in 1983 holed one of the most electrifying shots of all time, a 128-yard wedge that bounced into the 72nd hole for an eagle that gave him a one-stroke victory. Short on length, the Waialae fives are long on drama.

Besides, they are not as short as they look. Golf at Waialae means golf in wind—constant, swirling, gusting,

confounding wind. About 80 percent of the time, it is a tradewind from the northeast, but occasionally a kona wind from the opposite direction will prevail. Still, since the par fives point in four different directions, neither condition offers an advantage. On a given day, a player might reach one green with a drive and a 5-iron, one with a drive and a 2-iron, one with a drive and a 3-wood, and one not at all.

Wind is an even greater factor on the par threes. The 193-yard fourth hole is called *Apiki*, the Hawaiian word for "tricky." Its elongated, two-level green, bunkered on both sides, is the toughest target on the course and is made more difficult because the hole normally plays upwind. Club selection varies from a 3-wood to a 4-iron.

Its sister, the 172-yard seventh, also plays into the wind and also is surrounded by sand. The elevated green on this hole is patterned after the green of the sixth hole at C. B. Macdonald's first and most famous project, the National Golf Links of America in Southampton, New York.

If you like to watch the pros sink mammoth putts, watch the midwinter telecast of the Hawaiian Open. The greens at Waialae are relatively large, but more important, they are among the fastest and best-conditioned surfaces anywhere in the world. They are grown with bermudagrass, not normally associated with smooth, true putting. But the constant sun in Hawaii is perfect for the Tifdwarf bermuda used at Waialae. Past champions such as Ben Crenshaw, Hale Irwin, Andy Bean, and Hubert Green will quickly admit that some of their hottest putting has occurred on Oahu.

The truth is that everything grows well on this island. The Waialae course is an arboretum with dozens of different trees and with flowering shrubs in bloom year around. Many of them have names as colorful as their blossoms: bauhinia, Chinese fan palm, graveyard plumeria, monkey pod, madre de coco, false kamani, wili-wili, Madagascar olive, be-still, tuckeroo, and cow-itch.

During the years of World War II, the tournament was played at other courses because Waialae's fairways were strung with barbed wire to prevent landings by Japanese aircraft. No damage was done to the course during the

ALL TIME TOURNAMENT RECORDS

Record	Player(s)	Score	Year
Low 18	Nick Faldo	62	1981
	Hale Irwin		1981
	Craig Stadler		1987
Low first 36	Vance Heafner	131 (66–65)	1983
Low 36	Hale Irwin	128 (66–62)	1981 (rounds 2–3)
Low first 54	Hale Irwin	196 (68–66–62)	1981
Low 54	Andy Bean	195 (63–66–66)	1980
Low 72	Hale Irwin	265 (68–66–62–69)	1981
Highest winning score	Dudley Wysong	284 (72–69–70–73)	1967
Largest winning margin	Hale Irwin (265)	6 strokes	1981
Largest 18-hole lead	Jack Nicklaus (63)	4 strokes	1969
Largest 36-hole lead	Jack Nicklaus (134)	4 strokes	1969
	Tom Watson (133)		1973
	Jack Nicklaus (132)		1974
Largest 54-hole lead	Jack Nicklaus (201)	6 strokes	1974
Lowest start by winner	Grier Jones	65	1972
	Jack Nicklaus		1974
	Corey Pavin		1987
Highest start by winner	Gay Brewer	74	1965
Lowest finish by winner	Grier Jones	64	1972
	Corey Pavin		1987
Highest finish by winner	Dudley Wysong	73	1967
Best final-round comeback	Grier Jones (210)	5 back	1972
Lowest 36-hole cut score		142	1979
Highest 36-hole cut score		152	1965

PAST WINNERS

Year	Winner	Score
1965	*Gay Brewer	281
1966	Ted Makalena	271
1967	*Dudley Wysong	284
1968	Lee Trevino	272
1969	Bruce Crampton	274
1970	No Tournament	
1971	Tom Shaw	273
1972	*Grier Jones	274
1973	John Schlee	273
1974	Jack Nicklaus	271
1975	Gary Groh	274
1976	Ben Crenshaw	270
1977	Bruce Lietzke	273
1978	*Hubert Green	274
1979	Hubert Green	267
1980	Andy Bean	266
1981	Hale Irwin	265
1982	Wayne Levi	277
1983	Isao Aoki	268
1984	*Jack Renner	271
1985	Mark O'Meara	267
1986	Corey Pavin	272
1987	Corey Pavin	270
1988	Lanny Wadkins	271

*Playoff

8th hole

4th hole

5th hole

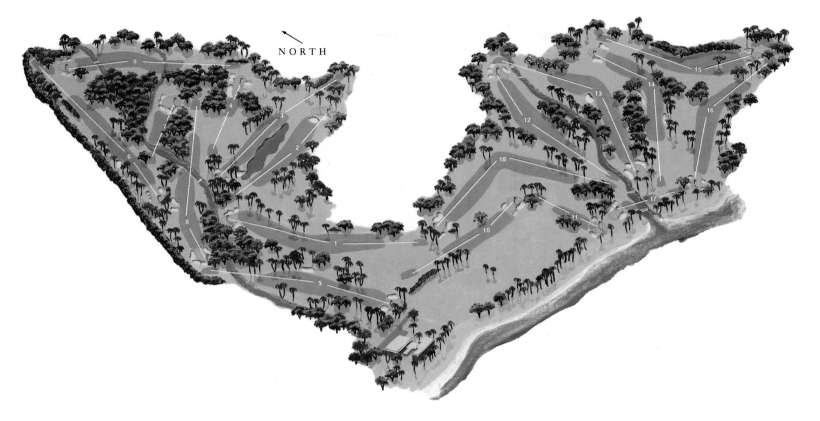

bombing of Pearl Harbor, but near a bunker on the first hole, Private Prewitt (Montgomery Clift) was "shot" during the filming of *From Here to Eternity*.

Today, club life at Waialae is, like Hawaii, a model of multi-ethnic harmony. The current membership is 58 percent Caucasian, 19 percent Japanese, 16 percent Chinese, 4 percent Hawaiian, and 2 percent Korean with a scattering of black, East Indian, Filipino, and other ethnic groups.

It is therefore somehow fitting that, on this course where several nationalities have long prospered, Isao Aoki became the first Japanese player to win an American PGA Tour event. And it is further appropriate on this serene democratic island that the man who took the impact of Aoki's electrifying final eagle, Jack Renner, came back a year later to have his own day in the Hawaiian sun.

SCORECARD

Hole	Yards	Par	PGA Tour Avg. Score
1	521	5	4.609
2	352	4	3.883
3	419	4	4.002
4	193	3	3.216
5	450	4	4.105
6	438	4	4.237
7	172	3	3.044
8	419	4	4.029
9	501	5	4.737
OUT	3465	36	35.862
10	349	4	4.032
11	178	3	3.071
12	424	4	4.024
13	500	5	4.422
14	407	4	4.015
15	394	4	4.136
16	434	4	4.098
17	191	3	3.057
18	539	5	4.595
IN	3416	36	35.450
TOTAL	6881	72	71.312

THE WEDGE FROM ROUGH
BY ISAO AOKI

The biggest thrill of my career came in the 1983 Hawaiian Open when, on the 72nd hole, I knocked a ball 125 yards out of the rough and into the cup for an eagle that beat Jack Renner by one stroke.

My style on the wedge shot is different than that of most American professionals. Take a narrow, open stance, with your body facing several degrees left of the target. Keep your head directly over the ball, which should be positioned about midway between your feet. The swing is made primarily with the upper body and is controlled by the right side.

I take the club away by pulling up with my right hand. My right arm bends immediately, allowing me to take the club back on an upright plane. On this shot, I rarely use more than a three-quarter backswing.

On the downswing I depend on my right hand for both power and accuracy. My key is to pull down with the right side, in a sort of chopping motion down and through the ball, taking a big divot. What little leg action I have is timed to coincide with my upper-body movement. The "firing" of my right knee toward the target occurs as the club moves through the hitting area, but this leg action is a natural reaction more than a conscious move. It's best, especially for older and/or less supple players, to key on the upper body and the upward-downward chop of the club, controlled by the right hand.

Isao Aoki's victory in the Hawaiian Open in 1983 made him the first Japanese player to win a PGA Tour event.

RIVIERA *Country Club*

LOS ANGELES
OPEN
PRESENTED
BY NISSAN
CALIFORNIA

George C. Thomas, whose inspired designs shaped several of America's most highly respected courses, was not a golf course architect.

Born into a wealthy Philadelphia family, Thomas never really worked for a living. He dabbled successively in his father's banking business, in the breeding of English setters, and in horticulture, becoming a nationally recognized expert and author on the care and cultivation of roses.

And he dabbled in golf course design. In 1908 he created a course on his father's estate in Chestnut Hill. It later became the Whitemarsh Country Club, the host for several years of a PGA Tour event known as the IVB Philadelphia Classic. During the twenties Thomas lived in California,

9th hole

where in collaboration with Billy Bell he designed more than two dozen courses, among them famed Bel-Air, Ojai, and the Los Angeles Country Club (North). But his last course was by popular agreement his finest: Riviera.

In 1925, the members of the Los Angeles Athletic Club decided to expand their facilities to include golf. They selected Thomas as their architect and summoned him to their proposed site in the center of the Santa Monica Canyon. There, Thomas stood on a precipice and surveyed the 240 acres of tangled brush, cactus, eucalyptus, pines, oaks, and sycamores, all threaded with a deep riverbed. After a time he offered the club fathers his opinion: He could build them a golf course, but it would not be much

of a layout because of the limitations of natural terrain. Still, he said, it would be "good enough for the Los Angeles Athletic Club."

Such arrogance did not sit well with the fathers, who informed Thomas that even the best course would be none too good for LAAC. They might also have hinted that the project was beyond Thomas's capabilities, for the architect had thrust himself into the job, offering his services without pay.

However, no other expense was spared in the construction of Riviera Country Club. A crew of more than 200 men hacked through the canyon for eighteen months, installing 100,000 feet of pipe, trucking in topsoil from the San Fernando Valley, sowing 19,000 pounds of grass seed, and depositing 1,350 tons of beach sand. Dozens of trees were cut down and dozens more were planted. In those days the cost of constructing an 18-hole layout ran roughly $100,000. The bill for Riviera came to over $650,000, making it, as nearly as anyone could determine, the most expensive golf course in the world.

But the money was well spent. Almost immediately the National Golf Foundation ranked Riviera third on a list of the world's top ten, behind Pine Valley Golf Club in New Jersey and Pinehurst Country Club in North Carolina. Today, despite sixty years and the blossoming of hundreds of impressive golf courses worldwide, Riviera retains its standing in the upper ranks of the world's greatest courses.

In Riviera, Thomas unveiled a collection of architectural gambits that grabbed the golf fraternity by its knickers. Among the innovations were a doughnut-shaped green with a pot bunker as its center, a par four with two alternate fairways, and a green half-barricaded by a grass mound the size of a diner. He also molded the final green into the base of a huge natural amphitheater, likely the first execution of what is now known as Stadium Golf.

On opening day in June of 1927, no one broke or equaled par on Riviera. Nor did anyone do so on the next day—or the next week—or the next month. In fact, after six months the best score anyone had squeezed from it was a 73, two-over par. Then, one of the club's glamorous Hollywood members, Douglas Fairbanks, posted a $1,000 purse for a medal tournament. The event attracted a strong and talented field, and Willie Hunter, the likable Scot who had won the 1921 British Amateur, did the deed with a 69.

Riviera has confounded and delighted both pros and amateurs ever since. Tom Watson, a two-time L.A. Open champion, says, "Riviera is the type of course that makes you want to shoot your very best." And you will have to. In 1984, when the PGA Tour issued its statistics on the 100 most difficult holes on the Tour, Riviera had eight of those holes, more than any other course.

The course starts literally on the edge of a cliff, the first tee overlooking the entire layout seventy-five feet below. The opening hole is a short but tight and ingeniously bunkered par five, giving the high-handicap player a good chance at an opening par while tempting the stronger player to go for birdie or even eagle.

The Tour players count on that birdie because the next three holes all are among those 100 toughest. The second is a members' par five, which has been converted into a 460-yard par four for the pros. It usually plays into a quartering wind, always plays into a narrow green. Says

Lee Trevino, "I have to hit two woods to get there, and the second one had better be a great shot."

Number three plays 434 yards dead into the wind. Here the green is relatively deep but narrow and guarded by gaping bunkers on both sides.

One of the largest bunkers on the course protects the entire front of the par-three fourth, forcing an all-carry tee shot of 238 yards. Ben Hogan, not one given to lavish praise, called this "the greatest par three in America."

The doughnut green is on the sixth hole. The little pot bunker in the center gets all the talk, but more sand in front and behind the green makes club selection harrowing on this 170-yard hole.

Number eight is the hole where Thomas offered two alternative fairways. However, one of them has since been eliminated. The result is a hole with half a fairway. "You have to drive the ball unbelievably straight to get through the narrow opening in the trees," says Gene Littler.

Riviera's 10th is one of golf's great short par fours, 311 yards of compressed architectural guile. As Jerry Pate sees it, "You can drive the green if you catch it with a little tailwind, or you can make 6 so fast you can't catch it."

How does a Tour pro make a quick 6 on a 311-yard hole? He flubs a chip shot from kikuyugrass. One of the foremost features of Riviera, kikuyu is an African strain, actually a weed, which grows in extreme density. When cut to a low height, it is perhaps the perfect fairway grass, perching the ball atop its leaves. But in the fringe and rough, where the height of the grass can be four or more inches, kikuyu grabs at the landing ball and swallows it deep into its tendrils, making crisp impact impossible. Faced with such lies, and chipping to Riviera's small, hard greens, even the pros can look like monkeys.

Dozens of eucalyptus trees make play difficult on the 413-yard 12th hole, but the real killer is a sycamore just to the left of the green. It is said to have caught more stray rubber than any guard rail on the L.A. freeway.

Big numbers are common on the 13th hole, where out-of-bounds stares the golfer in the face from tee to green.

Riviera's 18th has been called 447 yards of heartbreak. The tee shot is blind to a plateau fairway that banks and doglegs gracefully to the right, like a turn at Indy. A drive to the left will leave a "shank" lie, with the ball below the feet. On the right the terrain is level, but a row of overhanging trees blocks a direct shot at the green. The meanest jail on the course may be the steep bank to the left of the green, particularly when the pin is cut on the left side of the green. The remaining shot can be as short as 10 feet long, but with a sharp slope, snatching kikuyu, and a green like waxed marble, most players—Tour pros included—will not get up and down.

2nd hole

Directly behind the 18th green is the imposing Riviera clubhouse, constructed in 1925 with the same meticulous care as the course. Riviera required a sumptuous clubhouse to accommodate the most glamorous membership in golf. In addition to the aforementioned Douglas Fairbanks, its well-known members have included Mary Pickford, W.C. Fields, Basil Rathbone, Spencer Tracy, Katherine Hepburn, Leslie Howard, Adolphe Menjou, Johnny Weissmuller, Jim Backus, Sammy Davis, Jr., Peter Falk, James Garner, Burt Lancaster, Dean Martin, Jerry Lewis, Peter Graves, Gregory Peck, Robert Wagner, Don Rickles, and Glen Campbell, who for several years was the official host of the L.A. Open.

In the thirties, a Mr. and Mrs. Taylor from England became equestrian members of the club. Their eleven-year-old daughter worked out daily on her horse Hal over the steeplechase course, for she had been selected after a five-year search to play the lead in an MGM feature called *National Velvet*. Her name was Elizabeth.

Many movies have been shot at Riviera, including *Follow the Sun*, starring Glenn Ford. Indeed, *Follow the Sun* belonged at Riviera for it is the life story of Ben Hogan, who won two Los Angeles Opens and a U.S. Open on it within eighteen months.

It was at Riviera in 1962 that Jack Nicklaus won his first check as a professional, but this remains to date one of the few courses where he has never notched a victory.

Both course records were set in the 1985 L.A. Open. Lanny Wadkins shot 63 in the opening round, lowering the old mark by one. He lost the next day, however, when a 62 was posted by Larry Mize. But it was Wadkins who set the four-day mark, with a 20-under-par total of 264, a superb performance that bettered Johnny Miller's 1981 total by six shots.

In the same tournament, Mike Reid recorded a feat that is undoubtedly an all-time PGA Tour record. In four trips through the par-three sixth hole, the quiet, lanky Reid took only seven strokes. On Thursday he made a hole-in-one, and on each of the following three days, he scored a two. Apparently, he likes doughnuts.

ALL TIME TOURNAMENT RECORDS

Record	Player(s)	Score	Year
Low 18	George Archer	61	1983
Low first 36	Jimmy Thomson	131 (66–65)	1938
	Gibby Gilbert	(65–66)	1983
Low 36	Arnold Palmer	128 (66–62)	1966 (rounds 2–3)
Low first 54	Lloyd Mangrum	200 (66–66–68)	1956
	Arnold Palmer	(72–66–62)	1966
	Lanny Wadkins	(63–70–67)	1985
Low 54	Arnold Palmer	199 (64–67–68)	1967
	Gil Morgan	(68–63–68)	1983
Low 72	Lanny Wadkins	264 (63–70–67–64)	1985
Highest winning score	Denny Shute	296	1930
Largest winning margin	Phil Rodgers (268)	9 strokes	1962
Largest 18-hole lead	Terry Mauney	4 strokes	1982
Largest 36-hole lead	Henry Ransom	4 strokes	1951
Largest 54-hole lead	Pat Fitzsimons	6 strokes	1975
Lowest start by winner	Charles Sifford Lanny Wadkins	63	1969 1985
Highest start by winner	Jimmy Thomson	75	1938
Lowest finish by winner	Phil Rodgers	62	1962
Highest finish by winner	Fred Wampler	75	1954
Best final-round comeback	Ken Venturi	7 back	1959
Lowest 36-hole cut score		143	1981
Highest 36-hole cut score		156	1952

PAST WINNERS

Year	Winner	Score	Year	Winner	Score
1926	Harry Cooper	279	1958	F. Stranahan	275
1927	Bobby Cruikshank	282	1959	Ken Venturi	278
1928	Mac Smith	284	1960	Dow Finsterwald	280
1929	Mac Smith	285	1961	Bob Goalby	275
1930	Densmore Shute	296	1962	Phil Rodgers	268
1931	Ed Dudley	285	1963	Arnold Palmer	274
1932	Mac Smith	281	1964	Paul Harney	280
1933	Craig Wood	281	1965	Paul Harney	276
1934	Mac Smith	280	1966	Arnold Palmer	273
1935	*Vic Ghezzi	285	1967	Arnold Palmer	269
1936	Jimmy Hines	280	1968	Billy Casper	274
1937	Harry Cooper	274	1969	*Charles Sifford	276
1938	Jimmy Thomson	273	1970	*Billy Casper	276
1939	Jimmy Demaret	274	1971	*Bob Lunn	274
1940	Lawson Little	282	1972	*George Archer	270
1941	Johnny Bulla	281	1973	Rod Funseth	276
1942	*Ben Hogan	282	1974	Dave Stockton	276
1943	No Tournament		1975	Pat Fitzsimons	275
1944	H. McSpaden	278	1976	Hale Irwin	272
1945	Sam Snead	283	1977	Tom Purtzer	273
1946	Byron Nelson	284	1978	Gil Morgan	278
1947	Ben Hogan	280	1979	Lanny Wadkins	276
1948	Ben Hogan	275	1980	Tom Watson	276
1949	Lloyd Mangrum	284	1981	Johnny Miller	270
1950	*Sam Snead	280	1982	*Tom Watson	271
1951	Lloyd Mangrum	280	1983	Gil Morgan	270
1952	Tommy Bolt	289	1984	David Edwards	279
1953	Lloyd Mangrum	280	1985	Lanny Wadkins	264
1954	Fred Wampler	281	1986	Doug Tewell	270
1955	Gene Littler	276	1987	*T.C. Chen	275
1956	Lloyd Mangrum	272	1988	Chip Beck	267
1957	Doug Ford	280	*Playoff		

4th hole

5th hole

6th hole

COPING WITH KIKUYU
BY HAL SUTTON

Kikuyugrass grows all over the Rivi-era course, and I both love it and hate it. When it's clipped tight, as it is on the Riviera fairways, it provides an ideal surface for playing approach shots. But when it's allowed to grow, as in the rough surrounding the greens, it serves up some of the most vexing lies in the game.

When you deal with this stuff, you're playing defense all the way. Never try to play a running shot through kikuyu. It will just snag your ball. If you do have a short pitch or chip, fly it at least to the fringe of the green, even if that means running the ball well past the hole. That's better than having to play your next shot from kikuyu.

Kikuyu is a very strong-bladed grass, and when you hit into it, the ball will either perch atop those wiry tendrils or settle down into a nest. The two lies require two different methods.

On the perched lie, I prefer to use a stiff-wristed method to chip the ball crisply off the bed of grass. It's almost a picking shot where you minimize club contact with the tangly grass. But when the ball's sitting down, the only alternative is to play it back in your stance and hit down on the shot with a wristy motion. With this more vertical attack, you'll be best able to excavate the ball from the greenery. In either shot, expect no backspin and lots of roll.

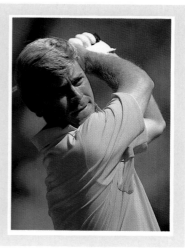

Hal Sutton won the 1983 PGA Championship at Riviera Country Club.

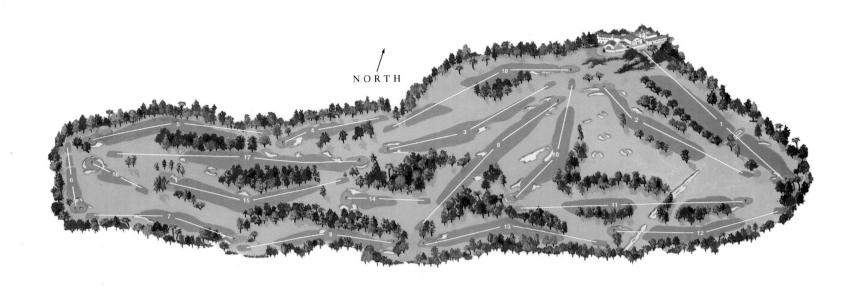

NORTH

SCORECARD

Hole	Yards	Par	PGA Tour Avg. Score
1	501	5	4.675
2	460	4	4.303
3	434	4	4.213
4	238	3	3.311
5	426	4	4.149
6	170	3	3.062
7	406	4	4.197
8	368	4	4.159
9	418	4	4.274
OUT	3421	35	36.343
10	311	4	3.954
11	561	5	4.939
12	413	4	4.228
13	420	4	4.147
14	180	3	3.075
15	447	4	4.241
16	168	3	3.091
17	578	5	4.996
18	447	4	4.335
IN	3525	36	37.006
TOTAL	6946	71	73.349

10th hole

59

$\mathcal{TPC}$ at EAGLE TRACE

THE HONDA CLASSIC FLORIDA

In its first two years at Eagle Trace, Honda got more mileage out of the Tour players than from its fuel-efficient cars. Both 1984 and 1985 produced gut-wrenching, down-to-the-wire final rounds capped by sudden-death playoffs.

Eagle Trace was the second of the Players Clubs designed for the financial benefit of the PGA Tour and the viewing advantage of the spectators. Westinghouse Properties joined with the Tour in creating the course and the surrounding houses. Their intent was to give a feel of

9th and 18th holes

northern courses, starting with the imposing Colonial clubhouse, a reproduction of the Carter's Grove Mansion in Williamsburg, Virginia.

The clubhouse is a faithful reproduction, but the golf course looks more Scottish than American. Windblown, comparatively treeless, and scored with sedge-covered humps and hillocks, it resembles a southern St. Andrews. The big difference is the water, a virtual canal system winding through 16 of the 18 holes. As a result, the course

demands a totally different game from the one played by the Scots. The original links courses encourage a low-lofted approach to the green. They call it a bump and run. At Eagle Trace they would call it a splash and sink.

Art Hills's design bears several likenesses to its older TPC brother at Sawgrass, created by Deane Beman and Pete Dye. There are the obvious marks of a stadium course—long, high mounds enclosing several of the greens. At Eagle Trace millions of cubic yards of earth were excavated, piled, and sculpted into natural amphitheaters. Some of them are nearly thirty feet high and afford views of more than a mile. Like Sawgrass, the course includes large expanses of untended sand and scrub known as "waste bunkers." Shots from these are played similarly to sand shots, but the areas are not regarded as hazards under the Rules of Golf. Grounding one's club is therefore permitted.

As at Sawgrass, the four par threes at Eagle Trace head in four different directions. The most difficult is number seven, which plays 193 yards over water and often into the wind. In the final round of the 1985 Honda Classic, Curtis Strange and Fred Couples came to this hole tied for the lead at 15-under par. Strange double-bogeyed it and Couples *triple*-bogeyed. Curtis survived to win a playoff against Peter Jacobsen, while Couples posted a 78 to finish fourth.

The ninth and 18th holes parallel each other on a line toward the clubhouse, which is thoughtful, because after playing these holes more than one golfer has been heard to mutter "I need a drink." The ideal drive on nine is to the right side of the fairway, since large mounds and deep rough line the left. A well-placed tee shot will leave a long-iron or wood approach, which must avoid a large bunker lapping at the left edge of the green. When the wind is up, few mortals are able to reach this par four in two.

The routing of this course is unusual: The front nine runs in a clockwise circle whereas the back runs counter-clockwise, a path first followed by the famed Muirfield links in Scotland. As such, the better player must switch his shot pattern in midstream. The front nine calls for a fade on most of the long holes, but the back favors a draw.

A controlled left-to-right tee shot leaves the best angle to the difficult 12th green, a banana-shaped peninsula with water on the right and grass bunkers on the left. The green is 58 yards long and mounded in the center. If the approach does not find the flagstick end of the banana, the first putt will have to go through a long stretch of fringe.

Fifteen is where the first two Honda Classics ended in the first hole of sudden death. In 1984 Bruce Lietzke edged Andy Bean here, and in 1985 it was Curtis Strange over Peter Jacobsen. It is a reflection of the difficulty of this hole that in both cases a par five was good enough to win. The tee shot must be hit accurately to miss a deep fairway bunker on the left and grassy mounds on the right. All but the longest, straightest drives will leave a second shot over water, then a pitch (on mild days) or a hard punch (into the wind) at the small green flanked by bunkers.

The toughest approach shot on the course may be to the 16th, a narrow green that is almost totally surrounded by water. Any shot that is pushed or sliced will be wet; a pulled or hooked ball will be "saved" from the water probably by falling into either the large sand bunker or one of the two grass bunkers.

The members at Eagle Trace compare their 17th hole to the famous par-three 12th at Augusta National. Slightly longer than that hole, it plays 171 yards, most of that over water, to a shallow amphitheater green that is backed by bunkers.

The huge green at the 470-yard 18th is nearly 60 yards long. In 1984, Andy Bean came to that hole and left his approach shot 70 feet short of the hole. Then, unbelievably, he sank the putt. But he was upstaged by Bruce Lietzke, whose high 6-iron landed just left of the pin, kicked down the bank, and finished six feet away. In went the putt for birdie, locking Lietzke into the playoff, which he won on 15.

ALL TIME TOURNAMENT RECORDS

Record	Player(s)	Score	Year
Low 18	Fred Couples	63	1985
Low first 36	Fred Couples	131 (63–68)	1985
	Curtis Strange	(67–64)	1985
Low 36	Jack Nicklaus	131 (66–65)	1978 (rounds 3–4)
	Fred Couples	(63–68)	1985
	Curtis Strange	(67–64)	1985
Low first 54	George Burns	200 (66–67–67)	1982
Low 54	George Burns	200 (66–67–67)	1982
Low 72	Hale Irwin	269 (65–71–67–66)	1982
Highest winning score	Kenny Knox	287 (66–71–80–70)	1986
Largest winning margin	Jack Nicklaus (275)	5 strokes	1977
Largest 18-hole lead	Grier Jones (67)	2 strokes	1978
	Fred Couples (63)		1985
Largest 36-hole lead	Jack Nicklaus (136)	4 strokes	1977
Largest 54-hole lead	Larry Nelson (208)	4 strokes	1979
Lowest start by winner	Hale Irwin	65	1982
Highest start by winner	Bruce Lietzke	72	1984
Lowest finish by winner	Jack Nicklaus	65	1978
Highest finish by winner	Curtis Strange	74	1985
Best final-round comeback	Bruce Lietzke (212)	4 back	1984
Lowest 36-hole cut score		143	1985
Highest 36-hole cut score		151	1987

7th hole

13th hole

16th hole

17th hole

64

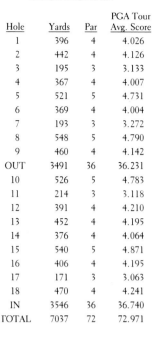

SCORECARD

Hole	Yards	Par	PGA Tour Avg. Score
1	396	4	4.026
2	442	4	4.126
3	195	3	3.133
4	367	4	4.007
5	521	5	4.731
6	369	4	4.004
7	193	3	3.272
8	548	5	4.790
9	460	4	4.142
OUT	3491	36	36.231
10	526	5	4.783
11	214	3	3.118
12	391	4	4.210
13	452	4	4.195
14	376	4	4.064
15	540	5	4.871
16	406	4	4.195
17	171	3	3.063
18	470	4	4.241
IN	3546	36	36.740
TOTAL	7037	72	72.971

PAST WINNERS

Year	Winner	Score
1972	Tom Weiskopf	278
1973	Lee Trevino	279
1974	Leonard Thompson	278
1975	Bob Murphy	273
1976	Hosted TPC	
1977	Jack Nicklaus	275
1978	Jack Nicklaus	276
1979	Larry Nelson	274
1980	Johnny Miller	274
1981	Tom Kite	274
1982	Hale Irwin	269
1983	Johnny Miller	278
1984	*Bruce Lietzke	280
1985	*Curtis Strange	275
1986	Kenny Knox	287
1987	Mark Calcavecchia	279
1988	Joey Sindelar	276

*Playoff

CROSS-HANDED PUTTING
BY BRUCE LIETZKE

In college I switched to a cross-handed putting grip, with my left hand positioned below my right on the shaft of the putter. This grip has worked for me ever since, and on fast, undulating greens such as those at Eagle Trace, it's an asset.

For years, the cross-handed grip has been regarded as a last-ditch effort, a refuge for players afflicted with the yips. But it's a lot more than that. It offers several advantages over a conventional putting grip.

First, the cross-handed grip puts the left hand in a strong, leading position. This prevents the right hand from overtaking the stroke and causing a collapse of the left wrist, one of the most common and destructive putting faults.

Another advantage is that the left hand resists the tendency of the right to lift the putterhead upward on the backswing. Thus it promotes the best type of stroke, one where the club swings as low to the ground as possible.

The cross-handed grip also allows the player to take a relatively short backswing and then accelerate through the ball. This Tom Watson-type of stroke is particularly useful on short putts of six feet or less, where a backswing of a few inches reduces the chance of opening or closing the face and thus hitting the ball off line.

———

Bruce Lietzke won the inaugural Honda Classic at Eagle Trace in 1984.

DORAL *Country Club*

18th hole

"It'll never work, Alfred. You're creating a monster." That's what everyone told Alfred Kaskel in 1960 when he decided to plunge his fortune into the construction of a golf resort smack in the center of a useless Florida swamp. His friends and business associates were unanimous in their disdain of the project they called "Kaskel's Folly."

Alfred called it Doral, a mellifluous meld of his own name and that of his wife, Doris. When he hired one of the era's preeminent golf architects, Dick Wilson, to construct a course, then grabbed an open date on the 1962 pro circuit and started a tournament with a purse of $50,000 (twice that of any other Florida event), the skeptics assumed Alfred had lost his marbles as well as his shirt.

To no one's surprise, both Doral Country Club and the Doral Open spewed red ink in their first year of operation. But in the two and a half decades since, the Doral Hotel has become one of the most popular destinations in Florida. Its success, in spite of its unlikely location miles from the nearest beach, proved that when every other aspect of a resort is top notch, the ocean is superfluous.

The critics were accurate, however, in one prediction. Kaskel and Wilson created a monster of a golf course—the Blue Monster—on which the Doral Ryder Open is annually staged.

It was first designated simply the Blue Course, to distinguish it from the Red, White, Green, Gold, and Silver Courses, which also snake through the Doral property. But this 6,939-yard demon is true blue, spread across almost as much water as grass.

The first difficult test comes at number four, a peninsular par three that preys on the mind as much as the muscles. It plays 237 liquid yards to a green guarded on both sides by sand.

The eighth has been called one of the world's best par fives. Its 528-yard fairway wiggles devilishly between two lakes. Anyone hoping to hit the green in two will have to slug a lengthy second shot over the right-hand lake and hope it holds the sand and water-surrounded green. Scores of 6 and 7 on this hole are not uncommon, even for the pros.

The ninth hole is a 163-yard par three that is similar in general design to its bigger sister, number four, playing entirely over water. The flip side to that short, tough par three is number 13, at 246 yards one of the longest short holes in golf. Most amateurs can not reach it, and most pros have trouble making par on it. The green is broad but unusually shallow, and it falls off quickly from front to back.

Seventeen is a classic par four requiring length and accuracy. A slight dogleg to the right of 406 yards, it calls for a drive down the right center, just inside a trio of bunkers. From there it is a middle iron for the pros to a long, narrow green guarded by six sprawling traps.

Raymond Floyd, a two-time winner at Doral, calls the 18th hole "the toughest par four in the world. I've made sixes and sevens on it hundreds of times," says Floyd, who lives in nearby Miami. A nerve-shattering journey of 425 yards, 18 plays along the edge of a big blue lake. Indeed, the name Blue Monster is often used to refer solely to this hole. The fairway is narrow and serpentine, with the water looming large on the left, trees on the right. The second shot is played to a green that is 175 feet long but very narrow, with the lake on the left and a bunker to the right.

When Tom Kite won in 1984, he became the eighth player to pass the $2-million mark in official earnings. Kite joined that elite club in style, birdieing four of the final six holes en route to a 65. The capper came at 18 where, from a poor lie in the right rough he summoned "as good a swing as I have ever made," knocking the ball onto the green. From there he sank a 30-footer for the final birdie and a two-stroke victory over Jack Nicklaus.

Nicklaus also finished second in 1978, when Tom Weiskopf edged him by a stroke. Jack nearly chipped-in on 18 to force a playoff. But do not feel too sorry for the Golden Bear. He has two victories and over a quarter million dollars in prize money to show for his efforts at Doral.

Weiskopf, though, has frequently suffered the role of victim. His saddest moment at Doral came exactly a decade before his victory. With a chance to win the tournament on the final hole, he took a double-bogey 6. The collapse became all the more tragic when the one man ahead of him, Gardner Dickinson, also double-bogeyed the hole yet still shaved Tom by one stroke.

The four-round record here belongs to Hubert Green, who shot 270 in 1976. "I almost didn't show up that year," Green says, "but my game was rusty at the time so at the last minute I decided to play myself into shape." It was a good decision. Green not only won Doral, he went on to win the Jacksonville Open and Heritage Classic in the next two weeks.

ALL TIME TOURNAMENT RECORDS

Record	Player(s)	Score	Year
Low 18	Jack Nicklaus	64	1969–1972
	Lee Trevino		1973
	David Graham		1976
	Hubert Green		1986
Low first 36	Tom Weiskopf	133 (67–66)	1968
	Jerry Heard	(65–68)	1974
Low 36	Gary Koch	132 (67–65)	1983 (rounds 2–3)
	Lanny Wadkins	(66–66)	1987 (rounds 2–3)
Low first 54	Hubert Green	201 (66–70–65)	1976
	Gary Koch	(69–67–65)	1983
Low 54	Hubert Green	201 (66–70–65)	1976
	Gary Koch	(69–67–65)	1983
Low 72	Hubert Green	270 (66–70–65–69)	1976
Highest winning score	Mark McCumber	284 (70–71–72–71)	1985
Largest winning margin	Hubert Green (270)	6 strokes	1976
Largest 18-hole lead	Lee Trevino (64)	4 strokes	1973
Largest 36-hole lead	Lee Trevino (134)	4 strokes	1973
Largest 54-hole lead	Lee Trevino (205)	4 strokes	1973
	Hubert Green (201)		1976
	Gary Koch (201)		1983
Lowest start by winner	Lee Trevino	64	1973
Highest start by winner	Dan Sikes	76	1963
Lowest finish by winner	Tom Kite	65	1984
Highest finish by winner	Gardner Dickinson	72	1968
	Andy Bean		1977
	Mark McCumber		1979
Best final-round comeback	Raymond Floyd (213)	3 back	1980
Lowest 36-hole cut score		144	1974–1983
Highest 36-hole cut score		153	1962

PAST WINNERS

Year	Winner	Score	Year	Winner	Score
1962	Billy Casper	283	1976	Hubert Green	270
1963	Dan Sikes	283	1977	Andy Bean	277
1964	Billy Casper	277	1978	Tom Weiskopf	272
1965	Doug Sanders	274	1979	Mark McCumber	279
1966	Phil Rodgers	278	1980	*Raymond Floyd	279
1967	Doug Sanders	275	1981	Raymond Floyd	273
1968	Gardner Dickinson	275	1982	Andy Bean	278
1969	Tom Shaw	276	1983	Gary Koch	271
1970	Mike Hill	279	1984	Tom Kite	272
1971	J. C. Snead	275	1985	Mark McCumber	284
1972	Jack Nicklaus	276	1986	*Andy Bean	276
1973	Lee Trevino	276	1987	Lanny Wadkins	277
1974	Brian Allin	272	1988	Ben Crenshaw	274
1975	Jack Nicklaus	276	*Playoff		

12th hole

3rd hole

4th hole

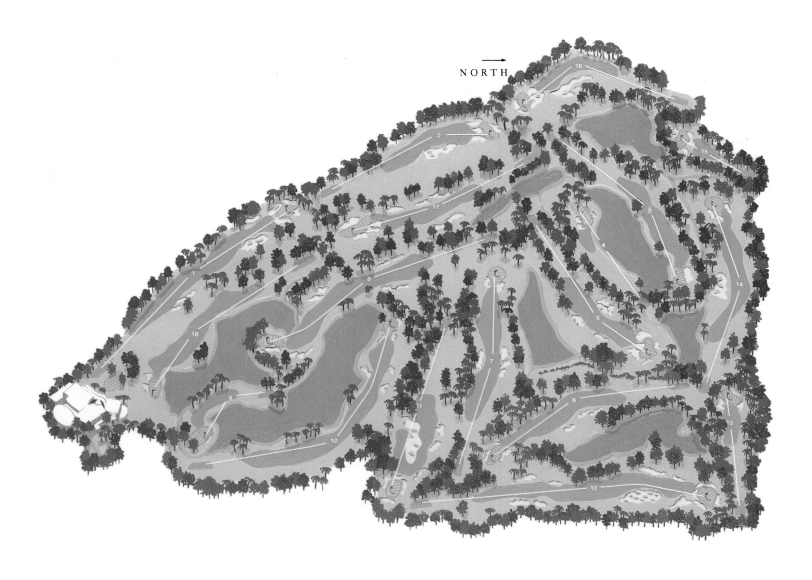

SCORECARD

Hole	Yards	Par	PGA Tour Avg. Score
1	514	5	4.668
2	355	4	4.015
3	398	4	4.243
4	237	3	3.151
5	371	4	4.002
6	427	4	4.090
7	415	4	4.081
8	528	5	4.900
9	163	3	3.016
OUT	3408	36	36.166
10	563	5	4.971
11	348	4	3.996
12	591	5	5.020
13	246	3	3.274
14	418	4	3.999
15	174	3	3.104
16	360	4	3.956
17	406	4	4.093
18	425	4	4.407
IN	3531	36	36.820
TOTAL	6939	72	72.986

HITTING A DRAW
BY RAYMOND FLOYD

The right-to-left shot, or draw, has helped me on a couple of occasions at Doral. First is the high-drawing 6-iron I hit over palm trees to salvage par on the 72nd hole in 1980. Then there's 1981, the year I beat David Graham in a playoff. I set up that victory with a long, low draw with a driver into the wind on the first playoff hole.

The key to the draw is to swing the club on a slightly flatter than normal plane inside the target line. You can set up such a swing at address by taking a closed stance, with your feet, knees, hips, and shoulders aligned several feet to the right of the target. I don't change my grip for this shot, but it doesn't hurt to rotate your hands a quarter-turn clockwise on the club.

I trigger the swing by rotating my right shoulder and concentrate on making a slow, strong turn. On the downswing the key is to make a good release. Be sure that your right hand crosses over your left. This action closes the clubface as you move through the hitting area, imparting the counterclockwise spin that creates the right-to-left flight path. You can check yourself for the proper release. Make a couple of swings and stop as your arms reach a full extension in the follow-through (pointing to nine o'clock). If in this position your right wrist is on top of your left, you've made the proper release.

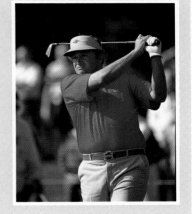

Raymond Floyd is a two-time winner (1980 and 1981) at Doral Eastern Open.

BAY HILL *Club and Lodge*

HERTZ BAY HILL CLASSIC FLORIDA

Arnold Palmer loved Bay Hill so much, he bought it. Then he remodeled it in his own image and invited the rest of the Tour. Now they too love it—and fear it.

Palmer first laid eyes on the course in 1965 when he played an exhibition match with Jack Nicklaus. So struck was he by the quality of Dick Wilson's design and the surrounding terrain that he immediately began pursuing its purchase. Arnie and several associates took over a lease on the property in 1970, and exercised a purchase option in 1976.

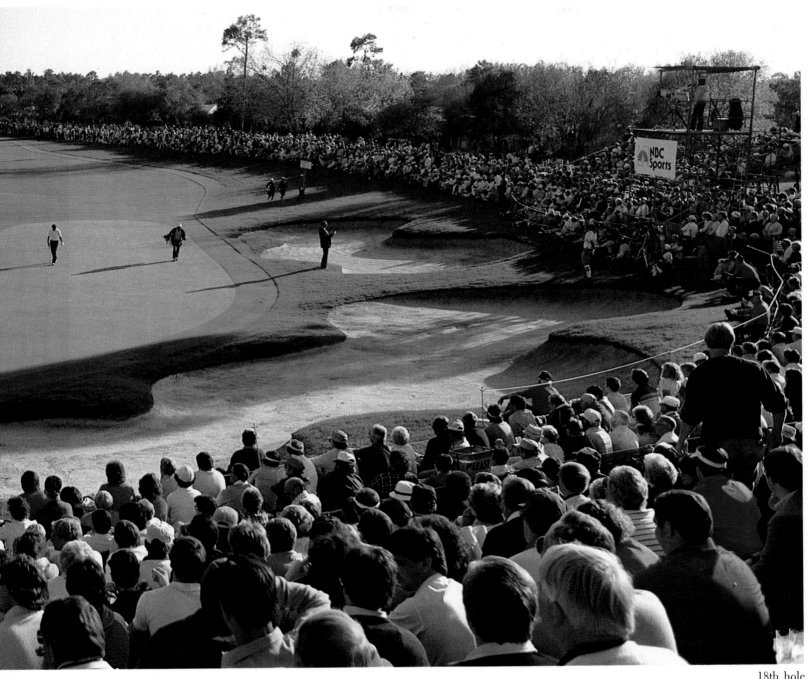

18th hole

Palmer's Bay Hill sharply reflects the personality of its owner, the most daring, aggressive player in modern golf. The course is long and tight, and most of the toughest par-four holes play into the face of a prevailing north wind, encouraging the hard, low, laserlike tee shot that was Arnie's trademark. When the holes dogleg, most of them turn from right to left, favoring the proprietor's preferred flight pattern, a draw.

Six water hazards and 108 bunkers testify to Palmer's love of gambling, scrambling, heroic golf. In almost every

round at Bay Hill there comes a moment when the player must hitch up his pants and go for broke.

The first such place is on the third hole, a sickle-shaped par four that has cut many a player to size. The hole doglegs sharply left around a lake, with the green perched a few feet from the water's edge.

Those who successfully pass through number three will be doubly blessed to survive the test that follows it. Number-one handicap hole for amateurs, the 468-yard fourth plays uphill, usually into the teeth of the wind,

forcing even the strongest players to approach its tightly guarded green with fairway woods.

Horror stories abound about the sixth hole, a mid-length par five that wraps in a counterclockwise semicircle around the largest lake on the course. Jim Colbert got an expensive lesson here.

"A few years ago I shot 65 at Bay Hill, including an eagle-three at number six," he says. "The next day when I got to the sixth tee I said 'Hell, I'm gonna make me another three.' Then I put two tee shots into the water and took 9. Since that day I've played the hole with much more respect."

Nine really was not that bad. Lee Trevino would have gladly taken 9 on the day in 1979 when he scored 11. After hitting a perfect drive, Supermex, whose celebrated fade is of little value on this hole, yanked three straight balls into the drink. Shortly thereafter he withdrew, muttering, "I can make more money selling soda pop at the gate." These days he spares himself the anguish of trying to play left-to-right golf on a right-to-left course. Instead,

Trevino sits in an NBC-TV tower in back of Bay Hill's 18th green, gleefully chronicling the plight of his colleagues.

It undoubtedly comes as little solace to Colbert and Trevino, but even the landlord has had his troubles at number six. In 1983 Arnold Palmer dumped two balls into the water and took a quintuple-bogey 10 en route to an 85, his highest round as a professional.

The ninth hole, a 467-yard par four, ranks second in difficulty for the pros, except for Tom Watson, who must rank it first, maybe even higher. In both 1980 and 1981, Watson came to this hole in contention in the third round. But on both occasions he whipped his tee shot into a parking lot and scored a triple-bogey.

The back nine at Bay Hill features two of the longest, most difficult par threes on the Tour. The first of them, number 14, plays 218 yards slightly uphill to a narrow green surrounded by six bunkers. Bob Gilder still winces over the experience he had here in the third round of the 1983 event. He was in second place when he pushed his tee shot high into the palm tree to the right of the green.

17th hole

1st hole

When the ball did not come down, Gilder tried to climb the tree to get at it, but abandoned his search when he drove a splinter into his left ring finger. Gilder eventually made a double-bogey and vanished from the leaderboard.

The other little devil is the 17th, a 223-yarder that annually ranks among the ten most difficult holes on the entire Tour. The green is tucked behind a large arm of water, and when the pin is cut to the right, as it is for virtually every final round, this is where the tournament is often lost and won. Palmer ranks this as one of the best eighteen golf holes he has ever played.

In 1984 the 18th hole at Bay Hill was statistically the most difficult par four on the PGA Tour, playing to an average of more than 4.5 strokes per round. And that average included a fourth-round eagle by J.C. Snead, who holed out a 4-iron. Snead, who refers to it as the greatest shot of his life, was so dumbfounded, he dropped his club and fell flat on his behind.

Eighteen was a quiet par five before Arnie worked it over, lowering the elevated green so that it cuddles at the edge of a pond. Large bunkers cling to the amphitheater at the left and rear of the green so that anyone who hits into them will face a downhill explosion, directly at water, across the fastest green on the course. In the words of Raymond Floyd, "the hole borders on the unfair."

With the bunkers on the left and water on the right, there is no safe approach to this green except to lay-up short. And that is often the way the pros play it. In fact, most of the players whose tee shots catch the rough to the left of this fairway do not even try for the green in two. On the Saturday round in 1983, commentator Trevino watched in amazement as twenty-seven consecutive players missed the green. He recalls, "All I kept saying was, 'Well, folks, there goes another one. . . .'"

Bay Hill consistently draws one of the strongest fields of the year, an invitation-only gathering of the best players in the United States and abroad. One reason for its popularity is the professional manner in which the tournament is conducted. Couple this with a challenging course, and two big attractions are in place. But the main reason the pros support this tournament is Arnold Palmer. Among the players on the PGA Tour, even more than among his fans, Arnie is regarded with a reverential love that knows no equal.

ALL TIME TOURNAMENT RECORDS

Record	Player(s)	Score	Year
Low 18	Andy Bean	62	1981
	Greg Norman		1984
Low first 36	Andy Bean	130 (68–62)	1981
	Tom Watson	(64–66)	1981 (rounds 2–3)
Low 36	Payne Stewart	128 (63–65)	1987
Low first 54	Andy Bean	197 (68–62–67)	1981
Low 54	Andy Bean	197 (68–62–67)	1981
Low 72	Payne Stewart	264 (69–67–63–65)	1987
Highest winning score	Mike Nicolette	283 (66–72–71–74)	1983
Largest winning margin	Andy Bean (266)	7 strokes	1981
Largest 18-hole lead	Dan Pohl (64)	2 strokes	1980
	Tom Watson (64)		1981
	Mike Nicolette (66)		1983
	Morris Hatalsky (66)		1985
Largest 36-hole lead	Mike Nicolette (138)	3 strokes	1983
	Greg Norman (133)		1984
Largest 54-hole lead	Mike Nicolette (209)	6 strokes	1983
Lowest start by winner	Mike Nicolette	66	1983
Highest start by winner	Fuzzy Zoeller	70	1985
Lowest finish by winner	Gary Koch	63	1984
Highest finish by winner	Dave Eichelberger	74	1980
Best final-round comeback	Tom Kite (209)	6 back	1982
	Gary Koch (209)		1984
Lowest 36-hole cut score		143	1982
Highest 36-hole cut score		152	1983

PAST WINNERS

Year	Winner	Score	Year	Winner	Score
1966	Lionel Hebert	279	1979	*Bob Byman	278
1967	Julius Boros	274	1980	Dave Eichelberger	279
1968	Dan Sikes	274	1981	Andy Bean	266
1969	Ken Still	278	1982	*Tom Kite	278
1970	Bob Lunn	271	1983	*Mike Nicolette	283
1971	Arnold Palmer	270	1984	*Gary Koch	272
1972	Jerry Heard	276	1985	Fuzzy Zoeller	275
1973	Brian Allin	265	1986	‡Dan Forsman	202
1974	Jerry Heard	273	1987	Payne Stewart	264
1975	Lee Trevino	276	1988	Paul Azinger	271
1976	*Hale Irwin	270			
1977	Gary Koch	274	*Playoff		
1978	Mac McLendon	271	‡Rain-curtailed		

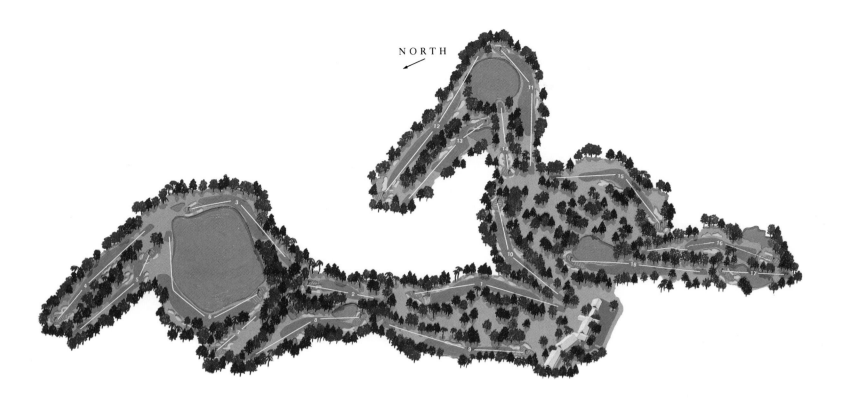

NORTH

HITTING LONG IRONS
BY ARNOLD PALMER

Bay Hill offers one of the most challenging finishes in golf. The last five holes are long and demanding—two par threes and three par fours. On almost every one of them, the shot to the green must be played with a long iron.

The pros don't have much trouble with these clubs, but many amateurs do. They look down at these shallow-faced clubs and wonder whether the loft is sufficient to get the ball airborne. As a result, they often hold back with their hands on the downswing and throw the club at the ball in an attempt to scoop it into flight.

Rule one on the long irons is to trust them. The loft on even a 1-iron is sufficient to put the ball high into the air. All you need is a swing that applies the clubhead squarely to the ball—a level swing.

The more level the swing arc—the longer it moves parallel to the ground—the better will be your chances of making solid impact. The best way to achieve this level clubhead path is to play the ball off your left instep and concentrate on making a smooth weight shift, to your right side on the backswing, then back to your left side on the downswing. One last point: Think of the ball simply as a point on your swing; don't hit at it, swing through it.

———

Arnold Palmer, winner of 61 Tour events, is the owner of the Bay Hill Club & Lodge and chairman of the Hertz Bay Hill Classic.

SCORECARD

Hole	Yards	Par	PGA Tour Avg. Score
1	511	5	4.657
2	214	3	3.271
3	407	4	4.215
4	468	4	4.316
5	367	4	3.973
6	553	5	4.848
7	198	3	3.084
8	391	4	4.169
9	467	4	4.268
OUT	3576	36	36.801
10	397	4	4.115
11	420	4	4.224
12	568	5	5.003
13	373	4	3.995
14	218	3	3.206
15	426	4	4.104
16	446	4	4.199
17	223	3	3.233
18	456	4	4.510
IN	3527	35	36.589
TOTAL	7103	71	73.390

LAKEWOOD *Country Club*

18th hole

In the 1965 New Orleans Open, Dick Mayer did the impossible. Tied with Bruce Devlin going to the last hole at the Lakewood Country Club, Mayer hit a poor drive, then left his second shot 35 yards short of the par-four hole. Devlin nailed his approach shot six feet from the flag and looked to have the tournament clinched.

Jack Nicklaus, the third member of the group, stood with Devlin at the edge of the green as Mayer played his third shot. "The ball was still about 30 feet from the hole," Nicklaus recalls, "when Devlin whispered to me, 'Good grief, that chip's going in.' He called it."

Devlin tried unsuccessfully to match Mayer's magic. "I was too stunned," he said later. "Everything around me was spinning. Frankly, I'm not sure if I could have made it from three feet."

Devlin perhaps should have known better. Lakewood is the type of course where birdies can be made from anywhere. It's not long, it's not tight, its greens are large, flat, and pleasantly fast. It's the place where Lee Trevino won in 1974 after playing 72 holes without a single bogey.

And yet, this is a deceptive course whose challenge is as subtle as a bayou breeze. The greens, although relatively easy to hit, are tough to read, and club selection is an acquired art. Because most of the greenside bunkers are separated from the green by five to ten yards, the flag often appears closer than it actually is on approach shots. The recessed bunkers also leave the toughest of all shots: the long explosion.

Keep the ball down the middle, and birdies will abound. But when shots stray the results can be double trouble, such as at the seventh hole. On this 405-yard par four, a trio of wide bunkers dots the left side of the fairway. Hit into any one of them, and an approach to the green will be blocked not only by the bunker's lip but by a stand of tall trees.

Even a drive down the center of the fairway sometimes will leave a difficult assignment, as at the par-four ninth where the terrain banks to the right. With the ball below their feet, most golfers will leave their shots to the right of target, and architect Robert Harris plotted a bunker to greet such mistakes, just to the right-front of this green. Water on the right side of this fairway and out-of-bounds all the way down the left make it the toughest hole on the front nine.

Thirteen water hazards earn Lakewood its name, and two of them flank the fairway at the 16th. This is a short,

tight dogleg right where treetops protrude into the fairway in front of the small green, creating a narrow tunnel for the approach. Only a good tee shot will stay dry; only an excellent one will leave a view of the target.

The longest and most difficult par three on the course is the 17th, a 210-yarder over water and normally into a wind. The green is large but tricky to read, and this hole sees lots of three-putts.

ALL TIME TOURNAMENT RECORDS

Record	Player(s)	Score	Year
Low 18	Bob Gilder	62	1979
Low first 36	George Archer	133 (66–67)	1970
	D. A. Weibring	(69–64)	1978
Low 36	Lon Hinkle	130 (64–66)	1978 (rounds 3–4)
Low first 54	Tom Watson	200 (66–68–66)	1980
Low 54	Lon Hinkle	197 (67–64–66)	1978
Low 72	Chip Beck	262 (69–64–65–64)	1988
Highest winning score	Mason Rudolph	293 (68–70–70–75)	1964
Largest winning margin	Lee Trevino	8 strokes	1974
Largest 18-hole lead	Lee Elder (65)	2 strokes	1973
	Mike Reasor (65)		1976
	Skip Dunaway (64)		1981
	John Mahaffey (63)		1985
Largest 36-hole lead	Bo Wininger (138)	2 strokes	1963
	Mason Rudolph (138)		1964
	Jack Nicklaus (134)		1965
	George Archer (133)		1970
	Billy Casper (134)		1972
	Bob Eastwood (134)		1984
Largest 54-hole lead	Calvin Peete	5 strokes	1986
	Billy Casper (201)		1975
Lowest start by winner	Tom Watson	66	1980
	Bob Eastwood		1984
	Ben Crenshaw		1987
Highest start by winner	Lon Hinkle	74	1978
Lowest finish by winner	Lee Trevino	65	1974
Highest finish by winner	Mason Rudolph	75	1964
Best final-round comeback	Larry Hinson	5 back	1969
Lowest 36-hole cut score		142	1981
Highest 36-hole cut score		151	1963–1964

The largest green on the course is at the 18th, and that's appropriate because this is the longest, hardest par four on the course. A mild dogleg to the right encourages a slight fade to avoid bunkers and heavy rough on the right side. Four more bunkers protect the green. Miss the fairway and you probably will not make the green. Miss the green and you probably will not make par. Unless, of course, you are Dick Mayer, in which case you still have a shot at birdie.

2nd hole

PAST WINNERS

Year	Winner	Score	Year	Winner	Score
1938	Harry Cooper	285	1968	George Archer	271
1939	Henry Picard	284	1969	*Larry Hinson	275
1940	Jimmy Demaret	286	1970	*Miller Barber	278
1941	Henry Picard	276	1971	Frank Beard	276
1942	Lloyd Mangrum	281	1972	Gary Player	279
1943	No Tournament		1973	*Jack Nicklaus	280
1944	Sammy Byrd	285	1974	Lee Trevino	267
1945	*Byron Nelson	284	1975	Billy Casper	271
1946	Byron Nelson	277	1976	Larry Ziegler	274
1947	No Tournament		1977	Jim Simons	273
1948	Bob Hamilton	280	1978	Lon Hinkle	271
1949–			1979	Hubert Green	273
1957	No Tournaments		1980	Tom Watson	273
1958	*Billy Casper	278	1981	Tom Watson	270
1959	Bill Collins	280	1982	‡Scott Hoch	206
1960	Dow Finsterwald	270	1983	Bill Rogers	274
1961	Doug Sanders	272	1984	Bob Eastwood	272
1962	Bo Wininger	281	1985	‡Seve Ballesteros	205
1963	Bo Wininger	279	1986	Calvin Peete	269
1964	Mason Rudolph	283	1987	Ben Crenshaw	268
1965	Dick Mayer	273	1988	Chip Beck	262
1966	Frank Beard	276	*Playoff		
1967	George Knudson	277	‡Rain-curtailed		

16th hole

17th hole

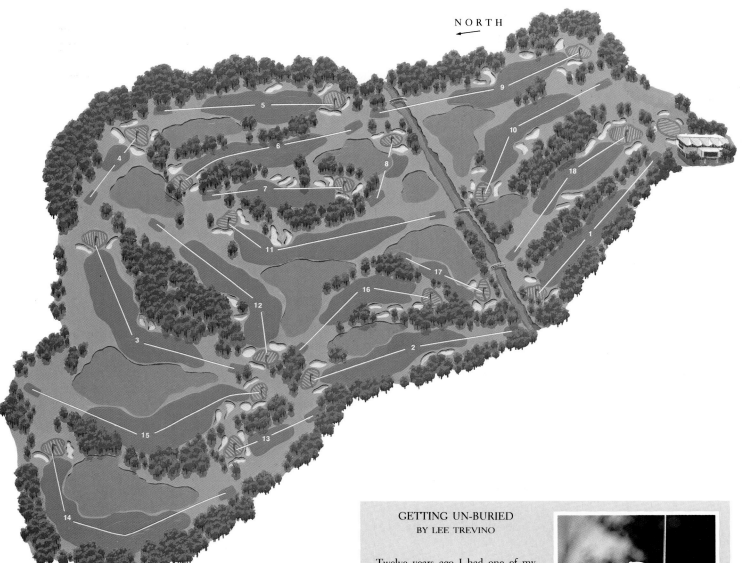

SCORECARD

Hole	Yards	Par	PGA Tour Avg. Score
1	440	4	4.126
2	560	5	4.880
3	390	4	4.016
4	195	3	3.075
5	410	4	4.119
6	540	5	4.681
7	405	4	4.036
8	165	3	2.951
9	430	4	4.132
OUT	3535	36	36.016
10	420	4	4.066
11	580	5	4.831
12	360	4	4.019
13	180	3	3.040
14	425	4	4.113
15	530	5	4.907
16	380	4	4.046
17	210	3	3.107
18	460	4	4.238
IN	3545	36	36.367
TOTAL	7080	72	72.383

GETTING UN-BURIED
BY LEE TREVINO

Twelve years ago I had one of my greatest weeks of golf at Lakewood Country Club. I won the New Orleans Open (now the USF&G Classic) by playing 72 holes without a single bogey. My swing was "on" that week, but I also saved a few pars from the bunkers. One of the most valuable shots I used that week, and every other week for that matter, is my "judo chop" explosion from buried lies in the sand.

Most golfers play the buried lie by cutting into the sand with the clubhead square or closed to the left to make sure the leading edge will dig well down and under the buried ball. Personally I don't care for that technique because the ball comes out too low and too hot. I want a softer shot with more backspin that will settle quickly on even a small area of green.

So I play the ball back about in the center of my stance with most of my weight on my left foot. I swing the club practically straight up and down and give the ball a judo chop with the clubface, just stick the clubhead into the sand with no fol-low-through. The ball rides up the clubface, taking on tremendous backspin, then flies up nice and high and floats onto the green like a feather dropping on a pond. I suggest, however, that you practice this shot a few times to see if you're precise enough to catch the ball itself instead of the sand behind it.

———————

Lee Trevino won the 1974 USF&G Classic.

$\mathscr{TPC}$ at SAWGRASS

THE PLAYERS CHAMPIONSHIP FLORIDA

It's Pine Valley with palm trees.

Not since curmudgeonly millionaire George Crump carved his fearsome masterpiece from the bleak Pine Barrens of New Jersey has the game seen anything quite like the TPC at Sawgrass. Here, on 415 heavily wooded acres in Ponte Vedra, Florida, Pete Dye crafted the ultimate examination in target golf.

The course and club are owned and operated by the PGA Tour and serve as the headquarters for the Commissioner and his staff as well as the permanent site of The Players Championship. The letters "TPC" refer to this club and to more than a dozen other such clubs now in exist-

17th hole

ence or under construction at various sites on the PGA Tour. The TPC at Sawgrass, however, is the grandfather of them all.

"Grandfather" may not be the ideal word, because this course is only a few years old. It is the brainchild of Commissioner Deane Beman, the fruition of his dream: to test the world's best players on the PGA Tour's own world-class course.

When the course opened in 1980, the initial reviews made that dream seem more like a nightmare. The design was too penal, an almost malevolent collection of par-defying gambits: narrow fingers of fairway lined with long strips of untended sand and marshgrass; dozens of deep, diabolically placed pot bunkers; scores of rough-covered knolls and craters; tall trees everywhere; and, meanest of all, 18 hard, fast greens contoured like clenched fists.

The loudest critics were the club's charter members, the Tour pros. During the inaugural Players Championship at the TPC in 1982, Jack Nicklaus was asked whether the layout suited his game. "No," he said, "I've never been very good at stopping a 5-iron on the hood of a car." Ben Crenshaw, normally the most diplomatic of players, pronounced the course "Star Wars Golf, designed by Darth Vader," and J.C. Snead, normally the most un-

1st hole

diplomatic, called it "90 percent horse manure and 10 percent luck."

But the winner of that initial TPC, Jerry Pate, had the best perspective. "It's too early to rate this course," he said. "It's like trying to rate girls when they're born. They get better with age."

In the ensuing months, architect Dye joined with an advisory group of players to rework every one of the 18 greens. Several bunkers also were altered, and subtle but important changes were made in some of the fairways. Quickly, the bulges of baby fat became graceful, shapely curves, the sharp teeth straightened into a comely smile. Today's TPC is a charmer, and most of her suitors savor the challenge of conquering her.

"Now it's a darn good golf course," says Crenshaw. "There are no weak holes." His opinion is shared by most of the selectors in *Golf Magazine*'s international panel, which ranks the TPC at Sawgrass among "The 100 Greatest Courses in the World."

4th hole

You *can* judge this book by its cover. The first tee at the TPC tells what's ahead in the next four hours. There is not so much a fairway as a landing strip. Miss it to the left and you are standing amid tall pines. Miss it to the right and you are in a waste bunker. The hole doglegs softly right to a narrow, heavily contoured green that is protected by sand and grass bunkers. Most of the pros play this hole with two irons, and respect.

Stand on that first tee, look down the fairway, and you know you are at an interesting golf course. But stand there and look to your right, your left, or your back, and you know you are at the TPC. For encasing you on three sides is a thirty-foot-high, bulkheaded, grass amphitheater, tiered like a wedding cake, with seating capacity for 20,000 people.

This course is equal parts a test of the player and a toast to the spectator. Earlier layouts, such as Nicklaus's Muir-field Village, had incorporated features that enhanced the visibility of tournament play, but the TPC was golf's first

stadium, a golf course designed with the dual intent of accommodating spectators and challenging the pros. Beman's bulldozers literally moved mountains of dirt to improve the spectator views. Like most of Florida, this is flat terrain; at no point does it rise higher than five feet above sea level. But this did not stop Beman and Dye; 850,000 cubic feet were excavated and elevated to create the massive gallery mounds that line many of the holes. The course was also routed so that play returns to, or near, the clubhouse several times, allowing spectators to mill out to many holes without having to walk over the property. Finally, most of the underbrush was cleared so that when the going gets rough, it does not get *too* rough.

At least not for the spectators. For the pros it is another story. The toughest stretch of the course begins early—at the fifth hole, the longest par four on the course. The 454-yard dogleg right banks softly to the right side. Mounds run along the left side of the fairway, and waste areas protect both the right and left sides of the landing area.

9th hole

11th hole

18th hole

The second shot is a long iron to a narrow and deep green that is guarded by tall palms and bunkers, and, as if that were not enough, tall palms *within* bunkers.

Few greens present a more intimidating target than that of the 381-yard sixth hole. The small, fiercely sloped putting surface is surrounded by a nest of deep bunkers and swales. If you fail to hit and hold this green on your second shot, you may not hit and hold it on your third.

Number seven is a demanding par four on a mild day; when played into a stiff breeze, it is a demanding bogey five. Back-to-back at the eighth and ninth holes are the hardest par three and par five on the course. The "short" hole plays 215 yards slightly downhill to a green that is as difficult to putt as it is to reach. Although the 17th hole gets most of the press, this par three without water taxes the pros for twice as many scores of bogey and worse.

The picturesque ninth hole is reachable in two, but no sane pro tries. The sensible second shot will carry over a stream that runs diagonally right to left away from the player. This leaves a wedge or short iron to the smallest green on the course, perched above a waste area on the left and a cluster of sand bunkers on the right. In 1984 this hole was played by the pros in an average of 5.123 strokes. That may not seem an awesome figure, but it was enough to make this the most difficult par five on that year's Tour.

Another of Beman's objectives was to give his course similar starts off the front and back nines. Since play during the first two rounds of the TPC begins simultaneously on both sides, the Commissioner felt that all players should have an equal opportunity to begin with a birdie—or a disaster.

The 10th is only seven yards longer than its sibling rival and in many ways is a mirror image. It doglegs slightly left in the same way that the first doglegs slightly right. The similar start continues with the par-five 11th hole as an analog to the second. Here is strategic golf course architecture at its intriguing best. Two routes are available off the tee. A drive down the left side of the fairway allows a safe second shot short of the green, leaving a wedge pitch. A long drive down the right leaves the better player an opportunity to go for the green in two. But that shot had better be a fine one. It must carry water and a waste bunker and then hold tight on an extremely narrow, rolling green surrounded by sand.

The second hardest hole on the course is number 14, a narrow, straightaway par four of 438 yards. A huge spectator mound looms up the right side of this right-to-left banked fairway, while a waste bunker runs down the left.

The last three holes at the TPC are as mind-warping a finish as there is in golf. The 16th is a gambler's.delight,

16th hole

a 497-yard par five that tempts the pros to go for it in two. The length of the second shot is no problem for most Tour players, but the lake on the right, the trees and bunkers on the left, and the terrifyingly terraced green are food for thought. In 1983 Hal Sutton came to this hole knowing he needed a birdie on one of the last three holes to win. After a 260-yard drive into position A, he slugged a 3-wood to the fringe of the green, chipped up and made the birdie. He won by a shot.

In only a few years, the island-green 17th hole has become the most famous par three in golf. Johnny Miller characterized this little devil aptly when he said, "I love it; every good golf course should have at least one hole that makes your rear end pucker."

The hole is only 132 yards long, but there is no margin for error. Except for a tiny pot bunker to the front-right of the green, there is no place to land the ball but green— or water. In the blustery opening round of the 1984 TPC, 64 balls plunked into the water here, and the stroke average for the day was 3.79, the highest ever recorded for a hole on the PGA Tour. John Mahaffey called it "the easiest par five on the course."

Number 18 is one of three or four closing par fours on the Tour that can be argued to be the toughest finishing hole in golf. A large lake embraces the entire left side of this doglegging, 440-yard demon, adding a special penalty for any player who tries to cut off too much or allows an overly active right hand. The safe shot is to the right, but not too far right because tall trees can block the lengthy approach. Near the green a cluster of thickly grown chocolate-drop mounds guard the right side, with grass bunkers in the back, sand, and the omnipresent lake on the left. If you do not think this is ample pressure for the pro, consider the 40,000 pairs of eyes peering down from the huge spectator mound to the right of the green.

Jerry Pate handled it nicely. On Sunday in 1982, he hit a drive down the center of the fairway, stung a 5-iron 18 inches from the cup, and made a birdie to win the TPC by two. It was *after* that tournament that the true theatrics began. Pate, in his prime years, was known for "celebratory aquatics," a predilection for capping his victories by diving into the nearest body of water. When that 5-iron came to rest, most of the gallery and television audience suspected the best was yet to come. Pate did not disappoint them. After signing his card, he did more than dunk himself, he grabbed course designer Dye and Commissioner Beman and tossed them in as well.

With that baptism, The Players Championship officially settled into its permanent home. During its first three years (1974–76), the event had floated from course to course—first at the Atlanta Country Club, then Colonial in Ft. Worth, Texas, then Inverrary in Ft. Lauderdale, Florida. The Tour had intended it to be a prestige event that would reward different Tour sites for excellence in staging their event. But instead, the TPC was viewed more as an interloper. Thus, in 1977, the Tour moved the event to what they thought would be a permanent home at the Sawgrass resort course just outside Jacksonville, an Arnold Palmer/Ed Seay design. But the chemistry still was not right. Sawgrass is set less than half a mile from the ocean, and in March it can be one of the windiest places in the world. In the first two years there, no one broke par for 72 holes. This was not the showcase Beman had in mind. So after a long search for a new home, Beman found it in the marshland across the street.

With the Players Club two miles farther inland and well protected by trees, the winds do not howl the way they did at the Sawgrass resort. The Tour also has pushed the date of its event back two weeks, from early March to mid-late March, and this has brought kinder conditions.

Beman's dream is thus fulfilled—or almost. His ultimate wish is for the TPC to be designated a major championship, equal in prominence to The Masters, U.S. Open, British Open, and PGA Championship. If golf can accommodate another major championship, this tournament would seem to be it.

PAST WINNERS

Year	Winner	Score
1974	Jack Nicklaus	272
1975	Al Geiberger	270
1976	Jack Nicklaus	269
1977	Mark Hayes	289
1978	Jack Nicklaus	289
1979	Lanny Wadkins	283
1980	Lee Trevino	278
1981	*Raymond Floyd	285
1982	Jerry Pate	280
1983	Hal Sutton	283
1984	Fred Couples	277
1985	Calvin Peete	274
1986	John Mahaffey	275
1987	Sandy Lyle	274
1988	Mark McCumber	273

*Playoff

ALL TIME TOURNAMENT RECORDS

Record	Player(s)	Score	Year
Low 18	Fred Couples	64	1984
Low first 36	Steve Jones	133	1987
	Mark O'Meara		1987
Low 36	Steve Jones	133	1987
	Mark O'Meara		1987
Low first 54	Larry Mize	200 (66–68–66)	1986
Low 54	Larry Mize	200 (66–68–66)	1986
Low 72	Calvin Peete	274 (70–69–69–66)	1985
	Sandy Lyle	(67–71–66–70)	1987
Highest winning score	Lanny Wadkins	283 (67–68–76–72)	1979
	Hal Sutton	283 (73–71–70–69)	1983
Largest winning margin	Calvin Peete	3 strokes	1985
Largest 18-hole lead	Bruce Lietzke (68)	1 stroke	1983
	Jim Thorpe (68)		1984
	Hale Irwin (67)		1985
Largest 36-hole lead	John Cook (139)	2 strokes	1983
	Fred Couples (135)		1984
	D.A. Weibring (136)		1985
Largest 54-hole lead	Larry Mize (200)	4 strokes	1986
Lowest start by winner	Jerry Pate	70	1982
	Calvin Peete		1985
Highest start by winner	Hal Sutton	73	1983
Lowest finish by winner	Calvin Peete	66	1985
Highest finish by winner	Fred Couples	71	1984
	John Mahaffey		1986
Best final-round comeback	Hal Sutton	4 back	1983
	John Mahaffey		1986
			1986
			1987
Lowest 36-hole cut score		143	1987
Highest 36-hole cut score		150	1983

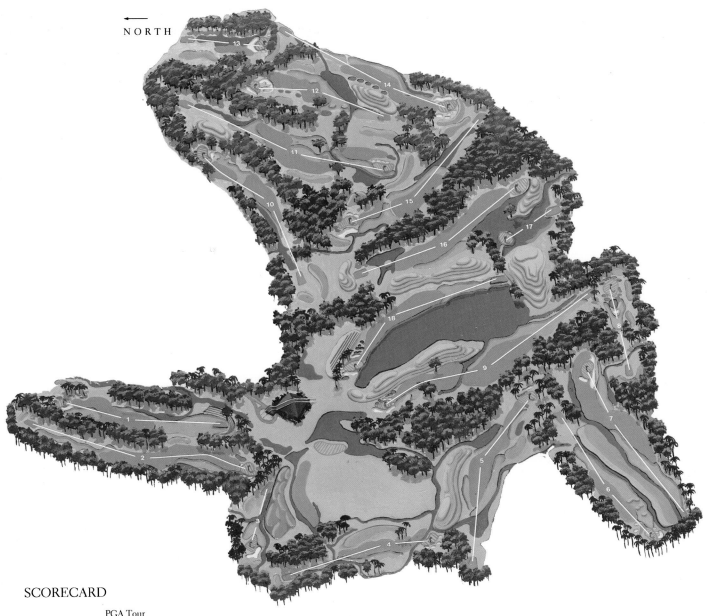

NORTH

SCORECARD

Hole	Yards	Par	PGA Tour Avg. Score
1	388	4	4.096
2	511	5	4.840
3	162	3	3.112
4	360	4	4.174
5	454	4	4.246
6	381	4	4.162
7	439	4	4.242
8	215	3	3.272
9	582	5	5.058
OUT	3492	36	37.202
10	395	4	4.121
11	529	5	4.944
12	336	4	3.935
13	172	3	3.146
14	438	4	4.303
15	426	4	4.173
16	497	5	4.749
17	132	3	3.174
18	440	4	4.435
IN	3365	36	36.980
TOTAL	6857	72	74.182

DRIVING FOR ACCURACY
BY CALVIN PEETE

With small targets and trouble on all sides, the TPC is a shotmaker's course, rewarding precision play far more than length.

The key to my accuracy is my controlled swing. I'm able to swing within myself for a couple of reasons. First, I don't put pressure on myself by trying to hit to precise areas of the fairways and greens. Anywhere on the fairway is fine with me; as for the greens, the fat part, not the pin, is usually my target.

I stay compact by keeping my left heel on the ground throughout the swing (in contrast to power players such as Tom Watson and Jack Nicklaus, both of whom allow their heels to lift). This limits my backswing turn a bit, but helps me build a tight coil for a powerful downswing.

I lead that downswing with my left wrist, pulling the club down to the ball. The left side for me is the control agent in the swing; the right side is the power producer. By keying on a strong, leading left wrist in the downswing, I'm able to guard against an overly powerful right side, which could cause my left wrist to collapse and lead to inaccuracy.

If you want more control, give yourself an ample target, anchor your left heel, and lead the downswing by pulling your left wrist toward the ball. These keys have worked for me.

Calvin Peete won the 1985 TPC with a record 274, 14-under par.

FOREST OAKS *Country Club*

3rd hole

K-MART GREATER GREENSBORO OPEN
NORTH CAROLINA

No one has measured the 1,000-odd greens on the PGA Tour, but one thing is certain: eighteen of the largest are at Forest Oaks Country Club. If you think that means this is an easy course, think again.

Although it may seem simple enough to plop a 5-iron approach onto a surface the size of a baseball diamond, consider having to get down in two from second base when the hole is at home plate. While playing 18 holes at Forest Oaks, virtually everyone meets at least one situation in which three-putting is not only a possibility, but an achievement.

Larry Nelson can tell you all about it. In 1981, a few months before he won the PGA Championship, Nelson led the Greater Greensboro Open by two shots over Mark Hayes, with four holes to go. But on the 15th hole, Nelson *four-putted*. Shaken, he then bogeyed the 16th. That opened the way for Hayes. As the two players approached the 18th green, Hayes, on the back fringe, was two strokes up and looked to be a winner over Nelson, whose approach had landed in a cavernous greenside bunker 50 feet from the hole.

But by this time Nelson, one of the hardest competitors on the Tour, had learned his lesson: rather than struggle with the green, he obviated it by blasting his ball out of the sand and directly into the cup for a birdie three. The shell-shocked Hayes three-putted, and both men went into a playoff, which Nelson won on the second hole, this time by hitting a bunker shot two feet from the cup.

Nelson's is the most famous shot in the history of the GGO, and that is saying something. Few tournaments can claim a longer history than this one. Besides, this is the event that Sam Snead won a record eight times between 1938 and 1965; where Tom Weiskopf says he played the best round of his career, a 64 amid 50-mile-an-hour winds; where Seve Ballesteros nearly missed the cut and then came back to win his first American event; and where virtually every top player in modern professional golf has won or come close to winning.

The first GGO was played in 1938 and won by Snead, who in accepting the winner's check of $1,200 served notice to The Masters and other events on the Tour. "I am happy to have won," he said, "and I'll be back next year to play in the finest tournament in which I have ever played." Over the next thirty years, the obverse would also be true—this is the tournament in which Sam Snead played his finest. Snead won Greensboro in 1938, 1946, 1949, 1950, 1955, 1956, 1960, and 1965. His total prize money from the years in which he played the GGO was $41,306. That type of performance today would be worth a little under $1 million.

No one has come close to Snead's dominance of a single event. In fact, in the history of the PGA Tour, there are only two other cases in which a player has compiled more than five victories in a tournament. One is Nicklaus's six Masters victories. The other is the Miami Open, won six times—by Sam Snead.

Snead won the first seven of his Greensboro victories at Starmount Country Club. Indeed, he won both the first and last GGO's played there. And, just to balance his words of praise after victory number one, he offered words of admonition following number seven. The course had been in sad shape for the tournament, and Snead let his feelings be known. His words were powerful. A five-year contract with Starmount was voided, and in 1961 the tournament moved to Sedgefield Country Club, where it stayed for sixteen years. In 1977 it moved to Forest Oaks.

Designed by Ellis Maples in 1964, the championship course is a par 72 of under 7,000 yards, and yet it is big. Large greens, large water hazards, large bunkers, and large trees make it play much longer than its 6,958 yards.

All these features come to bear on the third hole, a 409-yard par four that is the toughest hole on the front nine. The tee shot must be played into a narrow fairway that has water running down the entire right side. The drive will have to be solidly struck to afford a reasonable shot at the elevated green, guarded on both sides by bunkers.

The 13th is a gambler's par five—a 503-yard dogleg left with the second shot 250 yards downhill and over water. But the water is at the first part of that 250, not up next to the green. The pros enjoy this hole to the tune of about 4.8 strokes on average. But the birdies are necessary to balance the difficulties of the 18th hole, a 426-yard dogleg, where fairway bunkers control the play of the drive and more bunkers offer plenty to think about on the long-iron approach shot. Unless, of course, you can play your explosion the way Larry Nelson did.

6th hole

10th hole

13th hole

17th hole

18th hole

ALL TIME TOURNAMENT RECORDS

Record	Player(s)	Score	Year
Low 18	John Schlee	63	1967
	Doug Sanders		1968
	Gary Player		1970
	Sandy Lyle		1988
Low first 36	George Archer	131 (67–64)	1967
	Arnold Palmer	(64–67)	1970
	Billy Casper	(67–64)	1973
Low 36	George Archer	131 (67–64)	1967
	Arnold Palmer	(64–67)	1970
	Billy Casper	(67–64)	1973
Low first 54	George Archer	199 (67–64–68)	1967
	Dave Stockton	(67–67–65)	1967
	Billy Casper	(67–64–68)	1973
	Lou Graham	(68–64–67)	1973
Low 54	George Archer	199 (67–64–68)	1967
	Dave Stockton	(67–67–65)	1967
	Billy Casper	(67–64–68)	1973
	Lou Graham	(68–64–67)	1973
Low 72	George Archer	267 (67–64–68–68)	1967
	Billy Casper	(65–67–69–66)	1968
Highest winning score	Vic Ghezzi	286 (69–72–72–73)	1947
Largest winning margin	Ben Hogan (270)	9 strokes	1940
Largest 18-hole lead	Sam Snead (64)	3 strokes	1964
	Tom Weiskopf (64)		1975
Largest 36-hole lead	Sam Snead (135)	5 strokes	1956
	Tom Weiskopf (135)		1975
	Sandy Lyle (132)		1986
Largest 54-hole lead	Ben Hogan (203)	7 strokes	1940
Lowest start by winner	Gary Player	63	1970
Highest start by winner	Brian Allin	75	1971
Lowest finish by winner	Gary Player	65	1970
Highest finish by winner	Dow Finsterwald	77	1959
Best final-round comeback	Raymond Floyd (215)	6 back	1979

PAST WINNERS

Year	Winner	Score	Year	Winner	Score
1938	Sam Snead	272	1964	*Julius Boros	277
1939	Ralph Guldahl	280	1965	Sam Snead	273
1940	Ben Hogan	270	1966	*Doug Sanders	276
1941	Byron Nelson	276	1967	George Archer	267
1942	Sam Byrd	279	1968	Billy Casper	267
1943–			1969	*Gene Littler	274
1944	No Tournaments		1970	Gary Player	271
1945	Byron Nelson	271	1971	*Brian Allin	275
1946	Sam Snead	270	1972	*George Archer	272
1947	Vic Ghezzi	286	1973	Chi Chi Rodriguez	267
1948	Lloyd Mangrum	278	1974	Bob Charles	270
1949	*Sam Snead	276	1975	Tom Weiskopf	275
1950	Sam Snead	269	1976	Al Geiberger	268
1951	Art Doering	279	1977	Danny Edwards	276
1952	Dave Douglas	277	1978	Seve Ballesteros	282
1953	*Earl Stewart	275	1979	Raymond Floyd	282
1954	*Doug Ford	283	1980	Craig Stadler	275
1955	Sam Snead	273	1981	*Larry Nelson	281
1956	*Sam Snead	279	1982	Danny Edwards	285
1957	Stan Leonard	276	1983	Lanny Wadkins	275
1958	Bob Goalby	275	1984	Andy Bean	280
1959	Dow Finsterwald	278	1985	Joey Sindelar	285
1960	Sam Snead	270	1986	Sandy Lyle	275
1961	Mike Souchak	276	1987	Scott Simpson	282
1962	Billy Casper	275	1988	Sandy Lyle	271
1963	Doug Sanders	270	*Playoff		

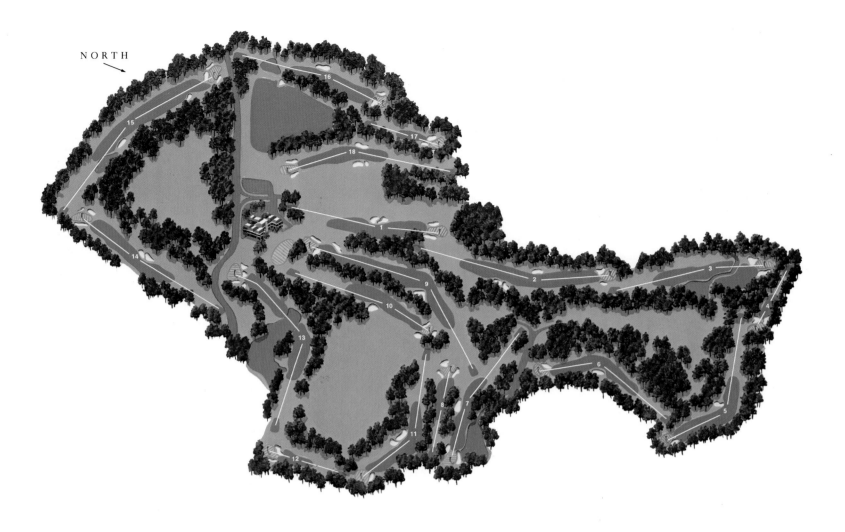

THE EXPLOSION
BY LARRY NELSON

The bunker at the 18th at Forest Oaks was about eight feet deep, and the pin was cut near the front lip, so I had to get the ball up quickly and make it stop just as quickly after it hit the green. To be honest I was trying to keep it within 10 feet of the flag, but to my good fortune it went into the hole to put me in a playoff that I eventually won.

The key to playing the explosion shot is to open the blade of the sand wedge as much as possible at address. The best way to do that is to turn the club to the open position in which you want to hold it, and then regrip it. The swing must be in the shape of a vee, with a sharply ascending takeaway, a just as sharply descending move into impact, and then another sharp ascent into the finish.

I try not to take too deep a divot of sand on this shot. I feel as if I'm bouncing the club off the bottom of the bunker at a point just underneath

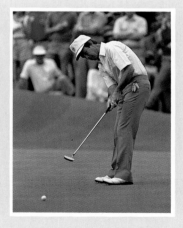

the ball. The main key, however, is to keep the sand wedge face open through impact. Do not let it close down by allowing your right hand to cross over your left the way it would in a normal release.

———————

Larry Nelson won the 1981 Greater Greensboro Open in a playoff after sinking an 18th-hole bunker shot to tie Mark Hayes.

SCORECARD

Hole	Yards	Par	PGA Tour Avg. Score
1	407	4	4.136
2	511	5	4.836
3	409	4	4.375
4	190	3	3.251
5	415	4	4.133
6	386	4	4.105
7	372	4	4.090
8	215	3	3.189
9	574	5	4.913
OUT	3479	36	37.028
10	393	4	4.180
11	383	4	4.122
12	186	3	3.214
13	503	5	4.808
14	438	4	4.154
15	554	5	4.970
16	408	4	4.325
17	188	3	3.245
18	426	4	4.257
IN	3479	36	37.275
TOTAL	6958	72	74.303

AUGUSTA

THE MASTERS
GEORGIA

More than a golf course, the Augusta National is the most famous "encore" in sports.

This was the project Bob Jones turned to in 1930 immediately after he had accomplished the impossible, after he had won the professional and amateur championships of both America and Great Britain in a single sensational year, a feat of such unimaginable proportions that there was no name for it at the time. Eventually a New York sportswriter tagged it the Grand Slam, borrowing a term from bridge.

At the age of 28, Jones had added this crowning achievement to a career that was already the most impressive the game had ever known, a career in which he had won

NATIONAL *Golf Club*

9th hole

more than 60 percent of the national championships he had entered, thirteen in all.

But after fourteen years in the cauldron of competitive golf, Jones was tired. Tired of trudging the circuit. Tired of the psychological strain that each victory increased. Tired of living in the public eye as a matinée idol. For years he had thought about quitting, and upon completing this "impregnable quadrilateral," he knew the time was right. Having played his masterpiece in four parts, Jones exited the stage of competitive golf, retiring to his law practice and business interests in Atlanta.

At the same time, he announced his intention to design and build a golf course. After playing on the finest venues

in the world for a decade and a half, he had developed some strong ideas about what a good golf course should and should not be. His course would incorporate those ideas. It would also be a place where he and his friends could enjoy golf in beautiful surroundings and with a degree of privacy.

Jones had hoped to find a site within reasonable distance of his home, and before long he did. Clifford Roberts, a tall, bespectacled Wall Street banker, had befriended Jones in the mid-1920s and knew of Jones's search. Roberts, who wintered in the antebellum resort of Augusta, home of Jones's wife Mary, knew of a unique property there that was for sale.

It was a place called Fruitlands, the first nursery in the South. It had been owned for seventy-five years by a Belgian nobleman named Baron Prosper Jules Alphonse Berckmans. Throughout the 365 acres of pine forests, Berckmans had indulged his horticultural interests in a dazzling assortment of trees, shrubs, and flowers. Azaleas flourished throughout the property, along with dogwood, redbud, daffodils, camellias, jasmine, woodbine, and a dozen types of plants and trees that existed nowhere else in the country—enough different varieties to name a hole after each one. Atop the highest hill on the property a long driveway, lined with a double row of magnolias, led to Berckmans's stately plantation home.

Alister Mackenzie, the famed Scottish golf architect, agreed to collaborate with Jones on the design of the course. Mackenzie had shown by his earlier work on Cypress Point that he knew how to take magnificent land and fashion an equally magnificent place to play golf.

From the start, the course reflected two of Jones's fundamental desires: first, that it have a natural look, that it rise out of the terrain rather than be stamped onto it. In this way, Jones hoped to recall the softly rolling feel of the Scottish linksland he so loved. Second, the design would be strategic. Each hole would offer several lines of attack, permitting the player to choose among conservative, mildly aggressive, and audacious tactics, with the rewards in proportion to the difficulty of the attempted shot and the skill with which the shot was brought off.

Jones was particularly determined to apply this philosophy to his par fives. He disdained long, unreachable holes where "you don't start playing golf until your third shot." He therefore designed four par fives; each could be reached in two by the game's strongest players. He also used menacing hazards, notably at the 13th and 15th holes, to punish the player who overestimated himself.

As Mackenzie drew the maps and oversaw the moving of the earth, Jones played thousands of experimental shots from planned tees to planned greens. When the course was completed in 1933, Mackenzie, who would die a few months later, said, "Augusta National represented my best opportunity and, I believe, my finest achievement."

Despite numerous changes, Augusta National today remains the golf course Bobby Jones wanted it to be: a masterpiece of strategic design and perhaps the finest thinking man's course since St. Andrews.

With expansive fairways, virtually no rough, and only 10 fairway bunkers, elbow room seems to abound on this course. And with enormous greens and only 34 greenside bunkers (fewer than two per hole) the targets seem unmissable. But these greens are awesomely fast and fearsomely swaled, and the combination of this speed and undulation is more lethal than at any other course on the PGA Tour.

Position play is therefore paramount. One must consistently play for the area of the green where putting will be least problematic. As Byron Nelson has said, "At Augusta, it's often better to be 20 feet to one side of the cup than six feet to the other side."

But to find that ideal patch of green, one must approach from the most propitious angle, which means the tee shot must be played not simply to the fairway but to the proper *sector* of the fairway, a task that requires great discipline when the general target is so wide. As Jones put it, "There is not a hole out there that can't be birdied if you just think; and there is not a hole out there that can't be double-bogeyed if you stop thinking."

Soon after the course was completed, Jones decided to hold a tournament, an informal get-together for his amateur and professional friends. Roberts urged Jones to play in the event and suggested it be called The Masters. Jones, after much reluctance, agreed to the former on condition that he not accept prize money, but refused the latter, arguing that "Masters" was too presumptuous a name for his clambake.

Jones was never a threat in his tournament, either in the first year or in any of the eleven times he competed, his best finish being a tie for 13th (although in 1936 he did record a practice round of 64, a record that stood for more than half a century of Masters competition). In 1947 he withdrew after two rounds with what was diagnosed as bursitis. Years later it became apparent that his condition was more serious. Eventually, the ailment was identified as syringomyelia, a crippling spinal disease. Soon Jones was forced to walk with a cane, then he was confined to a wheelchair. The last Masters he attended was 1968, and he died in December 1969.

But Bob Jones left behind a tournament that will live as long as golf is played. The first Augusta Invitational (1934) was won by young Horton Smith. This also was the last "Augusta Invitational." The press somehow got wind of the name "Masters," and by the end of the first week the newspaper reports carried the new name.

A year later the tournament had not only a new name but a storied tradition when Gene Sarazen surged to victory on the heels of "the shot heard round the world," an incredible 220-yard 4-wood that sailed across the water and into the hole at the par-five 15th in the final round. It enabled Sarazen to tie Craig Wood, whom he beat the next day in an 18-hole playoff.

Ever since that year, it seems, the Augusta National has had a gift for supplying the dramatic, the unexpected. It

Clubhouse

is difficult to pick a hole on the course where something dramatic has not happened. It was at the first hole in 1968 that Argentinian Roberto DeVicenzo smashed an enormous drive and then holed out a 9-iron for eagle to take the lead in the final round, a lead he lost *after* the tournament when it was discovered that he had signed an incorrect scorecard.

The second hole, one of those reachable par fives, was hit in dramatic style by Seve Ballesteros in 1983. In the last round Ballesteros knocked a 4-wood 15 feet from the hole and sank the putt for an eagle. That day he scorched through the first four holes in birdie-eagle-par-birdie to jump over former winners Raymond Floyd, Craig Stadler, and Tom Watson en route to his second Masters victory.

Mackenzie modeled the par-four fifth after the famous and feared Road Hole (17) at the Old Course at St. Andrews. As at that hole, the nemesis is the large, treacherously sloped green. One year Sam Snead stood at the front edge of the fifth, facing a 50-foot birdie putt up the steep bank to the second tier. He stroked it smoothly—too smoothly. The ball climbed to the crest of the slope, stopped, and then rolled back to Snead's feet. From there, unbelievably, the Slammer holed it for par.

During the 1960s and early 1970s, the original bermudagrass greens began to lose speed. They were still fast, to be sure, but not as fast as originally designed. So, in a daring gamble The Masters people simple dug up all 18 greens and reseeded them with speedier bentgrass. Tradi-

tionally, bentgrass flourishes only in cooler climates, but at Augusta National, which closes from May to September each year, the changeover and the new greens were given the necessary amount of tender, loving care. The switch was a success, and today Augusta's bent greens are every bit as fast as the bermuda greens were, at times even faster.

Another tough target greets mid-iron shots from the elevated tee of the par-three sixth. Amateur Billy Joe Patton solved this one in the last round of the 1954 Masters when he holed out his 5-iron shot for a 1. Patton led most of that tournament, but in one of the saddest chapters in Masters history, the likable North Carolinian gave it back on the finishing par fives, where he took a calamitous 13 strokes. He finished one stroke out of the Snead-Hogan playoff won by Sam.

The back nine of the Augusta National has produced more cliffhanging finishes than Edgar Allan Poe, Agatha Christie, and Alfred Hitchcock combined. It was at the green of the cathedral-like 10th hole in 1984 that Ben Crenshaw thrilled his fans with a 60-foot birdie putt that launched him to his only major championship victory.

It was at the daunting 11th in 1982 that Fuzzy Zoeller bravely stung an 8-iron 15 feet, then sank a birdie—simultaneously sinking opponents Watson and Ed Sneed—in The Masters' first sudden-death playoff.

And it is the devilish little 12th that has caused more competitors more consternation than any hole on the course. A windy, 155-yard shot over water to a green that

10th hole

is 105 feet wide but at its shallowest point only 28 feet deep, the Golden Bell has wrung every top player in the game. Gary Player calls it "the toughest par three in the world." Who knows what Tom Weiskopf calls it; in 1982 he took a 13 on it, the highest single-hole score in Masters history.

The 11th, 12th, and 13th holes comprise Augusta's Amen Corner. It is at the 13th hole that players have an opportunity to redress—or amplify—their sins at 11 and 12. Surely, this picture-perfect, 465-yard dogleg has produced more triumphs and tragedies than any par five in golf.

It was here in 1937 that Byron Nelson sank a 50-foot eagle chip to surge toward his first Masters victory. And it was here, five years later, that he completed a three-birdie sweep of Amen Corner while beating Ben Hogan in a playoff. Much later, Hogan did the same thing, birdieing 11, 12, and 13 at the age of 54 for a record 30 on the back nine, one of the most inspiring moments in golf history.

Thirteen was where the aforementioned Billy Joe Patton saw his title hopes go awry when his daring second shot fell into Rae's creek. Three decades later, Curtis Strange suffered the same fate in the final round of the 1985 Masters.

The original design of the Augusta National has undergone many changes, but none more radical than that of the 16th hole, which in 1947 got a complete facelift from Robert Trent Jones. Alister Mackenzie's par three was 150 yards, with a small creek to the right of the green and two alternate tees, one to the left of the 15th green and one to the right. Jones abolished the right-hand tee, lengthened the hole 20 yards, enlarged the creek into a pond, and repositioned the green to the right of that pond, banking the putting surface sharply from back-right to the water at

6th hole

12th hole

15th hole

16th hole

the front-left. The new green, he said, was far more receptive to the type of shots being played into it.

This was the site of the most famous putt in Masters history when in 1975 Jack Nicklaus rolled in an uphill-sidehill 40-footer for birdie in the final round. At the time he was in a wild three-way shootout with Johnny Miller and Tom Weiskopf, both playing directly behind him. Nicklaus's birdie gave him the lead, and when the other two missed birdie putts on 18, Jack won a record fifth Masters, a record which stood until he himself broke it in 1986.

Eleven holes on the course are doglegs, but only two—the first and the last—move from left to right. With trees lining the right side of 18 and two large bunkers on the outside corners, few players have the courage for an aggressive tee shot. Many in fact hit fairway woods or long irons to this fairway, which flows uphill to the green. The resulting mid-iron shot is played to a narrow target that slopes severely from back to front.

Virtually every top player of the last half century has won The Masters, and the best have won it more than once: Nicklaus (6 times), Palmer (4 times), Jimmy Demaret, Player, Sam Snead (3 times each), Ballesteros, Horton Smith, Hogan, Nelson, and Watson (2 times each).

Masters tickets simply are not for sale, at least not for the four days of the tournament proper. Daily tickets may be purchased for the three practice rounds and the traditional Par-3 Contest, but once the serious play begins, access to the course is limited to players and their immediate families, officials, press, and a few thousand lucky people called "patrons." These are the folks who years ago began coming to The Masters and have wisely retained their passes from year to year.

Each January the Augusta National Golf Club quietly invites patrons to renew their privilege for the upcoming tournament. Any patron who does not respond quickly and in the affirmative is summarily debadged, and a salivating member of the waiting list—cut off years ago and now estimated at about 10,000—gets the nod. The patrons' badges may not be willed or transferred in any way.

"You'd be surprised at the amount of correspondence we get from attorneys in divorce cases," says Masters Tournament Director Colonel Dave Davis. "If he gets the house and she gets the car, he gets the silver and she gets the kids, then who gets the Masters ticket? It's a sticky question."

Most Masters patrons could never make it inside the ropes, but most are avid if not accomplished golfers, and the Augusta gallery is generally regarded as the best informed and best mannered on the Tour.

More exclusive than the annual roster of players or the patrons' list is the Augusta National Golf Club membership

ALL TIME TOURNAMENT RECORDS

Record	Player(s)	Score	Year
Low 18	Nick Price	63	1986
Low first 36	Raymond Floyd	131 (65–66)	1976
Low 36	Raymond Floyd	131 (65–66)	1976
	Johnny Miller	(65–66)	1975 (rounds 3–4)
Low first 54	Raymond Floyd	201 (65–66–70)	1976
Low 54	Raymond Floyd	201 (65–66–70)	1976
Low 72	Jack Nicklaus	271 (67–71–64–69)	1965
	Raymond Floyd	(65–66–70–70)	1976
Highest winning score	Sam Snead Jack Burke, Jr.	289	1954 1956
Largest winning margin	Jack Nicklaus	9 strokes	1965
Largest 18-hole lead	Craig Wood	5 strokes	1941
Largest 36-hole lead	Herman Keiser Raymond Floyd	5 strokes	1946 1976
Largest 54-hole lead	Raymond Floyd	8 strokes	1976
Lowest start by winner	Raymond Floyd	65	1976
Highest start by winner	Craig Stadler	75	1982
Lowest finish by winner	Gary Player	64	1978
Highest finish by winner	Arnold Palmer	75	1962
Best final-round comeback	Jack Burke, Jr.	8 back	1956
Lowest 36-hole cut score		145	1979
Highest 36-hole cut score		154	1982

itself, a collection of American titans of industry. As one reporter wrote, "The Augusta National is a golf club that looks as if it dropped out of heaven, and it's just as hard to get into." Dwight Eisenhower was a member, both before and during his presidency, and the club also erected a small white cottage for him and Mamie. It still stands behind the 18th green.

Tradition and privilege also pervade the clubhouse itself, which includes a special grill room restricted to Masters champions and their guests, a "crow's nest" dormitory on the third floor, reserved each year for a handful of young amateurs who bunk there during the tournament, and a special window box on the main floor displaying one valued club from each of the past Masters champions.

Other events have often imitated this tournament, which has originated so many enduring aspects of championship competition. The whole idea of stadium golf arguably had its roots here in the many grassy knolls and terraces surrounding the fairways and greens. The concept of multiple

7th hole

18th hole

13th hole

leaderboards also was born at The Masters, where an army of 200 scorekeepers relays up-to-the-minute results via underground telephone wires.

Most of the gallery agree that the spectating is the easiest, the refreshments the tastiest (and most moderately priced) of any tournament in golf. Most of the press agree the facilities are the finest and most efficiently run. Most of the competitors agree that The Masters is the one golf tournament in the world they would most like to win. That is a fitting legacy to Bobby Jones.

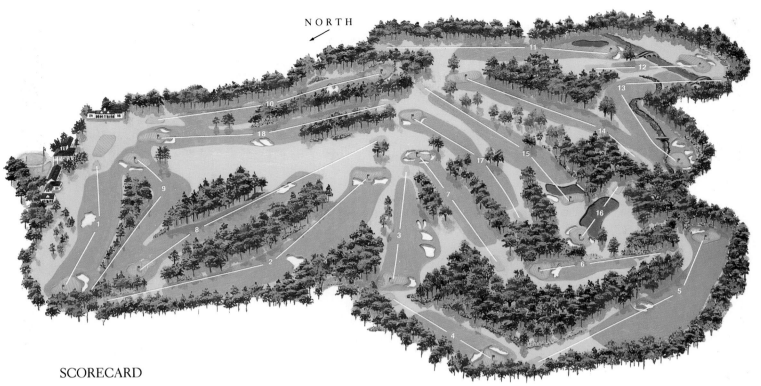

SCORECARD

Hole	Yards	Par	PGA Tour Avg. Score
1	400	4	4.198
2	555	5	4.803
3	360	4	4.145
4	205	3	3.178
5	435	4	4.259
6	180	3	3.177
7	360	4	4.062
8	535	5	4.793
9	435	4	4.100
OUT	3465	36	36.715
10	485	4	4.278
11	455	4	4.264
12	155	3	3.261
13	465	5	4.839
14	405	4	4.094
15	500	5	4.629
16	170	3	3.157
17	400	4	4.044
18	405	4	4.205
IN	3440	36	36.771
TOTAL	6905	72	73.486

HIGH SOFT IRONS
BY SEVE BALLESTEROS

The most important thing at Augusta is to hit your irons to the correct part of the green. Since the greens are usually hard, fast, and fiercely sloped, it's particularly important to hit the ball high and soft with the long and middle irons.

I have three keys I practice each year before playing The Masters. First, I position the ball a bit more forward in my stance than I do on other courses. This helps ensure that I make impact on a slightly upward angle, helping to lift the ball upward. Second, I make a big turn, getting my arms well into the air on the backswing. Third, I stay back behind the ball on the downswing while letting my arms swing through the ball. You must not attack or hit at these shots. Perhaps more than in any other situation, you must make a smooth, flowing swing. In the follow-through, it's important to have the arms reach high into the air. Remember, hit high, finish high.

Seve Ballesteros, a two-time Masters champion (1980, 1983), is also the youngest player (23 in 1980) to win a green jacket.

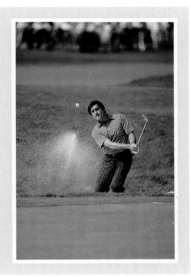

PAST WINNERS

Year	Winner	Score	Year	Winner	Score	Year	Winner	Score	Year	Winner	Score
1934	Horton Smith	284	1949	Sam Snead	282	1963	Jack Nicklaus	286	1977	Tom Watson	276
1935	*Gene Sarazen	282	1950	Jimmy Demaret	283	1964	Arnold Palmer	276	1978	Gary Player	277
1936	Horton Smith	285	1951	Ben Hogan	280	1965	Jack Nicklaus	271	1979	*Fuzzy Zoeller	280
1937	Byron Nelson	283	1952	Sam Snead	286	1966	*Jack Nicklaus	288	1980	Seve Ballesteros	275
1938	Henry Picard	285	1953	Ben Hogan	274	1967	Gay Brewer, Jr.	280	1981	Tom Watson	280
1939	Ralph Guldahl	279	1954	*Sam Snead	289	1968	Bob Goalby	277	1982	*Craig Stadler	284
1940	Jimmy Demaret	280	1955	Cary Middlecoff	279	1969	George Archer	281	1983	Seve Ballesteros	280
1941	Craig Wood	280	1956	Jack Burke, Jr.	289	1970	*Billy Casper	279	1984	Ben Crenshaw	277
1942	*Byron Nelson	280	1957	Doug Ford	282	1971	Charles Coody	279	1985	Bernhard Langer	282
1943–			1958	Arnold Palmer	284	1972	Jack Nicklaus	286	1986	Jack Nicklaus	279
1945	No Tournaments		1959	Art Wall, Jr.	284	1973	Tommy Aaron	283	1987	*Larry Mize	285
1946	Herman Keiser	282	1960	Arnold Palmer	282	1974	Gary Player	278	1988	Sandy Lyle	281
1947	Jimmy Demaret	281	1961	Gary Player	280	1975	Jack Nicklaus	276			
1948	Claude Harmon	279	1962	*Arnold Palmer	280	1976	Raymond Floyd	271	*Playoff		

HARBOUR TOWN *Golf Links*

M C I   H E R I T A G E
C L A S S I C
S O U T H
C A R O L I N A

"It's different, but then, so was Garbo."

With those words, Pete Dye defended his design of the Harbour Town Golf Links, a design that in 1969 violated nearly every rule of the prevailing school of golf course architecture.

It was the height of the macho era of course design. The trend was toward brutishly long courses, with airstrips for tees, broadly sweeping fairways, yawning ink-spot bunkers, and greens large enough to encircle the Houston Astrodome.

Even then, Dye was the *enfant terrible* of his profession. His early work at The Golf Club in Ohio and Crooked Stick in Indiana had shown a disdain for bigness. But his design for South Carolina's Sea Pines Plantation was ex-

13th hole

pected to be traditional. For one thing, it was slated to host a PGA Tour event. For another, Dye's consultant on the project was Jack Nicklaus, the embodiment of "brutishly long."

But the course they produced was unlike anything the Tour had ever seen. And yet it needed no defense, for by unanimous agreement it was brilliant.

Spread among 300 acres of trees and marshland on the inland coast of Hilton Head Island, Harbour Town has been variously nicknamed "Pebble Beach East," "Pine Valley South," and "St. Andrews with Spanish Moss." The references involve three courses as different from one another as California, New Jersey, and Scotland. Yet in each case the comparison to Harbour Town is a valid one.

And in each comparison is a key to the magnificence of this course.

Pebble Beach and Harbour Town both enjoy the most treasured asset a course can have: a spectacular natural setting. Sea Pines Plantation's founder Charles Fraser wisely parceled a huge chunk of his prime Hilton Head property to the golf course. Dye took advantage of it by winding the fairways through dense forests of oak, pine, magnolia, and Spanish moss and placing the greens in menacing proximity to a dozen small lakes, ponds, and lagoons.

Most of the holes are scenic, but the 17th and 18th are Monterey-spectacular. The 176-yard 17th plays directly over water and is guarded by an 80-yard-long bunker that

7th hole

8th hole

9th hole

is bulkheaded with Dye's most familiar "signature," railroad ties. The wind invariably is in one's face. Because there is no real terrain between tee and green, the tee-shot distance is difficult to judge. To compound this problem, during the late afternoon finish of the Heritage Classic, the hole plays directly toward the setting sun.

Eighteen is almost identical in design to the 18th at Pebble Beach, except that it is a par four instead of a par five. The hole snakes around the edge of Calibogue Sound (pronounced Cali-bogey); the tee, the landing area, and the green sit on small promontories. Too far left and you are in the salt marshes; too far right and you are out-of-bounds. Depending on the wind, the 465 yards can be a driver and a soft 7-iron, or be unreachable in two. A tall, red-and-white striped lighthouse, the Harbour Town trademark, stands behind this green, adding a touch of man-made beauty to one of the most scenically splendid finishing holes in the world.

Famous and feared, Pine Valley Golf Club is carved from the wild Pine Barrens of southern New Jersey. It is one huge, magnificent bunker, dotted at perilous intervals

with tees, fairways, and greens. In the same way, Harbour Town is cleverly cleaved from the swampland of coastal South Carolina. Both Pine Valley and Harbour Town are relatively short by championship standards—about 6,800 yards. But each course is, in the words of golf writer Bernard Darwin, "an examination in golf."

Harbour Town is a rigorous examination, even for those who know the subject cold; in fact, even for those who prepared the test. Says co-designer Nicklaus: "I get angrier here than anywhere else we [Tour pros] play. This place is designed for some shots I'm not supposed to be able to hit, and that's a challenge. Then, when I can't hit them, it just burns my rear end."

Indeed, perhaps no golfer can play all the shots that Harbour Town demands: punches under the wind and cuts over mammoth trees, splashes from bunkers and thrashes from pampas grass, careful chips from clinging, centipede rough, and just plain old impossible straight shots.

The fairways are amply wide, but the groves of trees often encroach to give tee shots a claustrophobic feeling. On almost every long hole, the terrain and placement of

14th hole

15th hole

hazards encourage the golfer to work the ball from left to right or right to left. ABC-TV commentator and former PGA champion Dave Marr, after playing a particularly frustrating round in an early Heritage Classic, captured the essence of Harbour Town in a wry comment to one of the tournament officials: "I never complain about pin positions," Marr said, "but you certainly have put the fairways in some strange places today."

The wise strategy is to find the fairway, and hew to the best part of it, for the greens at Harbour Town are tiny, so tiny, in fact, that Harbour Town is the site of the PGA Tour record for fewest putts over 72 holes. In 1980 George Archer got through four rounds of the Heritage with only 94 rolls, an average of 23.5 putts per 18 holes. His "secret"? He missed a lot of greens, then chipped up close for short putts. Despite the hot blade that week, Archer finished tied for 10th.

When you miss a green at Harbour Town, par can be as elusive as Garbo, especially if your ball finds one of the bunkers. There are only 35 on the course, but they are not wasted. Sand completely encircles the par-three seventh, where the bunker also houses a large tree. The ninth hole, one of the world's classic, short par fours, was made more difficult in 1981 with the addition of a pot bunker behind the heart-shaped green. In the same year, another pot bunker was added to the back-left of the par-three 14th. A tee shot into that bunker leaves the golfer with a difficult explosion to a shallow green backed by deep water.

The 15th hole, a 556-yard par five, is the one Lee Trevino once rated as his favorite on the Tour. "It's so long that it doesn't favor the long hitters," he said. "Even King Kong couldn't get on that hole in two." The green has been reached a few times in tournament play, but the hole normally demands three thoughtfully executed shots. The drive and second shot should leave a pitch of about 100 yards to the narrowest opening on the course, between water and sand left and more sand right.

Perhaps the finest par four is number 13. Symbolic of the course, this 358-yard hole demands accuracy rather than power. The tee shot must be positioned to the right side of the fairway to set up the second shot, played between two huge oak trees. A large U-shaped bunker, banked with cypress planks, awaits a misplayed approach. Early during Heritage week, the pros can be seen practicing unusual sand shots in anticipation of a lie that is up against the planks. They normally choose a middle iron and try to explode the ball in such a way that it climbs up the planks and rolls softly onto the green.

In 1983 a survey asked Tour pros the question, "Which Tour course is your favorite, a layout so sound that you

18th hole

wish you had designed it yourself?" The course mentioned most frequently was Harbour Town.

"Heritage" was not a capricious choice for the name of the tournament hosted at Harbour Town. A substantial body of evidence indicates that South Carolina's low country is the birthplace of American golf.

The English and Scottish settled in this region, and by the end of the eighteenth century they had civilized their society to the extent that their thoughts had turned to golf. In 1786 a group of Charleston men founded the South Carolina Golf Club, more than a century before the famous "Apple Tree Gang" established the first permanent club in Yonkers, New York. Sometime in the 1900s, the South Carolina Golf Club dissolved, but with the birth of the Heritage Classic the club was rechartered and given a home at Harbour Town, making that club arguably the St. Andrews of America.

The Harbour Town club today houses a valuable collection of antique golf clubs, assembled and curated by Laurie Auchterlonie, the honorary professional of The Royal and Ancient Golf Club of St. Andrews, Scotland. Each spring for several years Auchterlonie came to Harbour Town for the "playing-in" of the Captain of the South Carolina Golf Club, a tradition celebrated with a parade of Scottish bagpipers and culminated with a tee shot by the defending Heritage champion, timed with the firing of a small cannon. It is the same ceremony staged in St. Andrews, Scotland, each fall to honor the incoming Captain of The Royal and Ancient Golf Club.

Of course, any comparison to Scotland's venerable Home of Golf is inherently strained. But if venerability grows from a highly revered course, Harbour Town has a fine start. And if additional prestige accrues from the list of champions who prevail on such a course, then Harbour Town already ranks ahead of nearly every Tour site. The first Heritage was won in 1969 by Arnold Palmer, and since then the list of champions has added Nicklaus, Tom Watson, Hale Irwin, Johnny Miller, Hubert Green, Fuzzy Zoeller, and Bernhard Langer, all winners of major championships. This heritage, although young, is already rich.

PAST WINNERS

Year	Winner	Score	Year	Winner	Score
1969	Arnold Palmer	283	1980	*Doug Tewell	280
1970	Bob Goalby	280	1981	Bill Rogers	278
1971	Hale Irwin	279	1982	*Tom Watson	280
1972	Johnny Miller	281	1983	Fuzzy Zoeller	275
1973	Hale Irwin	272	1984	Nick Faldo	270
1974	Johnny Miller	276	1985	Bernhard Langer	273
1975	Jack Nicklaus	271	1986	Fuzzy Zoeller	276
1976	Hubert Green	274	1987	Davis Love III	271
1977	Graham Marsh	273	1988	Greg Norman	271
1978	Hubert Green	277			
1979	Tom Watson	270	*Playoff		

ALL TIME TOURNAMENT RECORDS

Record	Player(s)	Score	Year
Low 18	Jack Nicklaus	63	1975
	Denis Watson		1984
	Jim Hallet		1988
Low first 36	Jack Nicklaus	129 (66–63)	1975
Low 36	Jack Nicklaus	129 (66–63)	1975
Low first 54	Tom Watson	199 (65–65–69)	1979
Low 54	Tom Watson	199 (65–65–69)	1979
Low 72	Tom Watson	270 (65–65–69–71)	1979
	Nick Faldo	270 (66–67–68–69)	1984
Highest winning score	Arnold Palmer	283 (68–71–70–74)	1969
Largest winning margin	Hale Irwin (272)	5 strokes	1973
	Hubert Green (274)		1976
	Tom Watson (270)		1979
Largest 18-hole lead	Jack Nicklaus (66)	3 strokes	1975
Largest 36-hole lead	Johnny Miller (134)	6 strokes	1974
	Jack Nicklaus (129)		1975
Largest 54-hole lead	Tom Watson (199)	8 strokes	1979
Lowest start by winner	Graham Marsh	65	1977
	Tom Watson		1979
Highest start by winner	Bob Goalby	74	1970
Lowest finish by winner	Bob Goalby	66	1970
Highest finish by winner	Arnold Palmer	74	1969
Best final-round comeback	Hubert Green (210)	5 back	1978
Lowest 36-hole cut score		144	1980
Highest 36-hole cut score		152	1971

17th hole

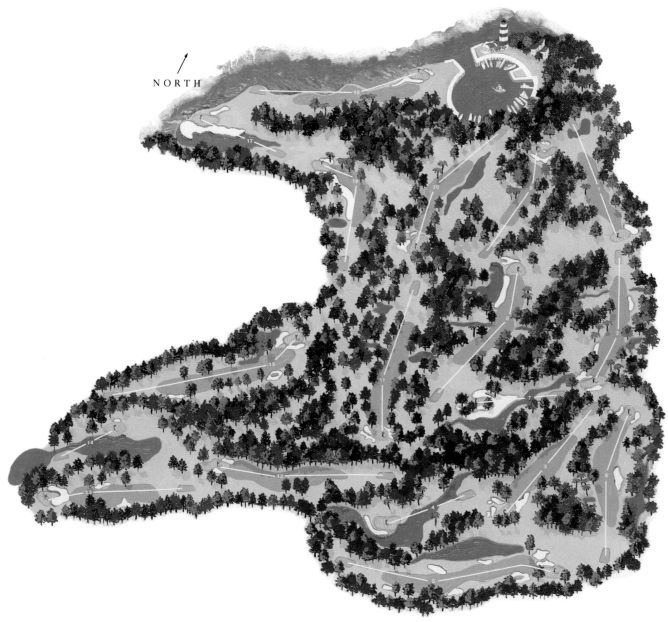

NORTH

SCORECARD

Hole	Yards	Par	PGA Tour Avg. Score
1	415	4	4.176
2	497	5	4.686
3	412	4	4.109
4	189	3	3.220
5	528	5	4.780
6	404	4	4.037
7	172	3	3.101
8	455	4	4.251
9	332	4	4.012
OUT	3404	36	36.372
10	443	4	4.227
11	423	4	4.264
12	420	4	4.152
13	358	4	4.153
14	165	3	3.012
15	556	5	4.998
16	398	4	3.990
17	176	3	3.078
18	465	4	4.143
IN	3404	35	36.017
TOTAL	6808	71	72.389

SHORT PUTTS
BY BERNHARD LANGER

At Harbour Town, where the greens are small, scoring usually depends on an ability to chip and putt for par. This puts a premium on those putts in the two- to five-foot range.

For several years, I was one of the worst players in the world at sinking short putts. I had the yips, that convulsive shaking in the hands and forearms that results from a deathly fear of missing three-footers. But over a period of time I overcame them, and today I consider myself one of the better putters on the Tour.

I wish I could give you a miracle cure for the yips, but I can't. Everyone has to fight through them as best he or she can. One thing that worked for me was switching to a new putter. Immediately after that, I started sinking short putts; that gave me confidence, and confidence gave me the ability to sink still more putts. I also became a better putter when I adopted my unique system of using a cross-handed grip on short putts and a conventional grip on long ones.

My point is that you must practice with the goal of finding something that will work for you—a new putter, a new method—because these artificial cures can lead you to the only true cure for the yips—a new attitude.

If you doubt your ability to make short putts, you won't make them; if you believe in yourself, you will.

———————

Bernhard Langer won the 1985 Heritage Classic one week after he won The Masters.

TPC at the
THE WOODLANDS

16th hole

THE INDEPENDENT
INSURANCE AGENT OPEN
TEXAS

Every golfer knows this heartache.

On a bright, crisp morning, you arrive at the course for your regular weekend match. The sun is shining, the birds are singing, and everything is right with the world. On the practice range, you strike the ball with the frightening precision of Ben Hogan. Striding confidently to the first tee, you tell yourself, "Today I will play like a champion."

Then you make nine on the first hole.

What ensues is a long day in the sun, a large number on the scorecard, a painful payout at the 18th, and a grim evening for the rest of the family.

Even the best players know what it is like to be crucified on the first hole. Even Tour pros. Even David Graham.

In 1983 Graham was one stroke out of the lead after 36 holes of what was then called the Houston Open. He was playing better than at any time since his impressive victory in the 1981 U.S. Open at Merion. A native Australian who had transplanted to Texas, Graham knew and loved the East course at The Woodlands. As the third round began, Lee Trevino held the lead, but the smart money said 43-year-old Lee would crack; bet on David.

At the very first hole, however, Graham was the cracker. A hooked tee shot into the woods, three more to get out, a fifth into a bunker, a sixth to the fringe of the green, on in seven and down in two for a quadruple-bogey 9.

Thereafter, however, Graham did play like a champion, taking 64 strokes for the remaining 17 holes. His 73 left him five strokes back after three rounds. On Sunday, as the leaders struggled, Graham opened with a birdie on his nemesis, went on to shoot a 64 and, incredibly, won the tournament by *five strokes*. The fact is, he could have made 13 on his disaster hole and still have won.

It is ironic that Graham blew to pieces on a course designed by his compatriot and close friend Bruce Devlin. And stranger still that the blowup occurred on the easiest hole on the course. Number one at The Woodlands is a comparatively straightforward par five of only 515 yards. Despite having a green that is literally surrounded by sand it annually crumbles under the pros' assault, yielding three times as many birdies as bogeys.

At The Woodlands there are many more likely places to score a 9. Designed by Devlin and his longtime associate, architect Bob Von Hagge, the East course at the Woodlands (there is also a West course) is a Texas-size par 72 of 7,042 yards carved from a huge forest of oaks and pines twenty-seven miles north of Houston.

The Tour moved the Houston Open here for a successful run beginning in 1975; in 1984 Commissioner Deane Beman announced that the course would be converted into a TPC stadium facility. Immediately architects Von Hagge and Devlin began toughening an already formidable design.

Ten bunkers were added, spectator mounds were sculpted into four holes, five tee boxes were relocated, one hole was completely overhauled, and another had its par changed.

One of the finest short par fours on the Tour is the 17th, a sharp dogleg of 383 yards, with water in play on the last 200. A large lake, one of nine water hazards on the course, guards the left side of the narrow fairway and pokes its nose directly in front of the green, actually tunneling under the last few yards of fairway. Because the hole plays downhill, even a good drive will leave an awkward stance for the approach to the extremely narrow green, guarded left, front, and right by water and in the rear by a treacherous bunker.

Flip the 17th hole on its back, move the lake from the left to the right, add 60 yards and you have an approximation of the 18th hole, a heroic finishing four. A new row of trees adds both definition and difficulty to the left side of the hole, while the lake wraps menacingly around the front part of the green. To the rear is a necklace of six bunkers. Even the pros play this approach with middle irons—and with caution.

The Woodlands has plans to expand to five golf courses by 1990. The golf facilities are part of one of the most successful residential developments in the country. Just as nearby Houston was the boomtown of the 1970s, The Woodlands seems to be the boom suburb of the 1980s. In its first ten years, the project grew from nothing to a community of 20,000 people. By the end of the decade, the population of its several connected villages is projected to top 40,000, with an ultimate goal of 55,000 residents.

Eventually, along with the other golf courses, the PGA Tour will build its own stadium facility from scratch. But until then, the East course at The Woodlands will host this event, as it has every year since 1975.

1st hole

ALL TIME TOURNAMENT RECORDS

Record	Player(s)	Score	Year
Low 18	Ron Streck	62	1981
Low first 36	Curtis Strange	129 (66–63)	1980
Low 36	Curtis Strange	129 (66–63)	1980 (rounds 1–2)
Low first 54	Curtis Strange	195 (66–63–66)	1980
Low 54	Curtis Strange	195 (66–63–66)	1980
Low 72	Curtis Strange	266 (66–63–66–71)	1980
Highest winning score	Cary Middlecoff	283	1953
Largest winning margin	Jack Burke, Jr.	6 strokes	1952
Largest 18-hole lead	Ed Furgol	2 strokes	1950
Largest 36-hole lead	Curtis Strange	4 strokes	1980
Largest 54-hole lead	Curtis Strange	6 strokes	1980
Lowest start by winner	Gary Player Ed Sneed	64	1978 1982
Highest start by winner	Bruce Crampton Curtis Strange	72	1973 1986
Lowest finish by winner	Ron Streck	62	1981
Highest finish by winner	Bill Collins	75	1960
Best final-round comeback	Ed Oliver Ed Sneed	5 back	1958 1982
Lowest 36-hole cut score		141	1979
Highest 36-hole cut score		159	1947

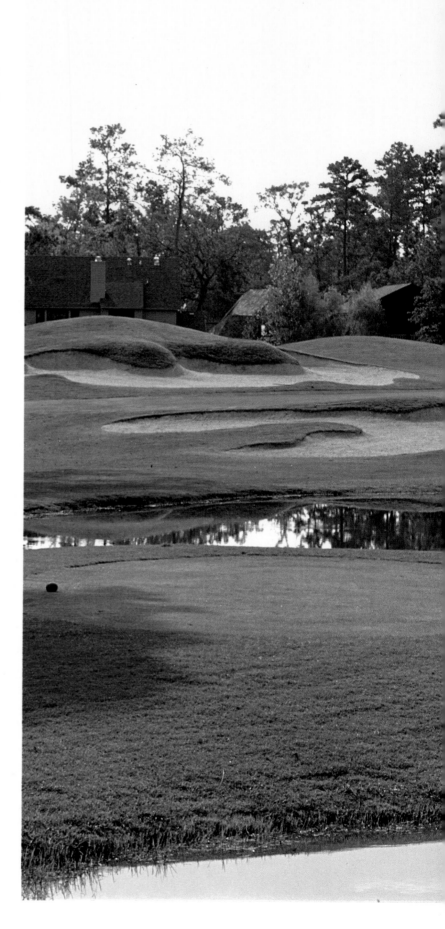

14th hole

13th hole

PAST WINNERS

Year	Winner	Score	Year	Winner	Score
1946	Byron Nelson	274	1968	Roberto De Vicenzo	274
1947	Bobby Locke	277	1969	No Tournament	
1948	No Tournament		1970	*Gibby Gilbert	282
1949	John Palmer	272	1971	*Hubert Green	280
1950	Cary Middlecoff	277	1972	Bruce Devlin	278
1951	Marty Furgol	277	1973	Bruce Crampton	277
1952	Jack Burke, Jr.	277	1974	Dave Hill	276
1953	*Cary Middlecoff	283	1975	Bruce Crampton	273
1954	Dave Douglas	277	1976	Lee Elder	278
1955	Mike Souchak	273	1977	Gene Littler	276
1956	Ted Kroll	277	1978	Gary Player	270
1957	Arnold Palmer	279	1979	Wayne Levi	268
1958	Ed Oliver	281	1980	*Curtis Strange	266
1959	*Jack Burke, Jr.	277	1981	‡Ron Streck	198
1960	*Bill Collins	280	1982	*Ed Sneed	275
1961	*Jay Hebert	276	1983	David Graham	275
1962	*Bobby Nichols	278	1984	Corey Pavin	274
1963	Bob Charles	268	1985	Raymond Floyd	277
1964	Mike Souchak	278	1986	*Curtis Strange	274
1965	Bobby Nichols	273	1987	*Jay Haas	276
1966	Arnold Palmer	275	*Playoff		
1967	Frank Beard	274	‡Rain-curtailed		

17th hole

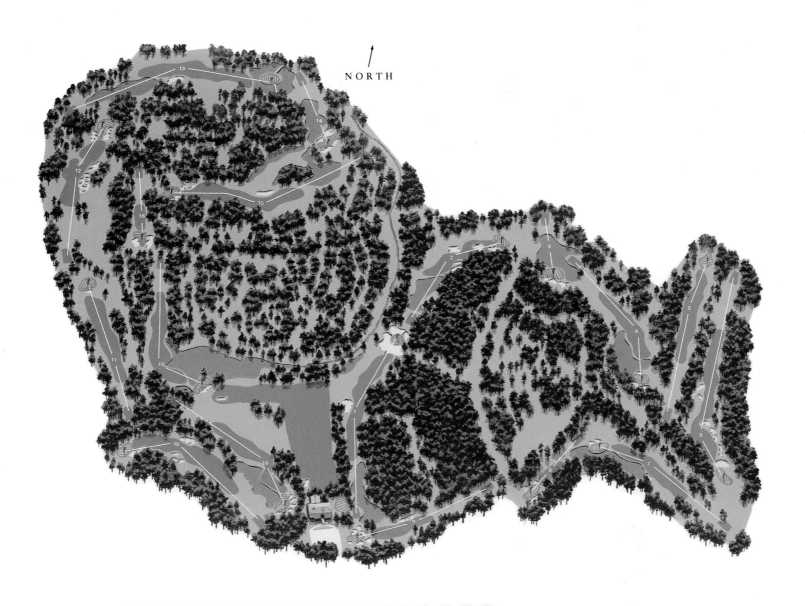

NORTH

TACKLING TEXAS WINDS
BY DAVID GRAHAM

The wind in Texas seems to blow constantly, and smart players know how to use it rather than be beaten by it.

Many players make the mistake of hitting the ball harder when playing into a headwind. As a result, they do one of two things: Most often, they mishit the shot—usually with a slice—and the wind exaggerates that bad shot, pushing it farther off line. If they do happen to make good impact, the result is often a high shot that gets caught by the wind and loses whatever extra distance the powerful swing had added.

The best way to battle a headwind is to make a shorter swing. When you make a shorter turn, your hands don't get as high on the backswing, your swing plane is thus a bit flatter, and you strike the ball with a less descending and more forward-driv-

ing impact. Such an impact produces a low, boring shot. Also, with a shorter swing you always have a better chance of making solid impact. So the best tactic in a strong wind is to keep your cool and make a controlled, compact swing.

———

David Graham won the 1983 Houston Open.

SCORECARD

Hole	Yards	Par	PGA Tour Avg. Score
1	515	5	4.673
2	365	4	4.091
3	165	3	3.029
4	413	4	4.193
5	457	4	4.133
6	577	5	4.958
7	413	4	3.967
8	218	3	3.162
9	427	4	4.053
OUT	3550	36	36.259
10	428	4	3.982
11	421	4	4.044
12	388	4	3.942
13	525	5	4.851
14	195	3	3.044
15	530	5	4.784
16	177	3	3.062
17	383	4	4.264
18	445	4	4.249
IN	3492	36	36.222
TOTAL	7042	72	72.481

LAS VEGAS
Country Club

DESERT INN
Country Club

SPANISH TRAIL
Golf and Country Club

PANASONIC LAS VEGAS INVITATIONAL, NEVADA

The most exciting gambling spot in Las Vegas is not the roulette wheel at the Sands or the slot machines at Caesar's Palace. It is the 18th hole at Las Vegas Country Club. Here, stretched over 500 yards of fairway and 25 yards of water, is a gambler's nirvana.

Should your drive reach the top of the hill at the corner of this par-five dogleg right, you will feel as if you have just been dealt 16 in blackjack. You can stay pat and lay up shy of the pond, taking your chances with a short but tricky pitch to the green; or you can go for it all—or nothing at all—with a wood shot that will have to carry not only the water but the stone wall at its far edge.

It is a great place to settle a Nassau, and millions of dollars of Nassaus have been decided here by the high-rolling members who haunt this, the first and only private country club on the Strip. One rumor is that in one foursome alone the payoff was $1.8 million.

Number 18 at LVCC is also a good place to settle a professional tournament, which is what happens every year in the Panasonic Las Vegas Invitational.

One of the youngest—and richest—events on the PGA Tour, it started in 1983 with a total purse of more than $1 million, at that time the highest on the Tour. The extra pay was for extra play—90 holes instead of 72—and for hazardous duty. Each pro plays with four different amateurs on each of the first four days of the tournament. In this sense, the format is similar to the Tour's only other five-day event, the Bob Hope Chrysler Classic. The only difference is that in the Las Vegas event each amateur gets three new amateur partners in each of the four days, whereas in the Hope event the four-man amateur team stays together throughout the tournament. On the final day it is pros only, with the low-70 players making the cut.

During the first four days, play is spread among the Las

Las Vegas, 9th hole

Las Vegas, 7th hole

Las Vegas, 13th hole

Vegas Country Club, Desert Inn Country Club, and Spanish Trail Golf and Country Club. On Sunday, all the pros return to LVCC.

Spanish Trail is one of the youngest courses on the PGA Tour. Designed by Robert Trent Jones, Jr., it was completed in late 1984 and joined the Panasonic fold eighteen months later.

A system of lakes brings water into play on seven holes and adds interest to the approach shots. The greens are seeded with bentgrass, a rarity for this area of the country. They are large, fast, undulating, and generally guarded by bunkers or water in front. When the wind blows, this 7,088 yards is a challenging par 72.

The oldest of the three venues is the Desert Inn course, which brought golf to Las Vegas in 1950 and three years later brought big-time golf by hosting the first fourteen editions of the Tournament of Champions. This is a flat but long course with several tough holes, notably the stretch from the seventh through the ninth. The sternest hole on the course is that seventh, a 206-yard par three surrounded by both sand and water. In 1983 it was the second toughest one-shotter on the Tour. The only par three that exacted more strokes from Tour players was the famed 16th at Cypress Point, California.

The Las Vegas Country Club course was designed by Ed Ault in 1967 and updated in 1979 by Ron Garl, who erected the stone wall at 18, brought water into play at the ninth hole, added a huge front bunker on the first, and remodeled the 17th green.

The toughest hole on the front nine is without question number seven, a 470-yard par four whose fairway is narrowed by bunkers on both sides. The longer the drive, the smaller the landing area. Traditionally, the pros make twice as many bogeys as birdies on this hole.

Then, of course, there is the closing game of chance. Even after a good drive and a straight, powerful second shot, this hole is full of treachery. Bunkers line the back of the green, and shooting out of them means exploding to a fast green that slopes down to the water, 22 yards away. Many a hapless power hitter has boomed his second shot over the water and into the trap, then watched in agony as his mediocre bunker shot trickled down the green and into the drink.

That is basically what happened to Rex Caldwell on the final hole of the 1983 event as he tried desperately to catch Fuzzy Zoeller. Caldwell had to hole his bunker shot to have a chance; he dumped it into the water and finished four back. Still, his runner-up finish was worth $81,000, more than any check he had ever cashed.

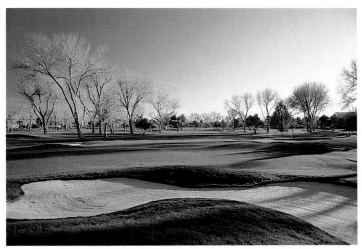

Desert Inn, 13th hole

ALL TIME TOURNAMENT RECORDS

Record	Player(s)	Score	Year
Low 18	Lon Hinkle	62	1984
	Bill Glasson		1985
	George Burns		1986
Low first 36	Lon Hinkle	130	1984
		(62–68)	
Low 36	Mike Smith	129	1984
		(63–66)	(rounds 2–3)
	Greg Norman	(64–65)	(rounds 4–5)
Low first 54	Tom Watson	199	1985
		(66–65–68)	
Low 54	Greg Norman	195	1986
		(63–68–64)	(rounds 2–3–4)
Low first 72	Fuzzy Zoeller	267	1983
		(63–70–70–64)	
Low 72	Fuzzy Zoeller	267	1983
		(63–70–70–64)	
Low 90	Greg Norman	333	1986
		(73–63–68–64–65)	
Highest winning score	Denis Watson	341	1984
		(69–66–68–70–68)	
Largest winning margin	Greg Norman	7 strokes	1986
Largest 18-hole lead	Bill Glasson (62)	3 strokes	1985
Largest 36-hole lead	Lon Hinkle (130)	3 strokes	1984
Longest 54-hole lead	Tom Watson (199)	3 strokes	1985
Largest 72-hole lead	Fuzzy Zoeller (267)	6 strokes	1983
Lowest start by winner	Fuzzy Zoeller	63	1983
Highest start by winner	Greg Norman	73	1986
Lowest finish by winner	Paul Azinger	64	1987
Highest finish by winner	Fuzzy Zoeller	73	1983
Best final-round comeback	Denis Watson (273)	3 back	1984
Lowest 72-hole cut score		283	1984
Highest 72-hole cut score		285	1985

PAST WINNERS

Year	Winner	Score
1983	Fuzzy Zoeller	340
1984	Denis Watson	341
1985	Curtis Strange	338
1986	Greg Norman	333
1987	Paul Azinger	271

Spanish Trail, 18th hole

TACKLING CROSSWINDS
BY FUZZY ZOELLER

Windy courses, such as those in Vegas, play differently every day, and anyone who wants to play them consistently had better have a good strategy for handling crosswinds.

The better player you are, the fancier you can get with the wind. If you're an average or less-than-average player, you probably shouldn't try to "doctor" shots to suit the wind. Go with your normal pattern, whether that is a low hook, a high fade, or whatever. Sometimes the wind can help you, sometimes it can hurt you, but the key is to take the breaks as they come. In windy conditions, you don't want to start trying low-percentage shots; let your opponent in the Nassau make that mistake.

If you have the ability to play both right-to-left and left-to-right shots with some degree of confidence, follow this general rule: When you want accuracy, fight the crosswind; when you want distance, ride it. On a tight tee shot or approach in a right-to-left wind, play a fade that will work against the wind and give you a more or less straight shot. But on a wide-open shot or in a situation in which you need maximum distance, take advantage of that right-to-left wind by playing a high draw or hook. Just allow plenty of room for the ball to work from right to left.

In 1983 Fuzzy Zoeller won the inaugural Panasonic Las Vegas Invitational, playing in 30-mile-an-hour winds.

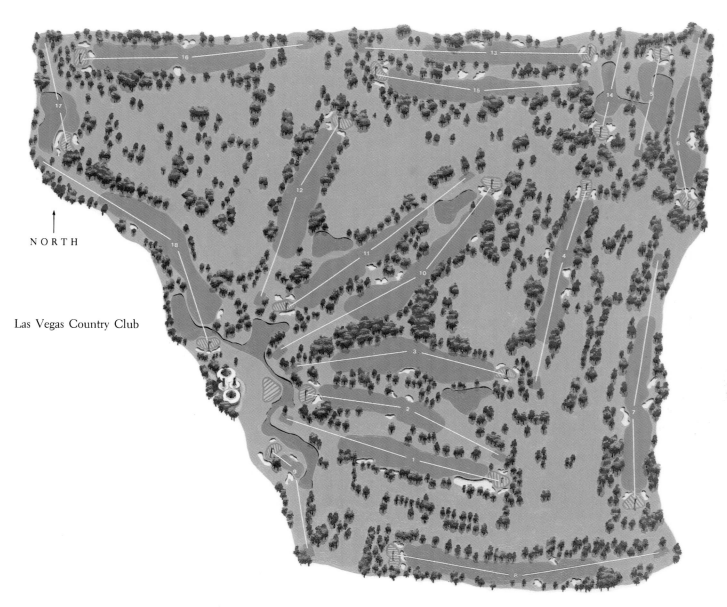

Las Vegas Country Club

NORTH

LAS VEGAS CC SCORECARD

Hole	Yards	Par	PGA Tour Avg. Score
1	416	4	4.100
2	420	4	3.994
3	440	4	4.046
4	405	4	3.972
5	198	3	3.007
6	365	4	3.867
7	470	4	4.263
8	546	5	4.654
9	176	3	3.013
OUT	3436	35	34.916
10	560	5	4.677
11	440	4	4.142
12	400	4	3.918
13	445	4	4.086
14	190	3	3.040
15	425	4	4.016
16	445	4	4.085
17	212	3	3.167
18	524	5	4.832
IN	3641	36	35.963
TOTAL	7077	71	70.879

DESERT INN CC SCORECARD

Hole	Yards	Par	PGA Tour Avg. Score
1	507	5	4.600
2	430	4	4.116
3	409	4	4.149
4	187	3	3.093
5	568	5	5.065
6	417	4	4.159
7	206	3	3.435
8	433	4	4.226
9	425	4	4.292
OUT	3582	36	37.135
10	511	5	4.625
11	208	3	3.159
12	413	4	4.102
13	399	4	4.053
14	406	4	4.154
15	504	5	4.693
16	175	3	3.120
17	399	4	4.123
18	421	4	4.191
IN	3436	36	36.220
TOTAL	7018	72	73.355

SPANISH TRAIL G&CC SCORECARD

Hole	Yards	Par
1	414	4
2	189	3
3	538	5
4	426	4
5	224	3
6	430	4
7	493	5
8	372	4
9	415	4
OUT	3501	36
10	463	4
11	193	3
12	405	4
13	362	4
14	220	3
15	573	5
16	431	4
17	424	4
18	516	5
IN	3587	36
TOTAL	7088	72

TPC at LAS COLINAS

5th hole

GTE BYRON NELSON
GOLF CLASSIC, TEXAS

Big-time golf came to Dallas, Texas, for the first time in 1944 in an event called the Texas Victory Open Golf Championship. At the time, World War II was winding toward a close with the Allied forces on top in all major theaters of operation. Optimism had replaced the austerity of a year earlier, and the War Commissioner had given tournament director Fred Corcoran permission to start a limited tour. The TVOGC was one of the twenty-two slots on the abbreviated circuit.

The favorite to win was a young army lieutenant named Ben Hogan. Stationed at Tarrant Field in Ft. Worth, Hogan had drawn cushy duty as the general's golf partner. On the Sunday before tournament week, he played Lakewood Country Club, the site of the event, in 66.

But Hogan finished that tournament in fifth place. The champion was, appropriately, the hometown hero, Byron Nelson, who triumphed by a whopping 12 strokes. Nelson would never again win this event, which a year later became known as the Dallas Open, but his brief eleven-year career was filled with other victories, 65 in all—including two in The Masters, two in the PGA Championship, and one in the U.S. Open. In 1968, the year the tournament moved to Preston Trail, Dallas honored its finest player by renaming its open the Byron Nelson Golf Classic, the first professional event ever named after a player.

Fifteen years passed and the tournament again changed venues before another native Texan stepped into the winner's circle. At the Las Colinas Sports Club in 1983, Austin native Ben Crenshaw broke a lengthy victory drought and edged Hal Sutton by a stroke.

One year after that—and exactly forty years after Nelson's inaugural win—the PGA Tour announced that Las Colinas would become the site of the Tour's seventh Tournament Players Course. Golf course architect Jay Morrish would design a new 18-hole layout on the existing site. And he would be aided by two player-consultants—Ben Crenshaw and Byron Nelson.

The original course at Las Colinas had been designed by Robert Trent Jones, Jr., son of the dean of American architects and a prolific, imaginative designer in his own right. Jones's course was as large and sprawling as Texas itself, with spacious fairways, expansive, heavily sloped greens, and mammoth flash bunkers. The course was big on everything but subtlety.

Enter understated Morrish and soft-spoken Crenshaw. Using the general route of Jones's back nine and blazing a new trail for the front, they created an entirely different golf course from the one that had been there.

Byron Nelson assumed a more passive, advisory role than did Ben Crenshaw. Las Colinas was Crenshaw's first real involvement with course design, but he had been a student of golf architecture ever since his early amateur days, with a decided predilection for the old-style layouts, particularly the links courses of Great Britain.

One of Ben's strong beliefs is that a well-designed golf course affords more than one route to most of its greens. Specifically on approach shots, such a course accommodates not only the high-floating darts played by the modern American pros but the low punches and run-ups that are the bread-and-butter of British golf. At Las Colinas, where the wind is every bit as strong and persistent as in Britain, Crenshaw insisted on providing low-road access to most of the targets.

So strong are the Texas winds that during the 1984 Nelson, Dave Eichelberger cranked out the longest drive in the history of the PGA Tour, a clout that traveled 397 yards. Also in that tournament, Hal Sutton holed out a 3-wood shot on one of the par fives for the first double eagle on Tour in two years.

In his routing plan, Morrish strove for balance vis-à-vis the prevailing southerly wind, with some holes playing against it, some with it, and some across it. He also gauged the yardages of several holes with the wind strongly in mind. A notable example is the third, a par four of 475 downwind yards. Tailwinds not only lengthen golf shots, they tend to straighten errant drives and irons. For the 70 percent or so of golfers who battle a slice, that notion will provide some degree of solace at number three because water lines the entire right side of the hole. The green is large but so is one of the two bunkers guarding it, and the other bunker is a deep pot. God help the soul who catches this one on a day when the prevailing wind is not prevailing.

Morrish likes each of his designs to include at least one par four that is drivable, under ideal conditions, by the game's strongest players. At Las Colinas, that hole is the 331-yard 11th. Since it also is a cuttable dogleg, the straight-line distance from tee to green is actually only 300

PUTTING BASICS
BY BEN CRENSHAW

The new TPC course at Las Colinas will have honest, straightforward greens with relatively mild undulations. Those are the kind I like, because they usually reward a solidly struck putt.

I think of the putting stroke as a miniature version of the golf swing. You should too. For example, if you're a wristy player you should putt using your wrists.

I swing more with my arms than wrists. Consequently, my stroke is slow and deliberate, my arms and shoulders swinging the putter back and through with my wrists firm.

I recommend a grip in which both thumbs are positioned on the top of the putter shaft. This grip helps give you a feel for the speed of a putt and is a must for holding the stroke on line.

Finally, get to know the various types of grass and grain and how they affect your putts. To save strokes on the green, know which putts must be lagged and which may be charged.

Ben Crenshaw was the design consultant on the TPC at Las Colinas and is also the 1983 Byron Nelson champion.

ALL TIME TOURNAMENT RECORDS

Record	Player(s)	Score	Year
Low 18	Sam Snead	60	1957
Low first 36	Sam Snead	126	1957
Low 36	Sam Snead	126	1957
Low first 54	Sam Snead	194	1957
Low 54	Sam Snead	194	1957
Low 72	Sam Snead	264	1957
Highest winning score	Ben Hogan	284	1946
Largest winning margin	Byron Nelson	10 strokes	1944
Lowest start by winner	Sam Snead	60	1957
Highest start by winner	Tom Watson	72	1975
Lowest finish by winner	Peter Thomson	63	1956
Highest finish by winner	Ben Hogan	73	1946
Lowest 36-hole cut score		139	1987
Highest 36-hole cut score		149	1970, 1984

PAST WINNERS

Year	Winner	Score	Year	Winner	Score
1944	Byron Nelson	276	1971	Jack Nicklaus	274
1945	Sam Snead	276	1972	Chi Chi Rodriguez	273
1946	Ben Hogan	284	1973	*Lanny Wadkins	277
1947–			1974	Brian Allin	269
1955	No Tournaments		1975	Tom Watson	269
1956	Don January	268	1976	Mark Hayes	273
1956A	*Peter Thomson	267	1977	Raymond Floyd	276
1957	Sam Snead	264	1978	Tom Watson	272
1958	*Sam Snead	272	1979	Tom Watson	275
1959	Julius Boros	274	1980	Tom Watson	274
1960	*Johnny Pott	275	1981	*Bruce Lietzke	281
1961	Earl Stewart, Jr.	278	1982	Bob Gilder	266
1962	Billy Maxwell	277	1983	Ben Crenshaw	273
1963	No Tournament		1984	Craig Stadler	276
1964	Charles Coody	271	1985	*Bob Eastwood	272
1965	No Tournament		1986	Andy Bean	269
1966	Roberto De Vicenzo	276	1987	*Fred Couples	266
1967	Bert Yancey	274			
1968	Miller Barber	270			
1969	Bruce Devlin	277	A: Two tournaments		
1970	*Jack Nicklaus	274	*Playoff		

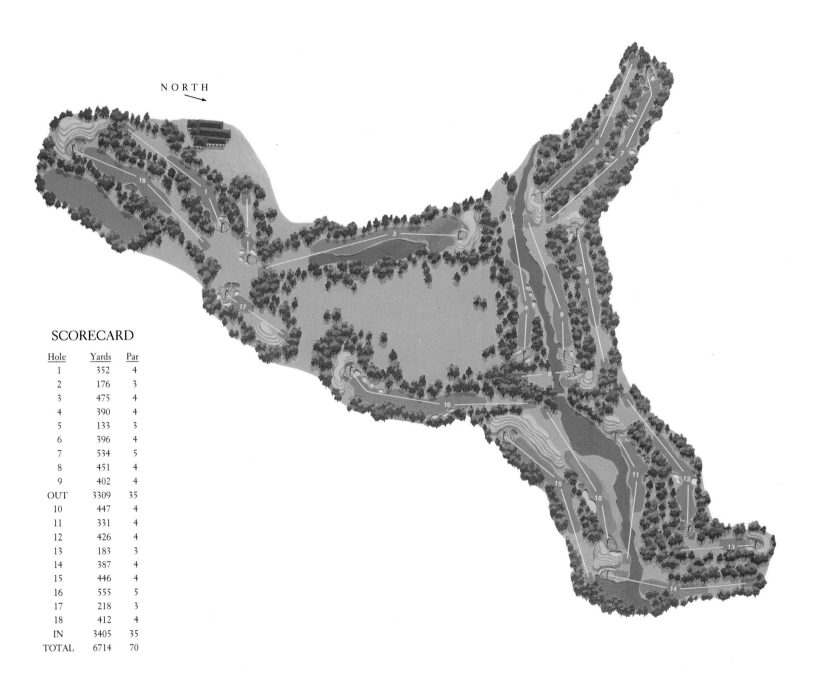

NORTH

SCORECARD

Hole	Yards	Par
1	352	4
2	176	3
3	475	4
4	390	4
5	133	3
6	396	4
7	534	5
8	451	4
9	402	4
OUT	3309	35
10	447	4
11	331	4
12	426	4
13	183	3
14	387	4
15	446	4
16	555	5
17	218	3
18	412	4
IN	3405	35
TOTAL	6714	70

yards. Aha! But 99 percent of that straight line runs across water. The 11th tee sits on the edge of a small river, and the fairway and green are on the other edge.

When the wind is right, long-hitting players can bite off most of this right-to-left hole, but they had better hit hard and straight. Furthermore, even a long drive may not be of help here, as the approach must be played with plenty of backspin in order to hold this, the smallest green on the course. At the back-right of the green, a four-foot-deep pot bunker adds interest to the assignment.

A gauntlet of bunkers greets assailants of the 16th hole, a 555-yard par five. The pleateaued teeshot landing area is fronted by three pot bunkers running diagonally across the left side of the fairway. Then, on the second shot,

three cross-bunkers run diagonally down the right, threatening to punish anyone who tries to take the short way home on the dogleg. At the green, roll-down bunkers guard the right while a grassy hollow catches missed shots to the left.

Most of the middle of the golf course passes through heavily wooded terrain, but the opening and closing holes have a landscaped look, especially the 15th through 18th, where the stadium mounds predominate. During construction of the course, however, thousands of live oaks, Mexican plums, and pine trees were added, many of them lowered by helicopter into waiting holes along the fairways. As these grow, so surely will the beauty and difficulty of the course.

COLONIAL *Country Club*

COLONIAL NATIONAL INVITATION TEXAS

They call it Hogan's Alley, but it is more than that. In one sense, Colonial Country Club *is* Ben Hogan. Linked together for nearly a half century, the course and the man developed a matchless affinity. Today, the terms that describe Hogan also describe the 18 holes he called home: proud, stern, brutally honest, and unremittingly tough; pursuant of precision, intolerant of mediocrity, and when in top form, virtually unbeatable.

Founded in 1935 by Texas businessman Marvin Leonard, this big golf course on the bank of Ft. Worth's Trinity River quickly became the favored practice ground of Hogan. When, in 1946, the first Colonial National Invitation tournament was played, Hogan won by a stroke, on a final round of 65, a score that would remain the

16th hole

course record for a quarter-century. In the next seven years, The Hawk won three more Colonials, adding a record fifth in 1959 at the age of 46.

At his peak, Hogan hit balls with a swing whose compact power and repetitive precision were likened to a machine stamping out bottle caps. So it is no wonder that he loved Colonial, a course that demands both accuracy and might, where one must be prepared either to hit the ball squarely or hit it often. It is said that Hogan, having played so much of his formative golf at Colonial, found most other courses easy.

Most of the PGA Tour players agree that this design by Texas architect John Bredemus is one of the finest and most difficult tests they play. An extremely tight 7,098

yards, it is, according to 1951 champion Cary Middlecoff, "the toughest par 70 in the world."

The cluster of holes three, four, and five is known as the Horrible Horseshoe. Number three is the longest par four on a course that is full of long par fours. A 470-yard dogleg left, it plays around a large tree and a trio of bunkers at the knee of the dogleg. The 226-yard fourth hole is a Texas-size par three. Hogan claimed it was "in between clubs; a 4-wood was too much and a 2-iron was not enough."

Number five is not simply the hardest par four at Colonial but the hardest par four on the PGA Tour. At least that is what the pros told a *Golf Magazine* survey in 1983. The 466-yard, left-to-right dogleg is tightly guarded by a

13th hole

17th hole

18th hole

treelined ditch on the left, trees to the shallow right, and the Trinity River to deep right, all made more difficult by a prevailing left-to-right wind. The ideal tee shot is a powerful fade, which the long hitters play with a 3-wood and with courage. This leaves a long-iron approach to the firm, well-trapped green. All of which explains why the nickname for this hole is Death Valley.

Middlecoff claimed he approached the fifth this way: "First I pull out two brand-new Wilson balls and throw them into the Trinity River. Then I throw up. Then I go ahead and hit my tee shot into the river." In 1951 he played it a bit differently than that. In the final round, Middlecoff whistled his approach shot 60 feet over the green, next to a concession stand. From there he took a putter and rapped the ball under the trees, onto the green, and into the hole for a birdie. He went on to win by one.

But if number five has been inspiring for some, it has been demoralizing for many. Imagine how Craig Wood felt during the 1941 U.S. Open. After only four holes of play in the second round, Wood was three-over par. To make matters worse, his chronic back ailment was bothering him so much that he was playing in a corset. That was aggravated still further by the heavy rains during round two that had soaked both the course and the corset. And as a final touch of agony, waterlogged Wood had hit his tee shot into the ditch at number five, only seconds before USGA officials had suspended play.

Wood did what most mortals would have done. He decided to quit and go home. But his playing partner, Tommy Armour, would not let him. "C'mon," said Armour, "everyone's struggling out here. Stick around."

Wood, the reigning Masters champion, decided that quitting was not such a good idea after all. When play resumed, he managed to get through number five with a bogey, then played even-par golf for the rest of the tournament. His 284 was good enough to win that Open by three strokes.

In 1968 the Army Corps of Engineers rerouted sections of the Trinity River as part of a major flood control project. At Colonial that meant rebuilding nine holes and relocating the 8th and 13th greens, although the greens have since been restored. When Kel Nagle got the news about 13, he was upset. It was on this 174-yard par three in 1961 that Nagle scored the first hole-in-one in Colonial history. But it is not the memory of that shot that he savors, but the reaction of his playing companion.

The affable Australian had been paired with Hogan, and the Ice Mon, as usual, had wrapped himself in a cocoon of concentration and not spoken a word during the round. But after Nagle's flawless 2-iron found its mark, Hogan cracked. After waiting for the yells and whoops of

the gallery to subside, he emerged from solitary confinement just long enough to mutter, "Nice shot."

When the powers at Colonial decided they wanted to host the U.S. Open, they knew they had to make one major accommodation for the USGA—they had to develop bentgrass greens. That is a tall order for a golf course based in a hot climate. Even today, the bent greens require delicate care to survive the dry summers, and many Colonial members rue that ancient decision. But one factor that has made growth and maintenance a bit simpler is the relative flatness of Colonial's greens. Only one of them has severe undulations—number 16. Jack Nicklaus claims that the 17-foot putt he made there in his victorious final round of 1982 is the most memorable shot he has ever played at the Colonial.

Mention "Big Annie" to Jack Nicklaus, and he may give you a dirty look. Big Annie was a woman from Nicklaus's past whom he would just as soon forget. She stood on the corner of the 17th hole, a 200-foot-high pecan tree that snagged second shots, turning pars into double bogeys. In 1974 Nicklaus was leading the tournament and figured he would beat Big Annie by playing over the top of her. But his strategy backfired when his shot flew over not only the tree but the green as well. A 6 went on his card, and Jack lost by a stroke. (Big Annie died during a 1986 storm.)

The 18th seems a straightforward if difficult hole on which to finish—a 434-yard par four that doglegs softly left, culminating at a green that is tucked between a large expanse of sand on the right and a large body of water on the left. But it is deceptive as well as difficult. A mound in the center of the fairway often produces a lie in which the ball is above the feet, a situation that encourages pull-hooks into the water. And the fickle wind can be a killer, as Jim Colbert will attest. In the final round of the 1983 Colonial, it nearly blew his chance of victory.

"The wind that day was blowing right to left and a little behind me," Colbert recalls. "I had 182 yards to the hole, and everything in my body told me to hit a 6-iron. But that's the chicken shot. I wanted to try to make birdie, par for sure, so I had to go to a 5-iron and shoot for the flag [which was toward the back-left of the green].

"It was the best shot I ever hit in a stress situation. Then the wind came right in behind me, and the ball carried 200 yards in the air [and into the lake]. It was a terrible break. If I had lost the tournament, I would have gone to my grave being the only person to know that I didn't choke on that second shot at 18." Colbert won the tournament in a six-hole sudden-death playoff with Fuzzy Zoeller.

Stranger things have happened on 18. One year, 280-pound George Bayer pumped his second shot high into the wind, and it sailed all the way to the roof of the

5th hole

clubhouse—at least that is where it is assumed to have finished. No one ever found the ball.

But the king of calamity at Colonial's home hole is Bruce Crampton, the Australian-turned-Texan who was among the top Tour players in the late sixties and early seventies. In 1962 Crampton came to 18 needing a par to win, a bogey to get into a playoff with Arnold Palmer and Johnny Pott. Instead, he pulled his approach shot into the lake, took a double-bogey 6, and went home a loser. A day earlier on the same hole, he had hit the same dreaded shot. Almost immediately, the water hazard became known as Crampton's Lake.

In 1965 Crampton had his revenge. On Sunday he made an uneventful par on 18 and won the tournament by three strokes. Eight years later, the Colonial folks decided to put up a plaque on the 18th. It reads "Crampton's Lake: Named for Bruce Crampton, who found water on the third and fourth rounds of the 1962 NIT and lost by one stroke. A true golf professional and champion, he returned and won a popular first-place victory in the 1965 NIT."

Five days after that plaque was erected, Crampton did it again. Just as in 1962, he came to the final hole needing a par for outright victory, a five to get into a playoff—this time with Tom Weiskopf. But he ran into tree trouble, then sand trouble, and once again took 6 to lose the tournament.

Like Crampton, the Colonial tournament has had its ups and downs. In 1949 the Trinity River flooded so badly that the tournament was called off. In 1953, the year Hogan scored his triple victories in the U.S. Open, the British Open, and The Masters, he also won an impressive five-shot victory at Colonial. But his performance was marred by the destruction of the clubhouse by fire only a month earlier—the third such fire in its short life.

Despite such disasters, the Colonial tournament has consistently ranked among the best run, most popular, and most prestigious events on the Tour. The superb course always attracts a strong field of players, and that field invariably produces an exciting tournament with a dramatic finish.

The story of Clayton Heafner, the 1948 champion, says a lot about the Colonial event and the course on which it is played. As part of his victory euphoria, Heafner issued one of those breathless compliments. "This is the way all golf tournaments should be run," he exclaimed. "Why, I'd rather finish last at the Colonial and get to take part than be up in the money at some other tournament."

In the very next Colonial, he got his wish. His seventy-two-hole total of 304 left him flat in the cellar.

ALL TIME TOURNAMENT RECORDS

Record	Player(s)	Score	Year
Low 18	Joey Sindelar	62	1985
Low first 36	Corey Pavin	130 (66–64)	1985
Low 36	Keith Clearwater	128 (64–64)	1987 (rounds 3–4)
Low first 54	Payne Stewart	198 (68–66–64)	1984
	Corey Pavin	(66–66–68)	1985
Low 54	Payne Stewart	198 (68–66–64)	1984
	Corey Pavin	(66–64–68)	1985
Low 72	Corey Pavin	266 (66–64–68–68)	1985
	Keith Clearwater	(67–71–64–64)	1987
Highest winning score	Ben Hogan	285 (69–67–77–72)	1959
Largest winning margin	Chandler Harper (276)	8 strokes	1955
Largest 18-hole lead	Dave Stockton (65)	2 strokes	1967
	Bruce Lietzke (63)		1980
Largest 36-hole lead	Chandler Harper (134)	7 strokes	1955
Largest 54-hole lead	Chandler Harper (204)	6 strokes	1955
Lowest start by winner	Bruce Lietzke	63	1980
Highest start by winner	Ben Hogan Mike Souchak	74	1952 1956
Lowest finish by winner	Keith Clearwater	64	1987
Highest finish by winner	Arnold Palmer	76	1962
Best final-round comeback	Ben Hogan (212)	6 back	1952
Lowest 36-hole cut score		141	1986
Highest 36-hole cut score		148	1971– 1973

PAST WINNERS

Year	Winner	Score	Year	Winner	Score
1946	Ben Hogan	279	1968	Billy Casper	275
1947	Ben Hogan	279	1969	Gardner Dickinson	278
1948	Clayton Heafner	272	1970	Homero Blancas	273
1949	No Tournament		1971	Gene Littler	283
1950	Sam Snead	277	1972	Jerry Heard	275
1951	Cary Middlecoff	282	1973	Tom Weiskopf	276
1952	Ben Hogan	279	1974	Rod Curl	276
1953	Ben Hogan	282	1975	Hosted TPC	
1954	Johnny Palmer	280	1976	Lee Trevino	273
1955	Chandler Harper	276	1977	Ben Crenshaw	272
1956	Mike Souchak	280	1978	Lee Trevino	268
1957	Roberto De Vicenzo	284	1979	Al Geiberger	274
1958	Tommy Bolt	282	1980	Bruce Lietzke	271
1959	*Ben Hogan	285	1981	Fuzzy Zoeller	274
1960	Julius Boros	280	1982	Jack Nicklaus	273
1961	Doug Sanders	281	1983	*Jim Colbert	278
1962	*Arnold Palmer	281	1984	*Peter Jacobsen	270
1963	Julius Boros	279	1985	Corey Pavin	266
1964	Billy Casper	279	1986	*Dan Pohl	272
1965	Bruce Crampton	276	1987	Keith Clearwater	266
1966	Bruce Devlin	280			
1967	Dave Stockton	278	*Playoff		

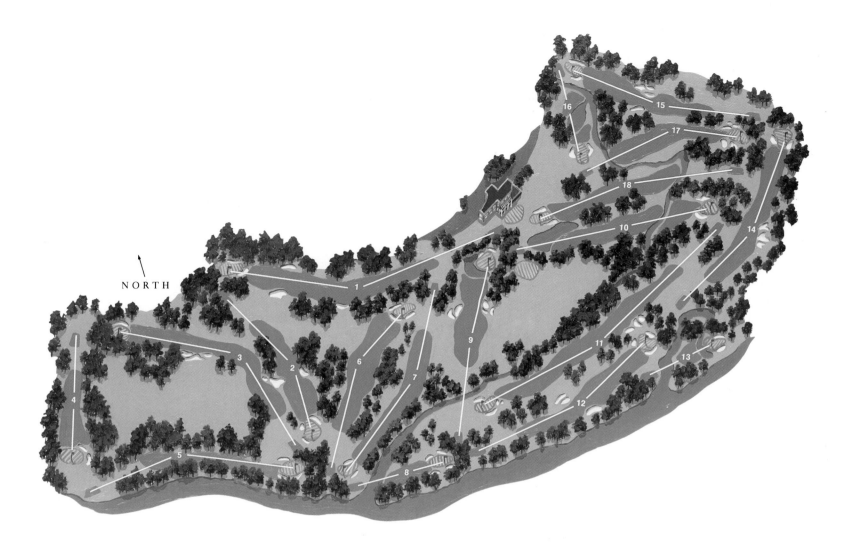

NORTH

SCORECARD

Hole	Yards	Par	PGA Tour Avg. Score
1	572	5	4.783
2	401	4	3.970
3	470	4	4.209
4	226	3	3.196
5	466	4	4.352
6	415	4	3.949
7	453	4	4.077
8	192	3	3.061
9	405	4	4.123
OUT	3600	35	35.720
10	416	4	4.088
11	609	5	4.930
12	435	4	4.154
13	174	3	2.986
14	431	4	4.076
15	436	4	4.159
16	176	3	3.163
17	387	4	4.010
18	434	4	4.103
IN	3498	35	35.669
TOTAL	7098	70	71.389

PLAYING A FADE
BY COREY PAVIN

Of all the courses on the Tour, none favors a fade as much as Colonial. By my count, 11 of the 14 par fours and fives are best attacked with left-to-right tee shots. My natural flight pattern is a fade, so I always enjoy playing the NIT.

I'm a believer in keeping golf as simple as possible; I don't do anything fancy when maneuvering the ball. My fade is pre-programmed entirely by my setup. I align my body—feet, knees, hips, and shoulders—open to the target, facing several yards left of it, while keeping the clubface square to the target (actually open to the orientation of my body). The more I want to fade the ball, the more open I stand.

When you set up in this open position, your right hip blocks the path of a takeaway straight from the target. Instead, you take the club back along the outside path that is parallel to your open alignment. You also swing back toward the ball on this out-to-in path. As a result, your shot starts out well to the left of the target. However, since your clubface was square to the target (open to your swing path), left-to-right spin is imparted and the ball curves to the right. It's that simple—after a few sessions of practice.

Corey Pavin won the 1985 Colonial with a tournament record score of 266, 16-under par.

MUIRFIELD VILLAGE
Golf Club

17th hole

In 1974, during the thirteenth year of his reign as the greatest professional golfer of all time, Jack Nicklaus created a championship golf course near his hometown of Columbus, Ohio. Today many claim that Jack's twenty major titles and countless records notwithstanding, this course is his most impressive achievement.

Nicklaus named it Muirfield Village, after the site of his first British Open victory. But he modeled it—and every aspect of the tournament staged on it—after another major championship. Jack's Memorial is The Masters of the Midwest.

From the wide, rolling fairways, menacing hazards, and fast, undulating greens to the tough ticket policy and invitational format, the course that Jack built is rooted firmly in the soil of the Augusta National.

Indeed, in the minds of some players, Nicklaus's Memorial has surpassed Bobby Jones's Masters. When a 1983 survey asked Tour players to name the event that is the best run and most enjoyable to play, the Memorial ranked first, ahead of the Colonial, the Hertz Bay Hill Classic, and The Masters in that order.

The first decade of Memorials produced a list of victors that included Hale Irwin, Tom Watson, David Graham, Raymond Floyd, and the architect himself—twice. Except for Irwin, Nicklaus is the only two-time winner of his tournament, a fact that fuels the argument that Jack designed the course to suit his own game.

Muirfield Village favors a fade, and a fade is the shot that won Nicklaus his millions. Muirfield Village favors long, high approach shots that can suck back on linoleum. Nicklaus's have always done that. And Muirfield Village favors a player who can play from tee to green with caution, then putt without fear. That's Jack Nicklaus.

But a case could also be made for the course fitting the piercing tee shots of Lee Trevino, the deft touch of Tom Watson, or the bunker genius of Gary Player. The fact is, just as the Memorial Tournament honors fine players of the past, the Muirfield Village course rewards the best players of the present.

Par fours are the strength of the course, and the front nine begins with two of the toughest. The 446-yard first plays from an elevated tee to a fairway that slopes from right to left while doglegging from left to right. Bunkers

2nd hole

3rd hole

guard the inside of the dogleg, woods and a creek run along the outside. The green is the largest on the course, but is surrounded by bunkers.

Number two is another monster—452 yards for the pros—and demanding of accuracy even more than length. The fairway slopes toward the right, where a creek runs along the entire length of the hole. Water seems omnipresent at Muirfield Village, and it almost is. Tom Weiskopf once observed incredulously, "Water comes into play on 18 shots here. That's *eighteen shots!*"

The longest and toughest of the short holes is number four, just as is the case at Augusta National. And also as. at The Masters it plays slightly downhill to a shallow, well-bunkered green.

Nicklaus saved the best hole on the front side for last, a taut 410-yard par four that calls for equal amounts of courage and finesse. The drive must thread through a chute of trees and find not simply the fairway but the best part of it to leave a good shot at the green, which is framed by a lake, a creek, two bunkers, and a hillside.

Masters mimicry returns with the 12th hole, a par three over water that closely resembles the famous 12th at Augusta. The winds do not swirl as capriciously as they do among the Georgia pines, and this hole plays downhill

9th hole

11th hole

16th hole

12th hole

18th hole

14th hole

instead of level, but its tiny, two-tiered green is far more difficult than that of its model.

The greens at Muirfield Village are among the fastest on the Tour—up to 12 and more on the Stimpmeter, the device used for measuring green speed. Together with the fierce slopes, they could almost be unfair were it not for their consistently superb condition. Says Trevino, "They should have slippers at every hole at Muirfield and pass a rule that you have to take off your shoes before walking on the greens. They shouldn't be walked on with cleats."

It is rare to see a professional golfer play his third shot on a par four *purposely* into a greenside bunker, but at Muirfield's 14th hole that happens with frequency. Just 363 yards long, this hole has quickly earned a reputation as one of the most testing holes in golf. Restraint is required from the tee, where most pros hit fairway woods and long irons to a valley just short of a creek that crosses the fairway. From there the target is a long, narrow strip of green, cut against a hill, with bunkers on the left and a steep bank down to the meandering creek on the right. A shot that strays left of the bunkers means that the next shot will not hold the green; that is why third shots are played safely *into* the sand. In 1980 John Fought was tied for the lead in the final round when he took a quadruple-bogey 8 here. Three players have made 9.

All the par fives at Muirfield Village are reachable in two to the long hitters on the Tour, but the 15th hole is hittable by everyone. Still, the 490 yards roll up and down hills and through a continuously tight cordon of trees.

The Memorial's most memorable moments have occurred on number 17, the 430-yard par four that winds past a 130-yard bunker through a valley of rough to a green flanked by a trio of the deepest bunkers on the course. It was here in the inaugural tournament that Roger Maltbie "staked" himself to victory in a playoff over Hale Irwin. When Maltbie's approach soared well left of the green, he looked to have blown any chance of victory. But the ball struck a gallery stake and bounded straight back onto the green. Roger got down in two and then birdied 18 to win the tournament.

Eight years later Jack Nicklaus chose this hole to play perhaps his worst tee shot under pressure. Tied with Andy Bean after 70 holes, Nicklaus slashed a rainbow slice so far and deep that it finished on the back porch of one of the Muirfield Village condos. But he rolled in a 25-foot putt for a bogey, then parred 18 as Bean missed a short putt. Nicklaus won the tournament in a playoff when Bean again missed a short one—on the 17th hole.

If 18 has occasionally been anticlimactic, it is nonetheless the most difficult hole on the course, having played to a stroke average of 4.3 in the first ten Memorials. A downhill-then-uphill dogleg right, it curls around a corner of trees and bunkers to a heavily contoured green that is as hard to putt as it is to hit and hold.

Although Muirfield is a terror to players, it is a pleasure for spectators. This was one of the first golf courses designed with tournament galleries in mind, predating all of the PGA Tour's Stadium Courses, and many of the tees and greens are situated within natural amphitheaters.

The Memorial is unique on the Tour because each year it produces not only a champion but a special honoree. The Captain's Club, a group of golfing graybeards led by Nicklaus, annually selects an individual who has "played golf with conspicuous honor" and dedicates the tournament to him or her. The first such honoree was Nicklaus's idol, Bobby Jones, and others have included Walter Hagen, Byron Nelson, Francis Ouimet, Chick Evans, Sam Snead, Gene Sarazen, Tommy Armour, Roberto De Vicenzo, and Glenna Collett Vare. But the perennial honoree is Nicklaus himself, who created this course and tournament, in the same way Jones did Augusta National, as his own memorial.

ALL TIME TOURNAMENT RECORDS

Record	Player(s)	Score	Year
Low 18	Mark McCumber	64	1984
Low first 36	Scott Hoch	131 (67–64)	1987
Low 36	Scott Hoch	131 (67–64)	1987
	Denis Watson	(66–65)	1987 (rounds 3–4)
Low first 54	Scott Hoch	198 (67–64–67)	1987
Low 54	Scott Hoch	198 (67–64–67)	1987
Low 72	Hal Sutton	271 (68–69–66–68)	1986
Highest winning score	Roger Maltbie	288 (71–71–70–76)	1976
Largest winning margin	Tom Watson (285)	3 strokes	1979
Largest 18-hole lead	Several Players	1 stroke	
Largest 36-hole lead	Roger Maltbie (134)	6 strokes	1982
Largest 54-hole lead	Tom Watson (214)	4 strokes	1979
	Scott Hoch (198)		1986
Lowest start by winner	Jim Simons Hale Irwin Hal Sutton	68	1978 1985 1986
Highest start by winner	Raymond Floyd	74	1982
Lowest finish by winner	Hal Sutton	68	1986
Highest finish by winner	Roger Maltbie	76	1976
Best final-round comeback	Hale Irwin Don Pooley	4 back	1983 1986
Lowest 36-hole cut score		146	1986–1987
Highest 36-hole cut score		157	1976–1979

N O R T H

PAST WINNERS

Year	Winner	Score
1976	*Roger Maltbie	288
1977	Jack Nicklaus	281
1978	Jim Simons	284
1979	Tom Watson	285
1980	David Graham	280
1981	Keith Fergus	284
1982	Raymond Floyd	281
1983	Hale Irwin	281
1984	*Jack Nicklaus	270
1985	Hale Irwin	281
1986	Hal Sutton	271
1987	Don Pooley	272

*Playoff

AVOIDING THREE-PUTTS
BY HALE IRWIN

Muirfield Village has some of the most beautiful and well-conditioned greens in the world—and some of the toughest. They were designed, after all, by one of the greatest putters in the history of the game. During the Memorial, the greens are very fast and full of subtle breaks; they demand nothing less than a Nicklaus touch.

One of the toughest aspects of putting fast bentgrass greens, such as those at Muirfield Village, is adopting the correct attitude: neither too aggressive nor too cautious. I'm sure you've heard the expression, "Never up, never in." There can be no argument with its message. But this does not mean that charging the ball six feet past the hole is better than being one foot short. Ideally, you should hit every putt at a speed that will take it one foot past the hole if you fail to hole it. Even on those rare occasions when you have hit a very bad putt and you can see it's going to miss the hole and finish well past—don't turn away in disgust. Watch the ball carefully. It could save you the embarrassment of missing the return. The amount of break the ball takes past the hole is exactly the amount of break you must allow for when trying to hole out. It is a perfect guide to the next putt, which many people never see.

Hale Irwin is a two-time winner (1983, 1985) of the Memorial Tournament.

SCORECARD

Hole	Yards	Par	PGA Tour Avg. Score
1	446	4	4.206
2	452	4	4.241
3	392	4	4.120
4	204	3	3.192
5	531	5	4.848
6	430	4	4.160
7	549	5	4.846
8	189	3	3.111
9	410	4	4.142
OUT	3603	36	36.866
10	441	4	4.199
11	538	5	4.957
12	158	3	3.157
13	442	4	4.125
14	363	4	4.185
15	490	5	4.732
16	204	3	3.190
17	430	4	4.216
18	437	4	4.226
IN	3503	36	36.987
TOTAL	7106	72	73.853

TPC at AVENEL

KEMPER OPEN
MARYLAND

Several of the world's most spectacular courses have taken shape on real estate only Mother Nature could love. Swamps, deserts, lava beds, rock quarries, and barren lowlands have given rise to many if not most of the outstanding playing grounds in golf.

On that basis, mark the TPC at Avenel as a shoo-in for greatness. Audacious site selection may have reached a new height with this course, which wraps itself around the intended home of a sewer plant.

7th hole

In 1979 Maryland developer Gene Holloway purchased Avenel Farm, a rolling, tree-clad 1,000-acre tract in Potomac, ten miles west of the White House. Almost immediately after he took possession, Holloway was informed that Montgomery County had designated part of Avenel as the future site of a waste-treatment facility.

Holloway was understandably concerned. "The county was talking about taking 500 acres, and we didn't think we could convince buyers that the other 500 acres would remain pristine. We needed a buffer between the plant and my homesites," he said.

Holloway found that buffer a few months later when he received a phone call from PGA Tour Commissioner Deane Beman. Beman's deal: Give the Tour 200 acres of land, free and clear, and Holloway could have a stadium course at Avenel. Seven years later, the plan came to fruition with the TPC at Avenel, already being hailed as one of the finest new courses in America.

ALL TIME TOURNAMENT RECORDS

Record	Player(s)	Score	Year
Low 18	Jerry McGee	61	1979
Low first 36	Craig Stadler	131 (62–69)	1979
Low 36	Craig Stadler	131 (62–69)	1979 (rounds 1–2)
	Dave Hill	(66–65)	1974 (rounds 3–4)
	Jerry Heard	(66–65)	1974 (rounds 2–3)
Low first 54	Jerry Heard	200 (69–66–65)	1974
Low 54	Jerry Heard	200	1974
Low 72	Bob Menne	270 (67–69–67–67)	1974
	Craig Stadler	(67–69–66–68)	1981
	Tom Kite	(64–69–68–69)	1987
Highest winning score	Fred Couples	287 (71–71–68–77)	1983
Largest winning margin	Craig Stadler (275)	7 strokes	1982
Largest 18-hole lead	George Burns (64)	4 strokes	1983
Largest 36-hole lead	Greg Norman (136)	4 strokes	1984
Largest 54-hole lead	Greg Norman (207)	7 strokes	1984
Lowest start by winner	Jerry McGee	61	1979
Highest start by winner	Dick Lotz Andy Bean Craig Stadler Bill Glasson	72	1970 1978 1982 1985
	Greg Norman		1986
Lowest finish by winner	Andy Bean Bill Glasson Greg Norman	66	1978 1985 1986
Highest finish by winner	Fred Couples	77	1983
Best final-round comeback	Bill Glasson (212)	6 back	1985
Lowest 36-hole cut score		144	1987
Highest 36-hole cut score		150	1983–1984

PAST WINNERS

Year	Winner	Score	Year	Winner	Score
1968	Arnold Palmer	276	1979	Jerry McGee	272
1969	Dale Douglass	274	1980	John Mahaffey	275
1970	Dick Lotz	278	1981	Craig Stadler	270
1971	*Tom Weiskopf	277	1982	Craig Stadler	275
1972	Doug Sanders	275	1983	*Fred Couples	287
1973	Tom Weiskopf	271	1984	Greg Norman	280
1974	*Bob Menne	270	1985	Bill Glasson	278
1975	Raymond Floyd	278	1986	*Greg Norman	277
1976	Joe Inman	277	1987	Tom Kite	270
1977	Tom Weiskopf	277			
1978	Andy Bean	273	*Playoff		

The designers were Ed Ault and Tom Clark. Ault is a Washington, D.C.-based architect whose prolific 40-year career has been highlighted by the courses at Baltimore's Five Farms and at Las Vegas Country Club, one of the sites of the Panasonic Las Vegas Invitational. Clark has been with him since 1971.

The Tour player-consultant on the project was Ed Sneed. Variety seems to have been his keynote. The four par threes, for example, measure 136, 182, 195, and 239 yards, calling for clubs ranging from a 9-iron to a 1-iron or wood.

"I don't know why more courses aren't designed this way," Sneed says. "We play so many courses where all the par threes are 200–220 yards and all you hit are 2- and 3-irons."

The par fours are similarly diverse, ranging in length from 301 to 461 yards. As for the par fives, the sixth hole at 480 yards will be reachable in two by virtually all Tour players, whereas almost no one will hit the 615-yard second. The overall length of the course will be 6,864 yards, with a par of 71.

The two nines emanate from different sides of the clubhouse and run independently of each other, each ending in a slight loop. The front nine heads directly north to the fourth hole, where it makes an about-face and returns to the clubhouse. The toughest tests on this half should be the 239-yard third, a downhill par three where seven bunkers wreathe the green, and number seven, a 461-yard par four where the teeshot will have to be placed carefully between a large bunker on the left and dense trees to the right.

Number ten heads on an eastward path and begins a series of five holes where the creek comes constantly into play. At the 454-yard 12th, water parallels the left side of the fairway and then crosses in front of the severely contoured green, making this potentially the most testing hole on the back. Turning toward home on the 15th, the remainder of the course winds through a corridor of massive spectator mounds. At the short 17th the effect is that of a colosseum, as the mound wraps not only around the back of the green but also extends more than halfway down from the fairway.

"Avenel will be plenty tough," says Sneed, "but if a Tour player is on his game, he'll be able to shoot 65. That's what I think should happen." The course gets its first test in the 1987 Kemper Open.

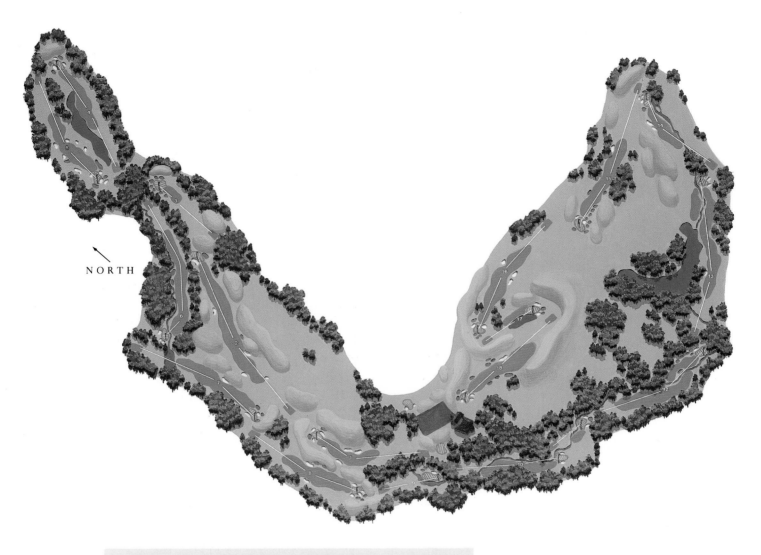

NORTH

RECOVERING FROM SWALES
BY ED SNEED

The TPC at Avenel offers opportunities to play a shot that heretofore had been restricted largely to courses in Great Britain: the swale shot. Several of the greens are set on mini-plateaus surrounded by steep-sided, moatlike swales.

I have a feeling that most amateur golfers approach these situations the wrong way—with wedges. They try to pop the ball softly to the top of the swale and let it roll to the pin. That's a very low-percentage shot, even for a pro.

It's far wiser to attack these shots the way the Brits do, with a putter. At Avenel the grass on the swales is not long or shaggy, so it's relatively easy to roll the ball up the banks. And when the pin is tight to the near edge of the green, there's no room to stop a wedge shot so the putter is the only sensible choice.

I play this shot a bit differently than I do a normal putt. I position the ball a bit farther back in my stance than for a putt, and instead

of stroking the ball, I give it a sharp rap. It's wise to rehearse this shot with a couple of serious practice swings in which you estimate the stroke that will propel the ball up the slope and across the green to the hole.

Ed Sneed is one of the architects of the TPC at Avenel.

SCORECARD

Hole	Yards	Par
1	393	4
2	615	5
3	239	3
4	430	4
5	340	4
6	479	5
7	461	4
8	424	4
9	182	3
OUT	3563	36
10	374	4
11	136	3
12	454	4
13	524	5
14	301	4
15	458	4
16	415	4
17	195	3
18	444	4
IN	3301	35
TOTAL	6864	71

WESTCHESTER *Country Club*

MANUFACTURERS HANOVER
WESTCHESTER CLASSIC
PRESENTED BY NYNEX
NEW YORK

8th hole

The first Westchester Classic took a week to play. Rain—nearly 72 hours of rain—caused a trio of postponed rounds and wrought havoc with the travel schedules of the players. By the time the tournament sloshed to its Wednesday afternoon finale, the New York press had baptized it "Wet-chester."

And yet, that inaugural classic had a silver lining, or a golden one; it was won by the game's most prominent player, Jack Nicklaus. The Golden Bear won the event again in 1972 and remains its only two-time champion. But the first decade at Westchester produced a string of distinguished victors: Julius Boros, Frank Beard, Bruce Crampton, Arnold Palmer, Bobby Nichols, Johnny Miller, Gene Littler, and David Graham.

Westchester is one of the oldest courses on the PGA Tour, designed in 1922 by "The Old Man," Walter J. Travis. During the twenties, 4,000 courses were built in America—four times the number then in existence. It was arguably the golden age of golf course design. One of the plum projects was John Bowman's plan for his Westchester Biltmore Hotel, where he sought to establish a golf complex par excellence—not simply a course but a 400-room

12th hole

18th hole

154

hotel, tennis courts, polo fields, all on a sprawling 500-acre tract perched on a hilltop in Rye, forty miles north of Manhattan.

Travis's assignment was to design 36 holes over the property—and he managed to fit in 45—two regulation 18s and a par-three course. The West course, on which the Classic is played, winds up and down rugged, rocky hills and loops through thick stands of pines, oaks, and maples. At 6,722 yards, it is not long, but it demands accuracy, particularly off the tees.

During the tournament, the front and back nines are reversed, with the result that the first hole is a par three. It seems an unassuming 192-yarder, but its guile was sufficient for Arnold Palmer to rank it among his favorite 54 holes in golf.

The fourth hole has been ranked as one of the finest in the New York area. A 422-yard par four, it begins with a blind tee shot to a relatively small landing area, then calls for a mid-iron uphill to a narrow, sloping green.

Water does not come into play until the eighth, a sharply doglegging par four that takes its hairpin left turn in front of a sizable pond. The pro must hit a draw off the tee or face a lengthy approach partially over the water.

Number nine is a short par five of 505 yards, but the second half is uphill. Still, lots of birdies are made here, and even more are made on the 304-yard 10th, which a few players drive each year. Such birdies are needed to balance the inevitable bogeys on holes 11 and 12.

The par-four 11th is a winding downhill dogleg left with tree trouble on both sides all the way to the two-level green. The second shot will be a long iron or wood. In 1983, the first year that scoring averages were computed, this was the sixth most difficult hole on the PGA Tour.

The *hardest* par four on the Tour that year was the hole that follows it. Normally a par five for the members and even for the Tour players until a few years ago, the 12th hole checks in at 467 yards. After another tight drive, the pros face a downhill/sidehill lie for a shot to a narrow green set at the top of a hill. Year in year out, the pros take more strokes on this par four—about 4.5 on average—than they do on a dozen or so *par fives* on the circuit.

Such sternness is balanced at Westchester by holes such as the 144-yard 14th. In 1975, Gene Littler made a hole-in-one here in the final round and went on to tie Julius Boros in regulation play. He won the tournament on the first hole of sudden death.

That hole happened to be the very difficult 15th. At 477 yards it is the longest of the several long par fours on the course. It doglegs sharply to the right, but a towering tree forbids all but the most aggressive players from trying to cut the corner. The downhill second shot is played with

a mid to long iron. Littler won his playoff with a one-putt par.

Westchester is blessed with a splendid finishing hole. It may not be as picturesque as the home hole at Pebble Beach or as intimidating as at Doral or as wind-blown as at Harbour Town, but the 18th at Westchester is as consistent at producing heart-stopping finales as any site on the Tour.

Two factors create the excitement. First is the hole's comparatively short length. At 535 yards it is reachable in two by any player who catches his drive on the screws. Second is the bunker that guards the right side of the green. Large, steep-faced, and cunningly placed, it does what a great hazard should—control the play of a scratch golfer from the moment he puts his tee in the ground. Together, the green and the bunker tug at the Tour pro, coaxing and conning him into a bold approach. It was on this hole in 1982 that Bob Gilder hit one of the most electrifying shots in golf, a 251-yard 3-wood that went into the hole for a double eagle. It gave Gilder a three-day total of 192, and spurred him to a record victory total of 261.

In 1983, major changes were made at Westchester. First, the tournament secured a new date in the Tour schedule, moving from mid-August to mid-June. Second, the club hired a new superintendent, Ted Horton, from nearby Winged Foot. Both changes had the same effect: a much harder golf course.

In one year Westchester was transformed from one of the Tour's pushovers to the bear of the Northeast. Horton contour-mowed the fairways, narrowing them substantially in spots, and let the rough sprout to four inches and more while also quickening the speed of the greens. Growing in the comparative coolness of early summer, the high grass was more thick and lush than the pros had ever seen it in August.

It killed them. Seve Ballesteros's winning score in 1983 was 15 strokes higher than Gilder's a year earlier and only four strokes lower than the winning total in the U.S. Open that followed a week later at formidable Oakmont.

Today, Walter Travis's compact little layout is a taut, nerve-wrenching test of shotmaking, loved by some, vilified by others, but respected by all who do battle with it. It retains its date a week before each year's U.S. Open, and several of the pros view the trip to New York as a valuable warm-up, reasoning, as the lyric goes, "if you can make it there you'll make it anywhere."

ALL TIME TOURNAMENT RECORDS

Record	Player(s)	Score	Year
Low 18	Dan Sikes	62	1967
	Jimmy Wright		1976
	Peter Jacobsen		1982
Low first 36	Bob Gilder	127 (64–63)	1982
Low 36	Bob Gilder	127 (64–63)	1982
Low first 54	Bob Gilder	192 (64–63–65)	1982
Low 54	Bob Gilder	192 (64–63–65)	1982
Low 72	Bob Gilder	261 (64–63–65–69)	1982
Highest winning score	Jack Renner	277 (69–71–70–67)	1979
Largest winning margin	Arnold Palmer	5 strokes	1971
	Bob Gilder		1982
	Scott Simpson		1984
Largest 18-hole lead	Tom Weiskopf (64)	3 strokes	1973
	David Graham (65)		1979
Largest 36-hole lead	Tom Weiskopf (129)	7 strokes	1975
Largest 54-hole lead	Bob Gilder (192)	6 strokes	1982
Lowest start by winner	David Graham	63	1976
Highest start by winner	Bob Tway	73	1986
Lowest finish by winner	Bobby Nichols	65	1973
	Scott Simpson		1984
Highest finish by winner	Jack Nicklaus	71	1967
	David Graham		1976
	Andy North		1977
Best final-round comeback	Bobby Nichols	5 back	1973
Lowest 36-hole cut score		141	1982
Highest 36-hole cut score		147	1983

9th hole

PAST WINNERS

Year	Winner	Score
1967	Jack Nicklaus	272
1968	Julius Boros	272
1969	Frank Beard	275
1970	Bruce Crampton	273
1971	Arnold Palmer	270
1972	Jack Nicklaus	270
1973	*Bobby Nichols	272
1974	Johnny Miller	269
1975	*Gene Littler	271
1976	David Graham	272
1977	Andy North	272
1978	Lee Elder	274
1979	Jack Renner	277
1980	Curtis Strange	273
1981	Raymond Floyd	275
1982	Bob Gilder	261
1983	Seve Ballesteros	276
1984	Scott Simpson	269
1985	*Roger Maltbie	275
1986	Bob Tway	272
1987	*J.C. Snead	276

*Playoff

TAMING THE ROUGH
BY JOHNNY MILLER

During the last few years, Westchester has earned a reputation for having some of the thickest, meanest rough on the PGA Tour. The best way to handle such heavy rough is to avoid it entirely. But since no one can do that, here are a few ways to cope with it.

First, play the ball back in your stance—the more severe the rough, the farther back the ball position. This encourages you to make a quick pickup of the club on the backswing and thus to make a sharply descending impact where the clubface is not deflected or twisted by the blades of grass.

Second, align your body 20 yards right of your target while toeing your clubface inward so that it faces the target. This will set you up for a pulled shot. As in baseball, a pull is the strongest shot you can hit, and that's exactly what you need when playing from thick rough.

Finally, because you're playing the ball back and closing your club-face (thus delofting it), never play this shot with a long iron. However, feel free to use the full range of middle irons and, of course, the lofted woods and utility clubs.

Johnny Miller won the Westchester Classic in 1974, a year in which he won eight tournaments on the PGA Tour.

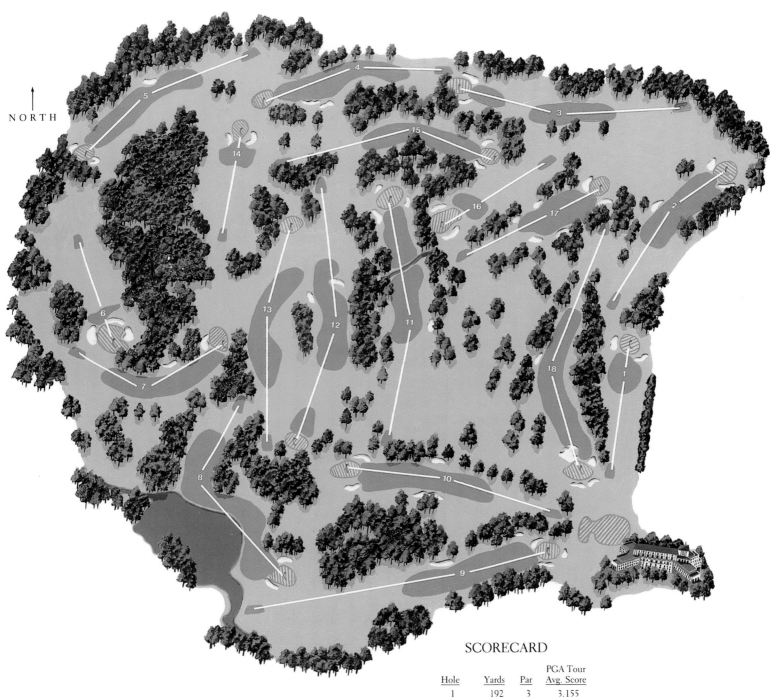

SCORECARD

Hole	Yards	Par	PGA Tour Avg. Score
1	192	3	3.155
2	359	4	4.018
3	419	4	4.121
4	422	4	4.351
5	573	5	4.899
6	133	3	2.827
7	333	4	4.080
8	455	4	4.357
9	505	5	4.902
OUT	3391	36	36.710
10	304	4	3.820
11	438	4	4.354
12	467	4	4.516
13	381	4	4.174
14	144	3	2.946
15	477	4	4.341
16	204	3	3.183
17	381	4	4.022
18	535	5	4.801
IN	3331	35	36.157
TOTAL	6722	71	72.867

ATLANTA *Country Club*

13th hole

GEORGIA–PACIFIC ATLANTA
GOLF CLASSIC, GEORGIA

Had you been a member of the gallery lining the right side of the 18th fairway at the Atlanta Country Club on March 15, 1979, you would have witnessed one of the cruelest crimes in the history of professional golf.

The hapless victim was Johnny Miller, U.S. and British Open champion, winner of 22 Tour titles. It was the final round of the Atlanta Classic, and Miller had a good chance to win. On the tee of the 72nd hole, he knew a birdie would give him victory, a par would create a playoff.

Because the second shot must be played over water, a long drive is desirable, preferably a ball that draws right to left around the banked corner of the dogleg. Miller hit just such a shot, or almost. It was a shade too far to the right. As the ball descended, Miller noticed it was coming down straight at a lone woman spectator perched on a metal seat just inside the gallery rope. The woman sensed she was in danger and quickly abandoned her post. A split-second later the ball pinged down onto the seat, bounced 100 feet into the air, and came to rest four inches out-of-bounds. Miller made a bogey 6 and lost the tournament by a shot.

Still, he lived to tell the tale. A century earlier, in the main events contested over this property, the rounds were fired not with golf clubs but with rifles. All over Georgia's Cobb County and particularly along the banks of Sope Creek, the armies of the North and South battled for the future of the Republic. The acreage that is now the golf course was the site of particularly furious action, in part because it housed a paper mill that was used to mint Confederate currency. In 1865, a brigade of Union soldiers finally torched the mill.

Exactly a hundred years later, an Atlanta businessman named Jim Clay formed a group of investors, purchased the historic land, and hired architect William Byrd to design a golf course, hoping to bring the pros to town.

By 1967 they had the tournament they wanted. With the inauguration of the Atlanta Classic, fast action returned to the banks of Sope Creek. Today the Atlanta Country Club is regarded as one of the finest battlefields on the PGA Tour.

During the past twenty years, the southern boys have won a few Classics and so have the northern boys. And ironically, on this acreage where black men once were slaves, the most electrifying victory was scored by Calvin Peete.

It was in 1983 when rain reduced the tournament to a 54-hole event. Peete, who had opened with a 68 but then slipped to a 75, began the final round seven strokes behind co-leaders Don Pooley and Jim Colbert. Playing two hours ahead of the leaders, Peete tore through the front side in 32, then made three more birdies in the first seven holes of the back nine. But at the 17th, a 421-yard par four, his second shot found the bunker to the right of the green, 70 feet from the pin.

Peete then played the best bunker shot of his life. The ball sailed high and far enough to land on the flat part of the green, then rolled into the heart of the hole for a birdie three. The shot sustained his momentum, and he birdied the home hole as well, coming in with a 31, a 63 for the day, and a three-round total of 206. No one would catch him.

Georgia-Pacific has sponsored the tournament since 1982, and that is appropriate; the layout has enough trees to choke a paper mill. Thousands of pines and oaks line the fairways of this difficult test of driving, where no two holes run parallel. Eight lakes and two creeks come continually into play, and the gently contoured greens, grown with bentgrass (unusual this far south), are normally fast and always in splendid condition. Even in its early years it was recognized as a strong layout. It was selected to host two different USGA championships and was also the first site of the Tournament Players Championship, in 1974.

Jack Nicklaus redesigned the course in 1980, and one of the first holes he changed was the third, a 196-yard par three. Although Nicklaus won the 1973 Atlanta Classic and six months later won that inaugural TPC (with identical scores of 272), he never did like the third hole. On one occasion, after pushing his tee shot into the tangly kudzu grass to the right of the green, he struggled to a quintuple-bogey 8. Nicklaus's version of number three is shorter (188 yards) and does not invite disaster to the degree its progenitor did.

The other par three on the front, number 6, is a testing tee shot, with a creek bordering the front and right of the green and four bunkers clasping the left and rear. But the toughest approach on the course is probably at the par-four seventh, a downhill shot over Sope Creek to one of the narrowest targets on either nine. Tommy Aaron once hit three balls into the water here en route to a 9.

159

2nd and 3rd holes

6th hole

15th hole

7th hole

The 13th hole is one of the prettiest par threes in the world. It is also one of the more historic, because the remains of that Confederate mint are just to the right of the green. On the left side is something even more arresting—a waterfall. The entire left side of the green is set against a sheer rock face that drops off 15 feet to a small patch of grass; then it drops off again to the waterfall. A tee shot that lands on that patch must be played almost vertically upward to get back onto the dance floor.

The final round of the 1982 Atlanta Classic proved that the 448-yard 15th hole is the most difficult on the course. A tantalizing par four, it invites a hard fade to the left-to-right-bending fairway. But a creek down the right side penalizes the overly zealous drive. The creek winds back across the fairway about 35 yards short of the green, adding interest to the approach.

In that final round, the top four finishing players—Keith Fergus, Raymond Floyd, Larry Nelson, and Wayne Levi—made scores of bogey 5, double-bogey 6, triple-bogey 7, and quadruple-bogey 8 respectively. Nelson, a former PGA and U.S. Open champion, should have known better. For one thing, he won this tournament in 1980 by seven strokes. For another, his address is Country Club Lane, Duluth, Georgia. Larry lives on the course!

ALL TIME TOURNAMENT RECORDS

Record	Player(s)	Score	Year
Low 18	Andy Bean	61	1979
Low first 36	Davis Love III	130 (65–65)	1987
Low 36	Andy Bean	128 (67–61)	1979 (rounds 2–3)
	Andy Bean	(61–67)	1979 (rounds 3–4)
Low first 54	Andy Bean	198 (70–67–61)	1979
Low 54	Andy Bean	195 (67–61–67)	1979 (rounds 2–3–4)
Low 72	Andy Bean	265 (70–67–61–67)	1979
	Dave Barr	(66–68–66–65)	1987
Highest winning score	Bob Charles	284 (72–71–69–70)	1967
Largest winning margin	Andy Bean (265)	8 strokes	1979
Largest 18-hole lead	Mark Lye (63)	4 strokes	1979
Largest 36-hole lead	Jack Nicklaus	4 strokes	1973
Largest 54-hole lead	Jack Nicklaus	6 strokes	1973
Lowest start by winner	Jack Nicklaus Hale Irwin Larry Nelson Keith Fergus	66	1973 1975 1980 1982
Highest start by winner	Bob Charles	72	1967
Lowest finish by winner	Calvin Peete	63	1983*
Highest finish by winner	Jack Nicklaus	73	1973
Best final-round comeback	Wayne Levi Bob Tway	4 back	1985* 1986
Lowest 36-hole cut score		141	1987
Highest 36-hole cut score		151	1967

*54 holes

PAST WINNERS

Year	Winner	Score
1967	Bob Charles	284
1968	Bob Lunn	280
1969	*Bert Yancey	277
1970	Tommy Aaron	275
1971	*Gardner Dickinson	275
1972	Bob Lunn	275
1973	Jack Nicklaus	272
1974	Host TPC	
1975	Hale Irwin	271
1976	Host U.S. Open	
1977	Hale Irwin	273
1978	Jerry Heard	269
1979	Andy Bean	265
1980	Larry Nelson	270
1981	*Tom Watson	277
1982	*Keith Fergus	273
1983	‡Calvin Peete	206
1984	Tom Kite	269
1985	*Wayne Levi	273
1986	Bob Tway	269
1987	Dave Barr	265

*Playoff
‡Rain-curtailed

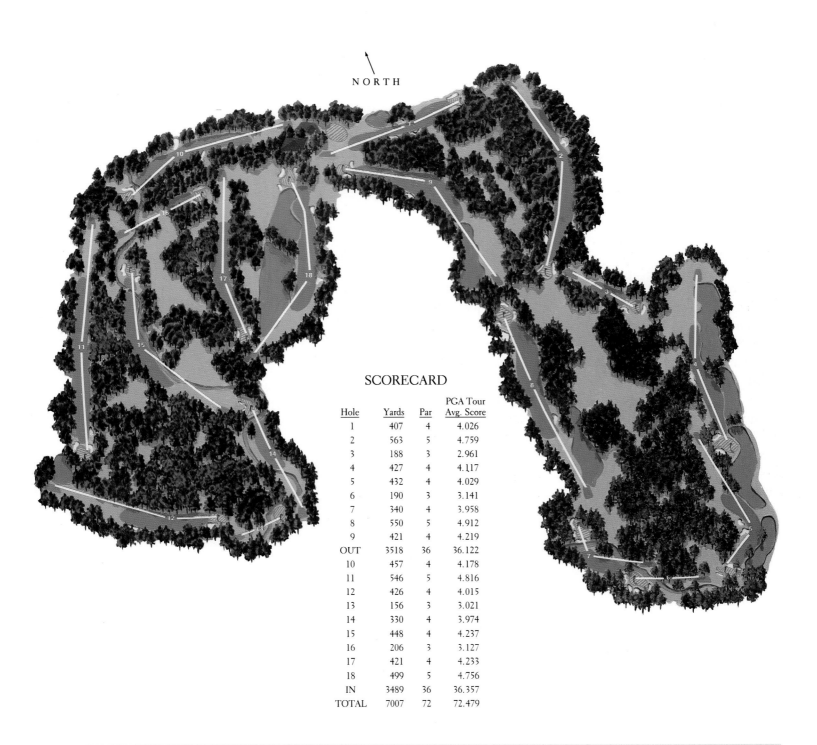

NORTH

SCORECARD

Hole	Yards	Par	PGA Tour Avg. Score
1	407	4	4.026
2	563	5	4.759
3	188	3	2.961
4	427	4	4.117
5	432	4	4.029
6	190	3	3.141
7	340	4	3.958
8	550	5	4.912
9	421	4	4.219
OUT	3518	36	36.122
10	457	4	4.178
11	546	5	4.816
12	426	4	4.015
13	156	3	3.021
14	330	4	3.974
15	448	4	4.237
16	206	3	3.127
17	421	4	4.233
18	499	5	4.756
IN	3489	36	36.357
TOTAL	7007	72	72.479

WHEN TO GAMBLE
BY ANDY BEAN

The 18th hole at the Atlanta Country Club is a great one: it's a very reachable—yet treacherous—par five. It coaxes and cons you into going for the green over the water. As such it produces an exciting finish nearly every year in the Atlanta Classic.

From time to time we all find ourselves with a lie in no man's land, where it's a tough choice whether to go for the green or lay up. Nobody makes the right decision every time, but you can improve your percentages by doing some homework.

First, know the carrying distance—the distance your ball flies in the air—on every one of your long irons and woods. (Assume that you will hit an *average* shot, not a maximum effort.) If your target is beyond the average distance of the club you must use, then lay up. The only exception would be if you had a flyer lie in light rough, where the grass will get between your club and ball, thereby inhibiting your ability to get backspin. Then you can figure on a few extra yards.

At the same time, consider the consequences of your worst shot. On some holes when you hit into the water, you can drop out, lieing three, very close to the green—sometimes even *on* the green. On others, the penalty for hitting into a hazard or unplayable lie can be very severe on both your score and your psyche. So think twice and then play the shot that you're sure is within your reach.

Andy Bean won the 1979 Georgia-Pacific Atlanta Classic on a record score of 265.

GLEN ABBEY *Golf Club*

CANADIAN
OPEN
CANADA

For Canadians, it is the national championship. For golf historians, it is the last of Byron Nelson's eleven straight wins. For Andy Bean, it is the scene of a colossally costly error.

The Canadian Open is one of the oldest tournaments in the world, dating back to 1904, and its glittering list of winners includes Walter Hagen, Tommy Armour, Sam Snead, Byron Nelson, Arnold Palmer, Gene Littler, and Lee Trevino, to name a few. But not Jack Nicklaus.

By 1966 Jack had won the four tournaments in the

13th hole

modern Grand Slam (as well as 13 other events on the Tour) but never the Canadian. By 1971 he had taken each of the majors twice (plus 29 other events) but still no Canadian. And by 1978, when his emotional victory in the British Open at St. Andrews completed an unprecedented triple grand slam and a total of 69 victories, the absence of a Canadian title had become a thorn in the Golden Bear's paw. Worst of all, when in 1985 he lost a fourth-round lead to Curtis Strange, Nicklaus recorded his

seventh second-place finish in the Canadian.

Nicklaus gets excited about the Canadian. And when Jack Nicklaus gets excited about something, so do the other players, the media, and the fans. Today, thanks in large part to Jacks's two-decade-long quest, the pros rank the Canadian Open among the dozen or so most coveted titles in the world of golf.

Part of Nicklaus's recent interest in the championship relates directly to the site on which the tournament is

played. In 1974 the Royal Canadian Golf Association commissioned Jack to design Glen Abbey, the course that would be the permanent home of the Canadian Open.

Glen Abbey is still a young course, and it will become more difficult with age as the thousands of planted trees begin to thicken. Nowhere is this more evident than at the fourth hole, a 417-yard par four that literally grows tougher each year. Trees down the right side of this slight dogleg suggest a drive to the left side of the fairway. The second shot here had better be a sharp one. Mounds behind the green make for tricky comeback chips and pitches, and the terraced green requires the touch of a safecracker.

The other short hole on the front nine—number seven—is 197 yards on the card, but can be stretched or compressed markedly by adjusting the tee blocks. Wind conditions also have a big influence on the playing distance of this hole.

The last 30 yards of the hole are over water, and the lightbulb-shaped green is surrounded by four sizable bunkers. It was here that Craig Stadler had one of his most embarrassing moments. In the middle of a less than stellar round, Stadler knocked his ball into the edge of the water

11th hole

12th hole

hazard. Without much preparation he waded in and whacked it, losing his balance just after impact. The ball came out, but the Walrus toppled backward and splashed into the lake.

Nicklaus says the eighth hole may be his favorite on the course, a par four of 433 yards that doglegs slightly right to a green that is raised in the center. Two bunkers down the right side of the landing area discourage boldness on the drive, and a grass bunker leads to a cluster of sand bunkers near the green.

The ninth through 12th holes represent one of the toughest stretches in competitive golf. Consider that in 1984 all four of them ranked statistically among the seventy toughest holes on the PGA Tour. Of the four, 9, 10, and 11 are par fours, averaging over 450 yards in length. The longest is nine, a 458-yarder that can seem like 548 yards when played into a headwind.

From day one of his career as a golf architect, Nicklaus has believed that the best golf hole is the one that plays downhill, where the golfer can see clearly from the tee everything that confronts him. Eleven is just such a hole. The tee sits 120 feet above the fairway. Two-thirds down

14th hole

the fairway a pair of bunkers wait, and a bit beyond that Sixteen Mile Creek crosses in front of the green, which is surrounded by pot bunkers. Not an encouraging sight, but at least it is all visible at the outset.

At the par-three 12th, swirling winds make club selection a constant challenge. The shot must carry water and avert sand in both the front and back.

Par for the incoming nine at Glen Abbey is 37, owing to the fact that three of the last six holes are par fives—reachable par fives. The 13th is the longest of them, at 529 yards, and the second shot must carry Sixteen Mile Creek as well as a front bunker, then grab tight on the fast, narrow green before rolling down into a deep, grassy swale toward the back left. Birdies here are frequent, but so are double bogeys.

Birdies are infrequent at the 14th, traditionally the hardest hole on the back nine. It is a moderate dogleg right that invites gambling players to take a big bite off the water-guarded corner. A large hollow cuts across the right-middle of the green, making every pin position a tough one. For the pros, par on 14 is about 4.5.

16th hole

The 15th is the site of Andy Bean's expensive blunder. In the third round of the 1983 Canadian Open, after narrowly missing his approach putt, Bean tapped in his ball billiard-style with the grip end of his putter. This was a miscue of Rule 14–1 of the Rules of Golf, which states: "The ball shall be fairly struck at with the head of the club and must not be pushed, scraped or spooned." At the time, of course, Bean did not realize his error; neither did his playing companions nor any of the officials or observers on the scene. But Clyde Mangum, deputy commissioner of the PGA Tour, happened to be watching the event on television and immediately recognized the infraction. He called the tournament headquarters and reported what he had seen, and in minutes Bean was assessed a two-stroke penalty for his violation.

Bean, who had been in the thick of contention, slipped quickly to a 77 and dropped well back in the pack. "If I lose by one or two strokes, I'll really have paid for it," he said.

He paid dearly. The next day, big Andy birdied eight of the first 11 holes, made the turn in 29, and came back

17th hole

18th hole

in 33 for a course-record 62. Into the clubhouse he went with a 279 while the leaders were still on the front nine. John Cook won that year in a five-hole playoff over Johnny Miller—both of them had finished at 277, two ahead of Andy, who finished tied for fourth and earned $14,166. Bean's mistake had cost him a berth in the playoff for the championship and first prize of $63,000.

The 16th hole was originally a par four, but in 1983 it was lengthened and is now a vulnerable five. With no water in front of the green, most of the field will go for this one, especially when it is downwind. In 1985 Nicklaus was two shots in back of Curtis Strange when he hit this green in two. Curtis was still in the fringe after three shots, and as Jack addressed his 30-foot eagle putt, it seemed as if this might be his year. But he left it two feet short, then

missed that one. Strange equaled the Bear's par, and two holes later Jack had his seventh bridesmaid finish.

It was the 17th that cost Nicklaus the 1981 tournament when he bogeyed the hole and then lost by one shot to Peter Oosterhuis. Fourteen bunkers, including 10 in the landing area of the drive, make this a very tough four.

Downwind, the 18th at Glen Abbey may be the shortest par five on the Tour. Only 500 yards long, it can play like 400. In 1985, defending champion Greg Norman reached it one day with an 8-iron. Nicklaus has grumbled that, with the 16th now a par five, the RCGA people should make this one a long four. But so far there has been no change. Evidently the officials like the notion of a player being able to eagle the final hole for victory. And who can argue with that?

ALL TIME TOURNAMENT RECORDS

Record	Player(s)	Score	Year
Low 18	Leonard Thompson	62	1981
	Greg Norman		1986
Low first 36	Johnny Palmer	131 (66–65)	1952
	Arnold Palmer	(64–67)	1955
Low 36	George Bayer	129 (64–65)	1958
	Doug Ford	(64–65)	1958
Low first 54	Arnold Palmer	195 (64–67–64)	1955
Low 54	Arnold Palmer	195 (64–67–64)	1955
Low 72	Johnny Palmer	263 (66–65–66–66)	1952
Highest winning score	Charles Murray	314 (n/a)	1911
Largest winning margin	J. Douglas Edgar (278)	16 strokes	1919
Largest 18-hole lead	Several Players	2 strokes	
Largest 36-hole lead	Nick Price (134)	6 strokes	1984
Largest 54-hole lead	Johnny Palmer (197)	8 strokes	1952
Lowest start by winner	Arnold Palmer	64	1955
Highest start by winner	Bruce Lietzke	76	1978
Lowest finish by winner	Leo Diegel	66	1929
	Johnny Palmer		1952
Highest finish by winner	Leo Diegel	78	1925
Best final-round comeback	Greg Norman (211)	4 back	1984
Lowest 36-hole cut score		145	1952
Highest 36-hole cut score		175	1922–1923

PAST WINNERS

Year	Winner	Score	Year	Winner	Score
1904	J. H. Oke	156	1948	C.W. Congdon	280
1905	George Cumming	148	1949	Dutch Harrison	271
1906	Charles Murray	170	1950	Jim Ferrier	271
1907	Percy Barrett	306	1951	Jim Ferrier	273
1908	Albert Murray	300	1952	John Palmer	263
1909	Karl Keffer	309	1953	Dave Douglas	273
1910	Daniel Kenny	303	1954	Pat Fletcher	280
1911	Charles Murray	314	1955	Arnold Palmer	265
1912	George Sargent	299	1956	**Doug Sanders	273
1913	Albert Murray	295	1957	George Bayer	271
1914	Karl Keffer	300	1958	Wesley Ellis, Jr.	267
1915–			1959	Doug Ford	276
1918	No Tournaments		1960	Art Wall, Jr.	269
1919	J. Douglas Edgar	278	1961	Jacky Cupit	270
1920	*J. Douglas Edgar	298	1962	Ted Kroll	278
1921	W.H. Trovinger	293	1963	Doug Ford	280
1922	Al Watrous	303	1964	Nel Nagle	277
1923	C.W. Hackney	295	1965	Gene Littler	273
1924	Leo Diegel	285	1966	D. Massengale	280
1925	Leo Diegel	295	1967	*Billy Casper	279
1926	Mac Smith	283	1968	Bob Charles	274
1927	T.D. Armour	288	1969	*Tommy Aaron	275
1928	Leo Diegel	282	1970	Kermit Zarley	279
1929	Leo Diegel	274	1971	*Lee Trevino	275
1930	*T.D. Armour	273	1972	Gay Brewer	275
1931	*Walter Hagen	292	1973	Tom Weiskopf	278
1932	Harry Cooper	290	1974	Bobby Nichols	270
1933	Joe Kirkwood	282	1975	*Tom Weiskopf	274
1934	T.D. Armour	287	1976	Jerry Pate	267
1935	Gene Kunes	280	1977	Lee Trevino	280
1936	Lawson Little	271	1978	Bruce Lietzke	283
1937	Harry Cooper	285	1979	Lee Trevino	281
1938	*Sam Snead	277	1980	Bob Gilder	274
1939	H. McSpaden	282	1981	Peter Oosterhuis	280
1940	*Sam Snead	281	1982	Bruce Lietzke	277
1941	Sam Snead	274	1983	*John Cook	277
1942	Craig Wood	275	1984	Greg Norman	278
1943–			1985	Curtis Strange	279
1944	No Tournaments		1986	Bob Murphy	280
1945	Byron Nelson	280	1987	Curtis Strange	276
1946	*George Fazio	278	*Playoff		
1947	Bobby Locke	268	**Amateur		

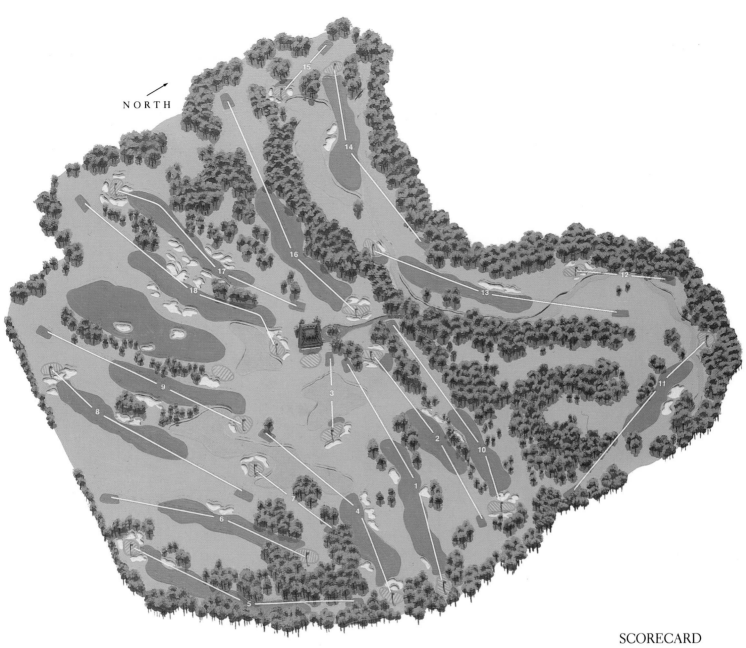

NORTH

SCORECARD

Hole	Yards	Par	PGA Tour Avg. Score
1	435	4	4.229
2	414	4	4.180
3	156	3	3.170
4	417	4	4.022
5	527	5	4.747
6	437	4	4.172
7	197	3	3.221
8	433	4	4.164
9	458	4	4.351
OUT	3474	35	36.256
10	443	4	4.312
11	452	4	4.289
12	187	3	3.307
13	529	5	5.009
14	426	4	4.420
15	141	3	3.060
16	516	5	4.724
17	434	4	4.266
18	500	5	4.808
IN	3628	37	38.195
TOTAL	7102	72	74.451

DRIVING FOR POWER
BY GREG NORMAN

One of the reasons I love the Glen Abbey course is that it suits my game. I'm a long hitter, and on a good day I can save a few strokes by hitting the par fives in two.

To me, the essence of power lies in the basics of grip, stance, and posture. In my grip the palms are parallel and face the target. I stand tall to the ball with my chin up, my back straight, and my knees slightly flexed.

A powerful swing begins with a takeaway in which everything moves together—hands, arms, and shoulders start away from the ball in one piece. Next is the turn—a full body turn—where hips and shoulders rotate around a firmly planted right leg. The resistance built up in that leg triggers an uncoiling into the forwardswing.

Just before my hands and club reach the top of the swing, I drive my right knee toward the left. This shifts my lower body laterally and allows my hips to clear the way so that my arms and hands can whip the club through the ball. There's nothing fancy to this swing, just sound fundamentals. But if you practice and learn to apply these fundamentals, you'll always hit the ball squarely and with good clubhead speed, and that's the only way to develop power.

Greg Norman is the 1984 Canadian Open champion.

$\mathcal{TPC}$ of CONNECTICUT

CANON
SAMMY DAVIS, JR.
GREATER
HARTFORD OPEN
CONNECTICUT

If Jekyll and Hyde had designed golf courses, their masterpiece would be the TPC of Connecticut. No other site on the PGA Tour—and perhaps none in the world—features back and front nines that are so dissimilar. Indeed, in this case, TPC stands for Two-Part Course.

But there are good reasons for the dissimilarity. Part one was designed in 1928; part two, in 1982. Part one was financed by a small, elite group of local businessmen; part two by a consortium of huge corporations. Part one was intended as a posh playground for the fortunate few; part two as a grass-covered Colosseum, capable of seating

17th hole

hundreds of thousands of spectators at the largest sporting event in the state.

For more than three decades, Connecticut had staged a major professional golf event near Hartford at the Wethersfield Country Club. Never one of the sternest tests on the Tour but ever among the finest-conditioned, it consistently produced birdie-filled, exciting tournaments.

But by the mid-1970s big-time golf had begun to outgrow Wethersfield, and when a rumor circulated that the Tour was planning to divide its forty-odd tournaments into "A" and "B" venues, with Wethersfield becoming one of

the "B"s, the sponsoring Greater Hartford Jaycees began to look for a new site.

Funding was secured through nine Hartford-area corporations, and the Jaycees commissioned Pete Dye to find and build a new home for their tournament. Dye, in characteristically meticulous manner, spent many weeks touring the countryside in search of suitable land before he found what he wanted just a few miles from Wethersfield.

On a snowy day in March of 1980, Dye visited the Edgewood Golf Club in Cromwell, Connecticut, and

came away impressed. Six months later he returned. This time he arrived on a morning when the course had been deluged with three and a half inches of rain in three hours. John Shulansky, the 1985 GHO chairman, recalls Dye's visit.

"Pete was sloshing across the course when he got to an area that intrigued him as a possible green site. It was one of the lowest points on the property, and the area was covered with a puddle the size of a small lake. He wanted to take a photograph of the spot, but had left his camera behind. 'Let's come back after lunch and be sure to get a picture,' he said.

"After lunch, the puddle was gone. It was then that Dye knew he had found his course. That night in a meeting with the Jaycees, he said, 'Today, I saw the perfect golf course. You could have a hurricane there Wednesday and play the tournament Thursday.'"

Edgewood was a classic old course in the Donald Ross mold, designed in fact by one of Ross's cousins, R. J. Ross, along with Maurice Kearney, and built by Ross's construction engineer, Orrin Smith. Despite its location in the wooded hills above the Connecticut River, the layout had a linkslike flavor. It was flat and relatively wide-open, with few trees and bunkers for definition. Today the front nine of the TPC of Connecticut is about 80 percent as it was then.

Dye's only major changes involved the first hole, a lengthy, rolling par four with an elevated green, which he created by combining the old first and second holes; and the construction of a new eighth hole, a vintage Pete Dye par four. Shortish at 178 yards, it greets its assailants with a profusion of perils—pot bunkers, grass bunkers, knobs, dips, knolls, and a long, narrow, undulating green.

This half of the course is set on a plateau about 100 feet higher than the rest. Water thus comes into play only once in the first nine, and even there it is only for amateurs because the teeshot on the par-five fourth calls for a carry from the back tees of about 218 yards over a pond.

The ninth hole is an interesting par five that snakes along the top of a ridge, culminating in a deep, narrow green. It is reachable only with two very strong shots, and that is what Jodie Mudd hit in the final round of the 1985 GHO. Mudd then sank an 80-foot eagle putt that helped him into a three-way tie for first after regulation play. Phil Blackmar, the man who beat Mudd in the playoff, also had good fortune here on Sunday, making a birdie after his third shot caromed off the forehead of an Associated Press photographer.

The back nine—Dye's nine—is only 3,254 yards long (278 yards shorter than the front), and its par is 35 to the front's 36. But this is the half of the course where high

18th hole

scores are made. Says Peter Jacobsen, the inaugural GHO champion of the new course, "You had better make your birdies on the front side when you can, because you won't find too many on the back."

Very few players can reach the par-five 10th in two. It is 558 yards long, up and down and up again to a green that is on one of the highest parts of the course. Most pros lay up about 80 yards short if they can avoid the large bunker in that area, then take their chances on an uphill wedge shot to a very shallow, very swift target.

Eleven plummets down a 100-foot chasm to a narrow, angled green. The scorecard says 194 yards, but many players choose 6-and 7-irons here where accurate club selection is as important as precise shotmaking.

One of the most thought-provoking tee shots on the course looms at 12, a 342-yard par four that most pros attack with an iron. Spectators tend to gather on the large mounds along the right side of this hole, and golf balls tend to gather in the large lake at the left. The green is elongated, two-tiered, and a place where two putts can quickly turn into three, maybe even four.

Some of the Tour players try to drive the tiny par-four 13th hole, but few hit it, and those who miss leave themselves short flicks and explosions that are more testing than the crisp wedges played by the guys who lay back. Raymond

Floyd, leading the tournament in 1985, took a quick 6 here, and he was one of the ones who layed up.

Tall trees, smack in the center of the line of flight, add interest to the tee shot at the dogleg 14th. And at the 15th, perhaps the best par four on the course, the drive must be both long and straight. This hole existed on the old layout, but Dye rerouted it with a severe dogleg to the right, around a thick stand of trees.

If one hole got complaints from the pros in the early years of the GHO at Cromwell, it was the par-three 16th, Dye's attempt to provide Connecticut with its own version of the famous island hole at Sawgrass. The green here is not an island; water guards only the left side. But this hole may be even tougher than that 17th. For one thing, it is 40 yards longer. For another, it plays into swirling, often undiscernible winds. And for another, the area to the right of the green is a steep, heavily grassed mound. The player who bails out to this area on his tee shot faces the strong possibility of pitching clear across the green and into the drink on his *second*. Jacobsen thinks the green area should be enlarged to allow for a safe tee shot away from the water. "The players on the Tour are aggressive," he says, "but they're not stupid."

In the sudden-death playoff of 1985, all three players gunned at the pin. Jodie Mudd, Phil Blackmar, and Dan

175

Pohl, all winless on the Tour, all nailed their tee shots within a few feet of the flag. Mudd missed, then Blackmar made his, then Pohl missed, and Blackmar, at six feet five inches and 270 pounds the biggest man on the Tour, scored the biggest win of his life.

As time passes, the most-talked-about hole at the TPC of Connecticut will surely be number 17, a 399-yard par four that plays completely around Dye's bulkheaded lake. The tee shot actually crosses paths with the tee shot at the 16th. Players marching off the championship tee at 17 have to pass beneath the descending tee shots of the group behind them. Dye proposed a novel solution to this traffic congestion: Push the championship tee even farther back, then let the pros hop a small motorized boat across the lake to their tee shots. It would have added a novel element, especially to the television broadcast of the event, but Commissioner Deane Beman nixed the idea as too gimmicky.

Most of the pros hit fairway woods or long irons to the ribbon of fairway, hoping to avoid rough-grown mounds on the left and the lake on the right. From there it is a white-knuckled short iron over the water to the shallow green. If there were statistics on the scariest holes on the Tour, this one would certainly rank in the top ten.

Even before it was opened, the 420-yard 18th hole was hailed as the greatest spectator hole in golf. The narrow fairway plays slightly uphill in its own mini-valley formed by the two huge ridges on either side. Behind the green those ridges join, forming an immense amphitheater around the long, thin green. And this stadium is truly natural, not bulldozed, bulkheaded, or bleachered. In the first year of the GHO at Cromwell, 40,000 fans flocked to 18 to witness the closing moments of play. Players walking to that green said the massive galleries gave them the goosebumps that signal the finish of a major championship.

ALL TIME TOURNAMENT RECORDS

Record	Player(s)	Score	Year
Low 18	Tommy Bolt	60	1954
Low first 36	Tim Norris	127 (63–64)	1982
Low 36	Tim Norris	127 (63–64)	1982
Low first 54	Tim Norris	193 (63–64–66)	1982
Low 54	Tim Norris	193 (63–64–66)	1982
Low 72	Tim Norris	259 (63–64–66–66)	1982
Highest winning score	Arnold Palmer Billy Casper	274	1956 1965
Largest winning margin	Sam Snead (269)	7 strokes	1955
Largest 18-hole lead	Several Players	2 strokes	
Largest 36-hole lead	Skee Riegel (133) Jack Burke, Jr. (130)	4 strokes	1952 1958
Largest 54-hole lead	Sam Snead (199)	5 strokes	1955
Lowest start by winner	Jack Burke, Jr. Tim Norris	63	1958 1982
Highest start by winner	Tommy Bolt Mac O'Grady	71	1954 1986
Lowest finish by winner	Mac O'Grady	62	1986
Highest finish by winner	Phil Blackmar Paul Azinger	72	1985 1987
Best final-round comeback	Billy Casper Mac O'Grady	5 back	1963 1986
Lowest 36-hole cut score		139	1981, 1982, 1983
Highest 36-hole cut score		152	1958

PAST WINNERS

Year	Winner	Score	Year	Winner	Score
1952	Ted Kroll	273	1971	*George Archer	266
1953	Bob Toski	269	1972	*Lee Trevino	269
1954	*Tommy Bolt	271	1973	Billy Casper	264
1955	Sam Snead	269	1974	Dave Stockton	268
1956	*Arnold Palmer	274	1975	*Don Bies	267
1957	Gardner Dickinson	272	1976	Rik Massengale	266
1958	Jack Burke, Jr.	268	1977	Bill Kratzert	265
1959	Gene Littler	272	1978	Rod Funseth	264
1960	Arnold Palmer	270	1979	Jerry McGee	267
1961	*Billy Maxwell	271	1980	*Howard Twitty	266
1962	Bob Goalby	271	1981	Hubert Green	264
1963	Billy Casper	271	1982	Tim Norris	259
1964	Ken Venturi	273	1983	Curtis Strange	268
1965	*Billy Casper	274	1984	Peter Jacobsen	269
1966	Art Wall	266	1985	*Phil Blackmar	271
1967	Charles Sifford	272	1986	*Mac O'Grady	269
1968	Billy Casper	266	1987	Paul Azinger	269
1969	*Bob Lunn	268			
1970	Bob Murphy	267	*Playoff		

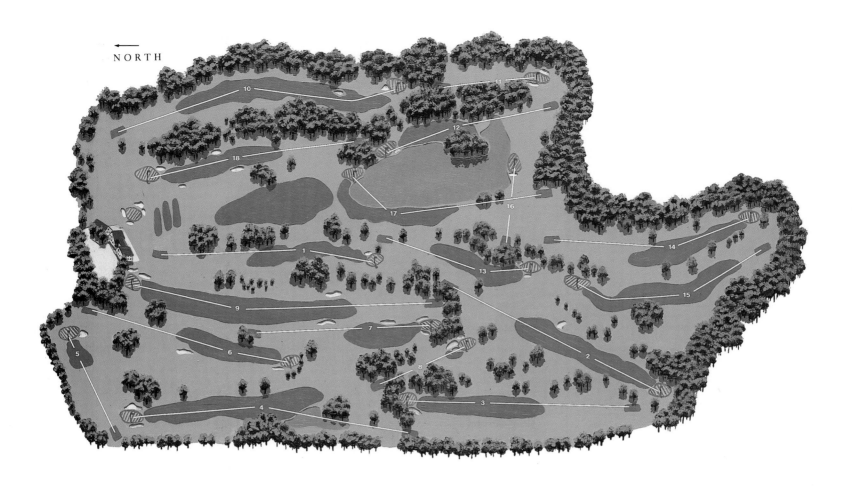

CHIPPING FROM HILLS
BY PETER JACOBSEN

At stadium courses such as the TPC of Connecticut, where several greens sit in grassy amphitheaters, errant approach shots often end up in the "grandstands" on hilly lies. Chipping from these positions requires a little extra attention.

When chipping from an uphill lie, I'll use a less-lofted club than I would from a flat fringe—a 6- or 7-iron instead of a sand wedge. The reason is that you naturally tend to lift the ball into the air when striking on an upward plane. A wedge shot tends to fly too high and come up short.

In setting up to the shot, I position the ball slightly more forward in my stance than for a standard chip—about midway between the feet—and I try to align my hips and shoulders parallel with the angle of the upward slope of the terrain. Many players will simply use their normal swing from this lie, but I use a slightly stiffer-wristed swing to guard against flipping the club into the ground in back of the ball or scooping it up too high.

From a downhill lie, I do the reverse of the above. I take as lofted a club as the lie will permit, play the ball back near my right foot, and use a wristier swing than normal to ensure hitting down and under the ball and to protect against a topped or skulled shot.

Peter Jacobsen won the inaugural (1984) Canon Sammy Davis, Jr. Greater Hartford Open at the TPC of Connecticut.

SCORECARD

Hole	Yards	Par	PGA Tour Avg. Score
1	410	4	4.121
2	453	4	4.157
3	433	4	4.038
4	528	5	4.601
5	218	3	3.110
6	384	4	3.926
7	343	4	3.830
8	178	3	3.059
9	585	5	4.894
OUT	3532	36	35.736
10	558	5	4.995
11	194	3	3.183
12	342	4	3.948
13	299	4	3.876
14	424	4	4.106
15	446	4	4.277
16	172	3	3.091
17	399	4	4.215
18	420	4	4.149
IN	3254	35	35.840
TOTAL	6786	71	71.576

KINGSMILL *Golf Club*

17th hole

ANHEUSER-BUSCH
GOLF CLASSIC
VIRGINIA

The PGA Tour is full of venerable events, but only one was sown in vintage wine country and aged in premium beer. The Anheuser-Busch Golf Classic—born the Kaiser Open—has enjoyed a twenty-year gestation that began in California's golden Napa Valley and now flourishes in Williamsburg, Virginia, on the 3,000-acre compound of America's largest brewmaster.

In 1968 Kaiser Aluminum staged its first Tour event at the famed Silverado Country Club course. The tournament stayed there for thirteen autumns. During the last six of those years, Anheuser-Busch was the sponsor, and in 1981 they brought the tournament East, switching to a midsummer date.

The move was part of the beermaker's grand design for the Williamsburg area, where its half-billion-dollar investment includes a huge brewery, the Busch Gardens amusement park, and Kingsmill-on-the-James, a residential resort community built around the Kingsmill course.

While the resort was being built, developers uncovered a pillar of exposed brick, down near the bank of the James River. An archaeologist from the Virginia Historic Landmarks Commission determined that the structure was a forty-foot-deep well shaft, built prior to the Revolutionary War. It contained a wealth of ceramics, glassware, coins, old farm implements, and a pewter bowl in mint condition.

Further excavation in the area uncovered some of Virginia's earliest settlements, including Burwell's Landing, Williamsburg's principal commercial wharf and outlet to the sea in Revolutionary times. Today, golfers pass near sites of a prehistoric Indian settlement, a Colonial tavern, Revolutionary breastworks, and the ruins of an eighteenth-century plantation.

But Pete Dye built a few memorable features of his own into the course. Ten of the greens are multi-tiered, and all of them have severe breaks, reminiscent of the Scottish courses after which Kingsmill was patterned.

Two stretches of the course are particularly testing, the first of these starting at the eighth hole. A narrow par four of 413 yards, it is the most difficult hole on the course. The landing area is severely banked. Hit the tee shot too far right, and the ball will pitch toward out-of-bounds. Hit it too far left, and it will bound into thick rough if you are lucky, or water if you are not. Most of the pros choose 1-irons off this tee, then take their chances on a mid-iron approach to the narrow, two-tiered green surrounded by sand.

179

5th hole

13th hole

16th hole

18th hole

In 1981 architect Ed Ault made several changes on the course in response to comments from the Tour players in the first Classic. One of his biggest moves was to add a new tee on the ninth hole. The Tour players now start that hole at a point 125 yards behind the members' tee. Even so, this is a wide-open hole, so the drive is not a difficult one. It is the second shot that is vexing, normally a mid-iron to a very shallow green that is guarded by sand and grass bunkers, with the latter variety the more difficult.

The second gauntlet is on the final three holes, a spectacular finish overlooking two miles of the James River. The 16th is thought by many to be the finest hole on the course. A dogleg par four of 427 yards, it normally plays into a headwind, increasing the need for both length and accuracy. The drive must be hit at least 240 yards to get past a long treeline on the right side and thereby leave a clear view of the green. Otherwise, the approach will have to be a slice or fade of nearly 200 yards. A half dozen bunkers and particularly deep rough surround this green.

Seventeen stretches 177 scenic yards along the bank of the James. The deepest green on the course allows for several pin positions, with all putts breaking softly toward the river. When the wind is up, par is a very welcome score here.

The final tee shot is played over water, ideally to the right center of the fairway. Too far left, and the water comes in play. The second shot is to a small well-trapped green below the club house.

ALL TIME TOURNAMENT RECORDS

Record	Player(s)	Score	Year
Low 18	Lanny Wadkins	63	1983
	Willie Wood		1984
	Wayne Levi		1984
	Ronnie Black		1984
	Mark O'Meara		1986
Low first 36	Willie Wood	131 (63–68)	1984
Low 36	Ronnie Black	129 (66–63)	1984 (rounds 3–4)
Low first 54	Willie Wood	197 (63–68–66)	1984
Low 54	Willie Wood	197 (63–68–66)	1984
Low 72	Ronnie Black	267 (69–69–66–63)	1984
	Mark McCumber	(65–69–67–66)	1987
Highest winning score	John Mahaffey	276 (72–67–70–67)	1981
	Calvin Peete	(66–75–66–69)	1983
Largest winning margin	John Mahaffey (276)	2 strokes	1981
	Calvin Peete (203)		1982*
Largest 18-hole lead	Scott Simpson (64)	2 strokes	1983
	Willie Wood (63)		1984
	Lon Hinkle (64)		1985
Largest 36-hole lead	Hal Sutton (132)	6 strokes	1983
Largest 54-hole lead	Hal Sutton (201)	6 strokes	1983
Lowest start by winner	Mark McCumber	65	1987
Highest start by winner	John Mahaffey	72	1981
Lowest finish by winner	Ronnie Black	63	1984
Highest finish by winner	Mark Wiebe	70	1985
Best final-round comeback	Ronnie Black (204)	7 back	1984
Lowest 36-hole cut score		142	1985 1986 1987
Highest 36-hole cut score		147	1983

*54 holes

PAST WINNERS

Year	Winner	Score	Year	Winner	Score
1968	Kermit Zarley	273	1980	Ben Crenshaw	272
1969	Miller Barber	135	1981	John Mahaffey	276
1969A	*Jack Nicklaus	273	1982	‡Calvin Peete	203
1970	*Ken Still	278	1983	Calvin Peete	276
1971	Billy Casper	269	1984	Ronnie Black	267
1972	George Knudson	271	1985	*Mark Wiebe	273
1973	*Ed Sneed	275	1986	Fuzzy Zoeller	274
1974	Johnny Miller	271	1987	Mark McCumber	267
1975	Johnny Miller	272			
1976	J.C. Snead	274			
1977	Miller Barber	272	A: Two tournaments		
1978	Tom Watson	270	*Playoff		
1979	John Fought	277	‡Rain-curtailed		

SCORECARD

Hole	Yards	Par	PGA Tour Avg. Score
1	360	4	3.986
2	204	3	3.113
3	514	5	4.795
4	437	4	4.278
5	183	3	3.167
6	365	4	3.938
7	516	5	4.862
8	413	4	4.334
9	452	4	4.250
OUT	3444	36	36.723
10	431	4	4.129
11	396	4	3.985
12	395	4	4.122
13	179	3	3.125
14	383	4	3.957
15	506	5	4.786
16	427	4	4.125
17	177	3	3.014
18	438	4	4.123
IN	3332	35	35.366
TOTAL	6776	71	72.089

BERMUDA VERSUS BENT GREENS

BY CURTIS STRANGE

Kingsmill is fortunate to be far enough north to be able to sustain bentgrass greens. Most of the courses north of here also have bent, but most of the courses farther south have bermuda greens. There's a big difference between the two types of grass.

Bermuda greens usually are slower and have a stronger grain than bent. Bentgrass is usually faster, smoother, and truer. A good putt on bent will usually go into the hole, a good putt on bermuda had better be perfect.

The bermuda's strong grain influences the break of a putt to the extent that, if it grows against the slope, it can negate up to three inches of break on a 10-foot putt. It also makes downgrain putts extremely fast and upgrain putts extremely slow.

I wouldn't recommend changing your stroke as you move from one type of grass to another unless you're making a permanent switch of residence. But it's worth observing that the players who have grown up on bermuda greens seem to have pop-type, rapping strokes, whereas the guys who have grown up on bentgrass have slower, silkier strokes.

Curtis Strange is the touring professional at the Kingsmill Golf Club course, site of the Anheuser-Busch Classic.

OAKWOOD *Country Club*

9th hole

Every summer during the third week of July, as millions of golf fans follow the dramatic twists and turns of the British Open, a few dozen good players and a few thousand loyal supporters get together in Coal Valley, Illinois, for a little excitement of their own. The Oakwood Country Club is the place where Fuzzy Zoeller birdied a record eight holes in a row. Quad Cities Open—now known as the Hardee's Golf Classic—is the tournament that produced the longest sudden-death playoff in Tour history. And it is the only event in which the commissioner of golf narrowly edged the game's only six-time Player of the Year.

The tournament began as a satellite event in 1971 and was won by Deane Beman, then a Tour player. The next year it was elevated to full Tour-event status, and Beman won again, this time finishing just ahead of an unknown pro named Tom Watson.

In those days, the Quad Cities was played at the Crow Valley Golf Club in Bettendorf, Iowa. But in 1975 it moved across the state line to a course designed by Pete Dye. Oakwood reflects Dye's belief that a testing layout does not have to be long; Oakwood is only 6,539. Beyond that, however, Oakwood does not feature many of the characteristics most observers associate with Dye. There are no railroad ties, no pot bunkers, no bulkheaded water hazards, and no small, gnarly greens. Dye began incorporating those ploys after his first visit to Scotland in 1963. By that time, Oakwood (1964) was already laid out and seeded.

It is true that more birdies are made on the front nine at Oakwood than on any nine holes on the Tour. The first two holes average about 370 yards, and birdie-birdie starts are not unusual. The second two, however, average 75 yards longer.

Out-of-bounds and a pond rise up on the left of the third fairway, and the approach shot to the narrow green is complicated by the presence of a bunker in back.

Number four, at 450 yards, is probably the hardest hole on the outward half. A pond and a fairway bunker are on the left side, and heavy rough is to the right, so accuracy is as important as distance off this tee. From position A, a middle iron will be needed for the approach to the huge, sloping green.

The 12th hole, a par three of 160 yards, looks harmless enough, but should the tee shot fall short, it will plunk into sand or water. Correct club selection is a must. In 1983 Curt Byrum came to this hole 12-under par for the tournament. He made a double bogey, then a bogey at 15,

another double at 16, and a bogey at 17. Byrum, who had opened the tournament with a 63, finished tied for 19th.

A deep gully runs along the left side of the 13th fairway, a 432-yard par four where the green plays tricks with the mind of everyone hitting into it. It slopes so steeply from front to back that when the pin is in the front portion of the green, a ball must pitch *short* of the putting surface to leave a short birdie putt. But a bunker guarding the front-right of the green adds risk to such a shot.

The longest par four on the back nine is the 442-yard 14th. Out-of-bounds on the left and heavy rough on the right narrow the fairway. The subtly sloped green is deep but narrow, and shots missed to the left invite disaster.

The 18th is one of the shortest finishing holes on the Tour—only 384 yards—but is also one of the tightest. To the left is a deep ravine, to the right, out-of-bounds. It is a good place to go for a finishing birdie, or to protect a

ALL TIME TOURNAMENT RECORDS

Record	Player(s)	Score	Year
Low 18	Jon Chaffee	62	1983
	Ron Streck		1985
Low first 36	Scott Hoch	129 (63–66)	1980
Low 36	Scott Hoch	129 (63–66)	1980 (rounds 1–2)
	Bill Kratzert	(65–64)	1984 (rounds 2–3)
Low first 54	Scott Hoch	197 (63–66–68)	1980
Low 54	Scott Hoch	197 (63–66–68)	1980
Low 72	Kenny Knox	265 (67–66–66–66)	1987
Highest winning score	Roger Maltbie	275 (74–65–72–64)	1975
Largest winning margin	Scott Hoch (266)	5 strokes	1984
Largest 18-hole lead	Scott Hoch (63)	2 strokes	1980
Largest 36-hole lead	Dave Eichelberger (132)	5 strokes	1975
Largest 54-hole lead	Dave Eichelberger (204)	3 strokes	1975
Lowest start by winner	Scott Hoch	63	1980
Highest start by winner	Roger Maltbie	74	1975
Lowest finish by winner	Payne Stewart	63	1982
Highest finish by winner	Victor Regalado	70	1978
Best final-round comeback	Roger Maltbie (211)	7 back	1975
Lowest 36-hole cut score		139	1987
Highest 36-hole cut score		146	1975

WEDGING IT CLOSE
BY SCOTT HOCH

A short course and not a particularly tight one, Oakwood Country Club always yields low scores. With a bunch of short par fours, the secret is to be able to hit wedge shots close to the hole.

One of the keys to good wedge play is often forgotten and has to do with the shot you play *before* the wedge. On a short par four, a strong player should hit his tee shot with the club that he knows will leave him at precisely the distance he hits a full wedge. Almost everyone has an easier time hitting full wedge shots than trying to throttle down for a half- or three-quarter shot. So if you're playing a 320-yard par four and you normally hit a full wedge 100 yards, select the club that will enable you to hit a tee shot of 220 yards.

Second, don't construe "full wedge" to mean hard wedge. The key to this shot is to maintain smoothness and control throughout the swing. On a wedge, you should use less leg action, a shorter backswing turn, and quieter hand action than on any other full shot.

Finally, since most wedge shots have enough backspin to stop quickly, be sure you get the ball to the hole. One good trick is to play your shot for the top of the flag, not the cup. With wedges as with short putts, never up, never in.

Scott Hoch is a two-time winner (1980, 1984) of the Hardee's Golf Classic.

good score with a cautious iron from the tee. In the first round of the 1976 tournament, Fuzzy Zoeller, then a rookie, came to this hole on the hottest of hot streaks. He had birdied holes 11 through 17, and he had an opportunity for yet another and a back nine score of 28 (63 overall). "As I stood over that putt, my caddie reminded me that I'd already birdied seven straight. The putt was about 25 feet, but by that time the hole looked like a barrel." In it went, and Fuzzy tied Bob Goalby's all-time Tour record, a mark that had stood since the 1961 St. Petersburg Open.

PAST WINNERS

Year	Winner	Score
1972	Deane Beman	279
1973	Sam Adams	268
1974	Dave Stockton	271
1975	Roger Maltbie	275
1976	John Lister	268
1977	Mike Morley	267
1978	Victor Regalado	269
1979	D.A. Weibring	266
1980	Scott Hoch	266
1981	*Dave Barr	270
1982	Payne Stewart	268
1983	*Danny Edwards	266
1984	Scott Hoch	266
1985	Dan Forsman	267
1986	Mark Wiebe	268
1987	Kenny Knox	265

*Playoff

2nd hole

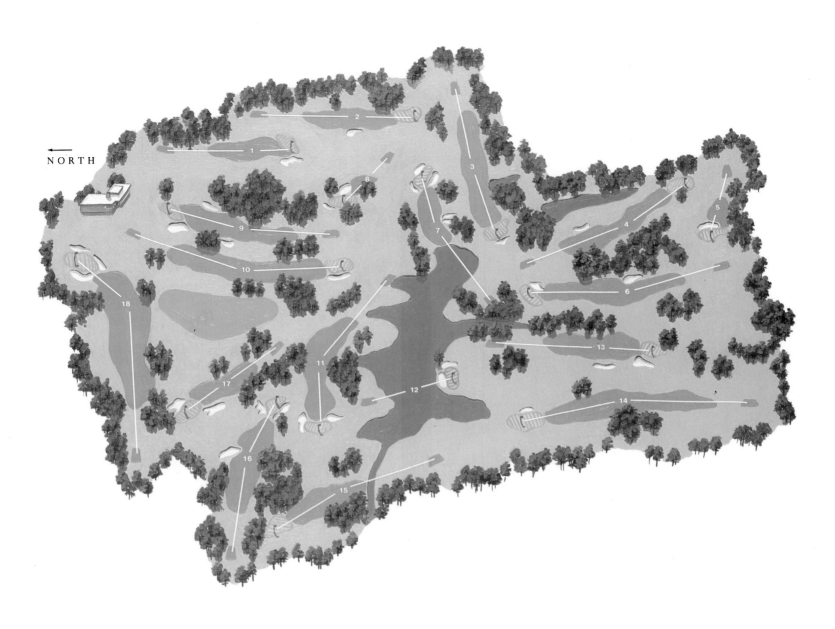

NORTH

3rd hole

SCORECARD

Hole	Yards	Par	PGA Tour Avg. Score
1	402	4	4.061
2	341	4	3.890
3	442	4	4.171
4	450	4	4.307
5	148	3	2.884
6	514	5	4.489
7	326	4	3.795
8	172	3	3.055
9	433	4	4.017
OUT	3228	35	34.669
10	508	5	4.635
11	386	4	3.955
12	160	3	3.072
13	432	4	4.196
14	442	4	4.130
15	405	4	4.021
16	384	4	3.960
17	210	3	3.121
18	384	4	4.099
IN	3311	35	35.189
TOTAL	6539	70	69.858

WARWICK HILLS
Golf and Country Clubs

14th hole

Soon after its launch in 1958 with the richest purse in professional golf ($52,000), the Buick Open developed problems. With an excruciatingly long course, lukewarm support from the sponsor, and unpropitious dates on the Tour calendar, the tournament failed to attract top players. It lurched through its first decade and sputtered to a halt in 1969. But in 1977 an updated model appeared on the Tour, and today, with a friendlier course, solid backing from General Motors, and loyal attendance from some of the game's most popular players, the Buick is back and stronger than ever.

Billy Casper won the inaugural event in 1958, on his twenty-seventh birthday, edging Arnold Palmer on the final hole. A year later, Art Wall added a Buick victory to The Masters jacket he had collected that spring. Mike Souchak took the 1960 title, and in 1961 another Masters champion, Jack Burke, Jr. was the winner. In those years, Buick presented cars to the top finishers. The money was good, and so were the fields.

Still, from the back tees the course was so lengthy and tough that one almost needed a Buick to get through it. At 7,280 yards, it was the longest track on the Tour. Most of the fairways were dead-straight, most of the greens were dead-flat. Sam Snead referred to it as "just a long walk." Charm was absent, and after a short time, so were the big-name players.

The 1963 event was also hurt by its slot on the schedule: a week before the U.S. Open. The big three—Arnold Palmer, Jack Nicklaus, and Gary Player—skipped it in favor of extra practice. But Julius Boros came, won, and then won the U.S. Open at Brookline, beating Palmer and Jackie Cupit in a playoff. A year later, the Buick preceded the British Open. Again, many stars stayed away. One exception was Tony Lema, who thrilled the fans by birdieing six holes in a row during the second round en route to victory. A day later he flew to Scotland where, without a single practice round on the inscrutable Old Course at St. Andrews, he won the British Open.

Lema was in fact the darling of the early Buick Open, winning again in 1965, this time on the 18th hole, over Jack Nicklaus. When Champagne Tony's plane crashed in 1966 the tournament began to sag. When General Motors canceled it, few expected it to return. But local golf supporters, led by club pro Larry Mancour, kept alive

an unofficial version of the tournament during the early and mid-seventies, while a complete redesign of the golf course grew to maturity. When Buick decided it was ready to try again, in 1977, a tournament administration and a tournament course were ready as well.

When Joe Lee took over the redesign of Warwick Hills, he had a mission. "Golfers want a challenge," he said, "but a fair one. They don't want to play a course feeling that the architect has his foot on their necks all the way around."

So Lee took 260 yards off the back markers, replacing the yardage with contours and curves on the fairways and undulations on the greens. Today the course demands only medium length, but requires a variety of shotmaking and short-game skills as well.

After a good birdie opportunity at the first hole, the challenge begins on number two, a 431-yard par four that plays through two rows of trees along with out-of-bounds on the left. The fairway slopes slightly downward, and the second shot calls for a mid-iron into a green guarded by a large bunker.

Long hitters will have to be careful off the tee of the fifth, where a slightly active right hand will yield a hook out of bounds or into the lake on the left side of the landing area. Still, it is best to favor the left of this mild dogleg right, where the right-hand greenside bunker, dotted with grassy mounds, is nearly as large as the green.

At the par-three eighth, Lee created a two-tiered green that is 43 yards from front to back. Pin position on this hole can thus make a difference of nearly three clubs. And whether it is playing at 150 yards or 200, the tee shot must be accurate because of the two bunkers to the left of the green and the one to the right.

Lots of birdies are made at the start of the back nine, but few players do what Ken Green did in the final round of the 1985 Buick. At the 11th hole he chipped in for a birdie, then made three more at 12, 13, and 14, in the process passing then leader Wayne Grady. Green's fast finish gave him a 67—268 (20-under par) and the first Tour victory of his career.

The pros had best collect their birdies by the time they leave the 14th green, because the final four holes at Warwick constitute as strong a finish as there is on the Tour.

It was at the 15th hole that architect Lee said "No more

1st hole

8th hole

13th hole

Mr. Nice Guy." A par four of 457 yards, this is a hole that only an architect's mother could love. With trees lining both sides and out-of-bounds on the left, it requires a hard, straight drive and then a hard, straight long-iron shot into a green whose entrance is protected by two violin-shaped bunkers.

Sixteen is a three-shot par five even for the pros. Again, accuracy is the number-one objective, with fairway bunkers on both sides of the tee shot landing area. The second must be threaded through a tight tunnel of trees to afford an unobstructed pitch to the angled, two-tiered green. In the Buick, pars and bogeys come with equal frequency on this hole.

In 1962 Jerry Barber scored the first televised hole-in-one on Warwick's 17th. Back then it played 222 yards. Today it is only 182, but four bunkers gape at approaching tee shots, and the green is the most fiercely sloped on the course. Lee also reworked this green so that it sits in a natural amphitheater, one of the first examples of stadium golf.

When Jack Nicklaus played in his first Buick Open as an amateur, he looked at the 18th and said, "Now this is a good finishing hole. It would be so easy to tighten up and sail one out-of-bounds on the left. I must remember to keep the tee shot way right." A few years later, Jack came to that hole needing a birdie to have a chance of tieing Tony Lema and forcing a playoff. In one of the rare instances in which he did not hit a good shot under pressure, Nicklaus unloaded a hook so wide and deep that it was still rising as it passed over the out-of-bounds fence.

The hole psyched-out Nicklaus, and it has conquered scores of lesser players in the past three decades. A par four of 435 yards, it plays into the teeth of the prevailing wind to the shallowest target on the course. Indeed, anyone who can birdie this monster deserves to win something.

And yet this hole, and the golf course in general, have won the praise of the pros. Players such as Ben Crenshaw, David Graham, Peter Jacobsen, Tom Kite, and Lanny Wadkins count Warwick II among their favorite courses on the Tour and prove their loyalty with consistent attendance at the Buick. General Motors is happy with its association with the tournament, and for the time being at least, the golf fans in Michigan have something to believe in.

ALL TIME TOURNAMENT RECORDS

Record	Player(s)	Score	Year
Low 18	Denis Watson	63	1984
	Mark Calcavecchia		1986
	Robert Wrenn		1987
	Trevor Dodds		1987
Low first 36	Robert Wrenn	128 (65–63)	1987
Low 36	Robert Wrenn	128 (65–63)	1987
Low first 54	Robert Wrenn	195 (65–63–67)	1987
Low 54	Robert Wrenn	195 (65–63–67)	1987
Low 72	Robert Wrenn	262 (65–63–67–67)	1987
Highest winning	Billy Casper	285	1958
Largest winning margin	Robert Wrenn (262)	7 strokes	1987
Largest 18-hole lead	Julius Boros (66)	2 strokes	1963
Largest 36-hole lead	Rex Caldwell (132)	5 strokes	1980
Largest 54-hole lead	Julius Boros (205)	6 strokes	1963
Lowest start by winner	Hale Irwin Robert Wrenn	65	1981 1987
Highest start by winner	Tom Weiskopf	73	1968
Lowest finish by winner	Lanny Wadkins Wayne Levi	65	1982 1983
Highest finish by winner	Art Wall Bill Collins Hale Irwin	72	1959 1962 1981
Best final-round comeback	Peter Jacobsen (209)	6 back	1980
Lowest 36-hole cut score		141	1986 1987
Highest 36-hole cut score		155	1958

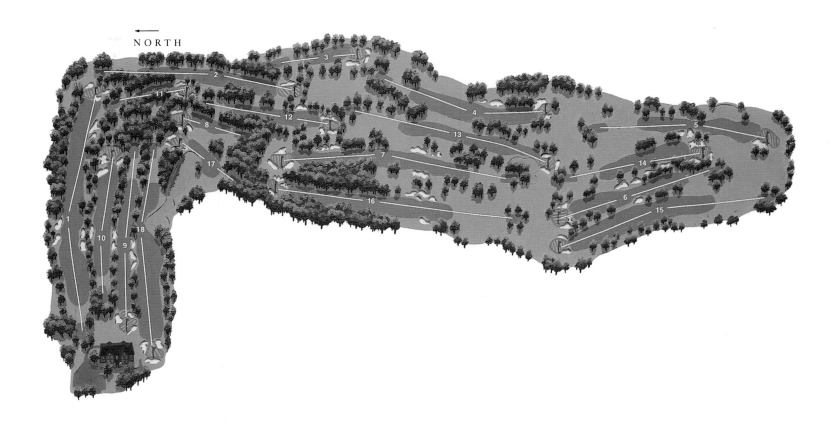

THE PRESSURE TEE SHOT
BY WAYNE LEVI

Holes, such as the 18th at Warwick Hills, where out-of-bounds looms down one side, present a challenge for all golfers. For better players, they also present a decision.

It's one of the age-old questions of golf instruction: Do you start the ball at the trouble and work it back into safety, or do you aim the ball well away from the trouble and play a straight shot or one that works from the safe side of the hole into the center of the fairway?

I tend to agree with the former strategy. Particularly if you have a consistent pattern to your shots, either a fade or draw, you should go with that pattern. Aim a fade or slice at trouble on the left, a draw or hook at trouble on the right, and then let the shot drift back into a good position.

I like this tactic because it's an aggressive, confident shot based on a known ability. When you take the other tack and try to play it safe, doubt invariably creeps in during the

swing. Fearing leads to steering and that leads to veering. So face up to intimidating tee shots—aim your drive at the worst trouble and work the ball back to position A.

Wayne Levi won the Buick Open in 1983.

SCORECARD

Hole	Yards	Par	PGA Tour Avg. Score
1	567	5	4.951
2	431	4	4.156
3	187	3	3.046
4	401	4	4.049
5	437	4	4.058
6	421	4	4.029
7	584	5	4.887
8	181	3	3.020
9	413	4	4.040
OUT	3622	36	36.236
10	401	4	4.021
11	190	3	3.011
12	335	4	3.786
13	490	5	4.491
14	332	4	3.794
15	457	4	4.221
16	580	5	4.924
17	182	3	3.026
18	435	4	4.152
IN	3402	36	35.426
TOTAL	7024	72	71.662

PAST WINNERS

Year	Winner	Score
1958	Billy Casper	285
1959	Art Wall	282
1960	Mike Souchak	282
1961	Jack Burke, Jr.	284
1962	Bill Collins	284
1963	Julius Boros	274
1964	Tony Lema	277
1965	Tony Lema	280
1966	Phil Rodgers	284
1967	Julius Boros	283
1968	Tom Weiskopf	280
1969	Dave Hill	277
1970–		
1974	No tournaments	
1975	(2T) Spike Kelley	208
1976	(2T) Ed Sabo	279
1977	Bobby Cole	271
1978	*Jack Newton	280
1979	*John Fought	280
1980	Peter Jacobsen	276
1981	*Hale Irwin	277
1982	Lanny Wadkins	273
1983	Wayne Levi	272
1984	Denis Watson	271
1985	Ken Green	268
1986	Ben Crenshaw	270
1987	Robert Wrenn	262

*Playoff

BUTLER NATIONAL
Golf Club

BEATRICE
WESTERN OPEN
ILLINOIS

When, in the late sixties, millionaire sportsman Paul Butler decided to bring golf to his Oak Brook recreation complex, he sought a course of championship caliber. George and Tom Fazio gave it to him in spades. Most of the pros agree that Butler National is the most demanding venue on the PGA Tour. Its USGA rating is 76.9, one of the highest in the *nation*.

What makes it tough? Everything. Gargantuan length, ubiquitous water, diabolical bunkering, unpredictable winds, trees everywhere, and greens that are tougher to read than the Koran. Indeed, among Butler's myriad perils, mere lightning may be the mildest.

8th hole

Butler National conjures bright memories for Tom Watson—and dark ones for Lee Trevino. Watson, with eight major championships, three dozen victories, and $4 million in prize winnings, is securely ranked among the greatest players in the history of golf. But he made his breakthrough pro Tour win at Butler, and he still sees that as the biggest thrill of his career.

Certainly, Butler National was the site of the worst moment in the career of Lee Trevino. It was here in the 1975 Western Open that he, along with fellow pros Jerry Heard and Bobby Nichols, was felled by lightning. Supermex was hospitalized briefly, and although he returned to the Tour the same year, the experience wrought permanent damage to his back. Today, however, he refers to it with characteristic good humor. His advice to anyone caught in a thunderstorm: "Grab a 1-iron and hold it high over your head; not even God can hit a 1-iron."

Butler National was founded as an all-male club, and the course requires an all-male game. For the pros in the Western Open it plays to 7,097 yards, but that is from just a bit past the middle tees. From the members' blue markers, it is 7,303 yards—and par is not 72 but 71!

Water comes into play nineteen times in 18 holes, sometimes in heroic proportion, such as at the fifth hole, a par

5th hole

three calling for a tee shot of more than 200 yards, the last 150 of which are liquid. In 1974 this hole yielded a hole-in-one to a most unlikely assailant, Bob Hope. He used a driver.

Paul Butler and his associates chose the Fazio team as their architects because of George's reputation for blending his courses inconspicuously into the natural terrain. Butler wanted to save as much of the character of his rolling, heavily wooded property as possible. At times, however, the owner's protective instinct impeded the design. Bill

Gahlberg, the real estate developer who first urged Butler to build the course, sympathized with the requirements of the Fazios and conspired with George and Tom behind the boss's back. Shortly after Butler's death, Gahlberg revealed the details of the subterfuge.

"The ninth hole was a forest from tee to green," he said, "but Paul wouldn't let us cut down any of the trees. Our solution was to give the trees 'Dutch elm disease,' at least that's what we told Paul. Actually, we used a bulldozer to crack the trees and break up their root systems. Within a few weeks they would begin to wilt. Then I'd bring Paul out and get his permission to cut the dying specimens. We went through this several times before we could clear a sufficient number of the huge oaks that were on that hole. And it's still one of the narrowest fairways in golf."

Fazio wanted to prune in other places, but Butler put his foot down. As a result, Butler National sports a couple of holes that only Paul Bunyan could love. The seventh, a 617-yard, double-doglegging par five, not only is lined by forest on both sides but actually has trees in the *center of the fairway* as well.

The eighth is a beautiful little par three across Salt Creek. It is, according to Tom Kite, "probably the best hole on the golf course." Water borders the front and right

14th hole

sides, trees crowd the left and back. Missing this green virtually guarantees a bogey or worse.

The 12th hole is a rarity on the PGA Tour—a par five for the pros that is a converted par four for members. The only real birdie hole on the course, it was played in an average of 4.45 strokes during the first ten years of Western Opens at Butler.

When Bill Shean, several times the club champion at Butler, was asked what advice he would give to visiting golfers, he said, "Bring two dozen balls and don't try to be a hero." That counsel could certainly apply to the 14th hole. It was here that two-time U.S. Open champion Julius Boros once made a 12 and that Bob Dickson, leading the tournament in the final round in 1976, made an 8.

Larry Nelson, the 1979 Western Open champion, calls Butler's 17th hole "one of the better holes we play on the Tour." At 459 yards, it requires power, but the approach must be played carefully to a bi-level green, one of the fastest on the course.

It was on this 17th green in 1985 that Western history was made, as Scott Verplank sank a six-foot par putt to defeat Jim Thorpe in sudden death, thus becoming the first amateur to win a Tour event since Gene Littler in the 1954 Andy Williams Open. Verplank, the defending U.S.

Amateur champion at the time, had also won the Western Amateur.

Butler saves its fiercest hole for last. The 18th is one of the grand finales in golf. It begins with a tight tee shot calling for a power fade between trees on the left and more trees and water on the right. Anything less than a grade-A drive will leave no view of the distant green, which is tucked to the left between two bends of Salt Creek. A large oak tree— one of the specimens that Paul Butler would not allow to be chopped—sits dead center in the fairway, about 70 yards short of the green, further complicating an already formidable assignment.

Without question, this is the meanest hole on a very mean golf course. When Bob Gilder shot a course-record 64 in 1982, he virtually mastered the first 17 holes, posting 10 birdies and an eagle, but then double-bogeyed 18. In the same year, Tom Weiskopf set the 72-hole record, thanks to a spectacular birdie on mean 18. "I was trailing Larry Nelson by a stroke when we came to the 18th tee," Weiskopf recalls. "He hit his second shot onto the green about 90 feet from the hole. I had about 170 yards and I hit a 6-iron that finished about six feet from the hole. Larry didn't get his approach putt inside mine, and then he missed his second putt. I made mine for a two-stroke swing and a one-stroke

18th hole

ALL TIME TOURNAMENT RECORDS

Record	Player(s)	Score	Year
Low 18	Cary Middlecoff	63	1955
Low first 36	Hugh Royer	132 (67–65)	1970
Low 36	Hugh Royer	132 (67–65)	1970
Low first 54	Sam Snead	201 (69–67–65)	1949
Low 54	Sam Snead	199 (67–65–67)	1949
Low 72	Sam Snead	268 (69–67–65–67)	1949
	Chi Chi Rodriguez	268 (64–69–68–67)	1964
Highest winning score	Alex Smith	318	1903
Largest winning margin	Walter Hagen (279)	9 strokes	1926
Largest 18-hole lead	David Graham (65)	3 strokes	1975
Largest 36-hole lead	Bob Dickson (136)	6 strokes	1976
Largest 54-hole lead	Tom Weiskopf (212)	5 strokes	1974
	Bob Dickson (210)		1976
	Scott Simpson (209)		1980
Best final-round comeback	Tom Kite (218)	7 back	1986
Lowest start by winner	Chi Chi Rodriguez	64	1964
Highest start by winner	Robert Simpson	84	1907
Lowest finish by winner	Cary Middlecoff	63	1955
Highest finish by winner	Jock Hutchison	80	1920
Lowest 36-hole cut score		147	1984
Highest 36-hole cut score		153	1974–1976

victory." Weiskopf calls that 170-yard 6-iron the finest shot of his pro career.

The victory was a meaningful one for the tall, talented, and tempestuous Ohioan, one of the most enigmatic players the game has produced. Twenty years earlier he had won the Western Amateur, thereby gaining a berth in the 1964 Western Open. In that tournament he earned his first paycheck as a pro, tieing for 30th place and a prize of $487.50. Each year since 1964, Weiskopf has sent a check for $487.50 to the Western Open's well-known charity, the Evans Caddie Scholar Program. When he won, he donated $4,875.

The Western Open is administered by the Western Golf Association, a non-profit organization of 450 clubs in the Midwest, with headquarters in the village of Golf, north of Chicago. The WGA was founded in 1899 by ten Chicago area clubs, and in the same year held its first Western Open. It was won by Willie Smith of Carnoustie, Scotland, who a week later won the U.S. Open, lapping the field by 11 strokes. Since then the Western has been won by nearly every major player in the game—Walter Hagen (five times), Tommy Armour, Gene Sarazen, Ralph Guldahl (three times), Byron Nelson, Jimmy Demaret, Ben Hogan (twice), Sam Snead (twice), Arnold Palmer (twice), Billy Casper (four times), Jack Nicklaus (twice), and Tom Watson (three times).

It is the second oldest professional championship in the United States (the U.S. Open is four years older), and with Butler National now its permanent site, it may be the most difficult to win.

PAST WINNERS

Year	Winner	Score	Year	Winner	Score	Year	Winner	Score	Year	Winner	Score
1899	*Willie Smith	156	1922	Mike Brady	291	1946	Ben Hogan	271	1969	Billy Casper	276
1900	No Tournament		1923	Jock Hutchinson	281	1947	Johnny Palmer	270	1970	Hugh Royer	273
1901	L. Auchterlonie	160	1924	W. Mehlhorn	293	1948	*Ben Hogan	281	1971	Bruce Crampton	279
1902	Willie Anderson	299	1925	Mac Smith	281	1949	Sam Snead	268	1972	Jim Jamieson	271
1903	Alex Smith	318	1926	Walter Hagen	279	1950	Sam Snead	282	1973	Billy Casper	272
1904	Willie Anderson	304	1927	Walter Hagen	281	1951	Marty Furgol	270	1974	Tom Watson	287
1905	Arthur Smith	278	1928	Abe Espinosa	291	1952	Lloyd Mangrum	274	1975	Hale Irwin	283
1906	Alex Smith	306	1929	Tommy Armour	273	1953	Dutch Harrison	278	1976	Al Geiberger	288
1907	Robert Simpson	307	1930	Gene Sarazen	278	1954	*Lloyd Mangrum	277	1977	Tom Watson	283
1908	Willie Anderson	299	1931	Ed Dudley	280	1955	Cary Middlecoff	272	1978	*Andy Bean	282
1909	Willie Anderson	288	1932	Walter Hagen	287	1956	*Mike Fetchick	284	1979	*Larry Nelson	286
1910	**Charles Evans, Jr.	6&5	1933	Mac Smith	282	1957	*Doug Ford	279	1980	Scott Simpson	281
1911	Robt. Simpson	2&1	1934	*Harry Cooper	274	1958	Doug Sanders	275	1981	Ed Fiori	277
1912	Mac Smith	299	1935	John Revolta	290	1959	Mike Souchak	272	1982	Tom Weiskopf	276
1913	J. J. McDermott	295	1936	Ralph Guldahl	274	1960	*Stan Leonard	278	1983	Mark McCumber	284
1914	Jim Barnes	293	1937	*Ralph Guldahl	288	1961	Arnold Palmer	271	1984	*Tom Watson	280
1915	Tom McNamara	304	1938	Ralph Guldahl	279	1962	Jacky Cupit	281	1985	**Scott Verplank	279
1916	Walter Hagen	286	1939	Byron Nelson	281	1963	*Arnold Palmer	280	1986	*Tom Kite	286
1917	Jim Barnes	283	1940	*Jimmy Demaret	293	1964	Chi Chi Rodriguez	268	1987	‡D.A. Weibring	208
1918	No Tournament		1941	Ed Oliver	275	1965	Billy Casper	270			
1919	Jim Barnes	283	1942	Herman Barron	276	1966	Billy Casper	283	*Playoff		
1920	Jock Hutchison	296	1943–			1967	Jack Nicklaus	274	**Amateur		
1921	Walter Hagen	287	1945	No Tournaments		1968	Jack Nicklaus	273	‡Rain curtailed		

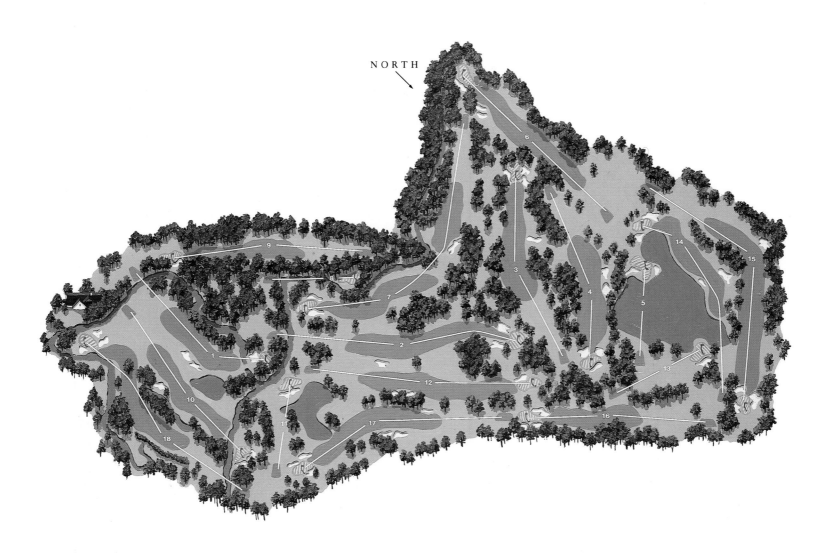

THE LOB SHOT
BY SCOTT VERPLANK

On a long, difficult golf course such as Butler National, everyone is bound to miss a few greens. And at Butler the recovery shots are tough because the rough is fairly heavy and the greens are hard and fast. Often the only way to get close to the pin is to play a lob shot.

The lob is golf's version of the knuckleball, a soft, spinless shot that plops down and sits where it hits, with almost no roll even on a slick green. I play the lob almost the same way I do an explosion from a bunker. I take an open stance, with my body aligned well to the left of the target. I also open and lay back the face of the sand wedge so that it points to the right of the target and has plenty

of loft. As with a sand shot, I hit about an inch behind the ball, assuming I'm in fluffy rough. The basic swing is a break-and-hold: I break my wrists quickly on the backswing to set up a steep angle of attack to the ball. But through impact, I swing only my arms with no uncocking of my wrists. This keeps the clubface open and lofted and also produces the knuckleball effect.

Once you've mastered this shot, you can be fairly aggressive with it. On most lobs you can fly the ball at least halfway to the hole, then let it trickle the rest of the way.

———————

Scott Verplank won the 1985 Western Open as an amateur, the first amateur to win a Tour event since Gene Littler in 1954.

SCORECARD

Hole	Yards	Par	PGA Tour Avg. Score
1	371	4	4.073
2	566	5	4.967
3	412	4	4.083
4	405	4	4.166
5	201	3	3.273
6	435	4	4.191
7	617	5	5.118
8	177	3	3.186
9	430	4	4.324
OUT	3614	36	37.381
10	392	4	4.373
11	176	3	3.140
12	478	5	4.615
13	167	3	3.084
14	405	4	4.339
15	583	5	5.067
16	381	4	4.119
17	459	4	4.245
18	442	4	4.314
IN	3483	36	37.296
TOTAL	7097	72	74.677

CASTLE PINES *Golf Club*

THE INTERNATIONAL COLORADO

Like most golfers, Jack Vickers uses fourteen clubs. Like many golfers, he has two sets of clubs at his disposal. Like no other golfer, however, Vickers's second set of golf clubs consists of the following: Augusta National Golf Club; Broadmoor Golf Club; Butler National Golf Club; Castle Pines Golf Club; Cherry Hills Country Club; Denver Country Club; Eldorado Country Club; Garden of the Gods Club; The Honors Course; La Quinta Golf Club; Old Baldy Club; Rolling Rock Club; Shinnecock Hills Golf Club; and The Vintage Club.

Vickers, chairman of The Vickers Company (a conglomerate of real estate, farming, stock investments, minerals,

and oil and gas properties), is a man of many interests, multiple talents, and much money. He usually gets what he wants. And for a decade or so, what he wanted most was his own world-class golf course and a major professional tournament to hold on it. In October of 1981, he got the former—Castle Pines—and in August of 1986, the latter—The International.

Neither came easily. For eleven years he tried to buy the rolling pine-clad land near Castle Rock, Colorado, about a half hour and 1,000 feet above Denver, and for eleven years he was unsuccessful. Then, in the late seventies, his perseverance was rewarded with an okay to purchase a 5,000-acre tract. Immediately Vickers called in Jack Nicklaus as his architect. Together, they walked across the land several times, then crossed several times more in a helicopter. In 1979 Nicklaus and his crew began construction, and in 1981 the course opened to strongly favorable reviews.

With the course in place, Vickers turned his attention to the matter of the golf tournament. With forty-odd events already crowding the calendar, the PGA Tour was not looking for another tournament. But Vickers had that problem solved; his would not be just another event. First, The International would be an invitational that would live

6th hole

10th hole

7th hole

18th hole

up to its name, with a field of pros from all over the world. Second, the prize money would be formidable—$1 million overall and a record $180,000 going to the winner. But the unique aspect—the hook—was Vickers's proposed format, the Stableford System, with points awarded in relation to par minus three points for double bogeys, minus one for bogeys, nothing for pars, two points for birdies, five for eagles, and a whopping eight points in the event of a double eagle. The Stableford has long been a popular format for club golf events, but until Vickers, no one had suggested it for the PGA Tour.

A gimmick? Perhaps, but it came at a time when the Tour was looking for new and different formats to help sustain interest in the professional side of the game. With events such as the Skins Game, the Nissan Cup, and the Legends of Golf attracting attention, Vickers's proposal seemed cogent. Commissioner Deane Beman decided it was good for golf—especially with a $1 million purse. The Tour found a spot for the tournament on the schedule and announced a multi-year agreement beginning in 1986.

The tournament itself runs for five days, with 162 pros competing on Wednesday and Thursday. On Thursday night the field is cut in half, with the top 78 point earners coming back Friday. Again on Friday the field is halved, to 39, with a final cut on Saturday night leaving 18 players for the shootout on Sunday. Since point totals are not cumulative from day to day, those 18 players begin the final round all even with $700,000 of the million dollars at stake.

"The Stableford format should bring a new aggressive approach to tournament golf," says Nicklaus. "In playing for points rather than protecting a total score, a player is forced to attack the course more than usual."

At 7,495 yards, this is the biggest battlefield on the Tour, and it begins with the Tour's longest hole, a 644-yard par five. If that sounds like an unlikely place to gun for birdies and eagles, keep in mind that the hole plays downhill all the way and that the Colorado air means a 10–15 percent diminution in distance. A player such as Greg Norman will reach this hole with a driver and an iron.

Wind is a factor at the linkslike third and fourth, the only area on the course not lined with trees. Into a stiff wind, the tee shot at the 205-yard fourth is one of the most difficult swings of the day. The hardest hole on the course is arguably number five, 477 uphill yards, with bunkers confronting both the drive and the approach.

One of Nicklaus's architectural preferences is for downhill holes, and the 10th at Castle Pines is a shining example. This par four is 485 yards long and almost that many yards down. A lush, tumbling carpet of fairway through

deep stands of pine and oak, it is reminiscent of—and every bit as beautiful as—the famed 10th hole at Augusta National. The major difference is that this hole is even more difficult.

Although the fairway is amply wide, the second shot of 200 yards or more will have to be played from a downhill and/or sidehill lie to an angled green that is guarded by a large pond. Four is an excellent score here.

Four is not a bad score on the 12th hole either, a tight 422-yarder where the approach is to a narrow green with a bunker on the right and a rocky stream on the left.

If Nicklaus had a weak moment in designing this course, it was at the par-three 16th where he plotted a "gathering bunker" at the front-left of the green. Gathering bunkers are throwbacks to the old pot bunkers of Scotland. They attract anything that bounces or rolls near their edges. The three such bunkers at Castle Pines have no sand but do have steep-faced banks. When the pin on this lengthy par three is at the brink of such a bank, at the top of the gathering bunker, there is virtually no way to get a ball close to it. Even some of Castle Pines's most loyal members concede that this gambit is contrived.

But if a four is wrought at the 16th, another four may easily be gotten at the par-five 17th, at 492 yards the shortest par five on the course.

Number 18 is marked by another Nicklaus signature, the double fairway. Long hitters usually will take the high road on the right, a tee shot over a bunker-filled hill which, once carried, allows for a long, bounding draw to within short-iron distance of the hole. Shorter hitters may opt for the lower fairway, actually a more direct route, where an accurate drive leaves a level lie and an approach over bunkers to the amphitheater green.

Unquestionably, one of the finest holes at Castle Pines is the 19th. This is an exclusive club with a clear taste for the finer things. Like Augusta National, membership is by invitation only, and it has been so from the beginning. Founder Vickers invited twelve of his friends to join as partners in his venture at a cost of $500,000 each. Then each of these twelve Disciples, as they are known, was asked to invite a few friends of his own. And so on until the membership of grand old men reached the planned number of 350.

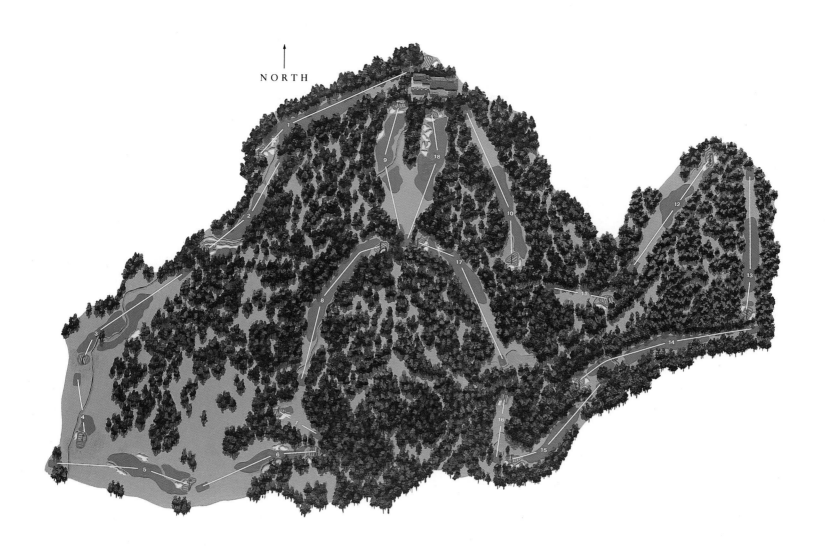

DOWNHILL LIES
BY JACK NICKLAUS

If I could design my ideal golf course, all of the holes would play downhill so that on each tee the golfer could see everything that he was about to play. At Castle Pines, each nine begins with a steeply downhill hole, and the second shots on those holes can be demanding ones.

When playing downhill from the fairway, the first key is to tilt yourself so that you're perpendicular to the slope. In effect, give yourself a flat lie. To prevent falling forward, put most of your weight on your back foot at address and keep it there throughout the swing. To help maintain balance, you should make this an arm-and-wrist swing and minimize your body turn. On the downswing, try to make your clubhead "chase" out after the ball through impact.

Off a downhill lie, the ball will tend to fly lower and thus travel farther than normal, so club appropriately. And if the slope is so severe that you are bound to lose balance, allow for a pushed shot by aiming a few yards left of your target.

Jack Nicklaus is the designer of the Castle Pines course.

SCORECARD

Hole	Yards	Par
1	644	5
2	408	4
3	452	4
4	205	3
5	477	4
6	417	4
7	185	3
8	535	5
9	458	4
OUT	3781	36
10	485	4
11	197	3
12	422	4
13	431	4
14	595	5
15	403	4
16	209	3
17	492	5
18	480	4
IN	3714	36
TOTAL	7495	72

FIRESTONE *Country Club*

16th hole

No one on the Tour can remember a shot equal to the one played by John Mahaffey in the 1984 World Series of Golf. On the 464-yard 18th hole at Firestone Country Club, Mahaffey's lengthy approach sailed well wide of the target and lodged briefly in the upper reaches of a large elm. Eventually tumbling earthward, it conked a female spectator on the head. From there the ball caromed toward the green, where it landed softly, rolled several feet across a slope, and plopped into the diametric center of the cup. Eagle two—the *first* eagle the hole had ever yielded.

The odds against such a shot are a million to one. That is why it happened at Firestone. Between 1954 and 1984, this golf course hosted more major professional tournaments by far than any other venue in America—fifty-five events in thirty years. And over that time, nearly one million competitive shots were played.

When Harvey S. Firestone opened his club in 1929, professional golf was the furthest thing from his mind. He had built the course purely as a recreational facility for the employees of his Firestone Tire and Rubber Company. Still, in 1954 it was strong enough to host the first Rubber City Open, in which Tommy Bolt shot a torrid 265—23-under par—and took home the first prize of $2,400.

The course lasted five more years, but when Firestone was nominated to host the 1960 PGA Championship, Robert Trent Jones was called in to stiffen the challenge. The result was major surgery; he built fifty new bunkers, added two ponds, enlarged the greens to twice their original size, and stretched the rubber man's course to a backbreaking 7,173 yards—all while reducing the par from 72 to 70.

That PGA was won by Jay Hebert on a score of 281—one-over par—and 14 strokes higher than Tom Neiporte's victory on the "same" course a year earlier. The success of that tournament spurred the birth of the American Golf Classic, which replaced the Rubber City at Firestone and ran for a decade and a half.

Two years later, a Chicago entrepreneur named Walter Schwimmer hatched the idea of bringing together the winners of the four major championships—The Masters, U.S. Open, British Open, and PGA Championship—in a late-season mini-event over 36 holes. In 1962 the World Series of Golf was born, with a field of just three players—Arnold Palmer (who had won both The Masters and British Open), Jack Nicklaus, and Gary Player. With golf's Big Three in its first event, the World Series got off to a flying start.

9th hole

2nd hole

10th hole

Nicklaus won the $50,000 first prize, and the tournament became a fixture on the PGA Tour. It has since expanded to include a large field of both American and international players.

During the sixties and seventies, Firestone hosted fourteen American Golf Classics, three PGA Championships, eight CBS Golf Classics, and the World Series every year. Since most of those events were televised, Firestone quickly became the most recognizable golf course in America.

Critics say the course is charmless, monotonous. Virtually all of its fairways run straight and parallel to one another, and few of the par threes and fours call for an approach shot with anything shorter than a long iron. Subtlety is not the strong suit at Firestone. However, the course has the near-unanimous admiration of the Tour players, who see it as a supremely honest, straightforward examination of their skills.

"It's a great test of golf. Every shot is demanding," says Nicklaus, whose record on the course is incredible even by his herculean standards. Jack has won seven tournaments at Firestone—five World Series, one American Golf Classic, and the 1975 PGA Championship. His prize winnings on this course alone total more than a half million dollars.

The front nine features a string of holes that perhaps only Nicklaus could love. After a comparatively benign (399-yard) opening par four and a bona fide birdie opportunity at the par-five second, Firestone bares its teeth with a stretch that includes five par fours averaging 458 yards and two "short" holes of 234 and 219 yards.

The back nine starts similarly to the front, with two relatively manageable par fours. Ten is the tougher of the two, calling for a pin-straight drive through a chute of trees. The greens at both 10 and 11 are closely bunkered and nightmarishly difficult to hold. Such is also the case at the par-three 12th, where an elevated green is guarded in front, left, and right by sand. Accuracy is doubly important here because the hole normally plays into the face of the wind.

Number 13 is thought by many to be the finest hole on the course, a 457-yard dogleg to the right. The tee shot landing area is guarded by a bunker on the left and a large, encroaching tree on the right, encouraging the golfer to play a fade between the two, and lengthening a long hole still further. Four bunkers ring the green, which slopes hard from back to front. A shot that strays into the heavy rough beyond the green virtually guarantees bogey or worse.

Par is a good score at the 221-yard 15th, where the narrow green is bunkered closely on both sides. The pros play anything from a 4-iron to a 3-wood. Gary Player would have been pleased to take par here one Monday morning in 1974, for it was on this hole that Lee Trevino sank a three-foot putt for par to beat Player in the longest playoff in the history of the series. The two had tied with one-under-par 139s that year, then had gone back to the 14th for sudden death. But they then tied five holes in a row. With darkness closing in, tournament director Jack Tuthill called an overnight moratorium. The next morning both teed off again on 14 and both made birdies. Then Trevino's 1-iron found the green at 15 while Player's 2-iron hit sand. Gary two-putted for bogey, and Lee sank a three-footer to win.

The 625-yard 16th hole is one of the most famous and feared in golf. For decades it has elicited the best and worst play. It was here in 1960 that Arnold Palmer saw the end of his bid to become the first player to win the American Slam. Palmer had won The Masters and the U.S. Open, and had finished second in the British Open. In the PGA at Firestone, he was in strong contention when he came to the 16th tee in the third round. But he hit a succession of less than desirable shots and finally wrote an 8 on his card. Later, he dubbed the hole "The Monster" and included it in a book listing his all-time

1st hole

11th hole

17th hole

18th hole

favorite eighteen holes in golf. "It has everything mean and nasty," Palmer wrote. "Bunkers, ditches, trees, water—you name it—everything that's troublesome, plus a green that is so hard the ball winces when it lands."

The hole plays downwind and sharply downhill, with the fairway banked hard from right to left. A well-hit, drawing drive can run a long way. Still, 625 yards is 625 yards; this is not a green that is reachable in two, at least not by mere mortals. Palmer and a few others have done it; but with a 50-yard pond smack in front of the green, a gambling 3-wood shot of 250 yards is generally not advised. Most players will cosy long irons to a position about 100 yards or so short of the green, then hit a fast-spinning wedge shot at the pin.

The hole has seen some great golf. In 1975 Jack Nicklaus hit his tee shot into trees on the left, took a penalty drop, and then hit his third shot into trees on the right; from there he played a gargantuan 8-iron over the tops of the trees and over the water to 20 feet from the pin. He sank the putt for a par and went on to win.

Somewhat less heroic was the par made by Lon Hinkle in the final round of the 1979 World Series. After pushing his third shot into trees on the right, Hinkle was blocked from the green. The trees blocked a high shot, the water prevented a low shot—at least that was the way it looked. But Hinkle closed the face on his iron, took the club back low and punched the ball straight at the water. It skipped once, twice, three times, and bumped up the bank and onto the green. He made his par and went on to win the tournament.

The 17th hole is short by Firestone standards—just 392 yards—but the driving area is pinched tight by four bunkers, so most players lead with an iron, then play a blind second shot over a pot bunker to the elevated green. A large hogback runs across this green, making it the site of frequent three-putts.

Eighteen is a superb finishing hole—464 treelined yards, slightly downhill, and turned softly from right to left. The best side of the fairway for the approach is the right, but two bunkers there caution against too aggressive a drive. The huge green is surrounded by bunkers and is nestled in a natural amphitheater. Hundred-foot putts are not uncommon here, and neither are three-putt bogeys. Like the course itself, 18 is long, tough, and pure golf from start to finish.

In the future, Firestone is likely to become even tougher. In 1986 Jack Nicklaus's design crew was called in to add more difficult contours to each of the 18 greens while providing additional spectator mounds. So these surfaces, heretofore among the world's hardest to reach, now will likely be among the most difficult to putt as well.

ALL TIME TOURNAMENT RECORDS

Record	Player(s)	Score	Year
Low 18	Denis Watson	62	1984
Low first 36	Denis Watson	131 (69–62)	1984
Low 36	Tom Watson	130 (65–65)	1980 (rounds 3–4)
Low first 54	Denis Watson	201 (69–62–70)	1984
Low 54	Lanny Wadkins	198 (66–67–65)	1977 (rounds 2–3–4)
Low 72	Lanny Wadkins	267 (69–66–67–65)	1977
Highest winning score	Gil Morgan	278 (71–72–67–68)	1978
	Craig Stadler	278 (70–68–75–65)	1982
Largest winning margin	Lanny Wadkins (267)	5 strokes	1977
Largest 18-hole lead	Andy Bean (64)	2 strokes	1979
	Tom Watson (65)		1980
	Bruce Lietzke (66)		1984
Largest 36-hole lead	Nick Price (134)	4 strokes	1984
Largest 54-hole lead	Raymond Floyd (208)	3 strokes	1982
Lowest start by winner	Tom Watson Roger Maltbie	65	1980 1985
Highest start by winner	Gil Morgan	71	1978
Lowest finish by winner	Lanny Wadkins Tom Watson Craig Stadler	65	1977 1980 1982
Highest finish by winner	Dan Pohl Curtis Strange	71	1986 1987
Best final-round comeback	Craig Stadler (213)	5 back	1982
No 36-hole cut score			

PAST WINNERS

Year	Winner	Score
1976	Jack Nicklaus	275
1977	Lanny Wadkins	267
1978	*Gil Morgan	278
1979	Lon Hinkle	272
1980	Tom Watson	270
1981	Bill Rogers	275
1982	*Craig Stadler	278
1983	Nick Price	270
1984	Denis Watson	271
1985	Roger Maltbie	268
1986	Dan Pohl	277
1987	Curtis Strange	275

*Playoff

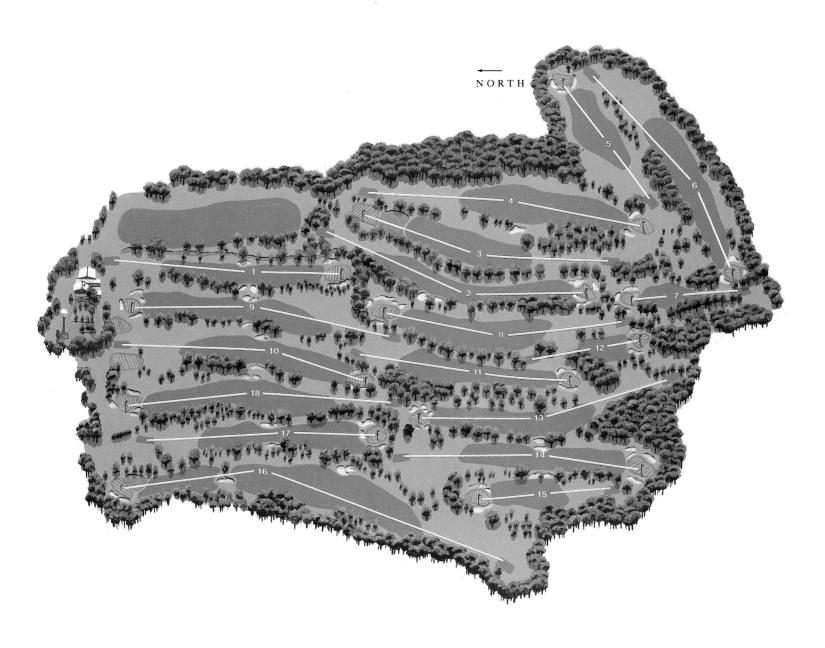

← NORTH

SCORECARD

GETTING UP AND DOWN
BY DENIS WATSON

Ironically, a long course such as Firestone puts a premium on the short game. The longer the holes, the less chance most players have of hitting greens in regulation. Thus, even more than usual, scoring depends on an ability to chip the ball close enough for one putt.

On a basic 20- to 40-foot chip shot from a good lie, I normally use a pitching wedge. I take an open stance and play the ball a little back from the middle, so that my hands are well ahead of the ball. About 60 percent of my weight is on my left side. From this position, I sense a slight hinging of the wrists going back and try to maintain the angle

I have set through impact by allowing my knees to lead the motion back to the ball. I make sure that I do not lose the angle at the back of my right hand, and this ensures a crisp downward stroke. Distance is governed by the length of the backswing, and the follow-through should be shorter than the backswing to maintain acceleration. A good rule is to try to get the ball rolling on the green as soon as possible rather than trying to fly it to the pin. Generally, you should figure on a chip shot to travel a quarter of its distance in the air and three-quarters of the way along the ground.

Denis Watson won the 1984 NEC World Series of Golf.

Hole	Yards	Par	PGA Tour Avg. Score
1	399	4	4.034
2	497	5	4.632
3	442	4	4.022
4	458	4	4.254
5	234	3	3.098
6	469	4	4.203
7	219	3	3.099
8	450	4	4.065
9	470	4	4.246
OUT	3638	35	35.653
10	410	4	3.958
11	370	4	3.875
12	178	3	3.030
13	457	4	4.190
14	418	4	4.054
15	221	3	3.123
16	625	5	4.976
17	392	4	3.952
18	464	4	4.129
IN	3535	35	35.287
TOTAL	7173	70	70.940

COLONIAL *Country Club*

FEDERAL EXPRESS
ST. JUDE
CLASSIC
TENNESSEE

Colonial Country Club is the second-longest course on the PGA Tour. It has treelined, hilly fairways, fast, contoured greens, and water hazards on eight of its last nine holes. Yet Colonial Country Club, in Memphis, Tennessee, is the site of the lowest single-round score in the history of the PGA Tour. It was here on June 10, 1977, that Al Geiberger sank an eight-foot birdie putt for a score of 59.

A 59 on the same course where only a day earlier he had been unable to break par. A 59 on the same day on which no one else shot below 65 and only two other players bettered 68. A 59 on a course where the tournament champions have averaged 69—10 strokes higher.

"I was hitting the ball well, was putting well, and was very confident," Geiberger recalls. "When in the middle of the round I strung together six birdies and an eagle, I knew I had a great round going, but I didn't know how many strokes I was under par. Then, when I got another birdie on my 15th hole of the day, the gallery started yelling '59! 59!' That was the first time I thought about it."

At the ninth hole (Geiberger's last of the day, since he began on the back nine), he hit a 9-iron eight feet from the cup, then ran his birdie putt dead into the center of the hole. His score broke the mark of 60 first set by Al Brosch at Brackenridge Park in San Antonio in 1951 and later tied by Bill Nary, Ted Kroll, Wally Ulrich, Tommy Bolt, Mike Souchak, and Sam Snead.

Colonial will always be remembered for Geiberger's round, but it had been the scene of plenty of excitement before 1977. Ben Hogan came close to winning the final event of his career there in 1960, losing a playoff to Tommy Bolt, who made up seven strokes in the final round.

In 1966 Bert Yancey, leading the tournament, overslept on the morning of the final round. A frantic call from his caddie roused Yancey with ten minutes to go before he had to tee off or be disqualified. Yancey bolted to the course, driving at speeds upwards of 100 miles an hour, and made it to the first tee with a few seconds to spare. Then he shot 66 and won by five strokes.

And in 1971 Lee Trevino used Memphis as a springboard for one of the finest months of golf the game has ever seen. After scoring a victory here, Supermex

16th hole

12th hole

18th hole

ALL TIME TOURNAMENT RECORDS

Record	Player(s)	Score	Year
Low 18	Al Geiberger	59	1977
Low first 36	Al Geiberger	131 (72–59)	1977
Low 36	Al Geiberger	131	1977 (rounds 1–2)
	Al Geiberger	131 (59–72)	1977 (rounds 2–3)
Low first 54	Cary Middlecoff	199 (67–68–64)	1961
	Bert Yancey	(63–69–67)	1966
	Mike Souchak	(65–66–68)	1967
Low 54	Billy Maxwell	198 (65–68–65)	1958
Low 72	Bert Yancey	265 (63–69–67–66)	1966
Highest winning score	Dave Hill	283 (68–69–74–72)	1973
Largest winning margin	Raymond Floyd (271)	6 strokes	1982
Largest 18-hole lead	Fred Marti (65)	2 strokes	1976
Largest 36-hole lead	Al Geiberger (131)	6 strokes	1977
Largest 54-hole lead	Gene Littler (204)	5 strokes	1975
	Raymond Floyd (202)		1982
Lowest start by winner	Bert Yancey Dave Hill	63	1966 1970
Highest start by winner	Tommy Bolt Al Geiberger Gil Morgan	72	1960 1977 1979
Lowest finish by winner	Billy Maxwell Mike Souchak Jack Nicklaus Hal Sutton	65	1958 1964 1965 1985
Highest finish by winner	Dave Hill	73	1967
Best final-round comeback	Hal Sutton (214)	8 back	1985
Lowest 36-hole cut score		144	1974–1983
Highest 36-hole cut score		150	1972–1973

went on in the next four weeks to win the Open Championships of the United States, Canada, and Britain, a feat that has never been equaled. Trevino is a three-time winner at Memphis (1971, 1972, 1980), and Dave Hill won the tournament four times in seven years (1967, 1969, 1970, 1973).

Colonial is also the site of perhaps the most famous non-pro hole-in-one of the modern age. In the same week that Geiberger fired his 59, former President Gerald Ford aced the 199-yard fifth hole. It was his first, and as nearly as anyone can determine, the only hole-in-one ever by a United States president.

PAST WINNERS

Year	Winner	Score	Year	Winner	Score
1958	Billy Maxwell	267	1974	Gary Player	273
1959	*Don Whitt	272	1975	Gene Littler	270
1960	*Tommy Bolt	273	1976	Gibby Gilbert	273
1961	Cary Middlecoff	266	1977	Al Geiberger	273
1962	*Lionel Hebert	267	1978	*Andy Bean	277
1963	*Tony Lema	270	1979	*Gil Morgan	278
1964	Mike Souchak	270	1980	Lee Trevino	272
1965	*Jack Nicklaus	271	1981	Jerry Pate	274
1966	Bert Yancey	265	1982	Raymond Floyd	271
1967	Dave Hill	272	1983	Larry Mize	274
1968	Bob Lunn	268	1984	Bob Eastwood	280
1969	Dave Hill	265	1985	*Hal Sutton	279
1970	Dave Hill	267	1986	Mike Hulbert	280
1971	Lee Trevino	268	1987	Curtis Strange	275
1972	Lee Trevino	281			
1973	Dave Hill	283	*Playoff		

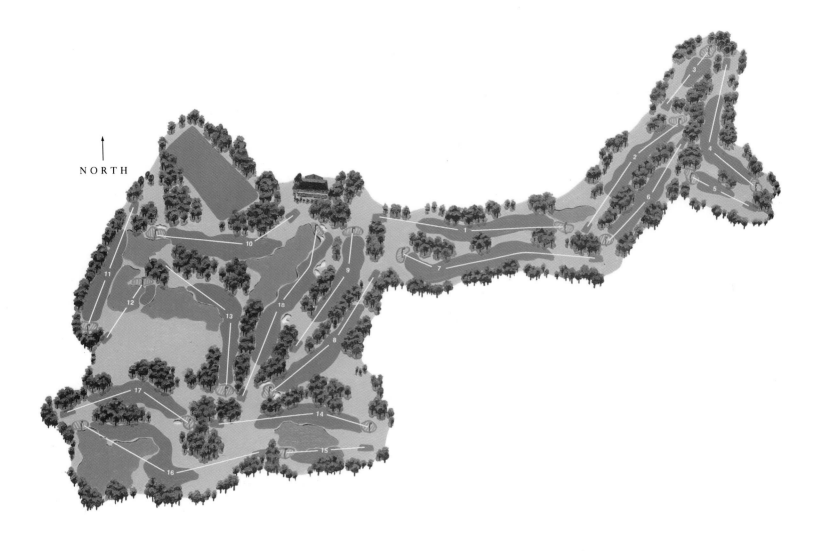

North

PRESSURE PUTTS
BY AL GEIBERGER

It was only the second round of the tournament, but as I stood over my 10-foot putt on the last hole, the pressure was as intense as any I had ever known. The putt was for a 59—and I made it.

I don't claim to be the finest pressure putter in the history of the game, but I do believe that I have the type of stroke that is pressure-resistant. Basically, it is a stiff-wristed pendulum method, a style that minimizes angles and movement in the hands, wrists, and arms.

When you're under pressure, you want to be able to move the putterhead to the hole with as simple an action as possible. The main key is to keep the left wrist firm throughout the stroke. Ideally, your hands should be set slightly ahead of the ball, and your wrists should arch slightly. This setup will give you firmness without tension.

The swing should also be as simple as possible, a simple straight-back movement initiated by the left hand and arm in unison. That causes a rocking of the shoulders, which is all the body movement you want. The right hand comes into play on the forwardswing, providing the feel for distance, but the left wrist remains firm throughout the stroke.

Al Geiberger won the 1977 St. Jude Memphis Classic after firing a second-round 59, the lowest score ever on the PGA Tour.

SCORECARD

Hole	Yards	Par	PGA Tour Avg. Score
1	582	5	4.961
2	414	4	4.045
3	182	3	2.958
4	423	4	4.145
5	199	3	3.042
6	388	4	4.052
7	564	5	4.952
8	479	4	4.227
9	403	4	3.946
OUT	3634	36	36.328
10	417	4	4.023
11	376	4	4.047
12	218	3	3.058
13	464	4	4.240
14	447	4	4.224
15	200	3	3.069
16	545	5	4.910
17	433	4	4.279
18	548	5	4.804
IN	3648	36	36.774
TOTAL	7282	72	73.102

EN-JOIE *Golf Club*

18th hole

Anyone who believes golf is a rich man's game should go to the B.C. Open, the Tour event where all men are created equal, played at the golf course of the people, by the people, and for the people.

The name of the club is "En-Joie," and that is more than a cute attempt at a Gallicism. "En" is short for "Endicott," the quiet town in upstate New York which is the home of the B.C. "Joie" stands for "Johnson," more specifically George F. Johnson, the man who built the course. Together they are Endicott-Johnson, one of America's largest shoe manufacturers, a company that was based in Endicott and owned by George F. Johnson.

Johnson had always wanted to build a golf course exclusively for the Endicott-Johnson employees. In 1927 he commissioned Ed Moran, who operated a steam shovel at a granite pit near the company plant, to take a crew of men and begin developing the course. Two years later Endicott-Johnson opened the doors to the first corporate golf course in America. Each hole was named after a different department in the company, and the 15th green was actually designed in the shape of a shoe. Golf clubs were sold to the workers for a dollar each, and group lessons were made available for fifty cents. The local paper hailed the project as the "first attempt by an industry to inject democracy into the white-collar men's game of golf."

The democratic spirit fostered by George Johnson has spread throughout much of New York's rural southern tier, where today hundreds of volunteers work to make the B.C. Open a big-time event with small-town charm. At perhaps no other tournament on the PGA Tour is there the same feeling of warmth, almost a familial bond between the players and the event. As Lee Trevino, a loyal B.C. supporter, puts it, "Most tournaments on the Tour cater to three or four big guns. At the B.C., a rookie gets the same treatment as a star."

Today the tournament is named in honor of Johnny Hart, the Endicott resident and golf fanatic whose comic strip, "B.C.," is syndicated all over the world. But in 1971, the event was known as the Broome County Open. At that time it was a one-day pro-am with a total purse of $10,000. A year later it expanded to 36 holes, with double the prize money. Then in 1973, the first full-scale Tour event took place as a satellite tournament opposite the Cleveland Open. Since then, the Cleveland tournament has vanished, while the B.C. has grown into one of the liveliest stops on the circuit.

But that growth has not come without some pain. In 1974 fire demolished the clubhouse just five weeks before the tournament. A distressed call was placed to PGA Tour Commissioner Deane Beman.

"Was there any damage to the course?" Beman asked.

"None," was the reply.

"Then we'll be there as scheduled," said the Commissioner. "We haven't played a clubhouse yet."

A year later, a raging storm hit Endicott on Tuesday night of tournament week, uprooting several trees and leaving some of the fairways under five feet of water. But the next morning more than 500 volunteers pitched in and raked, pumped, shoveled, and squeegeed the course into playable condition in time for the pro-am.

That same year, Andy North opened the tournament with an incredible back nine score of 27, an all-time PGA Tour record, which apparently caught the eye of the Commissioner. Not long thereafter Beman began to question the quality of the En-Joie course and the viability of the rural New York market as a tournament site.

When tournament officials got wind of Beman's feelings, they invited the Commissioner to Endicott to see for himself. Beman came and rapidly changed his mind. Today the B.C. tournament is secure, and although the En-Joie course has had a redesign, it will remain the permanent site.

The most drastic change in the golf course came on the first hole. In 1983 the opening par four was the easiest hole on the course. At the suggestion of 1979 champion Howard Twitty, a lake was added near the green. In 1984 the pros played this hole in an average of 4.35 strokes. It was not only the most difficult hole on the course, it was one of the hardest par fours on the PGA Tour. Lake Twitty took its toll.

The relatively easy par five 15th was changed in yardage and par to a 476-yard par four. Set as it is among par threes at the 14th, 16th, and 17th, this hole stands out like King Kong in a kindergarten. It is by far the longest par four on the back nine, but it is not the sternest test— number 13 is. An extremely tight 441-yarder, played to an elevated green, this is the hole that beckons the best from the pros. At least it did from Calvin Peete, who in 1982 laced a 2-iron into the cup for an eagle two, spurring him to a three-stroke victory.

The final tee shot on most courses is a psychologically demanding one, but at En-Joie it is made doubly difficult by out-of-bounds to the right and two large ponds to the

7th hole

14th and 4th holes

16th hole

left. Adding to the intimidating beauty of the ponds is a waterfall that connects them, with the cascading waters very much in play.

The waterfall, unquestionably the most distinctive feature on the En-Joie layout, was, appropriately, the idea of a fellow named Alex Alexander. Since the inception of the B.C., Alexander has been a combination tournament director, traffic cop, social secretary, messiah, and den mother. He has guided the tournament from its modest beginning, nursing and nurturing it every step of the way. It was he who made the frantic call after the clubhouse fire, he who marshaled the cleanup effort after the storm, he who stood up to the doubting Commissioner. Alexander also founded an annual golf championship for the caddies.

It is all part of that spirit of democracy, of favoritism to no man, commitment to every man. At no time was that spirit more clearly reflected than in 1974, a year when the B.C. produced one of the most surprising victors in modern golf.

Richie Karl, a struggling twenty-nine-year-old pro, had earned only $256 when the Tour arrived in Endicott. But Richie had reason for hope. Endicott was his home, and he had played at the En-Joie course since the age of six. When he had turned professional, he had gone to work at En-Joie as the assistant to head pro Bill Dennis. Outside Endicott, no one knew Richie, but Richie knew Endicott inside-out.

He opened the tournament with a 70, then followed with rounds of 67 and 68. On Sunday Karl blitzed through the front nine in 31. With nine holes to go, he had a six-stroke lead and a gallery of 30,000 friends and neighbors.

At the 10th tee, however, Karl made a mistake; he looked at the leaderboard. Seeing his huge lead, he began to play defensively. He bogeyed 10 and 13 while one of his pursuers, Bruce Crampton, birdied 12 and 13. Karl three-putted the 16th, and with a 37 on the back nine, he had blown six shots in nine holes. The law of momentum said Crampton would win the sudden-death playoff.

But the spirit of the B.C. said otherwise. Crampton failed to reach the green of the first playoff hole and chipped to within a foot of the hole for a sure par. Karl, however, stroked his uphill putt directly into the hole for a victorious birdie. The crowd erupted into one of the wildest whoops Broome County had ever heard.

"The first thing I saw was my caddie running up to me. He was crying," said a joyous Karl. "Then something dressed in white [Natalie, his wife] was in my arms and she was sobbing, and I guess, well, I was sobbing a little, too."

ALL TIME TOURNAMENT RECORDS

Record	Player(s)	Score	Year
Low 18	Fuzzy Zoeller	62	1982
	Jay Delsing		1985
Low first 36	Joey Sindelar	128 (65–63)	1987
Low 36	Calvin Peete	127 (63–64)	1982 (rounds 2–3)
Low first 54	Calvin Peete	196 (69–63–64)	1982
Low 54	Calvin Peete	196	1982
	Calvin Peete	(63–64–69)	1982
Low 72	Calvin Peete	265 (69–63–64–69)	1982
Highest winning score	Wayne Levi	275 (67–71–71–66)	1984
Largest winning margin	Calvin Peete (265)	7 strokes	1982
Largest 18-hole lead	Calvin Peete (64)	3 strokes	1981
	Mark O'Meara (63)		1983
Largest 36-hole lead	Joey Sindelar (128)	7 strokes	1987
Largest 54-hole lead	Hubert Green (199)	5 strokes	1973
	Tom Kite (199)		1978
Lowest start by winner	Bob Wynn	65	1976
	Rick Fehr		1986
	Joey Sindelar		1987
Highest start by winner	Pat Lindsey	71	1983
Lowest finish by winner	Wayne Levi	66	1984
Highest finish by winner	Bob Wynn	69	1976
	Gil Morgan		1977
	Jay Haas		1981
	Calvin Peete		1982
Best final-round comeback	Wayne Levi (209)	3 back	1984
Lowest 36-hole cut score		142	1986
Highest 36-hole cut score		146	1984

PAST WINNERS

Year	Winner	Score
1973	Hubert Green	266
1974	*Richie Karl	273
1975	Don Iverson	274
1976	Bob Wynn	271
1977	Gil Morgan	270
1978	Tom Kite	267
1979	Howard Twitty	270
1980	Don Pooley	271
1981	Jay Haas	270
1982	Calvin Peete	265
1983	Pat Lindsey	268
1984	Wayne Levi	275
1985	Joey Sindelar	274
1986	Rick Fehr	267
1987	Joey Sindelar	266

*Playoff

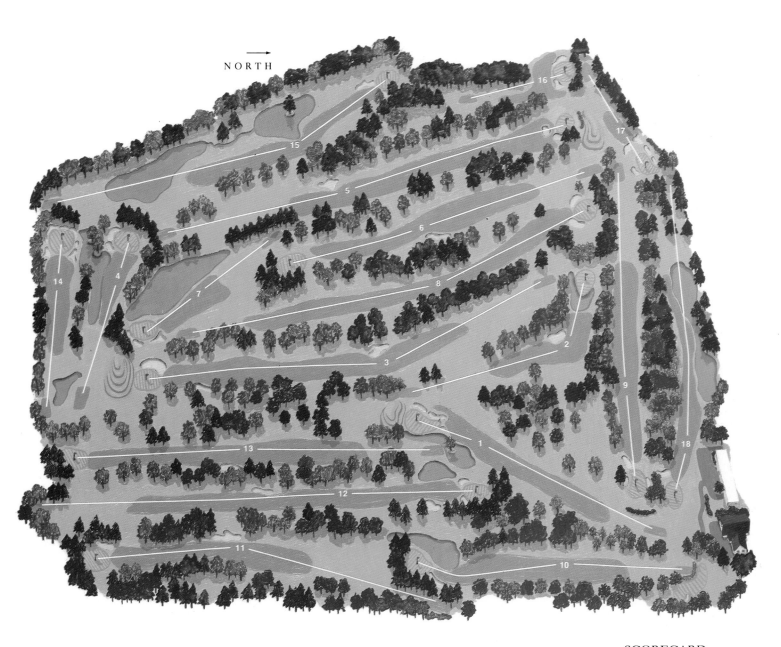

SCORECARD

TEE SHOT STRATEGY
BY TOM KITE

I like the En-Joie course a lot because it's one of the few remaining old-style courses on the PGA Tour. It's not enormously long, but it is tight and full of strategy.

On a course like this one, there's no advantage to taking a driver and trying to blast it off the tee of every par four and five. En-Joie is a thinking-man's course where it pays to play every hole backward in your mind before you play it forward from the tee. And that mental exercise is good discipline for anyone who wants to get the most out of his or her game.

If you haven't gone through this shot-planning on your home course,

do so now. For each hole, ask yourself what spot in the fairway affords the ideal approach to the green. Take into consideration hazards as well as the slopes on the green, but also factor in the pattern of your shots. Position A for a person who hits a draw is probably on the left side of the fairway, while the player with a fade will usually prefer the right. On short par fours, the best position may be well short of the green, where you can make a full swing, rather than up close where you'd have to play a finesse shot.

Once you know where you want your tee shots to finish, ask yourself which clubs on your tee shots will give you the best opportunities to find those spots. Once you have that strategy, you've taken a big step toward good course management.

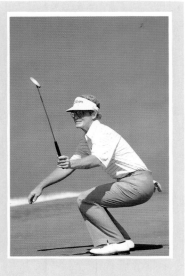

Tom Kite won the 1978 B.C. Open.

Hole	Yards	Par	PGA Tour Avg. Score
1	388	4	4.356
2	363	4	4.069
3	554	5	4.912
4	221	3	3.150
5	565	5	4.892
6	433	4	4.097
7	200	3	3.129
8	553	5	4.869
9	425	4	4.076
OUT	3702	37	37.550
10	360	4	4.019
11	433	4	4.137
12	556	5	4.763
13	441	4	4.185
14	212	3	3.132
15	476	4	4.292
16	182	3	3.016
17	198	3	3.046
18	406	4	4.115
IN	3264	34	34.705
TOTAL	6966	71	72.255

PLEASANT VALLEY
Country Club

BANK OF BOSTON
CLASSIC
MASSACHUSETTS

Number 17 is *the* hole at Pleasant Valley. It is the postcard hole and the killer. Peaceful, picturesque, and pugnacious, this lengthy par four looms over the back nine, ready to break the back of anyone who dares treat it lightly.

The view from the tee at 17 tells a lot about Pleasant Valley. A weather-worn, covered bridge says this is the heart of New England. Rolling, densely wooded terrain suggests immediately that this young course was not planted, it was hewn. A pond fronting the tee hints at other, more formidable carries over water. A sharp downhill dog-

17th hole

leg at the far edge of the landing area speaks of a layout where two-thirds of the holes bend right or left, and nearly all of them slope up or down. Finally, the length of number 17—441 yards from the championship tee—suggests that this is a long course.

Sculpted from a huge apple orchard in the heart of Massachusetts, Pleasant Valley is the fruit of one man's dream. Cosmo E. "Cuz" Mingolla was a contractor who loved golf and believed that New England deserved and would support a major professional tournament. In 1961

he designed a golf course with the help of local pro Don Hoenig. Four years later, Pleasant Valley Country Club hosted the $200,000 Carling World Open, at that time the largest purse on the pro Tour.

The tournament attracted a spectacular field that included Ben Hogan, Arnold Palmer, Jack Nicklaus, and Gary Player among many others. After 70 holes, Palmer was tied with Tony Lema. Then number 17 asserted itself. Both golfers played overly strong approaches to the water-guarded green. Lema's ball struck in the gallery and

bounced back to the edge of the green, but Palmer's sailed over everything and finished in a brook. Champagne Tony went on to win the final tournament of his brief, brilliant career.

After a hiatus of two years, tournament golf returned to Pleasant Valley, this time as the Kemper Open. Palmer returned as well. In the final round he charged from three strokes back to take a four-shot victory over Bruce Crampton. The winner's check made him the first player to win over $1 million in career earnings.

In 18 years the tournament has had 18 different winners and almost as many different names: Carling World, Kemper Open, Avco Invitational, Avco Classic, Massachusetts Classic, USI Classic, Pleasant Valley Classic, American Optical Classic, Pleasant Valley Jimmy Fund Classic. The Bank of Boston took over sponsorship in 1980, however, and its current contract runs through 1989.

The weather has also been fickle. During the first year the event was televised, a storm interrupted play at 5:50 P.M. in the first round, with only twenty-one of the 150-odd competitors still on the course, none with more than

six holes to play. Tour officials ruled that the round would have to be aborted and replayed the next day. George Archer was the biggest victim. His 65 was rained out, and in his second start he posted a 73. Eventually, he finished in a tie for 13th.

But like Palmer, Archer came back. Nineteen years later, in 1984, at the age of forty-four, he once again shot a 65, but this time it was in the final round and this time it gave him a record six-stroke victory.

Pleasant Valley is a superb spectator course. Eight of the 18 holes have their tees or greens within proximity of the clubhouse. Indeed, at times the clubhouse comes into play, as in 1972 when Larry Ziegler pitched his third shot to the ninth green from the floor of the bag room. In 1976 New England architect Geoffrey Cornish redesigned the 18th with an amphitheater green that now holds several thousand spectators.

But no changes were made to number 17. "That hole is a monster," says Raymond Floyd, the 1977 champion who won *in spite of* 17. Leading the tournament by five shots in the final round, Floyd pushed his tee shot into

13th hole

7th hole

ALL TIME TOURNAMENT RECORDS

Record	Player(s)	Score	Year
Low 18	Rik Massengale	63	1977
	Lennie Clements		1985
Low first 36	Mark Hayes	133	1978
		(67–66)	
	George Burns	(67–66)	1985
Low 36	Mike McCullough	130	1982
		(64–66)	(rounds 2–3)
Low first 54	John Mahaffey	201	1983
		(65–69–67)	
	George Burns	(67–66–68)	1985
Low 54	John Mahaffey	199	1978
		(65–67–67)	
Low 72	George Burns	267	1985
		(67–66–68–66)	
Highest winning score	Tom Shaw	280	1969
		(68–68–67–77)	
Largest winning margin	George Archer (270)	6 strokes	1984
	George Burns (267)		1985
Largest 18-hole lead	Fred Marti (64)	3 strokes	1977
Largest 36-hole lead	Tom Shaw (136)	5 strokes	1969
Largest 54-hole lead	Tom Shaw (203)	7 strokes	1969
Lowest start by winner	Raymond Floyd	67	1977
	Bob Gilder		1982
Highest start by winner	Roger Maltbie	72	1975
	Brian Allin		1976
Lowest finish by winner	Mark Lye	64	1983
Highest finish by winner	Tom Shaw	77	1969
Best final-round comeback	Mark Lye	8 back	1983
Lowest 36-hole cut score		143	1980–1982
Highest 36-hole cut score		150	1969

PAST WINNERS

Year	Winner	Score
1965	Tony Lema	279
1966–		
1967	No Tournaments	
1968	Arnold Palmer	276
1969	Tom Shaw	280
1970	Billy Casper	277
1971	Dave Stockton	275
1972	Bruce Devlin	275
1973	Lanny Wadkins	279
1974	Vic Regalado	278
1975	Roger Maltbie	276
1976	Brian Allin	277
1977	Raymond Floyd	271
1978	John Mahaffey	270
1979	Lou Graham	275
1980	Wayne Levi	273
1981	Jack Renner	273
1982	Bob Gilder	271
1983	Mark Lye	273
1984	George Archer	270
1985	George Burns	267
1986	*Gene Sauers	274
1987	‡Sam Randolph	199

*Playoff
‡Rain curtailed

the right-hand woods and made double-bogey 6 as his playing companion and closest pursuer, Jack Nicklaus, birdied, cutting the lead to two. On the last hole, a par five, Nicklaus nearly chipped in for eagle, but his birdie left him one short of Floyd in the most exciting finish in the history of the tournament.

The crowds at Pleasant Valley have been consistently among the largest on the Tour. "Cuz" Mingolla was right —the locals would indeed support a pro event. Mingolla died in 1979, but his son, Ted, continues to run the Pleasant Valley tournament with the same loving hand. In 1984 he hired an architectural firm to recommend long-term changes in the course, changes that would ensure the best possible test for the Tour players without sacrificing the enjoyment of the members who have made the tournament work.

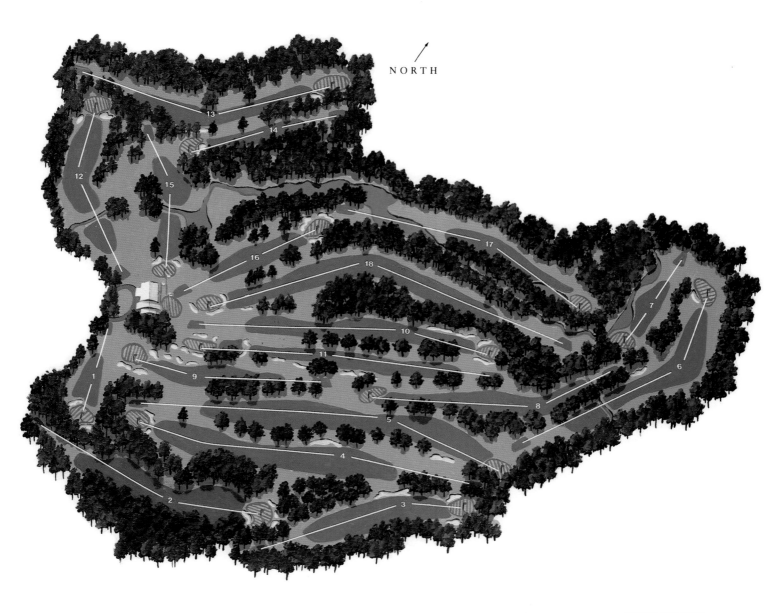

NORTH

SCORECARD

Winner at Pleasant Valley in 1984 at age 44, George Archer also holds the PGA Tour record for fewest putts in a 72-hole event (94 in the 1980 Sea Pines Heritage Classic).

LONG PUTTS
BY GEORGE ARCHER

With some of the largest greens on the Tour, Pleasant Valley puts a premium on the ability to handle lengthy putts.

When I practice putting before or after a round, I concentrate on long putts rather than mid-length or short ones. My reasoning is that if I can make a solid stroke on a 50-footer, I can surely make a solid stroke on a five-footer.

It's a waste of time to agonize over the precise amount of break on a long putt. Too many golfers create unnecessary pressure by worrying about whether to hit the ball at the right-center or right lip of the cup. As a result they either leave the ball 10 feet short or slug it well past. On putts of just a few feet, it's fine to aim the putter as you would a rifle, but on the long ones, think of the putter more as a shotgun. Concentrate not on line but on distance; if you hit the ball with the right pace you'll almost always finish within a couple of feet of the hole.

The type of stroke you make is a matter of personal choice. Just be aware that even stiff-wristed putters must allow a bit of hinging and unhinging on the longer strokes. Other than that, the secret is to develop feel, and the only way to do that is to hit lots of practice putts—long ones.

Hole	Yards	Par	PGA Tour Avg. Score
1	185	3	3.040
2	395	4	4.194
3	386	4	3.956
4	547	5	4.655
5	606	5	4.866
6	443	4	4.164
7	180	3	3.007
8	455	4	4.139
9	414	4	3.874
OUT	3611	36	35.895
10	441	4	4.266
11	437	4	4.140
12	425	4	3.973
13	394	4	4.113
14	230	3	3.162
15	357	4	4.043
16	183	3	3.114
17	441	4	4.173
18	583	5	4.847
IN	3492	35	35.831
TOTAL	7102	71	71.726

TUCKAWAY *Country Club*

GREATER
MILWAUKEE
OPEN
WISCONSIN

In 1984 Mark O'Meara came to Milwaukee amid the most successful—and frustrating—season of his young career. During the first nine months of the PGA Tour, no one had played more consistently, no one had made more birdies, no one had compiled more top-ten finishes than O'Meara. Yet the cherubic-cheeked Californian had not produced the most valued statistic of all—a victory. In fact, in his four years on the Tour, O'Meara had been winless. The Rookie of the Year in 1981, he was generally regarded as the best player never to have won. Skeptics

said that he would never break through. And, after he finished second in five 1984 events, two of them back-to-back, even O'Meara himself began to wonder.

All that changed at Milwaukee. With rounds of 67–68–69–68—272, O'Meara stilled his worst critics and quelled his deepest fears. As for the folks in Milwaukee, well, O'Meara's victory was no big surprise. In fact, in Brewertown it was business as usual.

Milwaukee has a way of raising fledging Tour players to maturity just as surely as it ages hops and barley. The Greater Milwaukee Open has been in continuous operation since 1968, and in most years it has produced a winner similar to O'Meara, a young player knocking at the door of success. On fourteen occasions, the triumph at Milwaukee has been either the first or second win of the victor's career. In fact, two of the tournament's three double winners, Calvin Peete and Dave Eichelberger, won this event twice before notching any other victories.

Two factors explain this phenomenon. The first relates to the timing of the Milwaukee event. For many years it

7th hole

10th hole

16th hole

was played during the week before the British Open. As a result, many of the top players were already en route to Great Britain. A recent change in the Tour schedule has shifted the date of the Milwaukee Open to mid-September.

The second factor is the Tuckaway Country Club course, site of the Milwaukee Open since 1973. At 7,010 yards it is long but not a backbreaker. It is wooded but not overly tight, and its greens are large, fast, gently contoured, and consistently among the finest conditioned on the Tour. This is a golf course where a player can get the putter going, generate some confidence, and play like a champion. It was here that Jim Thorpe broke through for his first win, after a third round of 62, sparked by five birdies in a row for a front nine of 29.

Simplistic as it may sound, the course is toughest at the beginning, the middle, and the end. Two of the first three holes are long, demanding par fours. Number one calls for a superstraight drive between bunkers left and right. A tee shot into the sand leaves a nearly 200-yard approach, usually into the wind, to an elevated, closely bunkered green. That is like facing the trickiest fingering in a piano concerto in the first four bars.

17th hole

After a par five that is a relative breather, the course jumps up again with a 437-yard par four, a dogleg that the pros play in an average of 4.159 strokes. The tee shot should be hit with a slight fade to curl with the fairway and leave the best approach to the angled green. When the pin is cut back-right, near two large bunkers, this one is especially tough.

The ninth hole, a 430-yard par four, requires a skillful second shot, played from a downhill lie to an elevated green. This is probably the second hardest hole on the course.

The hardest is the one that follows it. Number 10 plays 444 yards steeply uphill, with the second shot blind, making club selection difficult. According to 1980 champion Bill Kratzert, "Once you get to the green, your work has just begun. The putting surface has a severe slope from back to front, and anything above the hole is treacherous."

Nor is the 18th good birdie territory at Tuckaway. It is a 445-yard, uphill dogleg right, with the second shot sharply uphill. When the pin is cut to the right, the approach is particularly tough, with bunkers in front and behind that area of the green. In 1983, Morris Hatalsky had a chance to win outright at 18. He had made six birdies on the back nine, including four in a row from 11 to 14. But George Cadle, who had begun the final day in 19th place, had made five birdies on the same stretch and had turned in a 64 for 275. Hatalsky needed a par on 18 to beat him. But it was not to be. He pushed his approach into a right-hand bunker then blasted out to 15 feet and missed the putt. Off they went to a playoff, which Hatalsky won on the second hole.

Shortly after his victory, Morris received his check in a novel way. A parachutist landed with it on the 18th green, touching down on almost the exact spot from which Hatalsky had missed the putt thirty minutes earlier.

ALL TIME TOURNAMENT RECORDS

Record	Player(s)	Score	Year
Low 18	Dave Stockton	63	1973
	Dave Eichelberger		1976
Low first 36	Dave Stockton	132 (69–63)	1973
	Fuzzy Zoeller	(66–66)	1976
Low 36	Dave Stockton	132 (69–63)	1973
	Fuzzy Zoeller		1976
	Gary McCord	(65–67)	1975 (rounds 3–4)
	George Cadle	(66–66)	1980 (rounds 3–4)
	Rex Caldwell	(65–67)	1981 (rounds 2–3)
Low first 54	Bill Kratzert	200 (67–66–67)	1980
Low 54	Bill Kratzert	199 (66–67–66)	1980
Low 72	Bill Kratzert	266 (67–66–67–66)	1980
Highest winning score	Dave Eichelberger	278 (71–68–69–70)	1977
Largest winning margin	Calvin Peete (269)	5 strokes	1979
	Mark O'Meara (272)		1984
Largest 18-hole lead	Ed Sneed (66)	2 strokes	1974
	Miller Barber (65)		1975
	Ken Still (64)		1976
Largest 36-hole lead	Dave Stockton (132)	4 strokes	1973
Largest 54-hole lead	Dave Stockton (203)	6 strokes	1973
Lowest start by winner	Ed Sneed	66	1974
	Dave Hill		1976
	Lee Elder		1978
	Corey Pavin		1986
Highest start by winner	Dave Eichelberger	71	1977
Lowest finish by winner	Calvin Peete	65	1979
Highest finish by winner	Dave Stockton	73	1973
	Jay Haas		1981
Best final-round comeback	Morris Hatalsky (209)	4 back	1983
Lowest 36-hole cut score		141	1980
Highest 36-hole cut score		148	1974–1977

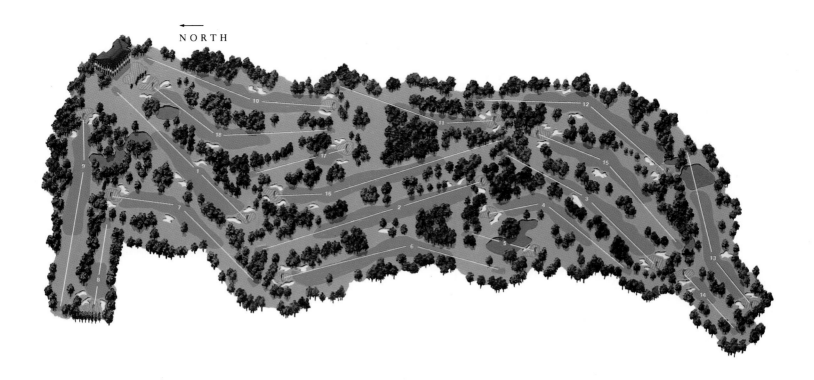

PAST WINNERS

Year	Winner	Score
1968	Dave Stockton	275
1969	Ken Still	277
1970	Deane Beman	276
1971	Dave Eichelberger	270
1972	Jim Colbert	271
1973	Dave Stockton	276
1974	Ed Sneed	276
1975	Art Wall	271
1976	Dave Hill	270
1977	Dave Eichelberger	278
1978	*Lee Elder	275
1979	Calvin Peete	269
1980	Bill Kratzert	266
1981	Jay Haas	274
1982	Calvin Peete	274
1983	*Morris Hatalsky	275
1984	Mark O'Meara	272
1985	Jim Thorpe	274
1986	*Corey Pavin	272
1987	Gary Hallberg	269

*Playoff

THE UPHILL APPROACH
BY MARK O'MEARA

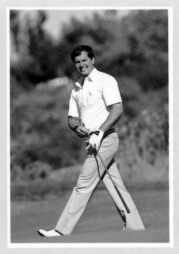

One of the keys to scoring well at Tuckaway is a solid iron game. Because the greens are fairly large, you need to hit the ball not simply onto the putting surface but in the vicinity of the flag. At holes such as nine and 18, the assignment is complicated by the way the fairway slopes steeply uphill to the green, leaving a semi-blind shot.

When playing such approaches, I use one club more than normal—a 4-iron instead of a 5-iron—and I concentrate on making a controlled swing. If I have an uphill lie, I position the ball a bit farther forward in my stance than usual and aim a few feet to the right of my target to compensate for the tendency to pull such shots to the left. I try to keep my backswing compact, but on the downswing I move my weight fully and aggressively to my left side. This is a bit tougher than usual when you're standing uphill because you're fighting gravity, but a good weight transfer and a full extension into the finish are important to the success of uphill shots.

Mark O'Meara's first Tour victory came in the 1984 Greater Milwaukee Open.

SCORECARD

Hole	Yards	Par	PGA Tour Avg. Score
1	415	4	4.124
2	527	5	4.806
3	437	4	4.159
4	390	4	3.985
5	170	3	2.996
6	524	5	4.573
7	393	4	4.066
8	197	3	3.101
9	430	4	4.240
OUT	3483	36	36.050
10	444	4	4.284
11	391	4	4.046
12	505	5	4.707
13	381	4	3.986
14	186	3	2.974
15	405	4	4.113
16	550	5	4.774
17	220	3	3.207
18	445	4	4.198
IN	3527	36	36.289
TOTAL	7010	72	72.339

FAIRWAY OAKS
Golf and Racquet Club

4th hole

GATLIN BROTHERS
SOUTHWEST GOLF CLASSIC
TEXAS

One of the youngest events on the PGA Tour, the Southwest Golf Classic, is nonetheless one of the most popular with the pros.

It started in the late seventies when oil men Hal and Jack McGlothlin and Tony Andress of the LaJet Company decided they wanted a Tour event in west Texas. So they bought one. They hired architect Ron Garl to build a golf course, lured Masters champion Charles Coody to become director of golf, and invited five of the game's top players—Ben Crenshaw, Lee Trevino, J.C. Snead, Don January, and Lou Graham—to baptize the place on .October 1, 1979. Trevino won the one-day exhibition with a score of 70. A year later, they held a $170,000 pro-am. A year after that their event hit the big time.

"The Tour was looking for a tournament to run opposite the 1981 Ryder Cup Matches," Coody recalls, "and when we approached them, they were receptive." Coody's bosses put up a $350,000 purse and attracted nearly every top player who was not locked into the matches against the Brits. The LaJet people wined, dined, and entertained them, took them on fishing trips and dove shoots after each day's golf competition, and generally served up one of the pleasantest work weeks of the year. Tom Weiskopf took home the first trophy, but LaJet was declared the big winner by the players.

The event and the golf course are monuments to the power of the purse. When architect Garl first set eyes on the property, it was as barren as a moonscape. Not only were there no oaks on the fairways of Fairway Oaks, there were no trees of any kind except the lowly mesquite, a pod-producing shrub that is to west Texas what the pigeon is to Manhattan.

But the LaJet people pumped money into the project and pumped water into the arid land. Hundreds of trees were introduced—specimens of live and red oak, poplar, maple, weeping willow, and Arizona ash. Streams and lakes were created, and ponds with fountains and reflecting pools. Around the tees and greens were planted flower beds full of petunias, roses, crape myrtle, and pansies. Pampas grass clumps were sown into the bunkers and now rustle in the breeze like stranded tumbleweeds. Fairways were planted with bermudagrass, the greens with bent, the combination that pros and better players prefer.

The oil barons also built a clubhouse that would make even J. R. Ewing jealous. Its size is 38,000-square feet—

about the same as fifteen middle-American houses—and in addition to the men's and women's locker rooms, it contains several dining areas, a huge wine cellar, an authentically reconstructed London pub, and a penthouse discotheque. Texas understatement at its subtle best.

At 7,156 yards, Fairway Oaks is a medium-long par 72, but it can play much longer or shorter depending on the weather. Wind is a constant in west Texas, and it normally comes from the south southwest, lengthening some of the toughest holes on the course. It also keeps the bentgrass greens dry, hard, and fast—very fast.

Ron Garl was born, reared, and trained in Florida, but his bunkering at the sixth hole is pure Pennsylvania. Stretched across the rough on both sides of this par four is a series of long troughs of sand. The locals call them "Venus's-flytraps," but students of the world's great courses know them as "church pews," the same church pews that Henry and William Fownes created at famed Oakmont Country Club near Pittsburgh. Eleven of them—five on one side, six on the other—add enormously to the difficulty of this 423-yard par four. And the pews on the right do double duty, acting as hazards for the ninth hole as well. On that par five of 536 yards, the pros will have a good chance of hitting the green in two—if they avoid hitting a church pew.

The toughest hole on the course is probably number 10, a 401-yard par four that usually plays into the teeth of the wind. This was a difficult hole from day one, but in 1982 it was lengthened to 425 yards. A year later it became one of the ten hardest fours on the Tour, taxing the pros for an average of 4.43 strokes. Trees on the left and water on the right make it the most demanding drive of the day, and most of the Tour players hit irons off the tee.

Number 14 is a classic do-or-die par five. Trees, traps, and water make the drive a challenging one, with only 25 yards of safe landing area. But once the strong player finds the fairway, he has a good chance of getting home in two, assuming he can jump the final hurdle, a guardian creek. The green is narrow, extremely long, and has three tiers. Frequently the Tour player will reach it with two fine shots only to three-putt for a par.

LaJet is not a slicer's course; almost all the trouble, particularly the water, is on the right. However, there is a glaring exception to that rule, number 16, a par three

15th hole

9th hole (left) and 6th hole (right)

6th hole

16th hole

that is one of the prettiest and most ticklish in pro golf. It is only 165 yards long, but water guards the front and left of the green, and the hole nearly always plays into a right-to-left wind. A pull, a hook, or a slightly heavy shot will all find the same watery fate.

Anyone who survives that water will face a 17th hole that calls for transaquatic maneuvers on both the drive and approach. The club members find this their stiffest assignment, and who could argue? This is a true Texas par four, at 471 yards. Granted, it normally plays downwind, but that is not as good as it sounds. About seven out of ten golfers have trouble hitting long irons, eight out of ten have trouble hitting long irons over water, nine out of ten have trouble hitting long irons over water to rock-hard greens, and ten out of ten have trouble hitting long irons over water to rock-hard greens while playing in a twenty-mile-per-hour tailwind.

The 18th hole is a climactic finale in the tradition of Pebble Beach, Harbour Town, and Doral, a twisting, tantalizing brute of a hole where wind and water coax and con the player every inch of the way. Under some conditions, this 562-yard par five can be reached in two by the stronger pros. The choice of whether to go for the green is complicated by a fairway that narrows into a bottleneck just in front of the target. Water guards the entire right side, and the green also slopes that way.

Jim Thorpe claims he hit the finest shot of his career on this hole. After a drive of 350 yards, a colossal shot even by his standards, he boomed a 4-iron that carried to the front edge of the green and rolled into the hole for a double-eagle two. "I was three-over par at the time," he recalls, "and then all of a sudden I was even."

When Rex Caldwell stepped to the 18th tee of the 1984 tournament, he figured he would need a birdie to beat Lee Trevino and win. It had been a strange year—both wonderful and terrible for Caldwell. Wonderful in that he had earned more money by far than in any other season. Terrible in that, during the first nine months of the Tour, he had finished second four times, including three weeks in a row, twice losing in playoffs. Caldwell, age 33, had never scored a Tour victory.

His fourth runner-up finish had come only a week earlier at the Las Vegas Pro-Celebrity Classic. On the eve of the last round there, he had aired his frustration. "I want to win," he said. "I've been on Tour for nine years now and I think I'm the only guy out here who hasn't won. Just one week I'd like to say I was the best, I beat them all. I don't care about the money. They can give me $10 if they want. I want to win."

Surely those words raced through Caldwell's mind again as he teed up his final drive at Fairway Oaks. Straight down the fairway it went. Once at his ball, Caldwell never hesitated. Out came the fairway wood, and he nailed it home. It finished in three-putt territory—70 feet from the hole. However, using the ultra-steady, lock-wristed stroke that is one of his trademarks, Rex hit such a spectacular putt that he nearly made eagle. The birdie was good enough to satisfy his quest.

ALL TIME TOURNAMENT RECORDS

Record	Player(s)	Score	Year
Low 18	Craig Stadler	63	1986
	Jay Haas		1983
Low first 36	Wayne Levi	135 (64–71)	1982
	Curtis Strange	(68–67)	1984
Low 36	Thomas Gray	133 (66–67)	1982 (rounds 3–4)
Low first 54	Curtis Strange	202 (68–67–67)	1984
Low 54	Curtis Strange	202 (68–67–67)	1984
Low 72	Wayne Levi	271 (64–71–68–68)	1982
Highest winning score	Rex Caldwell	282 (68–72–76–66)	1983
Largest winning margin	Wayne Levi (271)	6 strokes	1982
Largest 18-hole lead	Tommy Valentine (66)	2 strokes	1981
Largest 36-hole lead	Wayne Levi (135)	2 strokes	1982
Largest 54-hole lead	Curtis Strange (202)	6 strokes	1984
Lowest start by winner	Wayne Levi	64	1982
Highest start by winner	Tom Weiskopf	73	1981
Lowest finish by winner	Rex Caldwell	66	1983
Highest finish by winner	Curtis Strange Mark Calcavecchia	71	1984 1986
Best final-round comeback	Rex Caldwell	6 back	1983
Lowest 36-hole cut score		146	1981–1982
Highest 36-hole cut score		149	1983

PAST WINNERS

Year	Winner	Score
1981	Tom Weiskopf	278
1982	Wayne Levi	271
1983	Rex Caldwell	282
1984	Curtis Strange	273
1985	*Hal Sutton	273
1986	Mark Calcavecchia	275
1987	Steve Pate	273

*Playoff

NORTH

SCORECARD

Hole	Yards	Par	PGA Tour Avg. Score
1	398	4	3.980
2	453	4	4.249
3	569	5	4.973
4	214	3	3.263
5	400	4	4.127
6	423	4	4.175
7	410	4	4.055
8	185	3	3.185
9	536	5	4.752
OUT	3588	36	36.759
10	425	4	4.283
11	198	3	3.162
12	425	4	4.121
13	399	4	4.026
14	528	5	4.848
15	395	4	4.017
16	165	3	3.178
17	471	4	4.253
18	562	5	4.901
IN	3568	36	36.789
TOTAL	7156	72	73.548

PUNCH IT UNDER THE WIND
BY CHARLES COODY

Even when it's calm in Abilene, Texas, we have a ten to fifteen mile-per-hour wind, and when it kicks up we get gusts of forty miles an hour or more. Under such conditions, it's vital to be able to hit the ball low and to punch shots into the greens.

Let's take a shot of about 100 yards. Under windless conditions, I'd probably loft a sand wedge into the green. But into a headwind, I'll grab an 8-iron and punch it. I play the ball back in my stance, about mid-way between my feet, and I choke down on the club a couple of inches for control. The backswing is a short, compact one. My hands don't go much higher than my waist. On the forwardswing, the key is to pull through impact with the left hand and to finish low. If you let your hands get too high on the follow-through, the ball will also get too high. So after impact, try to stop in the extension position, with your arms and club pointing straight down the fairway at your target. This is a great shot, not only for cutting through a headwind but in any situation where you want to keep the ball low.

Charles Coody is the director of golf at Fairway Oaks Golf and Racquet Club.

GREEN ISLAND *Country Club*

SOUTHERN
OPEN
GEORGIA

5th hole

A few yards from the first tee of the Green Island Country Club is a large lake. It is called Swan Lake because, ever since anyone can remember, it has been the home of a pair of mute swans. So entrenched are these birds that the swan has become the symbol of the club.

For many PGA Tour players, the Southern Open held at Green Island is the swan song for the season, scheduled as it is near the end of the playing year. And yet, for those who have won the Southern, it has been not an end but a beginning. Perhaps more than any other event on the Tour, the Southern Open has been a springboard to greatness. In Columbus, Georgia, they call it magic.

It dates back nearly seventy years to 1919, when the tournament was played at Atlanta's East Lake Country Club. In that year, Long Jim Barnes played a spectacular final round that included a stretch of birdie-eagle-birdie on the front nine to edge a seventeen-year-old local boy. Later that year, Barnes also won the PGA Championship and two years later, the U.S. and British Opens, thus securing himself an honored place in the history of golf. The local boy also developed into a pretty fair player—his name was Bobby Jones.

In 1922 it was Gene Sarazen's turn to feel the magic, winning the first big tournament of his career by eight strokes over Leo Diegel, the host pro. Sarazen, only twenty years old, went on that year to win the U.S. Open and PGA Championship, and fast became one of the major players of his era.

In 1927 the Southern Open was discontinued. Not until 1970 did the event—and the magic—resume. In 1971 twenty-four-year-old Johnny Miller broke through for the first career win that many had been waiting for him to register. Immediately thereafter, he won the Heritage Classic. Over the next six years, Miller scored seventeen victories, including the 1976 British Open at Birkdale and the 1973 dramatic U.S. Open at Oakmont in which he charged past a dozen players with a record-breaking final round of 63.

In 1973 the magic came to Gary Player, who had just returned to the Tour after major back surgery. Limping slightly and hoping to regain some confidence, Player scored perhaps the most courageous victory of his career. It marked a return to top form, which he capped a year later by winning The Masters and British Open.

1st hole

Hubert Green, playing in his third full season as a pro, won the 1975 Southern, and it launched him toward the finest season of his career in 1976, a year in which he won three straight tournaments. A year later he scored his most prestigious triumph in the U.S. Open at Southern Hills. Nearly a decade later in 1984, Green again won the Southern, this time after a prolonged and painful slump. Again the magic worked. The victory marked the beginning of a comeback, which Hubert capped in 1985 with a stirring victory in a head-to-head battle with Lee Trevino for the PGA Championship at Cherry Hills.

Green Island is similar to Cherry Hills, the famous Denver course, which has played host to five major championships. Green Island both demands and rewards good shotmaking. At 6,791 yards, it is one of the shortest tests on the Tour, but what it lacks in length it makes up for in narrowness. George Cobb designed the course in 1961, winding it up and down the red clay hills of Georgia and through a forest of tall loblolly pines dotted with a half dozen lakes and ponds.

The opening hole at most courses is intimidating simply because it is the opening hole. At Green Island, number one is not simply intimidating, it is the hardest hole on the course. From the back tee, the hole plays 426 yards, across Swan Lake and uphill to a narrow landing area that falls sharply from left to right into a dense stand of trees. Assuming the pro passes that test, he will be standing at the edge of a chasm, facing a downhill approach to a slender, tightly bunkered green.

Green Island's steep hills increase the difficulty of several key holes. One of them is number five, played as a par five by the members but converted into a long four for the tournament. The tee shot is semiblind and downhill, with the fairway bending softly from left to right. The nearly 200-yard approach must be played to an elevated green that is bunkered to the left, right, and rear.

The longest hole on the course—indeed, one of the longest holes anywhere—is the 594-yard eighth, a classic three-shot par five. A large pond stretches across this fairway at about the halfway mark, providing food for thought on both the drive and second. The tee shot must be hit solidly and straight to afford a confident shot across the water.

The most challenging aspect of the Green Island course is its greens, which at tournament time are usually at top speed. The fiercest of them is at the par-three 17th, a 165-yard hole where any tee shot that leaves a downhill putt is a bad tee shot. In 1976 Gibby Gilbert was in strong contention in the Southern Open when he knocked his ball stiff to the flag, just five feet from birdie—but the five feet was all downhill. Gilbert actually five-putted the green and was never seen on the leaderboard again.

Seventeen is not a hole to fool with, but the par five that follows it is a gambler's delight. The 585-yard finish calls for a good drive, then dares the well-positioned player to go for the green with a long fairway wood that must carry "Pate's Pond," named for two-time champion and sometime aquanaut Jerry Pate, a close friend of Southern Open chairman Gunby Jordan.

"We think that pond is an appropriate place for Jerry's next victory dive," says Jordan, referring to Pate's distinctive celebrations at the 1981 Memphis Classic and 1982 TPC. "We just hope he has the good taste to make it a *swan* dive."

The swan is Green Island's symbol.

1st hole

8th hole

18th hole

ALL TIME TOURNAMENT RECORDS

Record	Player(s)	Score	Year
Low 18	Hale Irwin	61	1982
	Rod Curl		1986
Low first 36	Ken Brown	129 (65–64)	1987
Low 36	Hale Irwin	129 (68–61)	1982 (rounds 3–4)
	Ken Brown	129 (65–64)	1987 (rounds 1–2)
Low first 54	Hubert Green	198 (65–66–67)	1984
Low 54	Hubert Green	196 (66–66–64)	1975
Low 72	Hubert Green	264 (68–66–66–64)	1975
	Tim Simpson	264 (64–64–69–67)	1985
Highest winning score	DeWitt Weaver	276 (65–67–72–72)	1972
Largest winning margin	Jerry Pate (266)	7 strokes	1977
	Ken Brown (266)		1987
Largest 18-hole lead	Johnny Miller (65)	2 strokes	1971
Largest 36-hole lead	Jerry Pate (131)	4 strokes	1977
Largest 54-hole lead	Mike Sullivan (200)	5 strokes	1980
Lowest start by winner	Jerry Pate	64	1977
Highest start by winner	Mason Rudolph	75	1970
Lowest finish by winner	Mason Rudolph	64	1970
	Hubert Green		1975
	Bobby Clampett		1982
Highest finish by winner	DeWitt Weaver	72	1972
Best final-round comeback	Mason Rudolph	4 back	1970
Lowest 36-hole cut score		141	1986
Highest 36-hole cut score		148	1976

PAST WINNERS

Year	Winner	Score
1970	Mason Rudolph	274
1971	Johnny Miller	267
1972	*DeWitt Weaver	276
1973	Gary Player	270
1974	Forrest Fezler	271
1975	Hubert Green	264
1976	Mac McLendon	274
1977	Jerry Pate	266
1978	Jerry Pate	269
1979	*Ed Fiori	274
1980	Mike Sullivan	269
1981	*J. C. Snead	271
1982	Bobby Clampett	266
1983	*Ronnie Black	271
1984	Hubert Green	265
1985	Tim Simpson	264
1986	Fred Wadsworth	269
1987	Ken Brown	266

*Playoff

NORTH

UPHILL AND DOWNHILL PUTTS

BY HUBERT GREEN

At southern courses such as Green Island, the greens are usually seeded with bermudagrass, which has a very strong grain. This grain not only affects the break; it influences the pace of roll, especially on uphill and downhill putts.

On holes such as the 17th at Green Island, if you leave your approach at the back of the green you'll face one of the toughest putts on the Tour—a downhiller that rolls with the bermuda grain. This putt is virtually impossible to sink, so the key is to keep the ball from sailing way past.

When I face such a putt, I tend to use a slightly shorter backswing than normal. Obviously, the key is to tap it as softly as possible. Still, you must not decelerate at impact. Keep your head and shoulders down (avoid the temptation to peek) and strike the putt solidly—gently, but solidly. Pretend that the hole is two feet shorter than it actually is.

If that putt sails well past the hole, you'll face another tricky assignment, an uphiller *against* the grain. The first thing you must do is forget how fast the previous putt was. When going uphill and into the grain, you have to hit the ball harder than under any other conditions. So stay down and concentrate on making a firmly accelerating stroke into the ball. Try to knock it a foot or so past the hole.

Hubert Green is a two-time winner (1975, 1984) of the Southern Open.

SCORECARD

Hole	Yards	Par	PGA Tour Avg. Score
1	426	4	4.299
2	177	3	3.050
3	378	4	3.883
4	384	4	3.960
5	487	4	4.279
6	335	4	3.932
7	226	3	3.132
8	594	5	4.925
9	425	4	4.160
OUT	3432	35	35.620
10	365	4	3.901
11	462	4	4.197
12	368	4	4.032
13	378	4	3.976
14	210	3	3.204
15	440	4	4.173
16	386	4	4.043
17	165	3	3.023
18	585	5	4.968
IN	3359	35	35.517
TOTAL	6791	70	71.137

PERDIDO BAY *Country Club*

9th hole

PENSACOLA OPEN, FLORIDA

Anyone who has studied a year of Spanish can tell you what *perdido* means: lost. And anyone who has played one round on Perdido Bay Country Club can tell you what that means: lost balls.

This is the Venice of the PGA Tour, with water, water everywhere. Indeed, for the most errant hitters, water comes into play on *every tee shot* and almost every second shot. There are 49 bunkers on the course, and almost that many ponds, lakes, drainage ditches, and streams. When the wind blows strongly, as it does during the fall and spring, this course is a strong par 71, especially at its championship length of 7,093 yards.

"Since there was so little elevation in the land, we made a special effort to add interest to the greens," says architect Bill Amick. "They are all contoured, but there is no pattern, no predictability to the contouring. Each hole is a separate challenge, both on the approach from the fairway and in putting."

The 10th hole is an amalgam of all that is good and testing at Pensacola. A 453-yard dogleg par four, it is completely wrapped in water. The tee shot must be a long draw. Too straight, and the ball will go into water on the right. Too short, and it will not leave a view of the green. A large bunker fronts the right side of the green, with water hazards to the left, right, and rear.

Perdido's toughest hole is without question number 14, another long (441-yard) par four, well bunkered both along the fairway and at the green. Water runs completely down the left side and pinches the edge of the green. The tee shot on this hole is particularly daunting, with the water left and a large bunker on the right. Should the ball finish in that bunker, the approach to the green must be played with a fade, otherwise it will find sand or water to the left of the green. In 1984 Bill Kratzert bogeyed this hole the last day and thought he had blown his lead. But he came back with three straight birdies on 15, 16, and 17 to score his first victory in four years.

Number 18, site of all the agony and ecstasy, is appropriately demanding. As usual, the drive must avoid water on both sides, and when the pin is cut to the right side of the green behind the large guardian bunker, additional pressure accrues to this final swing of the year.

The Pensacola Open has been at Perdido Bay since 1978, but the tournament dates back to 1929, when it was won by Horton Smith, the same player who won the inaugural Masters tournament. Johnny Farrell won the next two stagings before the event was discontinued for

twelve years. In 1945 it returned and Sam Snead took first prize, then Lloyd Mangrum won in 1946, before another hiatus, this one lasting until 1955, when it returned with a spring date. The tournament soon became sponsored by Monsanto, and the Monsanto Open was won by Arnold Palmer, Doug Sanders, Art Wall, and Gene Littler, among others. In 1976 Monsanto withdrew sponsorship, leaving the tournament sponsorship to the local businessmen. At around the same time, the PGA Tour shuffled it from early spring to mid-fall and switched its site from the Pensacola Country Club to Perdido Bay. The complete change —of sponsor, time, and venue—was painful at first, but today the tournament flourishes.

ALL TIME TOURNAMENT RECORDS

Record	Player(s)	Score	Year
Low 18	Gay Brewer	61	1967
Low first 36	Gay Brewer	130 (66–64)	1967
	Ernie Gonzalez	128 (65–63)	1986
Low 36	Gay Brewer	125 (64–61)	1967 (rounds 2–3)
Low first 54	Gay Brewer	191 (66–64–61)	1967
Low 54	Gay Brewer	191 (66–64–61)	1967
Low 72	Gay Brewer	262 (66–64–61–71)	1967
Highest winning score	Johnny Farrell	287 (71–74–74–68)	1930
Largest winning margin	Sam Snead (267)	7 strokes	1945
	Calvin Peete (268)		1982
Largest 18-hole lead	Mark Lye (63)	3 strokes	1983
	Ralph Landrum (63)		1984
Largest 36-hole lead	Mac McLendon (132)	5 strokes	1978
Largest 54-hole lead	Gay Brewer (191)	9 strokes	1967
Lowest start by winner	Dave Hill	64	1972
Highest start by winner	Johnny Farrell George Archer	73	1931 1968
Lowest finish by winner	Calvin Peete Mark McCumber	65	1982 1983
Highest finish by winner	Homero Blancas	75	1973
Best final-round comeback	Dan Halldorson	3 back	1980
Lowest 36-hole cut score		139	1986
Highest 36-hole cut score		144	Several years

12th hole

PAST WINNERS

Year	Winner	Score	Year	Winner	Score
1929	Horton Smith	274	1969	Jim Colbert	267
1930	John Farrell	287	1970	Dick Lotz	275
1931	John Farrell	286	1971	Gene Littler	276
1932–			1972	Dave Hill	271
1944	No Tournaments		1973	Homero Blancas	277
1945	Sam Snead	267	1974	*Lee Elder	274
1946	*Ray Mangrum	277	1975	Jerry McGee	274
1947–			1976	Mark Hayes	275
1955	No Tournaments		1977	Leonard Thompson	268
1956	Don Fairfield	275	1978	*Mac McLendon	272
1957	Art Wall	273	1979	Curtis Strange	271
1958	Doug Ford	278	1980	Dan Halldorson	265
1959	Paul Harney	269	1981	Jerry Pate	271
1960	Arnold Palmer	273	1982	Calvin Peete	268
1961	Tommy Bolt	275	1983	Mark McCumber	266
1962	Doug Sanders	270	1984	Bill Kratzert	270
1963	Arnold Palmer	273	1985	Danny Edwards	269
1964	*Gary Player	274	1986	‡Ernie Gonzalez	128
1965	*Doug Sanders	277	1987	Doug Tewell	269
1966	Gay Brewer	272			
1967	Gay Brewer	262	‡Rain curtailed		
1968	George Archer	268	*Playoff		

18th hole

10th hole

NORTH

SCORECARD

Hole	Yards	Par	PGA Tour Avg. Score
1	379	4	3.873
2	460	4	4.156
3	419	4	4.062
4	210	3	3.054
5	411	4	4.101
6	560	5	4.652
7	445	4	4.151
8	173	3	2.957
9	378	4	4.110
OUT	3435	35	35.116
10	453	4	4.165
11	508	5	4.756
12	422	4	4.080
13	236	3	3.129
14	441	4	4.244
15	560	5	4.691
16	390	4	4.047
17	194	3	3.003
18	454	4	4.136
IN	3658	36	36.251
TOTAL	7093	71	71.367

SPLASHING OUT OF WATER
BY MARK McCUMBER

Water comes into play on virtually every hole at Perdido Bay. Usually, once you see the ball splash, you can reach into your bag for another one. Occasionally, however, you'll find the ball on or near the bank, either fully or partially submerged in water.

The trickiest thing is deciding whether or not the ball is playable. A good general rule is that if at least half of the ball is above water, you can safely give it a whack. If it's totally submerged, your chances are pretty slim.

To play the shot, I recommend using a pitching wedge rather than a sand wedge. You want to be able to slice into the water with as little splash as possible, so the thick-flanged sand wedge is the last weapon to select.

You should explode a ball from water much the same way you would a ball buried in sand. Assuming you can get a comfortable stance, play the ball about midway between the feet and stand open to your target with the blade of the wedge facing the target. Cock your wrists quickly on the backswing and hit down sharply on a point about two inches in back of the ball. Give it a good hard whack—the last thing you want to do is leave the ball in the water.

Mark McCumber won the 1983 Pensacola Open.

MAGNOLIA
Golf Course

PALM
Golf Course

LAKE BUENA VISTA
Golf Course

WALT DISNEY WORLD/OLDSMOBILE
CLASSIC, FLORIDA

Tour brats—that lucky/unlucky pack of boys and girls whose fathers play the pro circuit—could not care less whether daddy ever gets to The Masters or the U.S. Open. The main event of the year is, after all, the Disney, that golden week in October when they get to eat lunch with sea lions, shake hands with Goofy and Pluto, and take thirty-seven trips a day down Space Mountain, while pop plies his trade on the three courses across the street.

It is not a bad week for father either. The late-fall date on the schedule usually means that the top players are overseas playing exhibitions and invitational events. Thus, the struggling dads have a good opportunity to bring home some extra bacon. And the three courses, although typical of most Florida layouts, could hardly be described as Mickey Mouse.

All three were produced by Joe Lee, the protégé and eventual partner of Dick Wilson. Lee designed dozens of resort and real estate community courses in the Sun Belt, collaborated with Ben Hogan on the Trophy Club in Ft. Worth (Hogan's only serious foray into architecture), and reworked the layouts of two other PGA Tour courses, Green Island (Southern Open) and Warwick Hills (Buick Open).

Although the three courses sit within a few thousand yards of each other and all three are par 72s, they do have separate personalities. The Magnolia is the long-ball course at 7,150 yards. When the wind is blowing, it is much longer, especially when playing across and around its 108 bunkers. This is the course played twice during the Disney and always used for the final round.

Magnolia, 4th hole

Magnolia, 12th hole

Palm, 18th hole

The Palm, which emanates from the same clubhouse as its big sister, is 233 yards shorter, but it sometimes seems as if those yards were pared from the *width* of the fairways. With encroaching trees and water in play on 10 holes, the average player has two options: keep in play or bring lots of balls.

Lake Buena Vista is shorter yet, at 6,655 yards, but may be the tightest of the three, and its Tifdwarf greens (a strain of grass, not a Disney character) are much faster than the bermudagrass surfaces at the other two courses.

The Palm and Magnolia were opened in 1970 and hosted the Disney Classic from 1971–73. In each of those years it was won by Jack Nicklaus. Perhaps the Bear's stranglehold reminded the promoters of a brutally one-sided boxing match, because after twelve rounds they stopped it. The tournament returned three years later in a pro-pro team format, where twosomes pooled their efforts, using the lower score on each hole. That lasted through 1981, when the event returned to the standard format, adding play on the Lake Buena Vista course.

Two holes at the Palm and two at Magnolia deserve special mention. The toughest test at the former is number six, a 412-yard bowling alley with water in the left gutter, trees and swamp in the right. Water also cuts directly in front of the green. The hole was immortalized in one Disney when Arnold Palmer took an 11 on it.

The longest par four on the course is the 454-yard 18th, where the last third of the hole is an island. The right edge of the green is hard by the water, while the left is guarded by four bunkers. The pros will tell you they are glad they have to tackle this hole only once a year.

The fourth hole at the Magnolia is a place only Lawrence of Arabia could love. From tee to green are scattered 14 bunkers—more than two acres of sand. Half of them are at the green, which they encircle like a malevolent gallery, in some spots hovering two-deep. Still, if you can keep yourself out of buried lies, this 512-yard par five may be the easiest hole on the course. One year it yielded 10 eagles, 115 birdies, and only two bogeys in two days' play as the pros ravaged it in 4.3 strokes.

The finishing hole at the Magnolia, as at the Palm, is the longest par four on the course. At 455 yards it is also in fact the longest par four in the tournament.

ALL TIME TOURNAMENT RECORDS

Record	Player(s)	Score	Year
Low 18	Mark Lye	61	1984
Low first 36	Chip Beck	130 (64–66)	1984
Low 36	Chip Beck	130 (64–66)	1984 (rounds 1–2)
	Larry Nelson	(66–64)	1984 (rounds 2–3)
	Mark Lye	(61–69)	1984 (rounds 3–4)
	Scott Hoch	(63–67)	1985 (rounds 2–3)
Low first 54	Larry Nelson	196 (66–66–64)	1984
Low 54	Larry Nelson	196 (66–66–64)	1984
Low 72	Larry Nelson	266 (66–66–64–70)	1984
Highest winning score	Jack Nicklaus	275 (70–71–67–67)	1973
Largest winning margin	Jack Nicklaus (267)	9 strokes	1972
Largest 18-hole lead	Mark McCumber (64)	2 strokes	1983
Largest 36-hole lead	John Mahaffey (137)	2 strokes	1973
	Chip Beck (130)		1984
	Gary Koch (132)		1985
Largest 54-hole lead	Jay Haas (197)	5 strokes	1982
Lowest start by winner	Larry Nelson	66	1984
Highest start by winner	Hal Sutton	71	1982
Lowest finish by winner	Lanny Wadkins Larry Nelson	63	1985 1987
Highest finish by winner	Ray Floyd	71	1986
Best final-round comeback	Hal Sutton (202)	5 back	1982
Lowest 36-hole cut score		144	1971
Highest 36-hole cut score		147	1973
Lowest 54-hole cut score		212	1984
Highest 54-hole cut score		215	1986, 1987

PAST WINNERS

Year	Winner	Score
1971	Jack Nicklaus	273
1972	Jack Nicklaus	267
1973	Jack Nicklaus	275
1982	*Hal Sutton	269
1983	Payne Stewart	269
1984	Larry Nelson	266
1985	Lanny Wadkins	267
1986	Ray Floyd	275
1987	Larry Nelson	268

*Playoff

Palm, 16th hole

Lake Buena Vista, 6th hole

Lake Buena Vista, 18th hole

Lake Buena Vista, 5th hole

Magnolia, 6th hole

PUTTING ON BERMUDA
BY PAYNE STEWART

Grainy bermudagrass greens, such as those on the courses in the Disney, demand a different stroke and a different strategy than on rye and bentgrass greens. Bermuda is a stiff-bladed strain, and when clipped short it looks like a crewcut except that the "hairs" all grow in the same direction. Nine times out of ten, it's toward the setting sun. This grain has a big impact on putts—a ball that rolls 10 feet downgrain will go only half that distance against the grain.

I make a couple of changes in my stroke when I play a Tour event that has bermuda greens. Generally, it's tough to get the ball rolling smoothly on bermuda, particularly when putting into the grain, so I position the ball a bit farther forward in my stance than normal. From that position, I'm able to hit slightly upward on the ball, promoting forward spin and an even roll. I also grip the putter a bit more tightly than usual and concentrate on staying down on the stroke to guarantee solid impact. My strategy on upgrain putts is to play them as aggressively as possible, to charge them. If you don't try to beat bermudagrass, it will almost certainly beat you.

_____

Payne Stewart won the 1983 Walt Disney World/Oldsmobile Golf Classic.

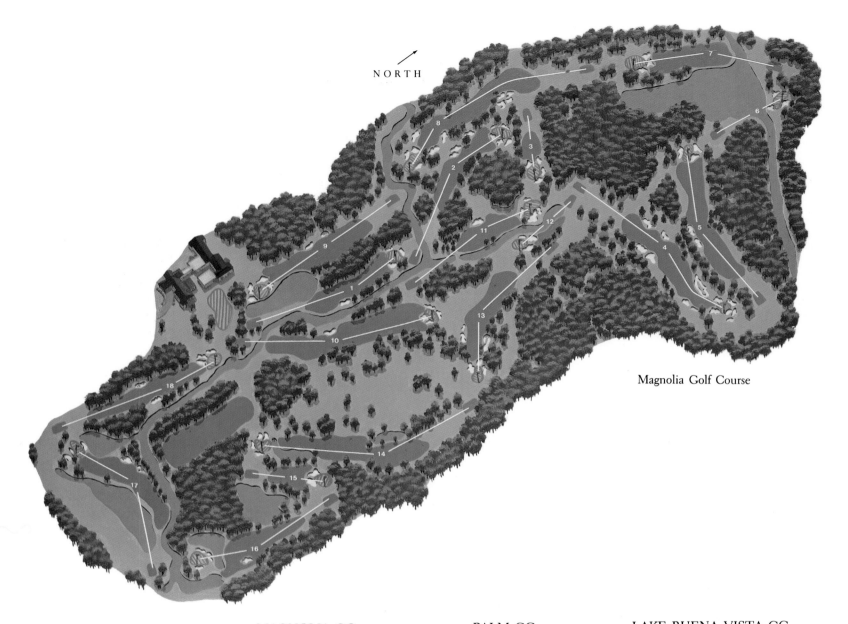

Magnolia Golf Course

MAGNOLIA GC
SCORECARD

Hole	Yards	Par	PGA Tour Avg. Score
1	428	4	4.066
2	417	4	4.024
3	160	3	2.871
4	512	5	4.387
5	448	4	4.240
6	195	3	2.971
7	410	4	3.976
8	614	5	4.908
9	431	4	4.134
OUT	3615	36	35.577
10	526	5	4.510
11	385	4	3.881
12	169	3	2.925
13	375	4	3.796
14	595	5	4.921
15	203	3	3.049
16	400	4	3.943
17	427	4	4.165
18	455	4	4.228
IN	3535	36	35.418
TOTAL	7150	72	70.995

PALM GC
SCORECARD

Hole	Yards	Par	PGA Tour Avg. Score
1	495	5	4.462
2	389	4	4.055
3	165	3	2.873
4	422	4	4.159
5	403	4	3.972
6	412	4	4.272
7	512	5	4.482
8	205	3	3.081
9	373	4	3.875
OUT	3376	36	35.231
10	450	4	4.231
11	532	5	4.682
12	199	3	3.112
13	364	4	3.848
14	547	5	4.921
15	426	4	3.944
16	172	3	2.967
17	397	4	3.949
18	454	4	4.283
IN	3541	36	35.937
TOTAL	6917	72	71.168

LAKE BUENA VISTA GC
SCORECARD

Hole	Yards	Par	PGA Tour Avg. Score
1	537	5	4.505
2	164	3	2.952
3	387	4	3.858
4	347	4	3.794
5	405	4	4.018
6	387	4	3.926
7	170	3	2.886
8	529	5	4.842
9	382	4	3.878
OUT	3308	36	34.659
10	379	4	3.827
11	437	4	4.069
12	196	3	3.061
13	348	4	3.843
14	508	5	4.569
15	364	4	3.939
16	185	3	2.990
17	519	5	4.850
18	411	4	4.182
IN	3347	36	35.330
TOTAL	6655	72	69.989

OAK HILLS *Country Club*

THE TEXAS OPEN PRESENTED BY NABISCO, TEXAS

18th hole

The PGA Tour record for 36 holes is 125, shot by Ron Streck in 1978. The site was the Oak Hills Country Club, designed by Albert W. Tillinghast, one of the giants of American golf course architecture.

"Golf's Forgotten Genius" was the title of a 1974 article by USGA Executive Director Frank Hannigan on this Philadelphia playboy who learned his trade in Scotland at the knee of Old Tom Morris. Tillinghast was not prolific, nor did he ever get a chance to design on scenically spectacular land, but his designs had an integrity, an artfulness, and an ability to test all levels of player. Today, "Tillie the Terror" continues to challenge all who are fortunate enough to play at Baltusrol Upper and Lower, Winged Foot East and West, Somerset Hills, Baltimore, Bethpage Black, Brook Hollow, and San Francisco golf clubs. At Oak Hills, Jay Morrish reworked the course in 1984, but the basic Tillinghast virtues remain intact.

"It has such great balance," says Ben Crenshaw, a Texan who made his Tour debut in 1971 in the Texas Open—and won. Although that victory came on another golf course, Crenshaw has fond memories of Oak Hills.

"I'll never forget the day I went to San Antonio with my Dad, at age eleven, and watched Arnold Palmer play. I particularly remember the third hole, one of the longest, toughest par fours on the course. It doglegs right, and the land also slopes to the right toward a series of mesquite trees. On that day, it was also playing straight into the face of the wind. I can recall standing in the gallery and watching my hero smack a long, low drive up the center of that fairway and then a tremendous 1-iron up to the green.

"Oak Hills is not an overpowering course," says Crenshaw, "but neither is it the kind of course that can be overpowered. Its strength, I believe, is its short par fours, some of the best I've ever seen."

Holes such as the first, sixth, eighth, and seventeenth average less than 350 yards yet provide some of the most testing golf on the course. All four demand tee shots into the ideal part of the fairway to ensure a good chance at birdie.

Miss a green, such as the one at number four, even by a little bit, and the ensuing assignment is a stern one. Like many a Tillinghast target, this green sits toward the player. Thus, an approach that goes into the swale beyond it will leave a difficult pitch to a severely canted surface.

Architect Morrish's main assignment was to reshape the

6th hole

6th hole

70-year-old greens on the course, most of which had developed drainage problems. At the seventh hole, a par four that doglegs slightly right, he created a double-tiered target. When the pin is on the back half, the approach shot had better find its way back there as well. If not, a three-putt is almost assured.

As at many Texas courses, two formidable opponents at Oak Hills are the wind and the mesquite tree. A southeaster blows almost constantly at fifteen miles per hour or so, guiding even slightly wayward shots toward the pesky mesquites. These are thorny, low-lying tree-bushes, rarely reaching more than twenty feet in height. They are easy enough to play over, but nearly impossible to play under, through, or out of. As such, mesquites are perhaps the most vexing of golf's deciduous perils.

All kinds of trouble come to bear at the 15th, a par five converted to a long, tough, downwind four for the pros. Trees line both sides of the fairway, including a tall live oak on the right edge. Crenshaw favors a "holding shot," a hard-hit fade down the left side of this slightly left-to-right fairway. Should that fade grow into a slice, the ball will go out-of-bounds.

Oak Hills is unique among the Tour courses, and rare

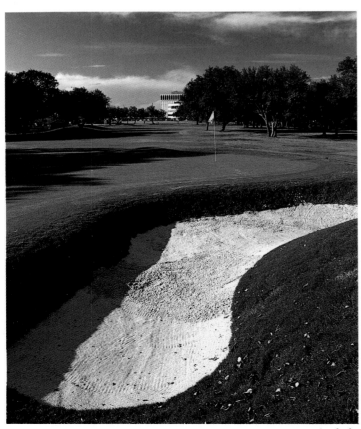

1st hole

265

among the world's courses, in that both its front and back nines conclude with par threes. Both the ninth and the 18th play over lakes and toward the clubhouse. The 18th is the more difficult of the two, a 6- or 7-iron to a broad, shallow green. In 1981, fellow Texans and close friends Crenshaw and Bill Rogers went into a playoff after Rogers made an eight-footer for birdie at 18. Rogers then birdied number one in sudden death for victory.

For more than sixty years, this tournament was known as The Texas Open. Then, in 1986 and 1987, the RJR Nabisco Company assumed title sponsorship and designated this event as the finale in a year-long points competition with $2 million in prize money at stake. In 1988, Nabisco shifted that competition to Pebble Beach, restoring its name to The Texas Open.

In 1986 the name of the tournament was changed from the Texas Open to the Vantage Championship, and the event was given a date later on the PGA Tour calendar. More important, it became the final opportunity for Tour players to earn points in the Vantage Cup program, a points competition designed to determine a national Tour champion. Sponsored by the R. J. Reynolds Tobacco Company, the program awards points to the highest finishers in each of the forty-four regular Tour events. At the end of the Vantage Championship, the player with the greatest number of points for the season wins a $500,000 first prize.

In addition, the tournament itself will have a purse of $1 million—Texas-size money, no matter what the name of the tournament.

ALL TIME TOURNAMENT RECORDS

Record	Player(s)	Score	Year
Low 18	Al Brosch	60	1951
	Ted Kroll		1954
	Mike Souchak		1955
Low first 36	Johnny Palmer	127 (65–62)	1954
Low 36	Ron Streck	125 (63–62)	1978
Low first 54	Johnny Palmer	191 (65–62–64)	1954
Low 54	Chandler Harper	189 (63–63–63)	1954
Low 72	Mike Souchak	257 (60–68–64–65)	1955
Highest winning score	Bill Mehlhorn	297	1928
Largest winning margin	Mike Souchak	7 strokes	1955
Largest 18-hole lead	Several Players	2 strokes	
Largest 36-hole lead	Arnold Palmer (130)	3 strokes	1961
	Jim Colbert (130)		1984
Largest 54-hole lead	Several Players	2 strokes	
Lowest start by winner	Mike Souchak	60	1955
Highest start by winner	Ron Streck	73	1978
Lowest finish by winner	Ron Streck	62	1978
Highest finish by winner	Bill Mehlhorn	79	1928
Best final-round comeback	Bruce Crampton (208)	6 back	1964
Lowest 36-hole cut score		139	1981–1983 1986
Highest 36-hole cut score		146	1962

PAST WINNERS

Year	Winner	Score	Year	Winner	Score	Year	Winner	Score
1922	Bob MacDonald	281	1946	Ben Hogan	264	1968	No Tournament	
1923	Walter Hagen	279	1947	Porky Oliver	265	1969	*Deane Beman	274
1924	Joe Kirkwood	279	1948	Sam Snead	264	1970	Ron Cerrudo	273
1925	Joe Turnesa	284	1949	Dave Douglas	268	1971	No Tournament	
1926	Mac Smith	288	1950	Sam Snead	265	1972	Mike Hill	273
1927	B. Cruikshank	272	1951	*Dutch Harrison	265	1973	Ben Crenshaw	270
1928	Bill Mehlhorn	297	1952	Jack Burke	260	1974	Terry Diehl	269
1929	Bill Mehlhorn	277	1953	Tony Holguin	264	1975	*Don January	275
1930	Denny Shute	277	1954	Chandler Harper	259	1976	*Butch Baird	273
1931	Abe Espinosa	281	1955	Mike Souchak	257	1977	Hale Irwin	266
1932	Clarence Clark	287	1956	Gene Littler	276	1978	Ron Streck	265
1933	No Tournament		1957	Jay Hebert	271	1979	Lou Graham	268
1934	Wiffy Cox	283	1958	Bill Johnston	274	1980	Lee Trevino	265
1935–			1959	Wes Ellis	276	1981	*Bill Rogers	266
1938	No Tournaments		1960	Arnold Palmer	276	1982	Jay Haas	262
1939	Dutch Harrison	271	1961	Arnold Palmer	270	1983	Jim Colbert	261
1940	Byron Nelson	271	1962	Arnold Palmer	273	1984	Calvin Peete	266
1941	Lawson Little	273	1963	Phil Rodgers	268	1985	*John Mahaffey	268
1942	*Chick Harbert	272	1964	Bruce Crampton	273	1986	‡Ben Crenshaw	196
1943	No Tournament		1965	Frank Beard	270	1987	Tom Watson	268
1944	Johnny Revolta	273	1966	Harold Henning	272	*Playoff		
1945	Sam Byrd	268	1967	Chi Chi Rodriguez	277	‡Rain curtailed		

NORTH

IN-BETWEEN SHOTS
BY BILL ROGERS

On short courses such as Oak Hills, where accuracy is more important than length, it's important to be able to hit your approach shots the proper distance every time. For many golfers this is difficult when the yardage is "in-between clubs." They try to manufacture a soft swing with the longer club or else overswing on the shorter club, and the results usually are less than ideal.

But there's a safe and simple way to hit those in-between distances: Take the longer club and simply choke down on it. Hold the club a little lower on the handle than you usually do, then simply put your normal swing on the ball. If you're worried that you'll lose distance by choking down, be aware that the shorter arc also has the effect of making you swing a little harder. Consequently, you won't miss as much distance as you think. For example, I can hit two shots with a 6-iron— one normal one and one when I've choked down a little—and there will

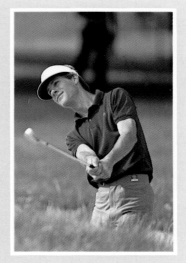

be a difference of only five yards or one-half club. Choking down also enhances control and usually produces a very solid hit.

————

Bill Rogers, a resident of San Antonio, Texas, won the 1981 Vantage Championship and is consultant on the event's new TPC course.

SCORECARD

Hole	Yards	Par	PGA Tour Avg. Score
1	349	4	4.048
2	175	3	2.979
3	456	4	4.224
4	389	4	4.155
5	604	5	4.834
6	352	4	4.019
7	460	4	4.243
8	309	4	3.892
9	155	3	3.013
OUT	3249	35	35.407
10	506	5	4.694
11	416	4	4.129
12	444	4	4.191
13	220	3	3.242
14	328	4	3.953
15	463	4	4.324
16	385	4	4.052
17	367	4	4.071
18	198	3	3.110
IN	3327	35	35.766
TOTAL	6576	70	71.173

TPC at STARPASS

StarPass is one of the newest among the recent crop of stadium courses commissioned by the PGA Tour. Each of these courses must follow a set of Tour specifications regarding spectator gallery areas. It is thus a challenge to the individual designers to keep their courses from looking too much like the already-existing TPC layouts.

Architect Bob Cupp had an additional challenge in working with the desert terrain, where footing is better suited to wild goats and rattlesnakes than to men. Thus, his spectator areas first had to be cleared of all rocks, crevices, and dangerous plants. The gallery mounds were then planted with bermudagrass and with six-weeks grass, a special strain that has a tan color that gives these areas a distinctive look. In addition, whereas the gallery areas at most spectator courses have a sort of long, straight, grandstand look, those at StarPass curl, leaving a bit more room for spectators. Also, some of the gallery areas are depressed, with the first few rows actually below the playing surface, so that a player sees only faces along the horizon, not entire bodies. Together, these innovations make Star-Pass a TPC course with its own strong personality.

The longest par three on the course is number eight, a 215-yard slightly downhill shot to a green that is bisected by a deep swale, leaving a distinct front, middle, and back. It is followed immediately by the longest par four on the course, 465-yard number nine. Bunkers guard the right side of this green, so the ideal approach is from the left. But the player who hits his drive in that direction will have to carry a trio of large, deep fairway bunkers, all of which sit well below fairway level. The right side of the fairway is lined by a rising slope and slightly rippled to offer irregular lies.

In complete contrast to nine—and more than 100 yards shorter—is number 15, 362 yards of compact guile. The teeshot can be played with almost any club from a middle iron to a driver, so long as the shot is straight. This is a thread-the-needle drive that must finish on a saddle of fairway between two craggy hills. If it does, the second shot will be a mere flick. If it does not, the second shot will have to be hammered out of sagebrush and rocks.

Only the bold—or desperate—will go for the 17th green in two, a 530-yard par five that plays against the backdrop of Tucson National Park. The hole will be won or lost on the third shot, a short iron to a smallish green protected by two deep bunkers on the right and a large pot bunker

StarPass, 16th hole

StarPass, 16th hole

StarPass, 15th hole

StarPass, 9th hole

on the left. The back part of the green is a foot higher than the front, and the gamblers will be counting on that when they bang their long, hard second shots home.

The finishing hole is a worthy place to settle matches, a 445-yard par four that puts a premium on both the tee shot and the approach. It is a straight hole, but the best approach to the green is from the right side of the fairway if the drive can avoid a cluster of bunkers near the ideal landing area. The small green will be a tough target, and if the Tour players are not happy with it, they can complain to Craig Stadler, the man who designed it. Stadler was the player-consultant on StarPass, his first venture into the business of golf course architecture.

Most of the Walrus's input related to the shape and contour of the greens, the feature that he feels is the make or break element of any course. One of the Tour's finest putters, Stadler favors fast greens, as does Cupp. In time they hope that the greens at StarPass will be the fastest on the Tour.

Cupp got his Ph.D. in putting-green construction in 1985 while he was an associate with Golforce, one of the architectural firms headed by Jack Nicklaus. In that year Golforce was called upon by the Augusta National Golf Club to rework the severely sloped 9th and 18th greens at The Masters course, where the challenge was to preserve the "treachery" that Bob Jones had intended half a century ago, while maintaining fairness.

ALL TIME TOURNAMENT RECORDS

Record	Player(s)	Score	Year
Low 18	Frank Stranahan	61	1952
	Buddy Sullivan		
	Johnny Miller		
Low first 36	Joe Campbell	129	1959
		(65–64)	
	Julius Boros	(65–64)	1959
	Bruce Lietzke	(63–66)	1979
	Craig Stadler	(65–64)	1982
Low 36	Johnny Palmer	126	1948
		(62–64)	(rounds 3–4)
Low first 54	Joe Campbell	194	1959
		(65–64–65)	
Low 54	Joe Campbell	194	1959
		(65–64–65)	
Low 72	Lloyd Mangrum	263	1949
	Phil Rodgers		1962
	Johnny Miller		1975
Highest winning score	Joe Campbell	278	1966
Largest winning score	Don January (266)	11 strokes	1963
Lowest start	Johnny Miller	62	1974
Highest start	George Knudson	70	1968
	Bruce Crampton		1973
	Johnny Miller		1976
	Bruce Lietzke		1977
Lowest finish	Johnny Miller	61	1975
Highest finish	Arnold Palmer	73	1967
	Miller Barber		1972
	Tom Watson		1978
Lowest 36-hole		139	1959
Highest 36-hole cut score		148	1964

SCORECARD

Hole	Yards	Par
1	365	4
2	510	5
3	445	4
4	400	4
5	530	5
6	200	3
7	420	4
8	215	3
9	465	4
OUT	3550	36
10	430	4
11	415	4
12	505	5
13	413	4
14	145	3
15	362	4
16	199	3
17	530	5
18	445	4
IN	3444	36
TOTAL	6994	72

STRIKING FROM THE SAND
BY CRAIG STADLER

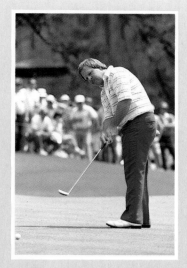

At StarPass sand is all around the course, not simply in the bunkers. If your ball finds the desert area, you had better be prepared to do some shotmaking.

Fundamentally, you play full shots from the desert floor the same way you would a ball from a fairway bunker. Give yourself good footing and take one club more than you would for a comparable distance from the fairway (assuming you don't have to fly the ball over any trees or vegetation). I try to play these shots with control, meaning relatively quiet leg action, and a more sweeping swing than usual to ensure that I contact the ball before the sand. It's important to trust the loft on the club and the power of your swing on this shot—be patient on the downswing and make a smooth, unhurried pass at the ball. The most common and damaging error on this shot is to throw your arms and club at the ball, to hit at it rather than swinging through it.

If you're an advanced player and you have a good clean lie from sand, you can try to play a controlled fade. Just take at least one club more than usual, set up for a fade, and pull through firmly, not letting the right hand cross the left. From this clean lie you can get a big left-to-right curve and lots of backspin.

Craig Stadler won the 1982 Tucson Open and was design consultant to the TPC at StarPass.

NORTH →

271

UNOFFICIAL MONEY EVENTS

ISUZU KAPALUA
INTERNATIONAL

KIRIN CUP
WORLD
CHAMPIONSHIP
OF GOLF

THE WORLD
CUP OF GOLF

THE SKINS GAME

JCPENNEY
CLASSIC

CHRYSLER TEAM
INVITATIONAL

In addition to the forty-one tournaments on its regular schedule, the PGA Tour co-stages six "unofficial" events each year. Prize winnings from these events are not applied to the official money winnings list, nor does a victory in any of these tournaments entitle the winner to any of the exemptions that accrue to victors in the core events. In most other ways, however, these six tournaments, each with a unique cachet, enjoy the full support of the Tour.

ISUZU KAPALUA INTERNATIONAL

This event is contested over the Bay Course at the spectacular Kapalua resort on Maui, Hawaii. The Isuzu Kapalua International began in 1982 as a limited field invitational event that included a few dozen top players from around the world. International is an apt description of its first four victors—local Hawaiian professional David Ishii in 1982, Australian superstar Greg Norman in 1983, Scotsman Sandy Lyle in 1984, and Mark O'Meara in 1985.

The Kapalua International has a major advantage over virtually every other tournament in golf. With a six-hour time difference between Maui and New York, its afternoon finish can be televised live during prime time evening hours on the East Coast.

The Bay Course, one of two designed by Arnold Palmer at the Kapalua resort, is a pleasurable place to play golf, but when the winds blow off Oneola Bay it is a daunting place to have to make a score. Most of the holes play up, down, or across hills above the dazzlingly blue Pacific, and many afford views that make keeping one's head down a true act of will.

The Kapalua tournament is a very young one, but in a short time it has engendered much loyalty among the world's top players. And why not? Win or lose, a week at Kapalua is about as close to paradise as the PGA Tour gets.

KIRIN CUP WORLD CHAMPIONSHIP OF GOLF

A week after the 1985 Kapalua International, the first Nissan (now Kirin) Cup World Championship of Golf was played on the same Bay Course at Kapalua. The event brought together for the first time teams from the four major professional golf tours around the world: the United States, European, Australian, and Japanese tours.

The format calls for four days of round-robin stroke play among the six-man squads, with team points awarded for

Kapalua, 17th hole

ties and wins in the individual matches. The inaugural matches were won by the American team.

Plans call for the Kirin Cup to rotate among the home countries of the four tours, returning to the United States once every four years.

THE WORLD CUP OF GOLF

In 1986 the World Cup of Golf became sanctioned as a coordinated tournament on the PGA Tour schedule. This international competition involves two-man teams from each of several nations around the globe, with prizes awarded for both individual and team competition. It is conducted by the International Golf Association under the motto "international good will through golf," and the site of the tournament shifts among the participating countries throughout the world.

Beginning with the 1986 staging, the World Cup will occupy a consistent date annually: the week before Thanksgiving. First choices to represent the two-man United States entry each year will be that season's TPC and Masters champions, provided both are citizens of the United States.

THE SKINS GAME

Most weekend golfers have played "skins" golf once or twice, the "two tie, all tie" format for three or more players. Each player competes against all others on a hole-by-hole basis, and the only way to win the hole (or skin) is to score lower than all other players. If Player A makes a par and Players B, C, and D make bogeys, Player A wins the skin. If, however, A and B both par the hole, then regardless of whether C and D make par, bogey, or quadruple bogey, all four players "tie" the hole, and the skin is carried over to the next hole. If the group is playing for a one-dollar skin, then the next hole is worth two dollars. Theoretically, the group could tie the first 17 holes and then one player could win it all—eighteen dollars from each of his or her opponents—with an outright victory on the 18th hole.

It is a format played all over the world, but never had the skins game found its way to the pro ranks until 1983, when Arnold Palmer, Jack Nicklaus, Tom Watson, and Gary Player teed up at Nicklaus's Desert Highlands course in Arizona. In their case, however, the skins were not a dollar a hole, they started at $10,000 per hole for the first six, doubled to $20,000 for holes seven through 12, then

PGA West, 17th hole

Bardmoor, 8th hole

Palm Beach, South Course 1st hole

upped to $30,000 on the final six holes. The total purse was $360,000, and with lots of ties along the way, large chunks of that total often hinged on single holes. Of course, in this case the players themselves did not ante up the cash, tournament sponsors did.

The 18-hole match is played over two days, to stretch the live television coverage. During the first two years, selection of the players was made by the tournament organizers, but beginning in 1985, when the PGA Tour adoped the skins as a co-sponsored event, the seeding system altered so that the foursome included the defending champion plus one player selected by the sponsors plus two players chosen by a blue-ribbon panel of golf officials and journalists.

After two years at Desert Highlands, the match moved to another Nicklaus course, Bear Creek, in Murietta, California. Now its home is the PGA West, Pete Dye's Stadium Course in Palm Springs. Opened in 1986, PGA West is already being called the hardest golf course in the world. Its rating is 77.1

JC PENNEY CLASSIC

Bardmoor Country Club in Largo, Florida, is the annual site of the only major tournament that teams PGA Tour pros with their counterparts from the Ladies Professional Golf Association (LPGA).

The event got its start in 1960 when it was known as the Haig & Haig Scotch Foursome. It ran for seven years, stopped for a decade, and returned in 1976. Virtually every top LPGA player has shared in a victory, beginning with Mickey Wright, Kathy Whitworth, and Ruth Jessen in the original version and continuing with Hollis Stacy, Pat Bradley, Nancy Lopez, Beth Daniel, JoAnne Carner, and Jan Stephenson in recent years.

Play is conducted according to the Pinehurst format, in which each member of the team plays a drive, then the partners hit second shots from each other's drives, then decide which of the two second shots offers the better potential for success. Once that choice is made, they take the other ball out of play and finish playing the hole with the selected ball, alternating shots until the ball is holed.

Strategy in this event is both more complicated and more important than in a standard tournament. On a 520-yard par five, for example, a male pro may hit a 260-yard drive, then his female partner will add a 210-yard fairway wood straight down the middle. They must weigh the promise of that position against that of their other ball, driven 240 yards by the female pro and boosted another 260 off the fairway wood of the male pro, but into a greenside bunker. Should the man play a 50-yard pitch shot or the woman play a 60-foot explosion? Such decision-making is the key to the excitement of this format for both players and spectators.

CHRYSLER TEAM INVITATIONAL

In 1983, Johnny Miller rallied support among his Tour colleagues for this event in which both pro-pro and pro-am teams compete. The field is composed of 112 pros and their 112 amateur partners, and in each foursome a score is recorded for the better ball of the pro-pro team and the better ball of each of the two pro-am teams. The tournament is played at the Palm Beach Polo and Country Club in Florida now, but for its first few years it was hosted by the Boca West resort in Boca Raton.

Miller, as founder, got first choice for his pro partner and made a good selection—Jack Nicklaus. During the mid-seventies when Miller was red-hot, he was seen as the top challenger to the supremacy of Nicklaus. At Boca the two giants teamed perfectly and won the rain-shortened inaugural tournament with a score of 191—25-under par. Nicklaus's amateur partner was his fourteen-year-old son, Gary. Said to be the most talented of the Nicklaus brood, Gary outdrove his dad on virtually every hole, sometimes by as much as 50 yards.

The second edition also produced an exciting finish as Ron Streck ran home a 15-foot birdie putt on 18 to carry himself and partner Phil Hancock to a one-stroke victory. And the third staging produced a gang-playoff with five teams (10 players) involved. Hal Sutton birdied the first hole of sudden death to win for himself and Raymond Floyd.

PAST WINNERS

KIRIN CUP WORLD CHAMPIONSHIP OF GOLF

Year	Winner	Score
1985	U.S. PGA TOUR Ind. Sandy Lyle	10–2 267
1986	JAPAN PGA Ind. Tommy Nakajima	8-4 270
1987	U.S. PGA TOUR Ind. Tom Kite	10-2 272

ISUZU/KAPALUA INTERNATIONAL

Year	Winner	Score
1983	Greg Norman	268
1984	Sandy Lyle	266
1985	Mark O'Meara	275
1986	Andy Bean	278
1987	Andy Bean	267

SKINS GAME

Year	Winner	Score
1983	Gary Player	$170,000
1984	Jack Nicklaus	$240,000
1985	Fuzzy Zoeller	$255,000
1986	Fuzzy Zoeller	
1987	Lee Trevino	$310,000

JC PENNEY CLASSIC

Year	Winner	Score
1960	*Jim Turnesa Gloria Armstrong	+ 139
1961	Dave Ragan Mickey Wright	272
1962	Mason Rudolph Kathy Whitworth	272
1963	Dave Ragan Mickey Wright	273
1964	Sam Snead Shirley Englehorn	272
1965	Gardner Dickinson Ruth Jessen	281
1966	Jack Rule Sandra Spuzich	276
1967 –75	No tournaments	

Year	Winner	Score
1976	Chi Chi Rodriguez JoAnn Washam	275
1977	Jerry Pate Hollis Stacy	270
1978	*Lon Hinkle Pat Bradley	267
1979	Dave Eichelberger Murle Breer	268
1980	Curtis Strange Nancy Lopez	268
1981	Tom Kite Beth Daniel	270
1982	John Mahaffey JoAnne Carner	268
1983	Fred Couples Jan Stephenson	264
1984	Mike Donald Vicki Alvarez	270
1985	Larry Rinker Laurie Rinker	267
1986	Tom Purtzer Juli Inkster	265

Note: From 1960–66, event was known as Haig & Haig Scotch Foursome. 1976–77 it was Pepsi-Cola Mixed Team.

CHRYSLER TEAM INVITATIONAL

Year	Winner	Score
1983	Jack Nicklaus Johnny Miller	191
1984	Phil Hancock Ron Streck	255
1985	Raymond Floyd Hal Sutton*	260
1986	Gary Hallberg Scott Hoch	251

SEIKO-TUCSON MATCH PLAY

Year	Winner	Score
1984	Tom Watson	2&1
1985	Jim Thorpe	4 & 3
1986	Jim Thorpe	67–71
1987	Mike Reid	268

*Playoff

THE WORLD CUP OF GOLF

Year	Winning Teams	Winning Individual
1953	ARGENTINA R. De Vicenzo, Antonio Cerda	Antonio Cerda, Argentina
1954	AUSTRALIA Peter Thompson, Kel Nagle	Stan Leonard, Canada
1955	UNITED STATES Ed Furgol, Chick Harbert	Ed Furgol, U.S.
1956	UNITED STATES Ben Hogan, Sam Snead	Ben Hogan, U.S.
1957	JAPAN T. Nakamura, Koichi Ono	T. Nakamura, Japan
1958	IRELAND Harry Bradshaw, C. O'Connor	Angel Miguel, Spain
1959	AUSTRALIA Peter Thomson, Kel Nagle	Stan Leonard, Canada
1960	UNITED STATES Arnold Palmer, Sam Snead	Flory Van Donck, Belgium
1961	UNITED STATES Sam Snead, Jimmy Demaret	Sam Snead, U.S.
1962	UNITED STATES Arnold Palmer, Sam Snead	R. De Vicenzo, Argentina
1963	UNITED STATES Jack Nicklaus, Arnold Palmer	Jack Nicklaus, U.S.
1964	UNITED STATES Jack Nicklaus, Arnold Palmer	Jack Nicklaus, U.S.
1965	SOUTH AFRICA Gary Player, Harold Henning	Gary Player, South Africa
1966	UNITED STATES Jack Nicklaus, Arnold Palmer	George Knudson, Canada
1967	UNITED STATES Jack Nicklaus, Arnold Palmer	Arnold Palmer, U.S.
1968	CANADA Al Balding, George Knudson	Al Balding, Canada
1969	UNITED STATES Lee Trevino, Orville Moody	Lee Trevino, U.S.
1970	AUSTRALIA David Graham, Bruce Devlin	R. De Vicenzo, Argentina
1971	UNITED STATES Jack Nicklaus, Lee Trevino	Jack Nicklaus, U.S.
1972	REP. CHINA Hsieh Min-Nan, Lu Liang-Huan	Hsieh Min-Nan, Rep. China
1973	UNITED STATES Johnny Miller, Jack Nicklaus	Johnny Miller, U.S.
1974	SOUTH AFRICA Bobby Cole, Dale Hayes	Bobby Cole, South Africa
1975	UNITED STATES Johnny Miller, Lou Graham	Johnny Miller, U.S.
1976	SPAIN Manuel Pinero, S. Ballesteros	Ernesto Acosta, Mexico
1977	SPAIN Antonio Garrido, S. Ballesteros	Gary Player, South Africa
1978	UNITED STATES John Mahaffey, Andy North	John Mahaffey, U.S.
1979	UNITED STATES John Mahaffey, Hale Irwin	Hale Irwin, U.S.
1980	CANADA Dan Halldorson, Jim Nelford	Sandy Lyle, Scotland
1981	No Tournament	
1982	SPAIN Manuel Pinero, Jose-Maria Canizares	Manuel Pinero, Spain
1983	UNITED STATES Rex Caldwell, John Cook	Dave Barr, Canada
1984	SPAIN Jose-Maria Canizares, Jose Rivero, Spain	Jose-Maria Canizares, Spain
1985	CANADA Dave Barr, Dan Halldorson	Howard Clark, Great Britain
1986	No Tournament	
1987	WALES David Llewelynn, Ian Woosnam	Ian Woosnam, Wales

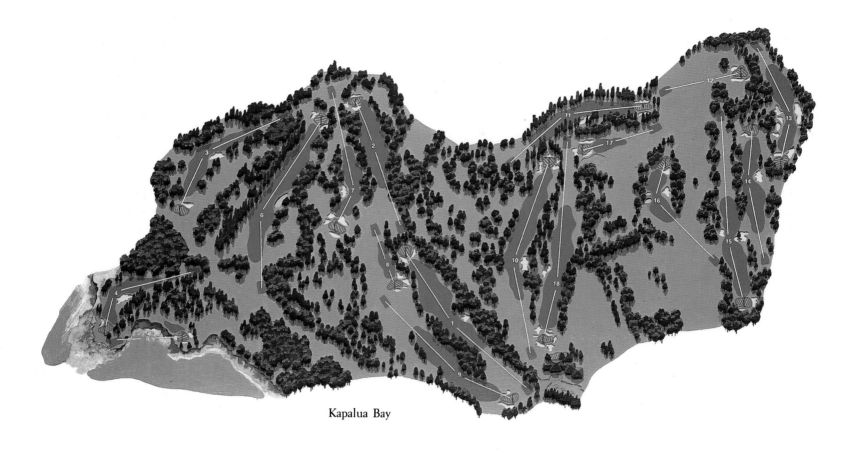

Kapalua Bay

RIDING A TAILWIND
BY SANDY LYLE

The wind blows constantly in Hawaii, but on certain holes at Kapalua, you have it at your back. That's the time to be aggressive on the tee shot.

You want to get your ball up high so that you can ride that wind. Some teachers recommend teeing the drive a bit higher than normal. I disagree, I think an abnormally high tee forces most golfers to make compensations in their swings. Very often, they end up hitting underneath the ball and popping it straight up. I prefer teeing the ball at its usual height but positioning it farther foward in my stance, up near my left instep where I'll be sure to hit it on the upswing.

Other than that, I concentrate on keeping my right shoulder below my left throughout most of the swing. This helps me stay behind and under the shot to ensure a high flight. You don't want to overswing on this shot and completely mis-hit it, but it's nice to know that on downwind shots you can afford to make a hard swing because the tailwind will straighten out a hook or a slice.

On downwind approach shots, bear in mind that your ball will not only fly farther than usual; it will tend to bounce and roll farther as well because the wind strips it of normal backspin. Thus, depending on the strength of the helping breeze, take one, two, three, or even four clubs less than normal for the distance in question.

Sandy Lyle won the 1984 Isuzu Kapalua International.

KAPALUA BAY GC
SCORECARD

Hole	Yards	Par
1	504	5
2	396	4
3	432	4
4	366	4
5	184	3
6	532	5
7	368	4
8	170	3
9	460	4
OUT	3412	36
10	552	5
11	416	4
12	198	3
13	360	4
14	352	4
15	457	4
16	397	4
17	178	3
18	557	5
IN	3467	36
TOTAL	6879	72

RECORDS AND STATISTICS

ALL-TIME PGA TOUR RECORDS

All Information Based on Official PGA Tour Co-Sponsored or Approved Events

SCORING RECORDS

72 holes:

257 — (60–68–64–65) by Mike Souchak, at Brackenridge Park Golf Course, San Antonio, Tex., in 1955 Texas Open (27 under par).

259 — (62–68–63–66) by Byron Nelson, at Broadmoor Golf Club, Seattle, Wash., in 1945 Seattle Open (21 under par).

259 — (70–63–63–63) by Chandler Harper, at Brackenridge Park Golf Course, San Antonio, Tex., in 1954 Texas Open (25 under par).

259 — (63–64–66–66) by Tim Norris, at Wethersfield CC, Hartford, Conn., in 1982 Canon Sammy Davis, Jr. Greater Hartford Open (25 under par).

Best under par performance:

— 27 Mike Souchak in winning the 1955 Texas Open with 257.

— 27 Ben Hogan in winning the 1945 Portland Invitational with 261.

— 26 Gay Brewer in winning the 1967 Pensacola Open with 262.

— 26 Robert Wrenn in winning the 1987 Buick Open with 262.

— 25 Chandler Harper in winning the 1954 Texas Open with 259.

— 25 Johnny Miller in winning the 1975 Tucson Open with 263.

— 25 Tim Norris in winning the 1982 Canon Sammy Davis, Jr. Greater Hartford Open with 259.

54 holes:

Opening rounds

191 — (66–64–61) by Gay Brewer, at Pensacola CC, Pensacola, Fla., in winning 1967 Pensacola Open.

192 — (60–68–64) by Mike Souchak, at Brackenridge Park Golf Course, San Antonio, Tex., in 1955 Texas Open.

192 — (64–63–65) by Bob Gilder, at Westchester CC, Harrison, N.Y., in 1982 Manufacturers Hanover Westchester Classic.

Consecutive rounds

189 — (63–63–63) by Chandler Harper in the last three rounds of the 1954 Texas Open at Brackenridge.

36 holes:

Opening rounds

126 — (64–62) by Tommy Bolt, at Cavalier Yacht & Country Club, Virginia Beach, Va., in 1954 Virginia Beach Open.

Consecutive rounds

125 — (63–62) by Ron Streck in the last two rounds of the 1978 Texas Open at Oak Hills Country Club, San Antonio, Tex.

126 — (62–64) by Johnny Palmer in the last two rounds of the 1948 Tucson Open at El Rio Country Club, Tucson, Ariz.

126 — (63–63) by Sam Snead in the last two rounds of the 1950 Texas Open at Brackenridge Park.

126 — (63–63) by Chandler Harper in the middle rounds and last two rounds of the 1954 Texas Open at Brackenridge Park.

126 — (60–66) by Sam Snead in the middle rounds of the 1957 Dallas Open at Glen Lakes Country Club, Dallas, Tex.

126 — (61–65) by Jack Rule, Jr. in the middle rounds of the 1963 St. Paul Open at Keller Golf Club, St. Paul, Minn.

126 — (63–63) by Mark Pfeil in the middle rounds of the 1983 Texas Open at Oak Hills CC, San Antonio, Tex.

18 holes:

59 — by Al Geiberger, at Colonial Country Club, Memphis, Tenn., in second round of 1977 Memphis Classic.

60 — by Al Brosch, at Brackenridge Park Golf Course, San Antonio, Tex., in third round of 1951 Texas Open.

60 — by Bill Nary, at El Paso Country Club, El Paso, Tex., in third round of 1952 El Paso Open.

60 — by Ted Kroll, at Brackenridge Park Golf Course, San Antonio, Tex., in third round of 1954 Texas Open.

60 — by Wally Ulrich, at Cavalier Yacht and Country Club, Virginia Beach, Va., in second round of 1954 Virginia Beach Open.

60 — by Tommy Bolt, at Wethersfield Country Club, Hartford, Conn., in second round of 1954 Insurance City Open.

60 — by Mike Souchak, at Brackenridge Park Golf Course, San Antonio, Tex., in first round of 1955 Texas Open.

60 — by Sam Snead, at Glen Lakes Country Club, Dallas, Tex., in second round of 1957 Dallas Open.

9 holes:

27 — by Mike Souchak, at Brackenridge Park Golf Course, San Antonio, Tex., on par-35 second nine of first round in 1955 Texas Open.

27 — by Andy North, at En-Joie Golf Club, Endicott, N.Y., on par-34 second nine of first round in 1975 B.C. Open.

Best Vardon Trophy scoring average:

69.23 — Sam Snead in 1950 (6646 strokes, 96 rounds).

69.30 — Ben Hogan in 1948 (5267 strokes, 76 rounds).

69.37 — Sam Snead in 1949 (5064 strokes, 73 rounds).

Most consecutive rounds under 70:

19 — Byron Nelson in 1945.

Most birdies in a row:

8 — Bob Goalby, at Pasadena Golf Club, St. Petersburg, Fla., during fourth round of 1961 St. Petersburg Open; Fuzzy Zoeller, at Oakwood Country Club, Coal Valley, Ill., during first round of 1976 Quad Cities Open.

Most birdies in a row:

8 — Bob Goalby, at Pasadena Golf Club, St. Petersburg, Fla., during fourth round of 1961 St. Petersburg Open; Fuzzy Zoeller, at Oakwood Country Club, Coal Valley, Ill., during first round of 1976 Quad Cities Open; Dewey Arnett, at Warwick Hills GC, Grand Blanc, Mich., during first round of 1987 Buick Open.

Best birdie-eagle streak:

6 — birdies and 1 eagle by Al Geiberger, at Colonial Country Club, Memphis, Tenn., during second round of 1977 Danny Thomas Memphis Classic.

Most birdies in a row to win:

5 — by Jack Nicklaus to win 1978 Jackie Gleason Inverrary Classic (last 5 holes).

Fewest putts, one round:

18 — Sam Trahan, at Whitemarsh Valley Country Club, in final round of 1979 IVB-Philadelphia Golf Classic.

18 — Mike McGee, at Colonial Country Club, in first round of Federal Express St. Jude Classic.

Fewest putts, four rounds:
94 — George Archer in 1980 Sea Pines Heritage Classic at Harbour Town Golf Links, Hilton Head Island, S.C.
99 — Bob Menne in 1977 Tournament Players Championship at Sawgrass, Jacksonville, Fla.
99 — Steve Melnyk in 1980 Sea Pines Heritage Classic at Harbour Town Golf Links, Hilton Head Island, S.C.

Fewest putts, nine holes:
8 — Jim Colbert, at the Deerwood Club, Jacksonville, Fla., on front nine of last round in 1967 Greater Jacksonville Open.
8 — Sam Trahan, at Whitemarsh Valley Country Club, on the back nine of the last round in the 1979 IVB-Philadelphia Golf Classic.

VICTORY RECORDS

Most victories during career (PGA Tour co-sponsored and/or approved tournaments only):
84 — Sam Snead
71 — Jack Nicklaus
62 — Ben Hogan
61 — Arnold Palmer
54 — Byron Nelson
51 — Billy Casper

Most consecutive years winning tournament:
17 — Arnold Palmer (1955–1971)
17 — Jack Nicklaus (1962–1978)
16 — Billy Casper (1956–1971)

Most consecutive victories:
11 — Byron Nelson, from Miami Four Ball, March 8–11, 1945, through Canadian Open, August 2–4, 1945. Tournament, site, dates, score, purse—Miami Four Ball, Miami Springs Course, Miami, Fla., March 8–11, won 8–6, $1500; Charlotte Open, Myers Park Golf Club, Charlotte, N.C., March 16–19, 272, $2000; Greensboro Open, Starmount Country Club, Greensboro, N.C., March 23–25, 271, $1000; Durham Open, Hope Valley Country Club, Durham, N.C., March 30–April 1, 276, $1000; Atlanta Open, Capital City Course, Atlanta, Ga., April 5–8, 263, $2000; Montreal Open, Islemere Golf and Country Club, Montreal, Que., June 7–10, 268, $2000; Philadelphia Inquirer Invitational, Llanerch Country Club, Phila., Pa., June 14–17, 269, $3000; Chicago Victory National Open, Calumet Country Club, Chicago, Ill., June 29–July 1, 275, $2000; PGA Championship, Moraine Country Club, Dayton, Ohio, July 9–15, 4–3, $3750; Tam O'Shanter Open, Tam O'Shanter Country Club, Chicago, Ill., July 26–29, 269, $10,000; Canadian Open, Thornhill Country Club, Toronto, Ont., August 2–4, 280, $2000; Winnings for streak: $30,250. NOTE: Nelson won a 12th event in Spring Lake, N.J. which is not accounted as official, as its $2,500 total purse was below the PGA $3,000 minimum.
4 — Jackie Burke, Jr. in 1952: From February 14 to March 9—Texas Open, Houston Open, Baton Rouge Open, St. Petersburg Open.
3 — Byron Nelson in 1944, 1945–46; Sam Snead in 1945; Ben Hogan in 1946; Bobby Locke in 1947; Jim Ferrier in 1951; Billy Casper in 1960; Arnold Palmer in 1960, 1962; Johnny Miller in 1974; Hubert Green in 1976; Gary Player in 1978.

Most victories in a single event:
8 — Sam Snead, Greater Greensboro Open: 1938, 1946, 1949, 1950, 1955, 1956, 1960, and 1965.
6 — Sam Snead, Miami Open: 1937, 1939, 1946, 1950, 1951, and 1955. Jack Nicklaus, Masters: 1963, 1965, 1966, 1972, 1975, and 1986.
5 — Walter Hagen, PGA Championship: 1921, 1924, 1925, 1926, and 1927. Ben Hogan, Colonial NIT: 1946, 1947, 1952, 1953, and 1959. Arnold Palmer, Bob Hope Desert Classic: 1960, 1962, 1968, 1971, and 1973. Jack Nicklaus, Tournament of Champions: 1963, 1964, 1971, 1973, and 1977. Jack Nicklaus, PGA: 1963, 1971, 1973, 1975, and 1980. Walter Hagen, Western Open: 1916, 1921, 1926, 1927, and 1932.

Most consecutive victories in a single event:
4 — Walter Hagen, PGA Championship, 1924–1927.
3 — Willie Anderson, U.S. Open, 1903–1905.
3 — Ralph Guldahl, Western Open, 1936–1938.
3 — Gene Littler, Tournament of Champions, 1955–1957.
3 — Billy Casper, Portland Open, 1959–1961.
3 — Arnold Palmer, Texas Open, 1960–1962; Phoenix Open, 1961–1963.
3 — Jack Nicklaus, Disney World Golf Classic, 1971–1973.
3 — Johnny Miller, Tucson Open, 1974–1976.
3 — Tom Watson, Byron Nelson Classic, 1978–1980.

Most victories in a calendar year:
18 — Byron Nelson (1945).
13 — Ben Hogan (1946).
11 — Ben Hogan (1948).
10 — Sam Snead (1950).
8 — Byron Nelson (1944).
8 — Lloyd Mangrum (1948).
8 — Arnold Palmer (1960).
8 — Johnny Miller (1974).
7 — Sam Snead (1938).
7 — Ben Hogan (1947).
7 — Arnold Palmer (1962, 1963).
7 — Jack Nicklaus (1972, 1973).

Most years between victories.
11 by Bob Rosburg (1961–1972).
11 by Bob Murphy (1975–1986).

Most years from first victory to last:
29 by Sam Snead (1936–1965).
27 by Jack Nicklaus (1962–1986).
23 by Gene Littler (1954–1977).
22 by Raymond Floyd (1963–1985).
22 by Art Wall (1953–1975).

Most first-time winners during one calendar year:
12 — 1968, 1969, 1979, 1980, 1986.

Youngest winners:
Johnny McDermott, 19 years and 10 months, 1911 U.S. Open.
Gene Sarazen, 20 years and 4 months, 1922 U.S. Open.
Horton Smith, 20 years and 5 months, 1928 Oklahoma City Open.
Raymond Floyd, 20 years and 6 months, 1963 St. Petersburg Open.
Seve Ballesteros, 20 years and 11 months, 1978 Greater Greensboro Open.

Oldest winner:
Sam Snead, 52 years and 10 months, 1965 Greater Greensboro Open.

MONEY-WINNING RECORDS

Most money won in a calendar year:
$925,941 by Curtis Strange in 1987.
$822,481 by Paul Azinger in 1987.
$653,296 by Greg Norman in 1986.
$638,194 by Ben Crenshaw in 1987.

Most money won by a rookie:
$320,007 by Keith Clearwater in 1987.
$260,536 by Corey Pavin in 1984.
$237,434 by Hal Sutton in 1982.
$198,537 by Phil Blackmar in 1985.

MISCELLANEOUS RECORDS

Most consecutive events without missing cut:

113 — Byron Nelson, during the 1940s.

105 — Jack Nicklaus, from Sahara Open, November 1970, through World Series of
Golf, September 1976 (missed cut in 1976 World Open).

86 — Hale Irwin, from Tucson Open, 1975, through conclusion of 1978 season.

Widest winning margin:

16 strokes — Bobby Locke, 1948 Chicago Victory National Championship.

14 strokes — Ben Hogan, 1945 Portland Invitational; Johnny Miller, 1975 Phoenix
Open.

13 strokes — Byron Nelson, 1945 Seattle Open.

12 strokes — Arnold Palmer, 1962 Phoenix Open.

Longest sudden-death playoffs:

11 holes — Cary Middlecoff and Lloyd Mangrum were declared co-winners by mutual
agreement in the 1949 Motor City Open.

8 holes — Dick Hart defeated Phil Rodgers in the 1965 Azalea Open.

8 holes — Lee Elder defeated Lee Trevino in the 1978 Greater Milwaukee Open.

8 holes — Dave Barr defeated Woody Blackburn, Dan Halldorson, Frank Conner and
Victor Regalado in the 1981 Quad Cities Open.

8 holes — Bob Gilder defeated Rex Caldwell, Johnny Miller and Mark O'Meara in
the 1983 Phoenix Open.

Youngest pro shooting age:

66 — (4 under), Sam Snead (age 67), 1979 Quad Cities Open.

ALL-TIME TOUR WINNERS

1. Sam Snead 84	16. Johnny Miller 23	T31. Bobby Cruickshank 16	Dave Hill 13
2. Jack Nicklaus 71	T17. Jim Ferrier 21	Mike Souchak 16	T47. Dow Finsterwald 12
3. Ben Hogan 62	Raymond Floyd 21	Lanny Wadkins 16	Bobby Nichols 12
4. Arnold Palmer 61	Gary Player 21	T34. Tommy Bolt 15	Curtis Strange 12
5. Byron Nelson 54	T20. Harry Cooper 20	Jack Burke, Jr. 15	T50. Miller Barber 11
6. Billy Casper 51	Doug Sanders 20	Bruce Crampton 15	Frank Beard 11
7. Cary Middlecoff 37	T22. Johnny Revolta 19	Dutch Harrison 15	Gay Brewer 11
8. Lloyd Mangrum 34	Doug Ford 19	Paul Runyan 15	Al Geiberger 11
9. Jimmy Demaret 31	Hubert Green 19	Tom Weiskopf 15	Bob Goalby 11
10. Tom Watson 32	T25. Julius Boros 18	T40. Ralph Guldahl 14	Don January 11
11. Horton Smith 30	Johnny Ferrell 18	Ken Venturi 14	Bobby Locke 11
12. Gene Littler 29	Gene Sarazen 18	Art Wall, Jr. 14	Dave Stockton 11
T13. Walter Hagen 27	T28. Harold McSpaden 17	T43. George Archer 13	Andy Bean 11
Henry Picard 27	Craig Wood 17	Ben Crenshaw 13	
Lee Trevino 27	Hale Irwin 17	Vic Ghezzi 13	

Note: Scorecards within chapters retain 1986 statistics

PGA TOUR COURSES RANKED BY LENGTH

	Course	Length	Par		Course	Length	Par		Course	Length	Par
1	Castle Pines GC	7503	72	21	Torrey Pines GC (South)	7021	72	40	TPC at Sawgrass	6857	72
2	Colonial CC (Tenn.)	7282	72	22	Warwick Hills G&CC	7014	72	41	Bermuda Dunes CC	6837	72
3	Magnolia GC	7190	72	22	Desert Inn CC	7018	72	42	Tamarisk CC	6829	72
4	Fairway Oaks G&RC	7189	72	23	TPC at StarPass	7010	72	43	Spyglass Hill GC	6810	72
5	Firestone CC	7173	70	24	Atlanta CC	7007	72	44	Pebble Beach GL	6799	71
6	Las Vegas CC	7162	71	25	TPC at Scottsdale	6992	71	45	Green Island GC	6791	70
7	Colonial CC (Tex.)	7116	70	26	Greenview Cover CC	6986	72	46	TPC of Connecticut	6786	71
8	Desert Inn CC	7111	72	27	Forest Oaks CC	6984	72	47	Kingsmill GC	6776	71
9	Pleasant Valley CC	7110	71	28	Waialae CC	6975	72	48	TPC at Las Colinas	6767	70
10	Muirfield Village GC	7106	72	29	Palm GC	6967	72	49	Kapalua Bay GC	6731	72
11	Bay Hill Club & Lodge	7103	71	30	En-Joie GC	6966	71	50	Westchester CC	6723	71
12	Glen Abbey GC	7102	72	31	PGA West/TPC Stadium	6961	72	51	Eldorado CC	6708	72
13	Butler National GC	7097	72	32	Bardmoor CC	6957	72	52	Lake Buena Vista CC	6706	72
14	Perdido Bay CC	7093	71	33	Riviera CC	6946	71	53	Torrey Pines GC (North)	6659	72
15	Spanish Trail G&CC	7088	72	34	Doral CC (Blue)	6939	72	54	Harbour Town GL	6657	71
16	Lakewood CC	7080	72	35	Wellington GC	6930	72	55	Oakwood CC	6602	70
17	Palm Beach Polo & CC	7050	72	T36	La Costa CC	6911	72	56	Oak Hills CC	6576	70
18	TPC at The Woodlands	7045	72	T36	La Quinta CC	6911	72	57	Cypress Point GC	6506	72
19	TPC at Eagle Trace	7037	72	38	Augusta National GC	6905	72	58	Indian Wells CC	6478	72
20	Tuckaway CC	7030	72	39	TPC at Avenel	6864	71				

TOUGHEST PGA TOUR COURSES 1983–1987

Rank	Golf Course	Par	Avg Score	Avg Over Under-Par	Eagles	Birdies	Pars	Bogeys	Double Bogeys	Triple Bogey +	Tournament Name
1	Butler National GC	72	74.629	2.629	39	4464	20277	6324	1160	208	Beatrice Western Open
2	Spyglass Hill GC	72	74.596	2.596	29	2047	9531	3320	431	50	AT&T Pebble Beach National Pro-Am
3	Cypress Point GC	72	74.381	2.381	46	2588	8991	3013	591	161	AT&T Pebble Beach National Pro-Am
4	Glen Abbey GC	72	74.203	2.203	110	5023	18944	6823	938	148	Canadian Open
5	PGA West/TPC Stadium	72	74.158	2.158	9	500	2294	614	121	26	Bob Hope Chrysler Classic
6	Forest Oaks CC	72	73.950	1.950	55	5240	24618	7948	717	104	K-Mart Greater Greensboro Open
7	Riviera CC	71	72.892	1.892	66	4520	19375	6374	663	70	Los Angeles Open Presented by Nissan
8	TPC at Eagle Trace	72	73.890	1.890	92	4749	19579	5868	891	177	Honda Classic
9	Westchester CC	71	72.829	1.829	76	6402	25197	8147	1094	142	Manufacturers Hanover Westchester Classic
10	Bay Hill Club & Lodge	71	72.740	1.740	89	4884	20343	6215	908	177	Hertz Bay Hill Classic
11	Augusta National GC	72	73.738	1.738	110	3763	14889	4944	558	72	The Masters
12	TPC at Avenel	71	72.651	1.651	22	1363	4939	1624	209	33	Kemper Open
13	Woodlands CC (West)	71	72.642	1.642	10	2341	10567	2973	335	64	Houston Open
14	Pebble Beach GL	72	73.622	1.622	77	3190	12343	3772	485	95	AT&T Pebble Beach National Pro-Am
15	Firestone CC	70	71.297	1.297	33	2283	9643	2812	248	29	NEC World Series of Golf
16	Harbour Town GL	71	72.246	1.246	79	5640	21798	6092	869	136	MCI Heritage Classic
17	TPC at Sawgrass	72	73.235	1.235	94	6295	23747	6649	1073	194	The Players Championship
18	Colonial CC (Tex.)	70	71.232	1.232	24	4397	19584	5229	528	64	Colonial National Invitation
19	Green Island CC	70	71.214	1.214	29	5753	26647	6942	612	103	Southern Open
20	Colonial CC (Tenn.)	72	73.181	1.181	68	6275	26789	7089	800	127	Federal Express St. Jude Classic
21	Fairway Oaks G&RC	72	73.016	1.016	106	6464	25096	6928	864	160	Gatlin Brothers Southwest Golf Classic
22	En-Joie GC	71	72.015	1.015	72	5876	25252	6469	760	91	B.C. Open
23	Muirfield Village GC	72	72.937	.937	110	5471	19283	5773	767	96	Memorial Tournament
24	Kingsmill GC	71	71.881	.881	122	6596	25325	7066	722	111	Anheuser-Busch Golf Classic
25	Pleasant Valley CC	71	71.759	.759	58	6213	26302	6306	674	119	Bank of Boston Classic
26	Doral CC (Blue)	72	72.756	.756	75	6311	25596	6684	631	87	Doral Ryder Open
27	TPC at The Woodlands	72	72.740	.740	46	4001	16040	3849	543	91	Independent Insurance Agent Open
28	TPC at Las Colinas	70	70.524	.524	24	2879	10742	2766	270	41	Byron Nelson Golf Classic
29	Desert Inn CC	72	72.506	.506	65	2483	9662	2552	274	30	Panasonic Las Vegas Invitational
30	Oak Hills CC	70	70.403	.403	86	5479	20929	5518	626	86	Texas Open Presented by Nabisco
31	TPC of Connecticut	71	71.324	.324	77	5550	21706	5038	511	76	Canon Sammy Davis, Jr. Greater Hartford Open
32	Perdido Bay CC	71	71.276	.276	123	6381	24667	6036	589	58	Pensacola Open
33	Lakewood CC	72	72.273	.273	103	6306	25091	5899	488	57	USF&G Classic
34	Eldorado CC	72	72.194	.194	22	897	2978	735	102	18	Bob Hope Chrysler Classic
35	La Costa CC	72	72.014	.014	26	1911	6981	1640	159	11	MONY Tournament of Champions
36	Oakwood CC	70	70.001	.001	122	6163	23440	5512	392	29	Hardee's Golf Classic
37	TPC of Scottsdale	71	70.968	.032–	38	1476	4905	1237	118	20	Phoenix Open
38	Atlanta CC	72	71.968	.032–	121	7329	25005	5620	793	120	Georgia-Pacific Atlanta Golf Classic
39	Tuckaway CC	72	71.919	.081–	153	6870	25447	6302	371	25	Greater Milwaukee Open
40	Phoenix CC	71	70.715	.285–	123	5821	20949	4720	437	44	Phoenix Open
41	Spanish Trail G&CC	72	71.522	.478–	39	1058	3549	821	66	11	Panasonic Las Vegas Invitational
42	Torrey Pines GC (South)	72	71.463	.537–	141	4918	16986	3792	273	26	Shearson Lehman Brothers Andy Williams Open
43	TPC at StarPass	72	71.459	.541–	59	1945	5008	1311	197	30	Seiko Tucson Open
44	Waialae CC	72	71.403	.597–	241	7999	24733	5629	611	99	Hawaiian Open
45	Palm GC	72	71.366	.634–	51	2406	7521	1613	188	29	Walt Disney World/Oldsmobile Golf Classic
46	Warwick Hills G&CC	72	71.248	.752–	133	7868	26885	5721	339	58	Buick Open
47	Magnolia GC	72	71.151	.849–	63	3573	12565	2244	241	34	Walt Disney World/Oldsmobile Golf Classic
48	La Quinta CC	72	71.111	.889–	39	1966	6687	1329	123	26	Bob Hope Chrysler Classic
49	Las Vegas CC	72	70.892	1.108–	132	4715	15124	3273	308	57	Panasonic Las Vegas Invitational
50	Tamarisk CC	72	70.823	1.177–	52	1375	4641	871	76	5	Bob Hope Chrysler Classic
51	Bermuda Dunes CC	72	70.783	1.217–	62	2883	10187	1726	121	15	Bob Hope Chrysler Classic
52	Torrey Pines GC (North)	72	70.211	1.789–	120	3105	8607	1667	123	22	Shearson Lehman Brothers Andy Williams Open
53	Lake Buena Vista GC	72	70.185	1.815–	69	2677	7610	1304	130	18	Walt Disney World/Oldsmobile Golf Classic
54	Indian Wells CC	72	70.178	1.822–	89	2935	8417	1462	141	24	Bob Hope Chrysler Classic
	Avg. Totals	71.537	72.079	.542							

TOUGHEST PGA TOUR HOLES 1983–1987

Rank	Golf Course	Hole	Par	Avg Score	Avg Over Under-Par	Eagles	Birdies	Pars	Bogeys	Double Bogeys	Triple Bogey +	Tournament Name
1	Cypress Point GC	16	3	3.678	.678		53	377	278	112	35	AT&T Pebble Beach National Pro-Am
2	Westchester CC	12	4	4.505	.505	1	127	1069	899	168	17	Manufacturers Hanover Westchester Classic
3	Pebble Beach GL	9	4	4.422	.422	1	72	599	369	56	12	AT&T Pebble Beach National Pro-Am
4	Spyglass Hill GC	8	4	4.409	.409		48	461	294	50	3	AT&T Pebble Beach National Pro-Am
5	Spyglass Hill GC	16	4	4.398	.398		50	469	293	37	7	AT&T Pebble Beach National Pro-Am
6	Palm GC	18	4	4.397	.397	1	39	372	205	35	4	Walt Disney World/Oldsmobile Golf Classic
7	Doral CC (Blue)	18	4	4.393	.393	1	182	1197	598	176	34	Doral Ryder Open
8	Cypress Point GC	17	4	4.392	.392		93	473	199	65	25	AT&T Pebble Beach National Pro-Am
9	Bay Hill Club & Lodge	18	4	4.391	.391	1	161	969	471	169	41	Hertz Bay Hill Classic
10	Desert Inn CC	7	3	3.380	.380		39	506	223	62	7	Panasonic Las Vegas Invitational
11	Glen Abbey GC	9	4	4.373	.373	2	159	992	452	148	24	Canadian Open
12	PGA West/TPC Stadium	9	4	4.369	.369		13	117	52	14	2	Bob Hope Chrysler Classic
12	Butler National GC	10	4	4.369	.369	1	165	1027	429	154	28	Beatrice Western Open
14	Westchester CC	15	4	4.368	.368	1	131	1318	713	106	12	Manufacturers Hanover Westchester Classic
15	Cypress Point GC	14	4	4.367	.367		57	504	225	53	16	AT&T Pebble Beach National Pro-Am
16	Glen Abbey GC	14	4	4.366	.366		150	976	523	109	19	Canadian Open
16	TPC at Sawgrass	18	4	4.366	.366		155	1276	477	160	46	The Players Championship
18	TPC at Eagle Trace	7	3	3.365	.365		147	1055	369	129	42	Honda Classic
19	Spyglass Hill GC	6	4	4.364	.364		52	488	275	38	3	AT&T Pebble Beach National Pro-Am
20	TPC at Avenel	12	4	4.363	.363		27	276	120	27	5	Kemper Open
21	Pebble Beach GL	10	4	4.360	.360		93	632	313	60	11	AT&T Pebble Beach National Pro-Am
22	Forest Oaks CC	3	4	4.356	.356	1	141	1236	643	110	18	K-Mart Greater Greensboro Open
23	Spyglass Hill GC	18	4	4.353	.353		62	485	265	38	6	AT&T Pebble Beach National Pro-Am
24	Colonial CC (Tex.)	5	4	4.344	.344	1	117	972	462	95	10	Colonial National Invitation
25	Woodlands CC (West)	10	4	4.338	.338		45	560	260	31	9	IIA Open
25	TPC at Avenel	15	4	4.338	.338		31	254	155	15		Kemper Open
27	Westchester CC	4	4	4.333	.333		168	1352	619	116	26	Manufacturers Hanover Westchester Classic
28	Westchester CC	11	4	4.331	.331	1	160	1308	708	92	12	Manufacturers Hanover Westchester Classic
29	En-Joie GC	15	4	4.325	.325		151	1261	642	72	14	B.C. Open
30	Butler National GC	18	4	4.322	.322		169	1047	457	108	23	Beatrice Western Open
31	Cypress Point GC	11	4	4.317	.317		48	535	236	31	3	AT&T Pebble Beach National Pro-Am
31	Pebble Beach GL	8	4	4.317	.317		95	639	326	37	12	AT&T Pebble Beach National Pro-Am
33	Firestone CC	4	4	4.314	.314		62	491	256	21	6	NEC World Series of Golf
34	Oakwood CC	4	4	4.313	.313		132	1153	644	49	3	Hardee's Golf Classic
35	Riviera CC	2	4	4.311	.311		137	993	523	68	5	Los Angeles Open Presented by Nissan
36	Westchester CC	8	4	4.309	.309		191	1334	615	120	21	Manufacturers Hanover Westchester Classic
37	PGA West/TPC Stadium	11	5	5.308	.308		17	119	53	6	3	Bob Hope Chrysler Classic
37	Green Island CC	1	4	4.308	.308		177	1340	580	113	17	Southern Open
39	Woodlands CC (West)	17	4	4.307	.307		62	534	280	27	2	IIA Open
39	Kingsmill GC	8	4	4.307	.307	1	167	1321	627	82	21	Anheuser-Busch Golf Classic
39	Harbour Town GL	8	4	4.307	.307		143	1199	465	106	10	MCI Heritage Classic
42	Eldorado CC	11	4	4.302	.302		12	175	64	11	2	Bob Hope Chrysler Classic
43	Butler National GC	14	4	4.301	.301		201	1096	312	140	55	Beatrice Western Open
43	En-Joie GC	1	4	4.301	.301		204	1228	574	111	23	B.C. Open
45	Tuckaway CC	10	4	4.300	.300		150	1282	695	45	4	Greater Milwaukee Open
46	Riviera CC	18	4	4.299	.299		116	1040	512	55	3	Los Angeles Open Presented by Nissan
47	Green Island CC	5	4	4.293	.293		158	1391	580	74	24	Southern Open
48	Riviera CC	4	3	3.286	.286	1	101	1069	516	38	1	Los Angeles Open Presented by Nissan
49	La Costa CC	5	4	4.283	.283		51	350	171	21	3	MONY Tournament of Champions
50	TPC at Eagle Trace	18	4	4.282	.282		116	1054	542	26	4	Honda Classic
51	Woodlands CC (West)	14	4	4.281	.281		69	559	236	37	4	IIA Open
52	Indian Wells CC	10	4	4.277	.277		64	434	203	19	6	Bob Hope Chrysler Classic
53	TPC at Avenel	7	4	4.275	.275		36	271	135	13		Kemper Open
53	Cypress Point GC	8	4	4.275	.275		131	447	197	60	20	AT&T Pebble Beach National Pro-Am
53	TPC at Eagle Trace	13	4	4.275	.275	1	154	1053	455	59	20	Honda Classic
53	TPC at Eagle Trace	16	4	4.275	.275		154	1080	396	101	11	Honda Classic
57	Torrey Pines GC (North)	11	4	4.274	.274		81	441	200	30	6	Shearson Lehman Brothers Andy Williams Open
58	Kingsmill GC	4	4	4.273	.273	1	183	1340	608	79	8	Anheuser-Busch Golf Classic
59	Oak Hills CC	15	4	4.272	.272	1	134	1099	497	65	22	Texas Open Presented by Nabisco

Rank	Golf Course	Hole	Par	Avg Score	Avg Over Under-Par	Eagles	Birdies	Pars	Bogeys	Double Bogeys	Triple Bogey +	Tournament Name
60	PGA West/TPC Stadium	3	4	4.268	.268		14	124	54	5	1	Bob Hope Chrysler Classic
61	Glen Abbey GC	10	4	4.266	.266	1	155	1053	516	43	9	Canadian Open
62	Colonial CC (Tenn.)	17	4	4.265	.265	1	221	1331	651	66	16	Federal Express St. Jude Classic
62	Torrey Pines GC (South)	12	4	4.265	.265		80	943	404	23	2	Shearson Lehman Brothers Andy Williams Open
64	Doral CC (Blue)	13	3	3.264	.264		126	1379	657	25	1	Doral Ryder Open
65	PGA West/TPC Stadium	6	3	3.263	.263		20	131	29	13	5	Bob Hope Chrysler Classic
66	Spyglass Hill GC	9	4	4.262	.262	1	63	526	243	23		AT&T Pebble Beach National Pro-Am
66	TPC of Connecticut	15	4	4.262	.262		148	1104	533	43	3	Canon Sammy Davis, Jr. Greater Hartford Open
66	Glen Abbey GC	11	4	4.262	.262	3	188	1044	437	94	11	Canadian Open
69	Spanish Trail G&CC	14	3	3.260	.260		12	207	86	3		Panasonic Las Vegas Invitational
70	TPC at Avenel	18	4	4.259	.259		40	271	131	12	1	Kemper Open
70	TPC at Las Colinas	3	4	4.259	.259		90	549	255	31	4	GTE Byron Nelson Golf Classic
72	TPC at StarPass	4	4	4.257	.257		47	294	108	24	2	Seiko Tucson Open
73	Firestone CC	9	4	4.255	.255	1	65	512	239	17	2	NEC World Series of Golf
73	Forest Oaks CC	16	4	4.255	.255		220	1248	585	79	17	K-Mart Greater Greensboro Open
73	TPC at The Woodlands	17	4	4.255	.255		195	791	250	108	21	IIA Open
76	Bay Hill Club & Lodge	4	4	4.254	.254		134	1100	516	54	8	Hertz Bay Hill Classic
77	Torrey Pines GC (South)	7	4	4.253	.253		118	912	382	31	9	Shearson Lehman Brothers Andy Williams Open
78	Butler National GC	9	4	4.251	.251		154	1073	497	66	14	Beatrice Western Open
78	Glen Abbey GC	12	3	3.251	.251	1	144	1119	448	50	15	Canadian Open
78	TPC at Sawgrass	7	4	4.251	.251		220	1266	529	85	14	The Players Championship
78	Augusta National GC	10	4	4.251	.251	1	113	833	355	44	6	The Masters
78	Augusta National GC	12	3	3.251	.251		165	803	294	66	24	The Masters
83	Glen Abbey GC	17	4	4.249	.249		167	1076	469	54	11	Canadian Open
83	Riviera CC	9	4	4.249	.249		179	1010	467	68	2	Los Angeles Open Presented by Nissan
85	Perdido Bay CC	14	4	4.248	.248		149	1369	506	68	11	Pensacola Open
85	Butler National GC	5	3	3.248	.248		138	1167	414	65	20	Beatrice Western Open
87	Eldorado CC	14	4	4.246	.246		17	186	44	13	4	Bob Hope Chrysler Classic
88	Cypress Point GC	4	4	4.243	.243		73	528	231	19	4	AT&T Pebble Beach National Pro-Am
88	Fairway Oaks G&RC	10	4	4.243	.243		189	1409	492	91	20	Southwest Golf Classic
88	Palm GC	6	4	4.243	.243	2	72	412	111	51	8	Walt Disney World/Oldsmobile Golf Classic
91	Augusta National GC	11	4	4.238	.238		118	862	305	62	5	The Masters
92	Butler National GC	8	3	3.237	.237		213	1153	315	99	24	Beatrice Western Open
92	Cypress Point GC	1	4	4.237	.237		79	523	227	24	2	AT&T Pebble Beach National Pro-Am
92	TPC at Sawgrass	8	3	3.237	.237		159	1335	571	47	2	The Players Championship
95	TPC at Avenel	9	3	3.235	.235		54	271	106	20	4	Kemper Open
96	Spanish Trail G&CC	5	3	3.234	.234		20	204	76	8		Panasonic Las Vegas Invitational
96	Green Island CC	14	3	3.234	.234		165	1428	596	35	3	Southern Open
98	Bay Hill Club & Lodge	2	3	3.232	.232		135	1136	501	36	4	Hertz Bay Hill Classic
99	TPC at Sawgrass	14	4	4.231	.231	1	215	1299	490	89	20	The Players Championship
100	TPC at Las Colinas	8	4	4.230	.230		78	581	250	17	3	GTE Byron Nelson Golf Classic
101	Fairway Oaks G&RC	4	3	3.229	.229	1	175	1461	459	81	24	Gatlin Brothers Southwest Golf Classic
101	Riviera CC	15	4	4.229	.229		155	1080	440	44	7	Los Angeles Open Presented by Nissan
103	Woodlands CC (West)	7	4	4.228	.228		99	551	214	34	7	IIA Open
103	Oakwood CC	13	4	4.228	.228		165	1254	516	44	2	Hardee's Golf Classic
105	TPC at Sawgrass	5	4	4.226	.226	2	191	1327	520	64	10	The Players Championship
105	Colonial CC (Tex.)	3	4	4.226	.226	2	134	1044	453	21	3	Colonial National Invitation
107	TPC at Eagle Trace	12	4	4.225	.225	1	193	1108	325	92	23	Honda Classic
107	Lakewood CC	18	4	4.225	.225		170	1349	542	44	3	USF&G Classic
107	TPC at The Woodlands	18	4	4.225	.225		127	891	279	60	8	IIA Open
110	Harbour Town GL	11	4	4.224	.224		192	1142	540	46	3	MCI Heritage Classic
110	Augusta National GC	18	4	4.224	.224		117	863	331	39	2	The Masters
112	Colonial CC (Tenn.)	14	4	4.223	.223	1	238	1407	539	95	6	Federal Express St. Jude Classic
113	PGA West/TPC Stadium	10	4	4.222	.222		26	119	37	15	1	Bob Hope Chrysler Classic
113	Forest Oaks CC	17	3	3.222	.222		176	1351	584	36	2	K-Mart Greater Greensboro Open
115	Torrey Pines GC (South)	4	4	4.221	.221	1	118	920	381	31	1	Shearson Lehman Brothers Andy Williams Open
115	Bay Hill Club & Lodge	9	4	4.221	.221	1	150	1143	474	38	6	Hertz Bay Hill Classic
117	Pleasant Valley CC	17	4	4.220	.220	1	279	1387	387	109	41	Bank of Boston Classic
117	TPC at Eagle Trace	9	4	4.220	.220	1	136	1111	471	21	2	Honda Classic
117	Forest Oaks CC	4	3	3.220	.220		182	1366	543	49	9	K-Mart Greater Greensboro Open
120	Glen Abbey GC	7	3	3.219	.219		182	1114	406	61	14	Canadian Open

Rank	Golf Course	Hole	Par	Avg Score	Avg Over Under-Par	Eagles	Birdies	Pars	Bogeys	Double Bogeys	Triple Bogey +	Tournament Name
120	Colonial CC (Tenn.)	8	4	4.219	.219	1	185	1471	572	52	5	Federal Express St. Jude Classic
122	Atlanta CC	15	4	4.219	.219		213	1372	484	84	13	Georgia-Pacific Atlanta Golf Classic
123	Westchester CC	16	3	3.218	.218	1	202	1462	551	61	4	Manufacturers Hanover Westchester Classic
124	Spyglass Hill GC	13	4	4.217	.217		77	538	219	22		AT&T Pebble Beach National Pro-Am
124	Firestone CC	6	4	4.217	.217		76	518	230	11	1	NEC World Series of Golf
126	Augusta National GC	4	3	3.214	.214		105	882	346	17	2	The Masters
127	Butler National GC	17	4	4.213	.213		176	1095	478	51	4	Beatrice Western Open
127	Las Vegas CC	7	4	4.213	.213		110	876	337	30	4	Panasonic Las Vegas Invitational
127	Augusta National GC	5	4	4.213	.213	2	125	830	361	33	1	The Masters
130	Pleasant Valley CC	10	4	4.211	.211		164	1437	553	46	4	Bank of Boston Classic
131	Colonial CC (Tenn.)	13	4	4.210	.210		236	1460	472	98	20	Federal Express St. Jude Classic
131	Fairway Oaks G&RC	16	3	3.210	.210	1	270	1370	434	104	22	Gatlin Brothers Southwest Golf Classic
131	TPC of Scottsdale	12	3	3.210	.210	1	31	292	96	11	2	Phoenix Open
131	Harbour Town GL	4	3	3.210	.210		202	1238	368	103	12	MCI Heritage Classic
135	Woodlands CC (West)	6	4	4.209	.209		92	590	178	34	11	IIA Open
135	Atlanta CC	9	4	4.209	.209		168	1423	532	41	2	Georgia-Pacific Atlanta Golf Classic
137	Phoenix CC	15	3	3.208	.208	1	157	1206	337	70	12	Phoenix Open
138	Kingsmill GC	9	4	4.208	.208	1	199	1393	581	37	8	Anheuser-Busch Golf Classic
138	Doral CC (Blue)	3	4	4.208	.208	1	234	1372	474	91	16	Doral Ryder Open
138	Forest Oaks CC	12	3	3.208	.208		171	1404	528	45	1	K-Mart Greater Greensboro Open
141	Muirfield Village GC	18	4	4.206	.206		193	1064	431	57	5	Memorial Tournament
142	Phoenix CC	13	3	3.205	.205	2	145	1177	421	36	2	Phoenix Open
142	Forest Oaks CC	10	4	4.205	.205	1	232	1315	542	55	4	K-Mart Greater Greensboro Open
144	Glen Abbey GC	1	4	4.204	.204		179	1101	454	42	1	Canadian Open
144	Warwick Hills CC	15	4	4.204	.204		196	1479	553	36	14	Buick Open
146	TPC of Connecticut	17	4	4.203	.203		260	1118	314	107	32	Canon Sammy Davis, Jr. Greater Hartford Open
146	Augusta National GC	1	4	4.203	.203	1	124	855	344	28		The Masters
148	Doral CC (Blue)	4	3	3.202	.202	2	180	1457	498	45	6	Doral Ryder Open
149	Forest Oaks CC	18	4	4.202	.202		229	1287	581	50	2	K-Mart Greater Greensboro Open
150	Oak Hills CC	13	3	3.200	.200	1	169	1199	374	63	12	Texas Open Presented by Nabisco
151	Atlanta CC	17	4	4.199	.199		266	1324	472	88	16	Georgia-Pacific Atlanta Golf Classic
151	Muirfield Village GC	2	4	4.199	.199		180	1098	411	54	7	Memorial Tournament
153	Bay Hill Club & Lodge	11	4	4.198	.198		207	1152	344	90	19	Hertz Bay Hill Classic
154	PGA West/TPC Stadium	1	4	4.197	.197		26	112	56	3	1	Bob Hope Chrysler Classic
154	Pleasant Valley CC	8	4	4.197	.197		209	1425	530	37	3	Bank of Boston Classic
156	Torrey Pines GC (South)	1	4	4.193	.193	1	116	963	352	19	1	Shearson Lehman Brothers Andy Williams Open
157	Augusta National GC	6	3	3.193	.193		128	870	325	27	2	The Masters
158	Desert Inn CC	9	4	4.192	.192		98	492	211	32	4	Panasonic Las Vegas Invitational
159	Tuckaway CC	9	4	4.191	.191		162	1460	516	36	2	Greater Milwaukee Open
160	Glen Abbey GC	2	4	4.190	.190		177	1124	440	34	2	Canadian Open
160	Palm GC	4	4	4.190	.190		69	415	156	14	2	Walt Disney World/Oldsmobile Golf Classic
162	Butler National GC	11	3	3.189	.189	1	219	1148	360	69	7	Beatrice Western Open
162	Bay Hill Club & Lodge	16	4	4.189	.189	1	199	1128	429	48	7	Hertz Bay Hill Classic
164	Firestone CC	13	4	4.188	.188	2	83	526	208	14	3	NEC World Series of Golf
164	Magnolia GC	18	4	4.188	.188		88	695	230	27		Walt Disney World/Oldsmobile Golf Classic
164	Spanish Trail G&CC	2	3	3.188	.188		25	217	55	7	4	Panasonic Las Vegas Invitational
164	Bay Hill Club & Lodge	3	4	4.188	.188	1	196	1124	422	58	11	Hertz Bay Hill Classic
168	Waialae CC	4	3	3.187	.187		181	1433	537	31	2	Hawaiian Open
169	Palm GC	10	4	4.184	.184		63	430	142	16	5	Walt Disney World/Oldsmobile Golf Classic
170	Waialae CC	6	4	4.183	.183	1	232	1378	495	72	6	Hawaiian Open
170	Riviera CC	3	4	4.183	.183		151	1136	414	23	2	Los Angeles Open Presented by Nissan
172	Spyglass Hill GC	5	3	3.182	.182		72	569	189	24	2	AT&T Pebble Beach National Pro-Am
172	TPC at Eagle Trace	3	3	3.182	.182		192	1107	386	48	9	Honda Classic
174	Fairway Oaks G&RC	17	4	4.181	.181		200	1454	465	74	8	Gatlin Brothers Southwest Golf Classic
174	Pebble Beach GL	12	3	3.181	.181		108	711	274	13	3	AT&T Pebble Beach National Pro-Am
176	Tuckaway CC	18	4	4.180	.180		195	1433	509	34	5	Greater Milwaukee Open
176	TPC of Connecticut	11	3	3.180	.180		196	1169	411	50	5	Canon Sammy Davis, Jr. Greater Hartford Open
176	En-Joie GC	13	4	4.180	.180	1	200	1388	515	32	4	B.C. Open
176	Cypress Point GC	18	4	4.180	.180	1	101	554	150	39	10	AT&T Pebble Beach National Pro-Am
176	Harbour Town GL	10	4	4.180	.180	2	210	1230	402	63	16	MCI Heritage Classic
181	Spyglass Hill GC	10	4	4.178	.178		101	527	205	21	2	AT&T Pebble Beach National Pro-Am

TOUGHEST PGA TOUR HOLES 1983–1987 (continued)

Rank	Golf Course	Hole	Par	Avg Score	Avg Over Under-Par	Eagles	Birdies	Pars	Bogeys	Double Bogeys	Triple Bogey +	Tournament Name
181	Green Island CC	9	4	4.178	.178	1	256	1400	501	60	9	Southern Open
181	TPC at Avenel	4	4	4.178	.178		63	270	103	17	2	Kemper Open
181	La Costa CC	18	4	4.178	.178		67	375	135	19		MONY Tournament of Champions
185	Fairway Oaks G&RC	8	3	3.177	.177	1	258	1355	531	51	5	Gatlin Brothers Southwest Golf Classic
185	Oak Hills CC	3	4	4.177	.177	2	178	1144	452	37	5	Texas Open Presented by Nabisco
185	Glen Abbey GC	8	4	4.177	.177	3	208	1071	462	33		Canadian Open
185	Cypress Point GC	9	4	4.177	.177	1	186	421	181	42	24	AT&T Pebble Beach National Pro-Am
189	Pleasant Valley CC	2	4	4.176	.176	4	237	1401	487	67	8	Bank of Boston Classic
189	Bay Hill Club & Lodge	8	4	4.176	.176	3	207	1159	373	60	10	Hertz Bay Hill Classic
189	TPC at The Woodlands	4	4	4.176	.176	1	164	883	245	65	7	IIA Open
189	Colonial CC (Tex.)	4	3	3.176	.176		141	1103	394	19		Colonial National Invitation
193	TPC at StarPass	12	4	4.175	.175		83	257	110	19	6	Seiko Tucson Open
193	Riviera CC	12	4	4.175	.175	1	210	1077	375	51	12	Los Angeles Open Presented by Nissan
195	Woodlands CC (West)	9	4	4.174	.174		99	584	193	24	5	IIA Open
196	Lake Buena Vista CC	18	4	4.173	.173		78	421	127	25	5	Walt Disney World/Oldsmobile Golf Classic
196	La Quinta CC	12	3	3.173	.173		54	352	144	13	2	Bob Hope Chrysler Classic
196	Atlanta CC	6	3	3.173	.173	2	253	1422	379	94	16	Georgia-Pacific Atlanta Golf Classic
199	PGA West/TPC Stadium	18	4	4.172	.172		27	125	32	13	1	Bob Hope Chrysler Classic
199	Perdido Bay CC	10	4	4.172	.172		216	1350	494	42	1	Pensacola Open
199	Fairway Oaks G&RC	2	4	4.172	.172	1	209	1408	541	39	3	Gatlin Brothers Southwest Golf Classic
202	La Quinta CC	2	4	4.170	.170	1	57	367	122	13	5	Bob Hope Chrysler Classic
203	Eldorado CC	17	4	4.169	.169		20	188	49	5	2	Bob Hope Chrysler Classic
204	Glen Abbey GC	6	4	4.168	.168	1	201	1117	417	38	3	Canadian Open
204	Muirfield Village GC	4	3	3.168	.168	2	210	1062	440	32	4	Memorial Tournament
204	TPC at Eagle Trace	2	4	4.168	.168	1	187	1130	369	50	5	Honda Classic
207	PGA West/TPC Stadium	15	4	4.167	.167		23	121	52	2		Bob Hope Chrysler Classic
207	Pleasant Valley CC	14	3	3.167	.167	1	188	1495	489	26	5	Bank of Boston Classic
207	TPC at Las Colinas	12	4	4.167	.167	1	105	589	208	23	3	GTE Byron Nelson Golf Classic
210	Green Island CC	11	4	4.166	.166		187	1487	541	11	1	Southern Open
210	Colonial CC (Tex.)	12	4	4.166	.166	1	193	1039	386	36	2	Colonial National Invitation
212	Phoenix CC	8	3	3.165	.165		154	1200	409	20		Phoenix Open
212	Firestone CC	18	4	4.165	.165	1	102	512	200	21		NEC World Series of Golf
212	Fairway Oaks G&RC	5	4	4.165	.165	3	262	1413	451	59	13	Gatlin Brothers Southwest Golf Classic
215	Butler National GC	6	4	4.164	.164		186	1171	392	53	2	Beatrice Western Open
215	Augusta National GC	16	3	3.164	.164		177	860	245	60	10	The Masters
215	TPC at Las Colinas	10	4	4.164	.164		98	593	226	11	1	GTE Byron Nelson Golf Classic
218	Oak Hills CC	7	4	4.163	.163		163	1138	482	33	2	Texas Open Presented by Nabisco
219	Cypress Point GC	12	4	4.162	.162		95	550	186	20	4	AT&T Pebble Beach National Pro-Am
220	Desert Inn CC	8	4	4.161	.161		95	525	190	24	3	Panasonic Las Vegas Invitational
220	Augusta National GC	3	4	4.161	.161	2	155	842	330	23		The Masters
220	TPC at Las Colinas	14	4	4.161	.161		152	533	192	46	6	GTE Byron Nelson Golf Classic
223	Harbour Town GL	1	4	4.160	.160	1	207	1263	391	52	9	MCI Heritage Classic
223	TPC at Avenel	16	4	4.160	.160		50	290	107	8		Kemper Open
225	Oakwood CC	3	4	4.159	.159	1	181	1334	433	32		Hardee's Golf Classic
225	Tuckaway CC	17	3	3.159	.159		219	1418	512	27		Greater Milwaukee Open
225	Muirfield Village GC	17	4	4.159	.159	1	220	1076	401	39	13	Memorial Tournament
228	Kingsmill GC	5	3	3.158	.158	1	256	1438	452	57	15	Anheuser-Busch Golf Classic
229	Tamarisk CC	3	4	4.156	.156		34	264	89	3		Bob Hope Chrysler Classic
230	TPC at Las Colinas	17	3	3.155	.155		84	629	205	9	2	GTE Byron Nelson Golf Classic
231	Woodlands CC (West)	8	3	3.154	.154		83	609	204	8	1	IIA Open
231	Perdido Bay CC	7	4	4.154	.154	1	218	1388	447	46	3	Pensacola Open
231	Desert Inn CC	11	3	3.154	.154		77	564	186	10		Panasonic Las Vegas Invitational
231	Pebble Beach GL	16	4	4.154	.154		123	725	235	21	5	AT&T Pebble Beach National Pro-Am
231	Waialae CC	5	4	4.154	.154		231	1456	449	46	2	Hawaiian Open
231	TPC at Las Colinas	4	4	4.154	.154		112	588	206	18	5	GTE Byron Nelson Golf Classic
231	TPC at The Woodlands	14	3	3.154	.154	1	112	911	310	28	3	IIA Open
231	Butler National GC	4	4	4.154	.154	1	196	1153	421	32	1	Beatrice Western Open
239	Kingsmill GC	18	4	4.153	.153	2	279	1424	439	61	14	Anheuser-Busch Golf Classic
240	Perdido Bay CC	13	3	3.152	.152	2	175	1464	425	37		Pensacola Open
240	Atlanta CC	10	4	4.152	.152		233	1419	461	45	8	Georgia-Pacific Atlanta Golf Classic
242	Glen Abbey GC	3	3	3.150	.150	1	220	1150	342	52	12	Canadian Open

Rank	Golf Course	Hole	Par	Avg Score	Avg Over Under-Par	Eagles	Birdies	Pars	Bogeys	Double Bogeys	Triple Bogey +	Tournament Name
242	Riviera CC	5	4	4.150	.150	1	184	1138	364	37	2	Los Angeles Open Presented by Nissan
242	Colonial CC (Tex.)	16	3	3.150	.150	1	171	1099	354	27	5	Colonial National Invitation
245	Pleasant Valley CC	11	4	4.149	.149	1	209	1477	495	22		Bank of Boston Classic
245	Colonial CC (Tex.)	15	4	4.149	.149		191	1068	361	32	5	Colonial National Invitation
245	La Costa CC	10	4	4.149	.149		68	386	124	16	2	MONY Tournament of Champions
245	La Costa CC	16	4	4.149	.149	1	68	380	135	12		MONY Tournament of Champions
249	Spyglass Hill GC	2	4	4.148	.148		89	581	161	22	3	AT&T Pebble Beach National Pro-Am
249	TPC at The Woodlands	5	4	4.148	.148	2	143	900	288	29	3	IIA Open
251	Eldorado CC	7	3	3.147	.147	1	31	168	57	6	1	Bob Hope Chrysler Classic
251	Desert Inn CC	18	4	4.147	.147		94	549	161	29	4	Panasonic Las Vegas Invitational
251	Cypress Point GC	7	3	3.147	.147	1	137	501	170	41	5	AT&T Pebble Beach National Pro-Am
251	Colonial CC (Tenn.)	12	3	3.147	.147	1	258	1562	373	82	10	Federal Express St. Jude Classic
251	Forest Oaks CC	8	3	3.147	.147	3	208	1417	496	22	3	K-Mart Greater Greensboro Open
256	Las Vegas CC	17	3	3.145	.145	1	130	919	278	27	2	Panasonic Las Vegas Invitational
256	Harbour Town GL	12	4	4.145	.145	1	244	1207	423	39	9	MCI Heritage Classic
256	Westchester CC	13	4	4.145	.145		285	1433	502	54	7	Manufacturers Hanover Westchester Classic
259	Eldorado CC	4	4	4.144	.144		26	180	52	6		Bob Hope Chrysler Classic
259	TPC of Connecticut	2	4	4.144	.144		180	1238	386	23	4	Canon Sammy Davis, Jr. Greater Hartford Open
259	Warwick Hills CC	18	4	4.144	.144		244	1512	481	30	11	Buick Open
259	Bay Hill Club & Lodge	17	3	3.144	.144	3	211	1147	369	77	5	Hertz Bay Hill Classic
263	Spanish Trail G&CC	10	4	4.143	.143		25	220	58	4	1	Panasonic Las Vegas Invitational
263	TPC at Eagle Trace	17	3	3.143	.143	1	210	1166	292	57	16	Honda Classic
263	TPC at Sawgrass	15	4	4.143	.143		238	1391	425	53	7	The Players Championship
263	TPC at Avenel	10	4	4.143	.143		75	276	76	23	5	Kemper Open
267	Lakewood CC	14	4	4.142	.142		235	1449	338	72	14	USF&G Classic
268	Green Island CC	15	4	4.141	.141		241	1472	468	40	6	Southern Open
268	Green Island CC	7	3	3.141	.141	1	233	1476	488	24	5	Southern Open
268	TPC of Scottsdale	7	3	3.141	.141		46	289	89	9		Phoenix Open
268	TPC of Scottsdale	18	4	4.141	.141		51	284	90	4	4	Phoenix Open
268	TPC at The Woodlands	8	3	3.141	.141	1	122	938	292	12		IIA Open
273	Firestone CC	15	3	3.140	.140		73	586	167	9	1	NEC World Series of Golf
273	Oak Hills CC	12	4	4.140	.140	1	194	1169	395	57	2	Texas Open Presented by Nabisco
273	Pleasant Valley CC	6	4	4.140	.140		250	1448	450	46	10	Bank of Boston Classic
273	Westchester CC	3	4	4.140	.140	1	283	1484	443	60	10	Manufacturers Hanover Westchester Classic
277	Fairway Oaks G&RC	12	4	4.139	.139		244	1478	430	38	11	Gatlin Brothers Southwest Golf Classic
277	En-Joie GC	18	4	4.139	.139	1	283	1363	423	63	7	B.C. Open
279	Forest Oaks CC	5	4	4.138	.138	1	230	1455	412	40	11	K-Mart Greater Greensboro Open
280	Torrey Pines GC (North)	6	3	3.137	.137		100	490	148	13	7	Shearson Lehman Brothers Andy Williams Open
280	Muirfield Village GC	16	3	3.137	.137		173	1173	380	23	1	Memorial Tournament
282	PGA West/TPC Stadium	13	3	3.136	.136		21	140	28	8	1	Bob Hope Chrysler Classic
282	Pebble Beach GL	1	4	4.136	.136		115	761	200	30	3	AT&T Pebble Beach National Pro-Am
284	Bay Hill Club & Lodge	14	3	3.135	.135		200	1159	420	27	6	Hertz Bay Hill Classic
285	Perdido Bay CC	2	4	4.134	.134	2	212	1415	434	39	1	Pensacola Open
285	Warwick Hills CC	2	4	4.134	.134	1	219	1559	467	28	4	Buick Open
285	TPC of Scottsdale	14	4	4.134	.134		48	288	89	7	1	Phoenix Open
285	Forest Oaks CC	14	4	4.134	.134		217	1450	453	28	1	K-Mart Greater Greensboro Open
285	TPC at Avenel	3	3	3.134	.134		41	315	96	3		Kemper Open
285	Tuckaway CC	3	4	4.134	.134	2	241	1423	483	27		Greater Milwaukee Open
291	Kingsmill GC	2	3	3.133	.133		223	1502	469	25		Anheuser-Busch Golf Classic
292	Magnolia Course GC	17	4	4.133	.133	1	147	686	135	57	14	Walt Disney World/Oldsmobile Golf Classic
293	Muirfield Village GC	10	4	4.132	.132		211	1114	390	32	3	Memorial Tournament
293	Muirfield Village GC	1	4	4.132	.132	2	211	1114	383	34	6	Memorial Tournament
295	Torrey Pines GC (North)	7	4	4.131	.131		78	513	147	19	1	Shearson Lehman Brothers Andy Williams Open
295	Fairway Oaks G&RC	6	4	4.131	.131	2	263	1400	496	39	1	Gatlin Brothers Southwest Golf Classic
295	La Quinta CC	14	4	4.131	.131	1	56	390	105	12	1	Bob Hope Chrysler Classic
295	TPC at StarPass	7	3	3.131	.131		65	298	99	11	2	Seiko Tucson Open
295	TPC at StarPass	18	4	4.131	.131		52	320	93	9	1	Seiko Tucson Open
295	Forest Oaks CC	1	4	4.131	.131	2	224	1434	466	22	1	K-Mart Greater Greensboro Open
301	Bermuda Dunes CC	16	4	4.129	.129		80	580	160	12	1	Bob Hope Chrysler Classic
301	Butler National GC	13	3	3.129	.129	1	216	1244	277	65	1	Beatrice Western Open
301	Westchester CC	1	3	3.129	.129	1	245	1525	471	34	5	Manufacturers Hanover Westchester Classic

Rank	Golf Course	Hole	Par	Avg Score	Avg Over Under-Par	Eagles	Birdies	Pars	Bogeys	Double Bogeys	Triple Bogey +	Tournament Name
301	Colonial CC (Tenn.)	4	4	4.129	.129	1	258	1536	439	37	15	Federal Express St. Jude Classic
305	Bermuda Dunes CC	17	3	3.128	.128		75	582	170	6		Bob Hope Chrysler Classic
305	Kingsmill GC	13	3	3.128	.128		235	1502	452	26	4	Anheuser-Busch Golf Classic
305	Forest Oaks CC	11	4	4.128	.128	2	264	1380	471	25	7	K-Mart Greater Greensboro Open
308	Desert Inn CC	3	4	4.127	.127		63	611	154	8	1	Panasonic Las Vegas Invitational
308	Pebble Beach GL	14	5	5.127	.127	1	178	659	221	39	11	AT&T Pebble Beach National Pro-Am
308	TPC at Avenel	17	3	3.127	.127		60	305	70	15	5	Kemper Open
308	TPC at Avenel	1	4	4.127	.127		49	304	97	5		Kemper Open
312	Tamarisk CC	14	3	3.126	.126		40	266	79	5		Bob Hope Chrysler Classic
312	Muirfield Village GC	14	4	4.126	.126	1	327	951	383	79	9	Memorial Tournament
314	Magnolia GC	9	4	4.125	.125	1	120	703	186	25	5	Walt Disney World/Oldsmobile Golf Classic
314	Phoenix CC	3	4	4.125	.125	1	198	1200	345	32	7	Phoenix Open
314	Harbour Town GL	18	4	4.125	.125		211	1302	371	32	7	MCI Heritage Classic
314	Augusta National GC	14	4	4.125	.125	1	175	845	316	15		The Masters
318	Pleasant Valley CC	13	4	4.123	.123	3	236	1495	430	38	2	Bank of Boston Classic
318	Desert Inn CC	16	3	3.123	.123	2	79	582	162	12		Panasonic Las Vegas Invitational
318	Indian Wells CC	11	4	4.123	.123		87	487	133	17	2	Bob Hope Chrysler Classic
318	Riviera CC	8	4	4.123	.123	2	234	1080	373	33	4	Los Angeles Open Presented by Nissan
318	Colonial CC (Tex.)	9	4	4.123	.123	1	236	1096	235	70	19	Colonial National Invitation
323	Lake Buena Vista CC	11	4	4.122	.122		74	451	116	14	1	Walt Disney World/Oldsmobile Golf Classic
323	Riviera CC	7	4	4.122	.122	1	255	1074	337	52	7	Los Angeles Open Presented by Nissan
325	Kingsmill GC	12	4	4.121	.121		334	1371	433	73	8	Anheuser-Busch Golf Classic
326	TPC of Connecticut	18	4	4.120	.120	1	231	1181	388	27	3	Canon Sammy Davis, Jr. Greater Hartford Open
326	En-Joie GC	4	3	3.120	.120		186	1529	396	28	1	B.C. Open
326	Waialae CC	16	4	4.120	.120	1	269	1448	418	42	6	Hawaiian Open
326	Lakewood CC	1	4	4.120	.120		224	1440	419	20	5	USF&G Classic
330	TPC at Sawgrass	10	4	4.119	.119	1	269	1366	437	38	3	The Players Championship
331	Oakwood CC	17	3	3.118	.118	2	202	1355	404	18		Hardee's Golf Classic
332	Tuckaway CC	1	4	4.117	.117		242	1460	450	22	2	Greater Milwaukee Open
333	Oakwood CC	14	4	4.116	.116	2	230	1314	404	29	2	Hardee's Golf Classic
334	En-Joie GC	14	3	3.115	.115	1	223	1486	384	43	3	B.C. Open
334	Desert Inn CC	14	4	4.115	.115		92	561	170	13	1	Panasonic Las Vegas Invitational
336	Firestone CC	8	4	4.114	.114		113	528	182	13		NEC World Series of Golf
337	TPC of Scottsdale	5	4	4.113	.113		45	302	79	6	1	Phoenix Open
337	Muirfield Village GC	12	3	3.113	.113		292	1060	306	80	12	Memorial Tournament
339	En-Joie GC	11	4	4.112	.112	1	216	1477	425	20	1	B.C. Open
339	Spyglass Hill GC	4	4	4.112	.112	3	155	495	163	35	5	AT&T Pebble Beach National Pro-Am
339	Indian Wells CC	13	3	3.112	.112		69	514	136	7		Bob Hope Chrysler Classic
342	Perdido Bay CC	9	4	4.111	.111	1	269	1376	404	50	3	Pensacola Open
342	Harbour Town GL	13	4	4.111	.111	1	292	1179	388	52	11	MCI Heritage Classic
344	Woodlands CC (West)	12	3	3.110	.110		98	620	176	11		IIA Open
344	Perdido Bay CC	12	4	4.110	.110	2	290	1373	365	60	13	Pensacola Open
344	Doral CC (Blue)	6	4	4.110	.110		264	1458	432	32	2	Doral Ryder Open
347	Kingsmill GC	10	4	4.109	.109		263	1480	447	26	3	Anheuser-Busch Golf Classic
347	Spyglass Hill GC	1	5	5.109	.109	2	131	516	182	21	4	AT&T Pebble Beach National Pro-Am
349	En-Joie GC	7	3	3.107	.107	1	274	1466	304	81	14	B.C. Open
349	Oakwood CC	12	3	3.107	.107		207	1391	357	23	3	Hardee's Golf Classic
351	Pleasant Valley CC	16	3	3.106	.106	1	246	1500	425	29	3	Bank of Boston Classic
351	Oakwood CC	1	4	4.106	.106	1	217	1358	381	24		Hardee's Golf Classic
351	Pebble Beach GL	7	3	3.106	.106	3	190	657	223	31	5	AT&T Pebble Beach National Pro-Am
354	Woodlands CC (West)	13	4	4.105	.105		129	577	178	18	3	IIA Open
354	Tamarisk CC	15	4	4.105	.105		48	266	63	13		Bob Hope Chrysler Classic
354	Tamarisk CC	11	3	3.105	.105		40	277	65	8		Bob Hope Chrysler Classic
354	La Quinta CC	10	4	4.105	.105		57	411	89	5	3	Bob Hope Chrysler Classic
354	Tamarisk CC	13	4	4.105	.105	1	40	274	64	8	3	Bob Hope Chrysler Classic
359	Bermuda Dunes CC	5	4	4.104	.104		104	553	159	16	1	Bob Hope Chrysler Classic
359	Las Vegas CC	13	4	4.104	.104	1	192	879	250	30	5	Panasonic Las Vegas Invitational
359	Butler National GC	15	5	5.104	.104		268	1178	302	48	8	Beatrice Western Open
359	TPC at The Woodlands	9	4	4.104	.104	2	177	876	276	29	5	IIA Open
363	Muirfield Village GC	6	4	4.103	.103	2	232	1164	288	64		Memorial Tournament
363	Muirfield Village GC	9	4	4.103	.103	1	262	1096	329	57	5	Memorial Tournament

Rank	Golf Course	Hole	Par	Avg Score	Avg Over Under-Par	Eagles	Birdies	Pars	Bogeys	Double Bogeys	Triple Bogey +	Tournament Name
365	Magnolia GC	15	3	3.102	.102		101	755	173	10	1	Walt Disney World/Oldsmobile Golf Classic
365	Bermuda Dunes CC	10	4	4.102	.102		78	589	159	5	2	Bob Hope Chrysler Classic
365	Oak Hills CC	4	4	4.102	.102		226	1174	369	46	3	Texas Open Presented by Nabisco
365	Fairway Oaks G&RC	11	3	3.102	.102	1	248	1494	417	36	5	Gatlin Brothers Southwest Golf Classic
365	Doral CC (Blue)	17	4	4.102	.102		268	1455	441	22	2	Doral Ryder Open
365	Lakewood CC	9	4	4.102	.102		271	1396	398	40	3	USF&G Classic
371	Augusta National GC	9	4	4.101	.101		174	888	270	19	1	The Masters
372	Desert Inn CC	2	4	4.100	.100		91	581	154	10	1	Panasonic Las Vegas Invitational
372	Colonial CC (Tenn.)	15	3	3.100	.100		280	1568	382	54	2	Federal Express St. Jude Classic
372	Atlanta CC	16	3	3.100	.100		234	1492	422	16	2	Georgia-Pacific Atlanta Golf Classic
372	TPC at The Woodlands	2	4	4.100	.100		161	927	254	20	3	IIA Open
376	Oak Hills CC	11	4	4.099	.099	3	236	1182	363	30	4	Texas Open Presented by Nabisco
376	Las Vegas CC	11	4	4.099	.099		170	890	273	21	3	Panasonic Las Vegas Invitational
376	TPC at Eagle Trace	6	4	4.099	.099	1	261	1099	330	48	3	Honda Classic
376	TPC at Sawgrass	6	4	4.099	.099		278	1390	387	51	8	The Players Championship
376	TPC at Avenel	8	4	4.099	.099		67	287	91	9	1	Kemper Open
381	Eldorado CC	15	4	4.098	.098		26	189	46	3		Bob Hope Chrysler Classic
381	Las Vegas CC	16	4	4.098	.098	2	177	903	244	26	5	Panasonic Las Vegas Invitational
381	Waialae CC	15	4	4.098	.098		289	1435	406	46	8	Hawaiian Open
381	TPC at Eagle Trace	11	3	3.098	.098		213	1183	308	34	4	Honda Classic
385	Bermuda Dunes CC	4	3	3.097	.097		69	604	151	8	1	Bob Hope Chrysler Classic
385	Butler National GC	7	5	5.097	.097		250	1168	336	42	8	Beatrice Western Open
385	Lakewood CC	17	3	3.097	.097		215	1492	383	18		USF&G Classic
388	Phoenix CC	10	4	4.096	.096		206	1203	348	24	2	Phoenix Open
388	Riviera CC	13	4	4.096	.096	2	272	1078	318	47	9	Los Angeles Open Presented by Nissan
388	Oakwood CC	18	4	4.096	.096	1	272	1327	311	58	12	Hardee's Golf Classic
391	Muirfield Village GC	13	4	4.095	.095		214	1181	322	31	2	Memorial Tournament
392	Phoenix CC	11	4	4.094	.094	2	210	1225	313	31	2	Phoenix Open
392	Spanish Trail G&CC	11	3	3.094	.094		30	225	47	6		Panasonic Las Vegas Invitational
392	Kingsmill GC	16	4	4.094	.094		316	1413	448	39	3	Anheuser-Busch Golf Classic
395	TPC of Connecticut	5	3	3.093	.093	1	211	1259	338	20	2	Canon Sammy Davis, Jr. Greater Hartford Open
396	Augusta National GC	7	4	4.092	.092	1	197	850	285	19		The Masters
397	Pebble Beach GL	18	5	5.090	.090	4	197	682	158	54	14	AT&T Pebble Beach National Pro-Am
398	Tuckaway CC	15	4	4.089	.089	1	262	1468	425	18	2	Greater Milwaukee Open
399	Eldorado CC	16	3	3.088	.088		30	184	47	2	1	Bob Hope Chrysler Classic
399	Palm GC	12	3	3.088	.088		76	452	122	6		Walt Disney World/Oldsmobile Golf Classic
399	Spyglass Hill GC	3	3	3.088	.088	1	124	545	169	15	2	AT&T Pebble Beach National Pro-Am
399	Muirfield Village GC	8	3	3.088	.088		199	1217	308	25	1	Memorial Tournament
399	TPC at Eagle Trace	14	4	4.088	.088	3	233	1143	337	22	4	Honda Classic
404	Magnolia GC	5	4	4.086	.086		137	670	211	18	4	Walt Disney World/Oldsmobile Golf Classic
405	Firestone CC	7	3	3.085	.085		94	586	147	9		NEC World Series of Golf
405	Pebble Beach GL	15	4	4.085	.085		149	755	178	23	4	AT&T Pebble Beach National Pro-Am
405	Harbour Town GL	17	3	3.085	.085	1	251	1297	337	33	4	MCI Heritage Classic
408	Waialae CC	17	3	3.084	.084	1	271	1504	376	30	2	Hawaiian Open
408	TPC of Connecticut	1	4	4.084	.084		252	1213	332	29	5	Canon Sammy Davis, Jr. Greater Hartford Open
408	Lakewood CC	4	3	3.084	.084		223	1509	359	16	1	USF&G Classic
411	Perdido Bay CC	3	4	4.083	.083	1	263	1439	370	26	4	Pensacola Open
412	En-Joie GC	6	4	4.082	.082	1	254	1465	402	17	1	B.C. Open
412	Lake Buena Vista CC	12	3	3.082	.082		67	473	111	5		Walt Disney World/Oldsmobile Golf Classic
412	Firestone CC	14	4	4.082	.082		114	552	162	7	1	NEC World Series of Golf
412	Desert Inn CC	17	4	4.082	.082		108	573	132	20	4	Panasonic Las Vegas Invitational
412	Torrey Pines GC (South)	16	3	3.082	.082	1	174	1021	236	19	1	Shearson Lehman Brothers Andy Williams Open
412	Riviera CC	16	3	3.082	.082	3	232	1136	330	23	2	Los Angeles Open Presented by Nissan
412	Harbour Town GL	7	3	3.082	.082		287	1220	380	33	3	MCI Heritage Classic
419	Palm GC	8	3	3.081	.081		73	464	112	7		Walt Disney World/Oldsmobile Golf Classic
419	Spanish Trail G&CC	1	4	4.081	.081		45	200	56	7		Panasonic Las Vegas Invitational
421	Perdido Bay CC	18	4	4.080	.080		240	1447	388	25	3	Pensacola Open
421	TPC at StarPass	17	3	3.080	.080		57	334	75	7	2	Seiko Tucson Open
421	Doral CC (Blue)	7	4	4.080	.080	2	291	1447	430	17	1	Doral Ryder Open
424	Firestone CC	5	3	3.079	.079	1	111	558	151	13	2	NEC World Series of Golf
424	Pleasant Valley CC	1	3	3.079	.079		253	1574	345	30	2	Bank of Boston Classic

TOUGHEST PGA TOUR HOLES FROM 1983–1987 (continued)

Rank	Golf Course	Hole	Par	Avg Score	Avg Over Under-Par	Eagles	Birdies	Pars	Bogeys	Double Bogeys	Triple Bogey +	Tournament Name
424	Perdido Bay CC	5	4	4.079	.079	1	246	1468	353	30	5	Pensacola Open
424	TPC of Scottsdale	11	4	4.079	.079	1	51	308	59	14		Phoenix Open
424	Bay Hill Club & Lodge	10	4	4.079	.079	2	236	1217	323	29	5	Hertz Bay Hill Classic
424	TPC at Sawgrass	17	3	3.079	.079	1	396	1352	180	154	31	The Players Championship
430	Phoenix CC	6	4	4.078	.078	2	218	1227	303	31	2	Phoenix Open
430	Spanish Trail G&CC	9	4	4.078	.078		37	214	54	2	1	Panasonic Las Vegas Invitational
430	La Quinta CC	15	3	3.078	.078		62	401	98	4		Bob Hope Chrysler Classic
430	Glen Abbey GC	15	3	3.078	.078		226	1221	296	34		Canadian Open
430	Colonial CC (Tex.)	14	4	4.078	.078		224	1103	310	19	1	Colonial National Invitation
435	Eldorado CC	12	3	3.077	.077		33	186	37	7	1	Bob Hope Chrysler Classic
435	Pebble Beach GL	13	4	4.077	.077		142	761	186	19	1	AT&T Pebble Beach National Pro-Am
437	Woodlands CC (West)	18	4	4.076	.076		125	601	166	11	2	IIA Open
437	Butler National GC	1	4	4.076	.076		284	1178	270	67	5	Beatrice Western Open
437	La Costa CC	14	3	3.076	.076		77	400	110	8	1	MONY Tournament of Champions
440	Harbour Town GL	3	4	4.075	.075	1	278	1250	352	38	4	MCI Heritage Classic
440	Butler National GC	16	4	4.075	.075	1	256	1166	335	40	6	Beatrice Western Open
442	Westchester CC	7	4	4.074	.074	5	414	1348	438	69	7	Manufacturers Hanover Westchester Classic
442	TPC of Connecticut	8	3	3.074	.074	1	222	1271	313	23	1	Canon Sammy Davis, Jr. Greater Hartford Open
442	Waialae CC	3	4	4.074	.074	1	319	1483	325	45	11	Hawaiian Open
442	Riviera CC	6	3	3.074	.074	4	250	1117	327	24	4	Los Angeles Open Presented by Nissan
442	Bay Hill Club & Lodge	15	4	4.074	.074	1	232	1234	312	26	7	Hertz Bay Hill Classic
447	En-Joie GC	9	4	4.073	.073		301	1424	372	42	1	B.C. Open
448	Oak Hills CC	18	3	3.072	.072		231	1222	330	33	2	Texas Open Presented by Nabisco
449	Lakewood CC	10	4	4.071	.071		282	1437	354	31	4	USF&G Classic
449	Colonial CC (Tex.)	10	4	4.071	.071		200	1163	267	25	2	Colonial National Invitation
451	Torrey Pines GC (North)	13	4	4.070	.070	1	94	520	133	9	1	Shearson Lehman Brothers Andy Williams Open
451	TPC at Eagle Trace	1	4	4.070	.070	2	214	1214	285	26	1	Honda Classic
451	La Costa CC	3	3	3.070	.070		57	444	91	4		MONY Tournament of Champions
451	Lakewood CC	5	4	4.070	.070		269	1439	374	20	6	USF&G Classic
455	Butler National GC	3	4	4.069	.069	1	263	1182	326	32		Beatrice Western Open
456	Colonial CC (Tex.)	18	4	4.068	.068	2	235	1095	287	33	5	Colonial National Invitation
456	Colonial CC (Tex.)	8	3	3.068	.068	2	203	1151	288	12	1	Colonial National Invitation
458	Harbour Town GL	6	4	4.067	.067		279	1300	300	37	7	MCI Heritage Classic
458	Forest Oaks CC	6	4	4.067	.067		286	1463	359	36	5	K-Mart Greater Greensboro Open
460	PGA West/TPC Stadium	14	4	4.066	.066		23	140	34	1		Bob Hope Chrysler Classic
460	PGA West/TPC Stadium	4	3	3.066	.066		31	126	39	1	1	Bob Hope Chrysler Classic
460	Desert Inn CC	6	4	4.066	.066		108	555	163	10	1	Panasonic Las Vegas Invitational
460	TPC at Sawgrass	13	3	3.066	.066		281	1464	305	53	11	The Players Championship
460	TPC of Connecticut	16	3	3.066	.066	2	277	1235	246	63	8	Canon Sammy Davis, Jr. Greater Hartford Open
460	Atlanta CC	4	4	4.066	.066	2	319	1452	317	71	5	Georgia-Pacific Atlanta Golf Classic
466	Warwick Hills CC	5	4	4.065	.065		304	1550	401	22	1	Buick Open
466	TPC at The Woodlands	11	4	4.065	.065	1	175	948	216	17	8	IIA Open
468	Eldorado CC	8	4	4.064	.064	1	29	193	34	7		Bob Hope Chrysler Classic
468	Cypress Point GC	15	3	3.064	.064		143	540	146	26		AT&T Pebble Beach National Pro-Am
468	En-Joie GC	17	3	3.064	.064	1	257	1515	346	19	2	B.C. Open
471	Colonial CC (Tenn.)	2	4	4.063	.063		313	1552	394	26	1	Federal Express St. Jude Classic
472	Pleasant Valley CC	7	3	3.062	.062	1	309	1571	239	74	10	Bank of Boston Classic
472	En-Joie GC	2	4	4.062	.062		361	1395	278	98	8	B.C. Open
474	Eldorado CC	2	3	3.061	.061		36	176	52			Bob Hope Chrysler Classic
474	PGA West/TPC Stadium	7	4	4.061	.061		38	124	23	12	1	Bob Hope Chrysler Classic
474	Eldorado CC	3	4	4.061	.061		38	177	44	5		Bob Hope Chrysler Classic
474	Torrey Pines GC (North)	12	3	3.061	.061		70	574	112	2		Shearson Lehman Brothers Andy Williams Open
478	La Quinta CC	17	4	4.060	.060		56	412	91	5	1	Bob Hope Chrysler Classic
478	Colonial CC (Tenn.)	11	4	4.060	.060	3	348	1496	398	37	4	Federal Express St. Jude Classic
478	TPC at Eagle Trace	4	4	4.060	.060		300	1104	278	54	6	Honda Classic
478	Warwick Hills CC	3	3	3.060	.060	1	262	1637	362	15	1	Buick Open
478	Lakewood CC	16	4	4.060	.060	1	325	1388	352	40	2	USF&G Classic
483	TPC at StarPass	9	4	4.059	.059	2	79	294	89	11		Seiko Tucson Open
483	Waialae CC	11	3	3.059	.059		267	1545	344	25	3	Hawaiian Open
483	La Costa CC	1	4	4.059	.059	1	75	415	98	7		MONY Tournament of Champions
486	TPC of Scottsdale	8	4	4.058	.058		69	275	84	5		Phoenix Open

Rank	Golf Course	Hole	Par	Avg Score	Avg Over Under-Par	Eagles	Birdies	Pars	Bogeys	Double Bogeys	Triple Bogey +	Tournament Name
486	Doral CC (Blue)	15	3	3.058	.058		263	1533	375	15	2	Doral Ryder Open
486	Colonial CC (Tenn.)	6	4	4.058	.058	4	304	1551	412	14	1	Federal Express St. Jude Classic
489	Tamarisk CC	10	4	4.057	.057		57	253	71	8	1	Bob Hope Chrysler Classic
489	TPC at StarPass	15	3	3.057	.057	1	68	322	71	13		Seiko Tucson Open
489	Augusta National GC	17	4	4.057	.057		182	930	225	13	2	The Masters
489	TPC at Las Colinas	9	4	4.057	.057		143	617	144	23	2	GTE Byron Nelson Golf Classic
493	Pebble Beach GL	11	4	4.056	.056	1	166	725	200	16	1	AT&T Pebble Beach National Pro-Am
493	Riviera CC	14	3	3.056	.056		208	1229	273	15	1	Los Angeles Open Presented by Nissan
495	Oak Hills CC	16	4	4.055	.055		261	1248	272	32	5	Texas Open Presented by Nabisco
495	Forest Oaks CC	7	4	4.055	.055		296	1458	364	27	4	K-Mart Greater Greensboro Open
497	TPC of Connecticut	3	4	4.054	.054	2	217	1317	270	23	2	Canon Sammy Davis, Jr. Greater Hartford Open
497	Waialae CC	7	3	3.054	.054	1	310	1482	361	26	4	Hawaiian Open
497	Warwick Hills CC	4	4	4.054	.054		343	1530	359	34	12	Buick Open
500	Oakwood CC	8	3	3.053	.053	1	269	1360	327	22	2	Hardee's Golf Classic
501	Spanish Trail G&CC	17	4	4.052	.052		45	209	49	3	2	Panasonic Las Vegas Invitational
501	Perdido Bay CC	4	3	3.052	.052		220	1565	307	11		Pensacola Open
501	Firestone CC	3	4	4.052	.052	1	131	557	123	23	1	NEC World Series of Golf
504	PGA West/TPC Stadium	16	5	5.051	.051	3	34	121	31	8	1	Bob Hope Chrysler Classic
504	Tamarisk CC	5	3	3.051	.051		49	273	67	1		Bob Hope Chrysler Classic
504	Torrey Pines GC (North)	8	4	4.051	.051		92	547	111	6	2	Shearson Lehman Brothers Andy Williams Open
504	Torrey Pines GC (South)	17	4	4.051	.051		207	996	217	27	5	Shearson Lehman Brothers Andy Williams Open
504	Muirfield Village GC	3	4	4.051	.051	1	338	1045	295	59	12	Memorial Tournament
504	Bay Hill Club & Lodge	7	3	3.051	.051		211	1308	282	11		Hertz Bay Hill Classic
510	TPC at Sawgrass	3	3	3.050	.050	1	263	1476	354	19	1	The Players Championship
510	Firestone CC	1	4	4.050	.050		132	549	139	15	1	NEC World Series of Golf
510	TPC at Las Colinas	15	4	4.050	.050		126	636	160	6	1	GTE Byron Nelson Golf Classic
513	Phoenix CC	17	4	4.049	.049		244	1241	276	20	2	Phoenix Open
514	Magnolia GC	1	4	4.049	.049	1	135	729	159	14	2	Walt Disney World/Oldsmobile Golf Classic
514	Pebble Beach GL	5	3	3.049	.049		154	758	176	20	1	AT&T Pebble Beach National Pro-Am
514	Atlanta CC	1	4	4.049	.049		316	1478	336	33	3	Georgia-Pacific Atlanta Golf Classic
514	Tuckaway CC	8	3	3.049	.049	2	255	1553	350	15	1	Greater Milwaukee Open
518	Woodlands CC (West)	3	4	4.048	.048		145	594	148	15	3	IIA Open
518	TPC at StarPass	16	4	4.048	.048		104	266	87	14	4	Seiko Tucson Open
518	Torrey Pines GC (South)	11	3	3.048	.048		190	1012	240	10		Shearson Lehman Brothers Andy Williams Open
521	Desert Inn CC	4	3	3.047	.047		109	586	136	6		Panasonic Las Vegas Invitational
521	Pebble Beach GL	3	4	4.047	.047	1	179	735	176	15	3	AT&T Pebble Beach National Pro-Am
521	Waialae CC	12	4	4.047	.047		275	1573	309	24	3	Hawaiian Open
524	TPC of Connecticut	14	4	4.046	.046		238	1292	285	13	3	Canon Sammy Davis, Jr. Greater Hartford Open
525	Las Vegas CC	14	3	3.045	.045	1	156	1002	185	10	3	Panasonic Las Vegas Invitational
525	Pebble Beach GL	17	3	3.045	.045		153	766	177	13		AT&T Pebble Beach National Pro-Am
525	Waialae CC	8	4	4.045	.045		331	1476	334	41	2	Hawaiian Open
525	Colonial CC (Tenn.)	5	3	3.045	.045	2	265	1661	343	15		Federal Express St. Jude Classic
529	Phoenix CC	9	4	4.044	.044		253	1221	287	22		Phoenix Open
529	Green Island CC	2	3	3.044	.044		261	1615	342	9		Southern Open
529	Warwick Hills CC	9	4	4.044	.044	1	327	1546	382	21	1	Buick Open
532	TPC at Sawgrass	4	4	4.043	.043	3	435	1243	314	101	18	The Players Championship
532	Lakewood CC	12	4	4.043	.043	1	334	1402	329	40	2	USF&G Classic
534	Spanish Trail G&CC	6	4	4.042	.042		41	215	51		1	Panasonic Las Vegas Invitational
534	Indian Wells CC	3	4	4.042	.042	1	82	546	85	11	1	Bob Hope Chrysler Classic
534	Torrey Pines GC (South)	14	4	4.042	.042		227	967	229	27	2	Shearson Lehman Brothers Andy Williams Open
534	TPC at Sawgrass	1	4	4.042	.042	2	299	1424	368	20	1	The Players Championship
538	Tamarisk CC	9	4	4.041	.041		45	288	53	4		Bob Hope Chrysler Classic
539	Lakewood CC	7	4	4.040	.040	2	272	1502	313	17	2	USF&G Classic
540	Bay Hill Club & Lodge	13	4	4.037	.037	1	339	1164	247	53	8	Hertz Bay Hill Classic
540	TPC at The Woodlands	16	3	3.037	.037		184	959	209	13		IIA Open
542	Tamarisk CC	6	4	4.036	.036		46	290	48	6		Bob Hope Chrysler Classic
542	Harbour Town GL	15	5	5.036	.036	2	401	1145	312	48	15	MCI Heritage Classic
544	Doral CC (Blue)	9	3	3.035	.035	1	312	1530	308	32	5	Doral Ryder Open
544	Colonial CC (Tex.)	7	4	4.035	.035		248	1105	287	16	1	Colonial National Invitation
546	Woodlands CC (West)	5	3	3.034	.034	1	118	644	135	5	2	IIA Open
546	Torrey Pines GC (North)	4	4	4.034	.034	1	115	507	126	8	1	Shearson Lehman Brothers Andy Williams Open

Rank	Golf Course	Hole	Par	Avg Score	Avg Over Under-Par	Eagles	Birdies	Pars	Bogeys	Double Bogeys	Triple Bogey +	Tournament Name
546	La Costa CC	17	5	5.034	.034		90	409	84	10	3	MONY Tournament of Champions
546	TPC at Las Colinas	13	3	3.034	.034		124	663	132	7	3	GTE Byron Nelson Golf Classic
550	Spyglass Hill GC	15	3	3.032	.032		135	587	110	22	2	AT&T Pebble Beach National Pro-Am
550	Harbour Town GL	9	4	4.032	.032		364	1191	324	41	3	MCI Heritage Classic
550	La Costa CC	15	4	4.032	.032		99	389	96	11	1	MONY Tournament of Champions
553	Spyglass Hill GC	17	4	4.030	.030	1	145	551	149	9	1	AT&T Pebble Beach National Pro-Am
553	La Quinta CC	8	4	4.030	.030	1	94	382	80	4	4	Bob Hope Chrysler Classic
553	Woodlands CC (West)	4	5	5.030	.030		184	555	128	33	5	IIA Open
556	Spyglass Hill GC	14	5	5.029	.029	2	150	557	124	18	5	AT&T Pebble Beach National Pro-Am
556	La Costa CC	7	3	3.029	.029		75	438	74	9		MONY Tournament of Champions
556	Warwick Hills CC	11	3	3.029	.029		327	1579	352	20		Buick Open
559	Magnolia GC	2	4	4.028	.028		151	729	143	15	2	Walt Disney World/Oldsmobile Golf Classic
559	TPC of Scottsdale	2	4	4.028	.028		78	272	77	5	1	Phoenix Open
559	TPC of Scottsdale	9	4	4.028	.028		72	287	68	4	2	Phoenix Open
562	Oak Hills CC	1	4	4.027	.027	2	337	1141	296	40	2	Texas Open Presented by Nabisco
563	Spanish Trail G&CC	13	4	4.026	.026	1	47	205	53	2		Panasonic Las Vegas Invitational
563	Perdido Bay CC	16	4	4.026	.026		348	1392	315	43	5	Pensacola Open
563	Tuckaway CC	11	4	4.026	.026	2	336	1466	347	25		Greater Milwaukee Open
563	TPC at The Woodlands	10	4	4.026	.026		189	964	200	12		IIA Open
563	Tuckaway CC	7	4	4.026	.026	1	297	1535	320	20	3	Greater Milwaukee Open
568	Colonial CC (Tenn.)	10	4	4.024	.024	2	366	1518	375	25		Federal Express St. Jude Classic
569	Westchester CC	17	4	4.024	.024	3	362	1530	352	29	5	Manufacturers Hanover Westchester Classic
570	Lakewood CC	13	3	3.023	.023	1	276	1513	310	8		USF&G Classic
571	Firestone CC	16	5	5.022	.022	1	193	492	109	32	9	NEC World Series of Golf
571	En-Joie GC	10	4	4.022	.022		338	1482	270	43	7	B.C. Open
571	En-Joie GC	16	3	3.022	.022		290	1531	301	18		B.C. Open
574	Waialae CC	14	4	4.021	.021		304	1556	307	12	5	Hawaiian Open
575	PGA West/TPC Stadium	5	5	5.020	.020	1	47	118	18	9	5	Bob Hope Chrysler Classic
575	Oak Hills CC	17	4	4.020	.020		306	1168	301	32	11	Texas Open Presented by Nabisco
577	Spyglass Hill GC	12	3	3.019	.019		133	601	102	18	2	AT&T Pebble Beach National Pro-Am
577	TPC at Las Colinas	2	3	3.019	.019		147	624	151	6	1	GTE Byron Nelson Golf Classic
579	La Quinta CC	18	4	4.018	.018		89	385	83	8		Bob Hope Chrysler Classic
579	Torrey Pines GC (North)	10	4	4.018	.018		99	549	107	3		Shearson Lehman Brothers Andy Williams Open
579	TPC of Scottsdale	4	3	3.018	.018		86	261	80	4	2	Phoenix Open
579	Green Island CC	16	4	4.018	.018		331	1544	329	18	5	Southern Open
579	Firestone CC	10	4	4.018	.018	1	138	565	119	12	1	NEC World Series of Golf
579	Harbour Town GL	14	3	3.018	.018		356	1271	216	70	10	MCI Heritage Classic
579	Colonial CC (Tex.)	13	3	3.018	.018		271	1172	160	47	7	Colonial National Invitation
586	Desert Inn CC	12	4	4.017	.017		105	602	122	6	2	Panasonic Las Vegas Invitational
586	TPC at The Woodlands	7	4	4.017	.017		220	936	160	42	7	IIA Open
588	Desert Inn CC	13	4	4.016	.016	1	115	595	122	4		Panasonic Las Vegas Invitational
589	PGA West/TPC Stadium	2	4	4.015	.015		28	141	27	2		Bob Hope Chrysler Classic
589	Tamarisk CC	16	4	4.015	.015		59	270	57	4		Bob Hope Chrysler Classic
589	Lake Buena Vista CC	16	3	3.015	.015		102	448	100	6		Walt Disney World/Oldsmobile Golf Classic
592	Las Vegas CC	3	4	4.014	.014		200	948	193	14	2	Panasonic Las Vegas Invitational
592	Bermuda Dunes CC	2	4	4.014	.014		100	620	107	4	2	Bob Hope Chrysler Classic
592	La Quinta CC	7	3	3.014	.014		86	391	82	6		Bob Hope Chrysler Classic
592	Phoenix CC	14	4	4.014	.014	2	282	1223	254	17	5	Phoenix Open
592	Indian Wells CC	17	4	4.014	.014		114	500	101	10	1	Bob Hope Chrysler Classic
592	Pebble Beach GL	4	4	4.014	.014	3	193	737	158	15	3	AT&T Pebble Beach National Pro-Am
592	Doral CC (Blue)	14	4	4.014	.014	1	336	1510	320	20	1	Doral Ryder Open
599	Firestone CC	12	3	3.013	.013	1	139	555	128	12	1	NEC World Series of Golf
600	TPC at The Woodlands	3	3	3.013	.013		200	991	149	19	6	IIA Open
601	Atlanta CC	5	4	4.012	.012		353	1479	292	39	3	Georgia-Pacific Atlanta Golf Classic
601	Pleasant Valley CC	15	4	4.012	.012		388	1456	300	50	10	Bank of Boston Classic
603	Fairway Oaks G&RC	13	4	4.011	.011	2	354	1498	307	37	3	Gatlin Brothers Southwest Golf Classic
603	Lake Buena Vista CC	5	4	4.011	.011		103	450	98	3	2	Walt Disney World/Oldsmobile Golf Classic
603	Torrey Pines GC (South)	3	3	3.011	.011	1	184	1072	188	7		Shearson Lehman Brothers Andy Williams Open
606	PGA West/TPC Stadium	17	3	3.010	.010		30	146	16	4	2	Bob Hope Chrysler Classic
606	Indian Wells CC	4	3	3.010	.010		103	506	113	3	1	Bob Hope Chrysler Classic
606	TPC at Sawgrass	9	5	5.010	.010	5	386	1352	318	44	9	The Players Championship

Rank	Golf Course	Hole	Par	Avg Score	Avg Over Under-Par	Eagles	Birdies	Pars	Bogeys	Double Bogeys	Triple Bogey +	Tournament Name
609	Oakwood CC	16	4	4.009	.009	2	316	1354	292	16	1	Hardee's Golf Classic
610	Las Vegas CC	9	3	3.008	.008	3	199	961	172	19	3	Panasonic Las Vegas Invitational
611	Las Vegas CC	5	3	3.007	.007	1	191	973	182	10		Panasonic Las Vegas Invitational
611	Perdido Bay CC	17	3	3.007	.007		312	1484	284	22	1	Pensacola Open
611	TPC of Scottsdale	1	4	4.007	.007	1	78	282	64	6	2	Phoenix Open
611	Green Island CC	17	3	3.007	.007	2	340	1543	324	18		Southern Open
615	Eldorado CC	10	4	4.004	.004		51	172	34	6	1	Bob Hope Chrysler Classic
616	Green Island CC	18	5	5.003	.003	7	429	1410	337	35	9	Southern Open
617	TPC of Scottsdale	6	4	4.002	.002		95	257	66	15		Phoenix Open
618	Palm GC	17	4	4.000			114	439	92	11		Walt Disney World/Oldsmobile Golf Classic
618	Woodlands CC (West)	15	3	3.000			139	638	117	11		IIA Open
618	Magnolia GC	12	3	3.000			168	733	127	11	1	Walt Disney World/Oldsmobile Golf Classic
618	Butler National GC	2	5	5.000		4	354	1136	287	22	1	Beatrice Western Open
618	Oakwood CC	15	4	4.000		1	280	1428	259	12	1	Hardee's Golf Classic
623	Colonial CC (Tex.)	17	4	3.999	.001 −		295	1092	245	23	2	Colonial National Invitation
623	Westchester CC	2	4	3.999	.001 −	2	374	1555	316	33	1	Manufacturers Hanover Westchester Classic
624	TPC at StarPass	6	4	3.998	.002 −		110	282	61	19	3	Seiko Tucson Open
624	Kingsmill GC	17	3	2.998	.002 −		332	1572	295	19	1	Anheuser-Busch Golf Classic
626	Phoenix CC	2	3	2.997	.003 −		282	1243	217	37	4	Phoenix Open
627	Cypress Point GC	13	4	3.996	.004 −	1	152	562	121	14	5	AT&T Pebble Beach National Pro-Am
627	Torrey Pines GC (South)	15	4	3.996	.004 −	3	243	973	216	16	1	Shearson Lehman Brothers Andy Williams Open
627	Firestone CC	17	4	3.996	.004 −	1	134	579	111	11		NEC World Series of Golf
630	Warwick Hills CC	8	3	2.995	.005 −		338	1629	295	16		Buick Open
630	TPC at Las Colinas	6	4	3.995	.005 −		166	616	133	12	2	GTE Byron Nelson Golf Classic
632	Palm GC	15	4	3.994	.006 −	3	95	462	95	1		Walt Disney World/Oldsmobile Golf Classic
632	Fairway Oaks G&RC	3	5	4.994	.006 −	8	456	1353	327	53	4	Southwest Golf Classic
632	Glen Abbey GC	4	4	3.994	.006 −	3	320	1161	270	23		Canadian Open
635	Las Vegas CC	15	4	3.993	.007 −		229	922	192	11	3	Panasonic Las Vegas Invitational
635	Kingsmill GC	11	4	3.993	.007 −	1	368	1525	302	20	3	Anheuser-Busch Golf Classic
635	La Costa CC	4	4	3.993	.007 −		104	400	84	8		MONY Tournament of Champions
635	Glen Abbey GC	13	5	4.993	.007 −	11	448	927	332	51	8	Canadian Open
639	Warwick Hills CC	17	3	2.992	.008 −	2	335	1619	310	8	4	Buick Open
640	Torrey Pines GC (North)	17	3	2.991	.009 −		120	536	91	11		Shearson Lehman Brothers Andy Williams Open
640	Phoenix CC	4	4	3.991	.009 −	1	298	1217	240	25	2	Phoenix Open
640	Bermuda Dunes CC	11	4	3.991	.009 −		132	578	109	13	1	Bob Hope Chrysler Classic
640	Atlanta CC	12	4	3.991	.009 −		350	1504	293	18	1	Georgia-Pacific Atlanta Golf Classic
640	Green Island CC	12	4	3.991	.009 −		356	1560	279	24	8	Southern Open
645	Spanish Trail G&CC	4	4	3.990	.010 −		59	199	44	6		Panasonic Las Vegas Invitational
645	Oakwood CC	9	4	3.990	.010 −	1	313	1385	269	13		Hardee's Golf Classic
647	TPC at StarPass	1	4	3.989	.011 −		86	315	68	5	1	Seiko Tucson Open
647	TPC at StarPass	2	4	3.989	.011 −		86	313	71	5		Seiko Tucson Open
649	La Costa CC	13	4	3.988	.012 −		114	383	91	8		MONY Tournament of Champions
649	TPC at The Woodlands	12	4	3.988	.012 −		235	914	195	18	3	IIA Open
651	Green Island CC	8	5	4.987	.013 −		419	1498	263	39	8	Southern Open
652	La Quinta CC	4	4	3.985	.015 −		98	372	77	14	4	Bob Hope Chrysler Classic
652	Warwick Hills CC	6	4	3.985	.015 −		371	1566	323	17	1	Buick Open
652	Forest Oaks CC	15	5	4.985	.015 −	3	397	1425	289	29	6	K-Mart Greater Greensboro Open
655	Phoenix CC	16	4	3.984	.016 −	1	285	1251	233	13		Phoenix Open
655	Cypress Point GC	3	3	2.984	.016 −		148	585	113	8	1	AT&T Pebble Beach National Pro-Am
655	Doral CC (Blue)	11	4	3.984	.016 −		366	1499	315	8		Doral Ryder Open
658	Las Vegas CC	4	4	3.983	.017 −	1	256	896	180	22	2	Panasonic Las Vegas Invitational
659	Las Vegas CC	2	4	3.982	.018 −	1	224	940	182	10		Panasonic Las Vegas Invitational
659	Atlanta CC	13	3	2.982	.018 −	1	384	1514	195	64	8	Georgia-Pacific Atlanta Golf Classic
661	Desert Inn CC	5	5	4.981	.019 −	5	162	529	126	15		Panasonic Las Vegas Invitational
663	Green Island CC	13	4	3.981	.019 −	2	388	1534	267	31	5	Southern Open
663	Palm GC	9	4	3.979	.021 −	1	109	474	64	5	3	Walt Disney World/Oldsmobile Golf Classic
663	Lakewood CC	3	4	3.979	.021 −	1	325	1507	256	17	2	USF&G Classic
663	TPC at Las Colinas	18	4	3.979	.021 −		140	675	107	6	1	GTE Byron Nelson Golf Classic
666	Fairway Oaks G&RC	7	4	3.978	.022 −	1	353	1515	319	12	1	Gatlin Brothers Southwest Golf Classic
667	La Quinta CC	3	3	2.977	.023 −		85	410	61	8	1	Bob Hope Chrysler Classic
668	Riviera CC	17	5	4.977	.023 −		310	1167	229	18	2	Los Angeles Open Presented by Nissan

Rank	Golf Course	Hole	Par	Avg Score	Avg Over Under-Par	Eagles	Birdies	Pars	Bogeys	Double Bogeys	Triple Bogey +	Tournament Name
670	Palm GC	2	4	3.976	.024 −		114	446	84	11	1	Walt Disney World/Oldsmobile Golf Classic
670	Lake Buena Vista CC	6	4	3.976	.024 −		110	466	74	5	1	Walt Disney World/Oldsmobile Golf Classic
670	Palm GC	16	3	2.976	.024 −		95	488	67	6		Walt Disney World/Oldsmobile Golf Classic
670	Kingsmill GC	1	4	3.976	.024 −	4	438	1409	344	24		Anheuser-Busch Golf Classic
674	Tuckaway CC	13	4	3.973	.027 −	2	353	1531	281	9		Greater Milwaukee Open
674	Green Island CC	4	4	3.973	.027 −	3	359	1592	250	20	3	Southern Open
676	La Quinta CC	16	4	3.972	.028 −	1	89	405	65	5		Bob Hope Chrysler Classic
676	Tuckaway CC	5	3	2.972	.028 −		384	1489	276	26	1	Greater Milwaukee Open
676	Waialae CC	10	4	3.972	.028 −	2	399	1475	252	48	8	Hawaiian Open
679	Spanish Trail G&CC	16	4	3.971	.029 −	1	38	239	29	1		Panasonic Las Vegas Invitational
679	Indian Wells CC	1	4	3.971	.029 −		116	522	77	10	1	Bob Hope Chrysler Classic
679	Indian Wells CC	9	4	3.971	.029 −	1	136	492	77	16	4	Bob Hope Chrysler Classic
679	Doral CC (Blue)	2	4	3.971	.029 −	2	411	1440	318	17		Doral Ryder Open
679	Colonial CC (Tenn.)	9	4	3.971	.029 −	1	406	1552	312	15		Federal Express St. Jude Classic
684	TPC of Scottsdale	16	3	2.970	.030 −		76	301	50	5	1	Phoenix Open
684	Magnolia GC	6	3	2.970	.030 −		156	766	112	5	1	Walt Disney World/Oldsmobile Golf Classic
684	Colonial CC (Tenn.)	1	5	4.970	.030 −		432	1522	307	23	2	Federal Express St. Jude Classic
684	Warwick Hills CC	10	4	3.970	.030 −		424	1519	314	21		Buick Open
684	Oak Hills CC	2	3	2.970	.030 −	2	313	1253	237	13		Texas Open Presented by Nabisco
689	Torrey Pines GC (North)	5	4	3.967	.033 −	2	135	519	93	8	1	Shearson Lehman Brothers Andy Williams Open
689	Woodlands CC (West)	2	4	3.967	.033 −	1	171	602	120	10	1	IIA Open
689	Eldorado CC	5	4	3.967	.033 −		53	174	31	4	2	Bob Hope Chrysler Classic
689	Pleasant Valley CC	3	4	3.967	.033 −	2	397	1503	281	19	2	Bank of Boston Classic
689	Doral CC (Blue)	12	5	4.967	.033 −	4	372	1505	286	18	3	Doral Ryder Open
694	TPC at StarPass	13	4	3.966	.034 −	1	84	328	54	8		Seiko Tucson Open
694	Harbour Town GL	16	4	3.966	.034 −		359	1298	233	30	3	MCI Heritage Classic
696	Fairway Oaks G&RC	15	4	3.965	.035 −	1	424	1436	309	25	6	Gatlin Brothers Southwest Golf Classic
697	TPC of Scottsdale	10	4	3.963	.037 −		77	300	51	5		Phoenix Open
698	Oakwood CC	11	4	3.963	.037 −	3	346	1373	241	17	1	Hardee's Golf Classic
698	Colonial CC (Tenn.)	3	3	2.963	.037 −	2	390	1607	268	17	2	Federal Express St. Jude Classic
700	TPC at Avenel	2	5	4.960	.040 −	1	109	259	80	5	1	Kemper Open
700	Westchester CC	14	3	2.960	.040 −	2	409	1581	263	25	1	Manufacturers Hanover Westchester Classic
702	Torrey Pines GC (South)	8	3	2.959	.041 −	2	208	1095	142	4	1	Shearson Lehman Brothers Andy Williams Open
702	Doral CC (Blue)	5	4	3.959	.041 −	3	397	1473	299	15	1	Doral Ryder Open
702	Bay Hill Club & Lodge	5	4	3.959	.041 −	1	312	1266	223	8	2	Hertz Bay Hill Classic
702	Oak Hills CC	6	4	3.959	.041 −	3	363	1175	228	41	8	Texas Open Presented by Nabisco
706	TPC of Scottsdale	17	4	3.958	.042 −	1	87	279	62	3	1	Phoenix Open
706	Torrey Pines GC (South)	5	4	3.958	.042 −	3	231	1051	158	9		Shearson Lehman Brothers Andy Williams Open
708	Waialae CC	2	4	3.957	.043 −	1	432	1470	255	23	3	Hawaiian Open
709	Torrey Pines GC (North)	15	4	3.956	.044 −		126	543	84	4	1	Shearson Lehman Brothers Andy Williams Open
709	Tuckaway CC	14	3	2.956	.044 −		356	1568	239	11	2	Greater Milwaukee Open
709	TPC at The Woodlands	6	5	4.955	.045 −	2	284	875	185	16	3	IIA Open
712	Oak Hills CC	9	3	2.954	.046 −	1	328	1229	225	33	2	Texas Open Presented by Nabisco
713	Cypress Point GC	2	5	4.951	.049 −		192	545	98	16	4	AT&T Pebble Beach National Pro-Am
713	Pleasant Valley CC	12	4	3.951	.049 −		419	1526	208	37	14	Bank of Boston Classic
713	Colonial CC (Tex.)	2	4	3.951	.049 −	1	337	1079	223	17		Colonial National Invitation
716	Palm GC	5	4	3.950	.050 −		116	462	73	5		Walt Disney World/Oldsmobile Golf Classic
716	TPC of Connecticut	12	4	3.950	.050 −		342	1273	183	30	3	Canon Sammy Davis, Jr. Greater Hartford Open
716	Doral CC (Blue)	16	4	3.950	.050 −		428	1458	286	16		Doral Ryder Open
719	Indian Wells CC	15	3	2.949	.051 −	1	142	480	99	4		Bob Hope Chrysler Classic
720	Bermuda Dunes CC	14	4	3.948	.052 −		147	595	78	13		Bob Hope Chrysler Classic
720	Magnolia GC	16	4	3.948	.052 −	1	187	740	93	16	3	Walt Disney World/Oldsmobile Golf Classic
722	Bermuda Dunes CC	15	4	3.947	.053 −	4	173	556	91	7	2	Bob Hope Chrysler Classic
722	Doral CC (Blue)	10	5	4.947	.053 −	5	491	1347	300	40	5	Doral Ryder Open
722	Kingsmill GC	6	4	3.947	.053 −	2	410	1524	270	13		Anheuser-Busch Golf Classic
722	Perdido Bay CC	8	3	2.947	.053 −		362	1501	230	10		Pensacola Open
726	Tamarisk CC	17	4	3.946	.054 −		72	271	43	4		Bob Hope Chrysler Classic
727	Colonial CC (Tenn.)	16	5	4.944	.056 −	26	623	1248	285	74	30	Federal Express St. Jude Classic
727	Magnolia GC	7	4	3.944	.056 −		184	740	106	10		Walt Disney World/Oldsmobile Golf Classic
729	Colonial CC (Tex.)	6	4	3.943	.057 −	1	315	1128	204	9		Colonial National Invitation
730	Lake Buena Vista CC	7	3	2.942	.058 −		123	451	79	3		Walt Disney World/Oldsmobile Golf Classic

Rank	Golf Course	Hole	Par	Avg Score	Avg Over Under-Par	Eagles	Birdies	Pars	Bogeys	Double Bogeys	Triple Bogey +	Tournament Name
730	Atlanta CC	3	3	2.942	.058 −	1	362	1572	219	11	1	Georgia-Pacific Atlanta Golf Classic
730	La Costa CC	8	4	3.942	.058 −		113	410	69	3	1	MONY Tournament of Champions
733	Tuckaway CC	4	4	3.941	.059 −	5	416	1459	282	13	1	Greater Milwaukee Open
734	Fairway Oaks G&RC	18	5	4.939	.061 −	14	578	1263	269	59	18	Gatlin Brothers Southwest Golf Classic
734	Atlanta CC	14	4	3.939	.061 −		461	1434	211	51	9	Georgia-Pacific Atlanta Golf Classic
736	La Quinta CC	9	4	3.938	.062 −		96	409	59	1		Bob Hope Chrysler Classic
737	La Costa CC	11	3	2.936	.064 −		118	404	68	6		MONY Tournament of Champions
738	Spanish Trail G&CC	12	4	3.935	.065 −		63	205	37	3		Panasonic Las Vegas Invitational
738	Las Vegas CC	12	4	3.935	.065 −		279	916	145	13	4	Panasonic Las Vegas Invitational
738	Lakewood CC	8	3	2.935	.065 −	2	357	1529	215	5		USF&G Classic
741	Green Island CC	6	4	3.934	.066 −	7	475	1419	310	16		Southern Open
741	Forest Oaks CC	9	5	4.934	.066 −	9	474	1348	297	18	3	K-Mart Greater Greensboro Open
743	Lake Buena Vista CC	2	3	2.933	.067 −		122	461	68	5		Walt Disney World/Oldsmobile Golf Classic
743	TPC at StarPass	10	4	3.933	.067 −	1	111	293	61	8	1	Seiko Tucson Open
745	Tamarisk CC	2	3	2.931	.069 −		63	293	32	2		Bob Hope Chrysler Classic
745	Magnolia GC	14	5	4.931	.069 −	3	219	683	119	15	1	Walt Disney World/Oldsmobile Golf Classic
747	PGA West/TPC Stadium	12	4	3.929	.071 −	1	39	135	19	4		Bob Hope Chrysler Classic
748	TPC of Connecticut	10	5	4.928	.072 −	7	389	1183	238	12	2	Canon Sammy Davis, Jr. Greater Hartford Open
749	Lake Buena Vista CC	15	4	3.927	.073 −		149	414	84	8	1	Walt Disney World/Oldsmobile Golf Classic
749	Riviera CC	11	5	4.927	.073 −	3	402	1069	225	24	3	Los Angeles Open Presented by Nissan
749	Atlanta CC	7	4	3.927	.073 −	2	480	1401	245	33	5	Georgia-Pacific Atlanta Golf Classic
749	Kingsmill GC	14	4	3.927	.073 −	1	464	1479	246	29		Anheuser-Busch Golf Classic
753	Bermuda Dunes CC	6	4	3.926	.074 −		149	600	82	1	1	Bob Hope Chrysler Classic
754	Fairway Oaks G&RC	1	4	3.926	.074 −	2	419	1506	261	11	2	Southwest Golf Classic
755	Colonial CC (Tenn.)	7	5	4.925	.075 −	5	510	1454	275	37	5	Federal Express St. Jude Classic
755	Westchester CC	5	5	4.925	.075 −	8	570	1359	292	45	7	Manufacturers Hanover Westchester Classic
757	Magnolia GC	3	3	2.923	.077 −	1	181	755	103			Walt Disney World/Oldsmobile Golf Classic
758	Spanish Trail G&CC	15	5	4.922	.078 −	4	67	194	36	6	1	Panasonic Las Vegas Invitational
758	TPC at StarPass	5	3	2.922	.078 −		114	290	65	6		Seiko Tucson Open
760	Torrey Pines GC (South)	10	4	3.921	.079 −		276	1010	155	10	1	Shearson Lehman Brothers Andy Williams Open
760	TPC at Las Colinas	11	4	3.921	.079 −	1	193	638	74	21	2	GTE Byron Nelson Golf Classic
762	Eldorado CC	6	4	3.920	.080 −	1	67	156	32	8		Bob Hope Chrysler Classic
762	Bermuda Dunes CC	7	3	2.920	.080 −		142	618	71	2		Bob Hope Chrysler Classic
762	Oak Hills CC	14	4	3.920	.080 −	1	367	1234	197	17	2	Texas Open Presented by Nabisco
762	Magnolia GC	8	5	4.920	.080 −		210	712	109	9		Walt Disney World/Oldsmobile Golf Classic
762	TPC at Sawgrass	12	4	3.920	.080 −		454	1388	256	15	1	The Players Championship
767	Lake Buena Vista CC	3	4	3.919	.081 −	1	126	469	54	5	1	Walt Disney World/Oldsmobile Golf Classic
768	Green Island CC	3	4	3.918	.082 −	1	477	1480	242	27		Southern Open
769	Bermuda Dunes CC	9	4	3.916	.084 −		148	620	60	4	1	Bob Hope Chrysler Classic
769	Oakwood CC	2	4	3.916	.084 −	3	386	1390	187	13	2	Hardee's Golf Classic
771	Torrey Pines GC (North)	3	3	2.912	.088 −		125	577	54	2		Shearson Lehman Brothers Andy Williams Open
771	Torrey Pines GC (North)	2	4	3.912	.088 −	1	141	542	72	2		Shearson Lehman Brothers Andy Williams Open
771	TPC of Connecticut	6	4	3.912	.088 −		366	1266	194	5		Canon Sammy Davis, Jr. Greater Hartford Open
774	Palm GC	3	3	2.910	.090 −		141	441	72	1	1	Walt Disney World/Oldsmobile Golf Classic
775	Spanish Trail G&CC	8	4	3.909	.091 −		75	191	37	5		Panasonic Las Vegas Invitational
776	La Costa CC	6	4	3.908	.092 −	2	130	387	75	2		MONY Tournament of Champions
777	Bay Hill Club & Lodge	12	5	4.907	.093 −	6	426	1096	240	36	8	Hertz Bay Hill Classic
777	Lakewood CC	15	5	4.907	.093 −	31	637	1015	366	55	4	USF&G Classic
777	Colonial CC (Tex.)	11	5	4.907	.093 −	7	381	1048	201	20		Colonial National Invitation
780	Phoenix CC	12	4	3.904	.096 −	5	382	1194	184	18		Phoenix Open
780	TPC of Connecticut	9	5	4.904	.096 −	8	377	1237	200	8	1	Canon Sammy Davis, Jr. Greater Hartford Open
782	Tamarisk CC	8	4	3.903	.097 −		70	290	28	2		Bob Hope Chrysler Classic
782	Palm GC	14	5	4.903	.097 −	4	168	383	89	10	2	Walt Disney World/Oldsmobile Golf Classic
782	Riviera CC	10	4	3.903	.097 −	1	430	1051	226	16	2	Los Angeles Open Presented by Nissan
782	Oakwood CC	5	3	2.903	.097 −		380	1419	177	5		Hardee's Golf Classic
786	Indian Wells CC	7	4	3.902	.098 −	2	141	512	68	3		Bob Hope Chrysler Classic
786	Indian Wells CC	16	4	3.902	.098 −		151	499	72	4		Bob Hope Chrysler Classic
786	TPC at Las Colinas	1	4	3.902	.098 −		216	600	102	10	1	GTE Byron Nelson Golf Classic
786	TPC at Las Colinas	5	3	2.902	.098 −		192	642	89	6		GTE Byron Nelson Golf Classic
790	Muirfield Village GC	11	5	4.900	.100 −	13	419	1073	206	37	2	Memorial Tournament
791	Eldorado CC	18	5	4.899	.101 −	3	74	140	41	5	1	Bob Hope Chrysler Classic

Rank	Golf Course	Hole	Par	Avg Score	Avg Over Under-Par	Eagles	Birdies	Pars	Bogeys	Double Bogeys	Triple Bogey +	Tournament Name
791	Lake Buena Vista CC	9	4	3.899	.101 –		125	475	53	3		Walt Disney World/Oldsmobile Golf Classic
793	Green Island CC	10	4	3.897	.103 –	5	501	1458	245	18		Southern Open
793	Torrey Pines GC (South)	2	4	3.897	.103 –	3	266	1065	113	5		Shearson Lehman Brothers Andy Williams Open
793	En-Joie GC	3	5	4.897	.103 –	16	501	1338	255	27	3	B.C. Open
793	Warwick Hills CC	1	5	4.897	.103 –	4	506	1503	235	23	7	Buick Open
793	TPC at Avenel	11	3	2.897	.103 –		119	283	41	8	4	Kemper Open
793	Bermuda Dunes CC	12	3	2.897	.103 –		158	591	81	1	' 2	Bob Hope Chrysler Classic
799	TPC of Connecticut	13	4	3.896	.104 –	6	398	1221	190	15	1	Canon Sammy Davis, Jr. Greater Hartford Oper
800	Woodlands CC (West)	11	4	3.895	.105 –		184	639	75	7		IIA Open
801	Bermuda Dunes CC	3	4	3.894	.106 –	8	154	592	76	3		Bob Hope Chrysler Classic
802	Indian Wells CC	2	4	3.893	.107 –	1	148	506	63	7	1	Bob Hope Chrysler Classic
803	Doral CC (Blue)	8	5	4.892	.108 –	18	526	1363	235	39	7	Doral Ryder Open
804	Magnolia GC	11	4	3.891	.109 –		207	746	80	7		Walt Disney World/Oldsmobile Golf Classic
805	Las Vegas CC	6	4	3.890	.110 –	4	291	920	134	8		Panasonic Las Vegas Invitational
805	TPC at Avenel	14	4	3.890	.110 –	1	115	280	52	6	1	Kemper Open
807	Pleasant Valley CC	9	4	3.889	.111 –	1	446	1562	187	8		Bank of Boston Classic
808	TPC at Sawgrass	11	5	4.887	.113 –	14	540	1242	285	31	2	The Players Championship
809	TPC at Eagle Trace	15	5	4.886	.114 –	5	437	1081	191	25	3	Honda Classic
810	Bay Hill Club & Lodge	6	5	4.880	.120 –	30	593	927	151	81	30	Hertz Bay Hill Classic
810	Firestone CC	11	4	3.880	.120 –		193	555	83	5		NEC World Series of Golf
812	Augusta National GC	13	5	4.876	.124 –	33	429	629	214	41	6	The Masters
813	Perdido Bay CC	1	4	3.875	.125 –	3	509	1360	209	20	2	Pensacola Open
814	Palm GC	13	4	3.872	.128 –	3	140	461	47	4	1	Walt Disney World/Oldsmobile Golf Classic
814	Tamarisk CC	7	4	3.872	.128 –	1	80	278	30	1		Bob Hope Chrysler Classic
814	TPC at The Woodlands	13	5	4.872	.128 –	5	353	842	136	24	5	IIA Open
817	La Quinta CC	1	4	3.871	.129 –		109	412	39	4	1	Bob Hope Chrysler Classic
818	Lake Buena Vista CC	10	4	3.870	.130 –		138	465	53			Walt Disney World/Oldsmobile Golf Classic
819	TPC at Avenel	13	5	4.868	.132 –	1	138	252	51	11	2	Kemper Open
820	Lakewood CC	2	5	4.866	.134 –	10	551	1288	233	19	7	USF&G Classic
821	Colonial CC (Tenn.)	18	5	4.865	.135 –	18	642	1293	292	33	8	Federal Express St. Jude Classic
822	Westchester CC	10	4	3.860	.140 –	7	654	1324	265	27	4	Manufacturers Hanover Westchester Classic
823	Kingsmill GC	7	5	4.857	.143 –	23	667	1236	208	70	15	Anheuser-Busch Golf Classic
824	Westchester CC	6	3	2.856	.144 –	2	554	1510	201	14		Manufacturers Hanover Westchester Classic
825	TPC at Avenel	5	4	3.855	.145 –		112	297	46			Kemper Open
826	Lake Buena Vista CC	13	4	3.854	.146 –		168	422	62	3	1	Walt Disney World/Oldsmobile Golf Classic
827	TPC at StarPass	8	5	4.851	.149 –	4	150	250	59	9	3	Seiko Tucson Open
827	Pebble Beach GL	6	5	4.851	.149 –	7	360	583	138	17	4	AT&T Pebble Beach National Pro-Am
829	Woodlands CC (West)	16	5	4.849	.151 –	5	247	551	87	12	3	IIA Open
829	TPC at Eagle Trace	10	5	4.849	.151 –	15	488	1020	188	26	5	Honda Classic
829	La Costa CC	9	5	4.849	.151 –		150	390	52	4		MONY Tournament of Champions
832	TPC at StarPass	14	5	4.846	.154 –	12	168	201	74	16	4	Seiko Tucson Open
833	Westchester CC	9	5	4.845	.155 –	21	605	1358	274	22	1	Manufacturers Hanover Westchester Classic
834	TPC at Eagle Trace	8	5	4.844	.156 –	7	475	1075	155	27	3	Honda Classic
835	Spyglass Hill GC	7	5	4.843	.157 –	13	223	515	96	7	2	AT&T Pebble Beach National Pro-Am
836	En-Joie GC	8	5	4.842	.158 –	6	560	1357	201	16		B.C. Open
837	Lake Buena Vista CC	4	4	3.841	.159 –		159	449	41	7		Walt Disney World/Oldsmobile Golf Classic
838	PGA West/TPC Stadium	8	5	4.838	.162 –	4	43	135	14	1	1	Bob Hope Chrysler Classic
839	Woodlands CC (West)	1	5	4.837	.163 –	3	252	559	78	7	6	IIA Open
840	En-Joie GC	5	5	4.836	.164 –	12	559	1336	212	20	1	B.C. Open
841	Atlanta CC	8	5	4.835	.165 –	11	591	1326	203	33	2	Georgia-Pacific Atlanta Golf Classic
841	TPC of Connecticut	7	4	3.835	.165 –	3	457	1216	150	5		Canon Sammy Davis, Jr. Greater Hartford Open
843	Eldorado CC	13	5	4.834	.166 –	1	96	124	35	5	3	Bob Hope Chrysler Classic
844	Torrey Pines GC (North)	16	4	3.832	.168 –	4	184	506	63	1		Shearson Lehman Brothers Andy Williams Open
845	Lakewood CC	11	5	4.831	.169 –	6	577	1307	205	12	1	USF&G Classic
846	Indian Wells CC	6	3	2.824	.176 –		173	508	45			Bob Hope Chrysler Classic
847	Spyglass Hill GC	11	5	4.823	.177 –	6	237	520	81	11	1	AT&T Pebble Beach National Pro-Am
847	La Quinta CC	11	5	4.823	.177 –		166	338	56	5		Bob Hope Chrysler Classic
847	Pleasant Valley CC	5	5	4.823	.177 –	7	567	1429	188	12	1	Bank of Boston Classic
850	Lake Buena Vista CC	17	5	4.822	.178 –	9	214	347	58	24	4	Walt Disney World/Oldsmobile Golf Classic
851	Warwick Hills CC	7	5	4.821	.179 –	6	596	1452	219	4	1	Buick Open
851	Pleasant Valley CC	18	5	4.821	.179 –	11	600	1376	195	18	4	Bank of Boston Classic

TOUGHEST PGA TOUR HOLES FROM 1983–1987 (continued)

Rank	Golf Course	Hole	Par	Avg Score	Avg Over Under-Par	Eagles	Birdies	Pars	Bogeys	Double Bogeys	Triple Bogey +	Tournament Name
853	Augusta National GC	8	5	4.820	.180 −	8	362	856	117	9		The Masters
854	Lake Buena Vista CC	8	5	4.817	.183 −	10	184	383	71	7	1	Walt Disney World/Oldsmobile Golf Classic
855	Magnolia GC	13	4	3.817	.183 −	1	265	698	75	1		Walt Disney World/Oldsmobile Golf Classic
856	Oakwood CC	7	4	3.814	.186 −	4	518	1310	140	9		Hardee's Golf Classic
857	Oak Hills CC	8	4	3.812	.188 −	4	444	1198	157	14	1	Texas Open Presented by Nabisco
858	Cypress Point GC	5	5	4.811	.189 −	8	264	473	102	8		AT&T Pebble Beach National Pro-Am
859	Westchester CC	18	5	4.808	.192 −	20	668	1347	225	19	2	Manufacturers Hanover Westchester Classic
860	Muirfield Village GC	5	5	4.806	.194 −	10	549	977	190	20	4	Memorial Tournament
860	Warwick Hills CC	14	4	3.806	.194 −	4	633	1448	187	6		Buick Open
862	Indian Wells CC	12	4	3.804	.196 −		190	492	40	4		Bob Hope Chrysler Classic
862	Warwick Hills CC	16	5	4.804	.196 −	12	617	1417	212	19	1	Buick Open
864	Bermuda Dunes CC	13	5	4.802	.198 −	3	209	579	34	8		Bob Hope Chrysler Classic
865	Glen Abbey GC	18	5	4.800	.200 −	33	613	851	241	33	6	Canadian Open
866	Phoenix CC	5	4	3.796	.204 −	7	488	1155	128	5		Phoenix Open
867	Oak Hills CC	5	5	4.793	.207 −	10	509	1118	169	11	1	Texas Open Presented by Nabisco
867	Augusta National GC	2	5	4.793	.207 −	18	436	731	143	21	3	The Masters
869	Harbour Town GL	5	5	4.788	.212 −	37	582	1103	167	26	8	MCI Heritage Classic
870	Tamarisk CC	12	5	4.787	.213 −	4	112	239	33	2		Bob Hope Chrysler Classic
871	Forest Oaks CC	13	5	4.787	.213 −	17	638	1301	167	21	5	K-Mart Greater Greensboro Open
872	Las Vegas CC	18	5	4.784	.216 −	40	500	604	158	36	19	Panasonic Las Vegas Invitational
873	Glen Abbey GC	5	5	4.780	.220 −	13	580	988	177	18	1	Canadian Open
874	TPC of Scottsdale	3	5	4.776	.224 −	2	133	261	35	1	1	Phoenix Open
874	Forest Oaks CC	2	5	4.776	.224 −	16	655	1280	168	25	5	K-Mart Greater Greensboro Open
876	Warwick Hills CC	12	4	3.771	.229 −	5	657	1476	135	5		Buick Open
876	TPC at Sawgrass	2	5	4.771	.229 −	25	701	1134	221	27	6	The Players Championship
878	Muirfield Village GC	7	5	4.768	.232 −	14	534	1037	151	13	1	Memorial Tournament
879	Augusta National GC	15	5	4.762	.238 −	43	481	660	138	22	8	The Masters
880	TPC at Eagle Trace	5	5	4.761	.239 −	54	639	796	191	46	16	Honda Classic
881	Colonial CC (Tex.)	1	5	4.760	.240 −	5	505	1027	112	7	1	Colonial National Invitation
882	Tuckaway CC	16	5	4.758	.242 −	29	698	1235	195	18	1	Greater Milwaukee Open
882	TPC at The Woodlands	15	5	4.758	.242 −	20	461	755	106	16	7	IIA Open
884	Kingsmill GC	3	5	4.757	.243 −	46	698	1239	212	20	4	Anheuser-Busch Golf Classic
885	Fairway Oaks G&RC	14	5	4.745	.255 −	32	779	1105	244	32	9	Southwest Golf Classic
886	TPC at Avenel	6	5	4.743	.257 −	19	177	178	67	12	2	Kemper Open
887	Tuckaway CC	2	5	4.742	.258 −	18	679	1309	164	5	1	Greater Milwaukee Open
887	Kingsmill GC	15	5	4.742	.258 −	39	764	1157	233	22	4	Anheuser-Busch Golf Classic
889	Tuckaway CC	12	5	4.731	.269 −	21	714	1280	151	10		Greater Milwaukee Open
890	Atlanta CC	11	5	4.729	.271 −	21	739	1225	158	18	5	Georgia-Pacific Atlanta Golf Classic
891	Tamarisk CC	4	5	4.728	.272 −	2	134	224	28	2		Bob Hope Chrysler Classic
892	Atlanta CC	2	5	4.727	.273 −	25	·753	1197	171	16	4	Georgia-Pacific Atlanta Golf Classic
893	Cypress Point GC	6	5	4.727	.273 −	10	304	454	83	3	1	AT&T Pebble Beach National Pro-Am
894	Atlanta CC	18	5	4.717	.283 −	56	854	971	230	38	17	Georgia-Pacific Atlanta Golf Classic
895	En-Joie GC	12	5	4.716	.284 −	31	718	1211	169	10	1	B.C. Open
896	Fairway Oaks G&RC	9	5	4.709	.291 −	36	783	1178	176	23	5	Southwest Golf Classic
897	TPC at The Woodlands	1	5	4.706	.294 −	11	499	739	99	15	2	IIA Open
898	TPC of Scottsdale	15	5	4.702	.298 −	20	184	147	70	11	1	Phoenix Open
899	TPC at Las Colinas	16	5	4.700	.300 −	12	356	476	69	12	4	GTE Byron Nelson Golf Classic
900	Torrey Pines GC (South)	13	5	4.695	.305 −	15	507	839	88	3		Shearson Lehman Brothers Andy Williams Open
900	TPC at Sawgrass	16	5	4.695	.305 −	39	815	1022	212	22	4	The Players Championship
902	Bermuda Dunes CC	1	5	4.691	.309 −	14	290	477	43	9		Bob Hope Chrysler Classic
903	Perdido Bay CC	6	5	4.687	.313 −	32	773	1132	153	13		Pensacola Open
903	Perdido Bay CC	11	5	4.687	.313 −	47	762	1081	183	25	5	Pensacola Open
905	Glen Abbey GC	16	5	4.683	.317 −	38	706	859	141	21	12	Canadian Open
906	La Costa CC	2	5	4.680	.320 −	11	219	318	46	2		MONY Tournament of Champions
906	Tamarisk CC	18	5	4.680	.320 −	4	144	219	19	3	1	Bob Hope Chrysler Classic
908	Lakewood CC	6	5	4.678	.322 −	48	763	1129	153	14	1	USF&G Classic
909	TPC at Las Colinas	7	5	4.675	.325 −	10	357	493	63	6		GTE Byron Nelson Golf Classic
910	Phoenix CC	7	5	4.674	.326 −	30	616	977	154	5	1	Phoenix Open
911	Cypress Point GC	10	5	4.673	.327 −	24	332	419	70	8	2	AT&T Pebble Beach National Pro-Am
912	Perdido Bay CC	15	5	4.672	.328 −	31	817	1063	169	22	1	Pensacola Open
913	Indian Wells CC	8	5	4.670	.330 −	14	261	406	32	9	4	Bob Hope Chrysler Classic

Rank	Golf Course	Hole	Par	Avg Score	Avg Over Under-Par	Eagles	Birdies	Pars	Bogeys	Double Bogeys	Triple Bogey +	Tournament Name
914	Oak Hills CC	10	5	4.668	.332 −	55	720	838	174	29	2	Texas Open Presented by Nabisco
915	Pleasant Valley CC	4	5	4.666	.334 −	25	816	1240	117	6		Bank of Boston Classic
916	Oakwood CC	10	5	4.660	.340 −	23	748	1093	113	4		Hardee's Golf Classic
917	La Costa CC	12	5	4.659	.341 −	11	236	303	37	9		MONY Tournament of Champions
918	Phoenix CC	18	5	4.656	.344 −	31	672	904	156	18	2	Phoenix Open
919	Waialae CC	1	5	4.655	.345 −	42	895	1088	126	25	8	Hawaiian Open
920	Muirfield Village GC	15	5	4.651	.349 −	63	707	781	159	31	9	Memorial Tournament
921	Riviera CC	1	5	4.650	.350 −	47	694	831	125	27	2	Los Angeles Open Presented by Nissan
922	Torrey Pines GC (South)	18	5	4.644	.356 −	47	578	687	125	15		Shearson Lehman Brothers Andy Williams Open
923	Las Vegas CC	10	5	4.643	.357 −	22	534	715	79	7		Panasonic Las Vegas Invitational
924	Bermuda Dunes CC	18	5	4.640	.360 −	19	360	389	56	8	1	Bob Hope Chrysler Classic
924	TPC of Scottsdale	13	5	4.640	.360 −	12	169	220	28	3	1	Phoenix Open
924	Desert Inn CC	15	5	4.640	.360 −	29	318	417	63	9	1	Panasonic Las Vegas Invitational
927	Palm GC	11	5	4.639	.361 −	6	274	329	42	3	2	Walt Disney World/Oldsmobile Golf Classic
927	Waialae CC	9	5	4.639	.361 −	58	974	926	138	63	25	Hawaiian Open
927	Waialae CC	18	5	4.639	.361 −	42	853	1148	134	7		Hawaiian Open
930	Torrey Pines GC (South)	6	5	4.637	.363 −	28	590	725	95	12	2	Shearson Lehman Brothers Andy Williams Open
931	Bermuda Dunes CC	8	5	4.637	.363 −	14	315	464	39	1		Bob Hope Chrysler Classic
932	Harbour Town GL	2	5	4.635	.365 −	33	782	963	123	20	2	MCI Heritage Classic
932	Phoenix CC	1	5	4.635	.365 −	38	731	885	115	13	1	Phoenix Open
932	La Quinta CC	5	5	4.635	.365 −	11	211	309	26	5	3	Bob Hope Chrysler Classic
935	Las Vegas CC	8	5	4.632	.368 −	18	570	676	77	14	2	Panasonic Las Vegas Invitational
936	Butler National GC	12	5	4.631	.369 −	29	756	895	116	7	1	Beatrice Western Open
937	Firestone CC	2	5	4.627	.373 −	23	330	422	58	3		NEC World Series of Golf
938	Indian Wells CC	18	5	4.625	.375 −	26	290	348	54	8		Bob Hope Chrysler Classic
938	Bay Hill Club & Lodge	1	5	4.625	.375 −	38	735	914	118	7		Hertz Bay Hill Classic
940	Doral CC (Blue)	1	5	4.620	.380 −	35	864	1173	112	3	1	Doral Ryder Open
940	Spanish Trail G&CC	18	5	4.620	.380 −	8	142	123	31	3	1	Panasonic Las Vegas Invitational
942	Torrey Pines GC (North)	1	5	4.603	.397 −	19	311	381	46	1		Shearson Lehman Brothers Andy Williams Open
943	Torrey Pines GC (South)	9	5	4.590	.410 −	36	605	735	71	5		Shearson Lehman Brothers Andy Williams Open
943	Desert Inn CC	10	5	4.590	.410 −	12	363	414	46	1	1	Panasonic Las Vegas Invitational
945	La Quinta CC	6	5	4.575	.425 −	9	250	280	24	2		Bob Hope Chrysler Classic
945	Tuckaway CC	6	5	4.575	.425 −	70	911	1078	107	10		Greater Milwaukee Open
947	Magnolia GC	4	5	4.573	.427 −	26	442	522	50			Walt Disney World/Oldsmobile Golf Classic
947	TPC of Connecticut	4	5	4.573	.427 −	46	789	913	67	15	1	Canon Sammy Davis, Jr. Greater Hartford Open
949	Eldorado CC	1	5	4.568	.432 −	5	127	116	9	7		Bob Hope Chrysler Classic
950	Desert Inn CC	1	5	4.568	.432 −	16	367	420	31	3		Panasonic Las Vegas Invitational
951	Indian Wells CC	5	5	4.559	.441 −	15	350	316	35	7	3	Bob Hope Chrysler Classic
952	La Quinta CC	13	5	4.556	.444 −	15	251	261	28	9	1	Bob Hope Chrysler Classic
953	Eldorado CC	9	5	4.545	.455 −	10	131	94	27	2		Bob Hope Chrysler Classic
954	TPC at StarPass	3	5	4.543	.457 −	17	226	195	31	6		Seiko Tucson Open
955	Spanish Trail G&CC	3	5	4.542	.458 −	8	136	153	11			Panasonic Las Vegas Invitational
956	Torrey Pines GC (North)	14	5	4.541	.459 −	17	360	336	44	1		Shearson Lehman Brothers Andy Williams Open
957	Indian Wells CC	14	5	4.530	.470 −	28	318	349	29	2		Bob Hope Chrysler Classic
958	Lake Buena Vista CC	14	5	4.526	.474 −	17	306	307	23	3		Walt Disney World/Oldsmobile Golf Classic
959	Magnolia GC	10	5	4.523	.477 −	28	475	503	33	1		Walt Disney World/Oldsmobile Golf Classic
960	Pebble Beach GL	2	5	4.505	.495 −	56	523	458	64	6	2	AT&T Pebble Beach National Pro-Am
961	Palm GC	1	5	4.495	.505 −	16	317	306	16	1		Walt Disney World/Oldsmobile Golf Classic
962	Palm GC	7	5	4.489	.511 −	15	331	285	24	1		Walt Disney World/Oldsmobile Golf Classic
963	TPC at StarPass	11	5	4.484	.516 −	21	255	156	35	7	1	Seiko Tucson Open
964	Warwick Hills CC	13	5	4.473	.527 −	97	1169	864	134	14		Buick Open
965	Lake Buena Vista CC	1	5	4.456	.544 −	32	329	258	32	4	1	Walt Disney World/Oldsmobile Golf Classic
966	Oakwood CC	6	5	4.450	.550 −	77	1001	842	57	4		Hardee's Golf Classic
967	Spanish Trail G&CC	7	5	4.435	.565 −	17	151	129	11			Panasonic Las Vegas Invitational
968	Waialae CC	13	5	4.415	.585 −	91	1167	857	63	5	1	Hawaiian Open
969	Torrey Pines GC (North)	18	5	4.390	.610 −	37	421	280	16	2	2	Shearson Lehman Brothers Andy Williams Open
970	Torrey Pines GC (North)	9	5	4.331	.669 −	38	453	246	20	1		Shearson Lehman Brothers Andy Williams Open
971	Las Vegas CC	1	5	4.317	.683 −	37	307	184	12			Panasonic Las Vegas Invitational
972	Tamarisk CC	1	5	4.179	.821 −	40	242	106	2			Bob Hope Chrysler Classic

ACKNOWLEDGMENTS

No book is a one-man show, but few books involve as many contributions or as diverse a group of contributors as did this one.

My first appreciation goes to the trio of photographers whose art makes these pages a visual feast: Brian Morgan, Jim Moriarty, and Tony Roberts. Brian's home is St. Andrews, Scotland, Jim lives near Pinehurst, North Carolina, and Tony is a native of San Francisco, three great places to live and especially to play golf. For nearly a year, however, these three spent most of their time *photographing* courses, not playing them, as they traced the transcontinental path of the PGA Tour, traveling to tournament sites from Massachusetts to Hawaii. The results testify to the reputations of these men as three of the finest photographers in sports.

But if this is a picture book, it also is a valuable reference, thanks to a fellow named Bill Inglish. A retired sportswriter from Oklahoma, Inglish is the official statistician for The Masters and the unofficial statistician for the rest of the world of golf. For each tournament on the PGA Tour he supplied a comprehensive list of scoring statistics, everything from course records to the best final-round comeback by a champion. No other book has this breadth and depth of statistical information on professional golf. (In fact, the only other place the information exists is in Inglish's den.)

In addition to Inglish's tournament data, a special appendix includes lists of the PGA Tour courses, ranked in order of difficulty and length, and a list of the almost 1,000 holes on the Tour, ranked by difficulty, based upon the three-year scoring averages (1983–1985) of the players on the Tour. These statistics are current through the 1985 Tour season and will be updated periodically in future editions of the book. For their help in supplying these statistics and for their patience in answering my myriad questions, I am deeply indebted to Steve Rankin and Denise Taylor of the PGA Tour.

Without the sanction of the Tour this book would not have the authority it carries. Thanks are therefore due Peter Davison, director of golf, for information on the new Tournament Players Club courses, which enable the book to be current through 1987, and, of course, Deane Beman, commissioner of the Tour, for his help in securing the cooperation of tournament officials and players, and for his kind contribution of the Foreword.

Literally dozens of men and women helped make my job easier by providing answers to a lengthy questionnaire, sharing anecdotes, and verifying facts with uncommon dedication and efficiency. I will list them tournament by tournament in the yearly chronology of the Tour events: MONY Tournament of Champions: Sam Cantor, Tommy Jacobs; Bob Hope Chrysler Classic: Ed Herodt; Phoenix Open: Willie Low, Jay Morrish, Joan Mutcher, Tom Weiskopf; AT&T Pebble Beach National Pro-Am: Carol Rissel; Shearson Lehman Brothers Andy Williams Open: Tom Morgan, Ralph Trembley; Hawaiian Open: Tom Hitch, Chester Kahapea, Dick Post; Nissan Los Angeles Open: Ron Rhoads; The Honda Classic: Janice Hamilton; Doral Ryder Open: Jim Montgomery; Hertz Bay Hill Classic: Jim Bell; USF&G Classic: Shirley Daniels, Tom Wulff; Greater Greensboro Open: John Hughes; The Masters: Jim Armstrong, Dave Davis, Hazel Salmon; Sea Pines Heritage Golf Classic: Mark King, Mike Stevens; Houston Open: Duke Butler, Burt Darden, Kent Wood; Panasonic Las Vegas Invitational: Jim Cook, Bill Farkas; Byron Nelson Golf Classic: Steve Barley, Jay Morrish, Joe Phillips, Phyllis Skidmore; Colonial National Invitation: Sandra Harder, Roland Harper; Memorial Tournament: Jim Wisler; Kemper Open: Ed Ault, Bill Love, Ed Sneed, Britt Stenson; Manufacturers Hanover Westchester Classic: Peter Bisconti, Noel Griffith, Charles McCabe; Georgia-Pacific Atlanta Golf Classic: Dixie Dunbar, David Kaplan; Canadian Open: Dick Grimm, Bill Paul; Canon Sammy Davis, Jr. Greater Hartford Open: Phil Bonee, Drew Pierson, Peter Pierson, Bill Reid, John Shulansky; Anheuser-Busch Golf Classic: Al Burns; Western Open: Brian Fitzgerald, Bill Shean; The International: Kaye Kessler, Jack Vickers; NEC World Series of Golf: Gary Robison; St. Jude Memphis Classic: Vernon Bell; B.C. Open: Alex Alexander; Bank of Boston Classic: Ted Mingolla; Greater Milwaukee Open: Arlene Erickson; Southwest Golf Classic: Hal McGlothlin; Southern Open: Gunby Jordan; Pensacola Open: Bud Cooper, Jerry Stephens; Walt Disney World/Oldsmobile Golf Classic: Eric Fredricksen, Dave Herbst; Vantage Championship: Ben Crenshaw; Seiko-Tucson Match Play Championship:

Bob Cupp, Bill Zmistowski; Isuzu Kapalua International: Christina Noah, Mark Rolfing, Craig Williamson; Chrysler Team Invitational: David Pearson.

In addition to the aforementioned Messrs. Crenshaw, Sneed, and Weiskopf, thanks are due to each of the players who contributed instructional tips. In alphabetical order, they are: Isao Aoki, George Archer, Seve Ballesteros, Andy Bean, Charles Coody, Raymond Floyd, Al Geiberger, David Graham, Hubert Green, Gary Hallberg, Scott Hoch, Hale Irwin, Peter Jacobsen, Tom Kite, Bernhard Langer, Wayne Levi, Bruce Lietzke, Sandy Lyle, John Mahaffey, Mark McCumber, Johnny Miller, Larry Nelson, Jack Nicklaus, Greg Norman, Mark O'Meara, Arnold Palmer, Corey Pavin, Calvin Peete, Bill Rogers, Craig Stadler, Payne Stewart, Curtis Strange, Hal Sutton, Lee Trevino, Scott Verplank, Lanny Wadkins, Denis Watson, Tom Watson, and Fuzzy Zoeller.

I would like to be able to say that the idea for this book was mine, but it belongs to Margaret Kaplan, senior vice president and executive editor of Harry N. Abrams, Inc. Margaret is not a golfer but is an avid golf-watcher, and she saw the necessity for a book that television viewers could read and refer to while they follow the telecasts of PGA Tour events. To Margaret, I owe a triple thanks—for choosing me to write the book, for allowing me generous latitude in developing the manuscript, and for her patience and professionalism in nurturing that manuscript through production.

The elegant design was created by Bob McKee, and the painstaking task of assuring consistency and accuracy was cheerfully performed by Pauline Crammer.

A special round of thanks goes to my colleagues on the editorial staff of *Golf Magazine* for their forebearance with an occasionally book-bound editor and to the management of Times Mirror Magazines not only for allowing me to get involved with this book but for encouraging the project.

Finally, to my collaborator in every sense, my wife Libby. During most evenings and weekends for nearly two years, we worked side by side, I on the words to the book, she on the oil-painted maps of the golf courses. It is incredible to me that she produced all forty-two technically complex yet artistically graceful paintings on deadline, but it seems a miracle that during the same period she not only took care of our house but supervised a change in our residence and not only tended to the needs of our four-year-old but gave birth to our second son, all while allowing me the lion's share of "book time." No one has meant more to the completion of this book than Libby, and no one means more to me.

George Peper
January 1986

Leonard Kamsler

The photographers, from left to right: James Moriarty, Brian D. Morgan, and Anthony Roberts.

BIBLIOGRAPHY

Allis, Peter. THE WHO'S WHO OF GOLF. Prentice-Hall, Englewood Cliffs, N.J., 1983.

Barkow, Al. GOLF'S GOLDEN GRIND. Harcourt, Brace, Jovanovich, London, 1974.

Cornish, Geoffrey S., and Ronald E. Whitten. THE GOLF COURSE. The Rutledge Press, New York, 1981.

Davis, Bill, and the editors of Golf Digest. THE 100 GREATEST COURSES AND THEN SOME. Simon & Schuster, New York, 1983.

Dobereiner, Peter. THE BOOK OF GOLF DISASTERS. Stanley Paul, London, 1983.

Flaherty, Tom. THE MASTERS. Holt, Rinehart & Winston, New York, 1961.

Hobbs, Michael (editor). IN CELEBRATION OF GOLF. Charles Scribner's Sons, New York, 1982.

Hope, Bob (with Dwayne Netland). CONFESSIONS OF A HOOKER. Doubleday, Garden City, N.Y., 1985.

Hunter, Robert. THE LINKS. Charles Scribner's Sons, New York, 1926.

Jones, Bobby. GOLF IS MY GAME. Chatto & Windus, London, 1959.

Mackenzie, Alister. GOLF ARCHITECTURE. Reissued by Grant Books, Worcestershire, England, 1982.

McCormack, Mark H. THE WONDERFUL WORLD OF PROFESSIONAL GOLF. Atheneum, New York, 1973.

————. THE WORLD OF PROFESSIONAL GOLF (editions for years 1966–85). Various publishers.

Miller, Dick. AMERICA'S GREATEST GOLFING RESORTS. The Bobbs-Merrill Company, New York, 1977.

Netland, Dwayne. THE CROSBY: GREATEST SHOW IN GOLF. Doubleday, Garden City, N.Y., 1975.

Nicklaus, Jack (with Ken Bowden). GOLF MY WAY. Simon & Schuster, New York, 1974.

Palmer, Arnold (with Bob Drum). ARNOLD PALMER'S BEST 54 GOLF HOLES. Doubleday, Garden City, N.Y., 1977.

————. (with William Barry Furlong). GO FOR BROKE. Simon & Schuster, New York, 1973.

Peper, George. GOLF'S SUPERSHOTS. Atheneum, New York, 1982.

PGA Tour. PGA TOUR MEDIA GUIDE (editions for years 1975–85). PGA Tour, Jacksonville, Fla.

Price, Charles. THE WORLD OF GOLF. Random House, New York, 1962.

Roberts, Clifford. THE STORY OF THE AUGUSTA NATIONAL GOLF CLUB. Doubleday, Garden City, N.Y., 1976.

Ross, John M. and the editors of Golf Magazine. GOLF MAGAZINE'S ENCYCLOPEDIA OF GOLF. Harper & Row, New York, 1978.

Steel, Donald, and Peter Ryde (editors). THE ENCYCLOPEDIA OF GOLF. Viking, New York, 1975.

Ward-Thomas, Pat, Herbert Warren Wind, Charles Price, and Peter Thomson. THE WORLD ATLAS OF GOLF. Mitchell Beazley, London, 1976.

Watson, Tom (with Nick Seitz). HOW TO GET UP AND DOWN. Random House, New York, 1984.

Wind, Herbert Warren. THE COMPLETE GOLFER. Simon & Schuster, New York, 1954.

————. THE STORY OF AMERICAN GOLF. Alfred A. Knopf, New York, 1975.

INDEX